Responsible AI

A GLOBAL POLICY FRAMEWORK

FIRST EDITION

Charles Morgan, Editor

McLean, Virginia, USA

International Technology Law Association
7918 Jones Branch Drive, Suite 300
McLean, Virginia 22102, United States
Phone: (+1) 703-506-2895
Fax: (+1) 703-506-3266
Email: **memberservices@itechlaw.org**
itechlaw.org

Cover and chapter title page designs by Stan Knight, MCI USA
Text design by Troy Scott Parker, Cimarron Design

This book is available at www.itechlaw.org.

ISBN-13: 978-1-7339931-0-4

Printed in the United States of America.

Printing, last digit: 10 9 8 7 6 5 4 3 2 1

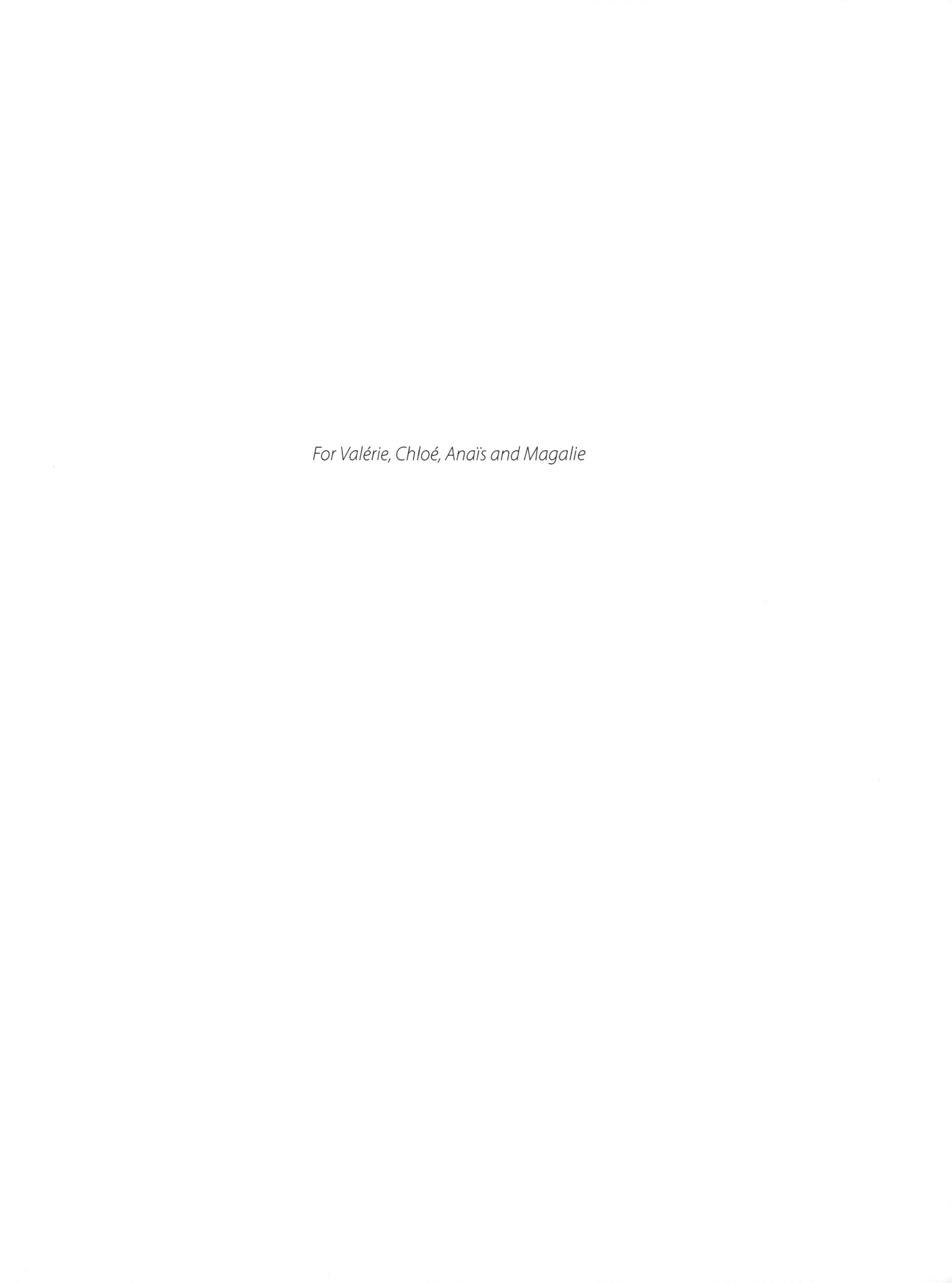

For Valérie, Chloé, Anaïs and Magalie

Contents

Acknowledgements

The publication of this Global Policy Framework for Responsible AI would not have been possible without the tireless efforts of a great number of participants. We would like to thank the following people who generously contributed to the publication of this book: two of our core project team members, who chose to remain anonymous; Emily Reineke, CAE, Executive Director of ITechLaw and her team; Troy Scott Parker of Cimarron Design; Gabriela Kennedy of Mayer Brown; George Takach, Kristian Brabander, Gong Ming Zheng and Linda Modica of McCarthy Tétrault (as well as the contributing members of McCarthy's document services group); Lindsay Morgan; and Dan Hunter, Swinburne University.

Foreword

The inspiration for this book came to me a year ago, almost to the day. ITechLaw members were gathering in Seattle for ITechLaw's annual World Technology Law Conference, held May 16-18, 2018. I was preparing for the association's board and executive committee meetings held at the offices of a leading local law firm whose offices had majestic views overlooking the Puget Sound. Quite naturally, the agenda for the board and executive committee meetings included time devoted to thinking about the strategic objectives and priorities for the association.

On the bedside table of my hotel room in Seattle were two publications that had captivated my attention.

The first was a whitepaper entitled *"The Future Computed: Artificial Intelligence and Its Role in Society"* that had been published by Microsoft a couple of months earlier and that included a Foreword written by Brad Smith (President and Chief Legal Officer, Microsoft) and Harry Shum (Executive Vice President, Artificial Intelligence and Research, Microsoft). That whitepaper made a compelling argument: in the same way that the field of privacy law had grown dramatically over the previous 20 years, it was very likely that a new field of "AI law" would develop over the next 20 years. Moreover, just as many of the core principles that form the basis of privacy and data protection legislation around the world today can be traced back to the "Fair Information Practices" that were developed in the early 1970's, the authors of *Future Computed* argued that the time had come to develop a set of core "responsible AI" principles that could provide the source of inspiration for policymakers considering the future regulation of artificial intelligence. In this context, *Future Computed* set out some preliminary thoughts regarding principles, policies and laws for the responsible use of AI.

The second publication on my bedside table was a book written in 2016 by the *New York Times* columnist Thomas Friedman called *Thank You for Being Late: An Optimist's Guide to Thriving in the Age of Accelerations.* In that book, Friedman argues that three disruptive forces—technological change, globalisation and climate change—are rapidly accelerating all at once and that they are transforming five fundamental spheres of our lives: the workplace, politics, geopolitics, ethics and community. His book offered stunning examples of the phenomenal rate of change in these areas, their impacts on society, as well as some thoughts on how best to embrace and shape these forces of change to positive effect. Although I'd seemingly placed a "tab" on every second page, there was one image that I found most arresting:

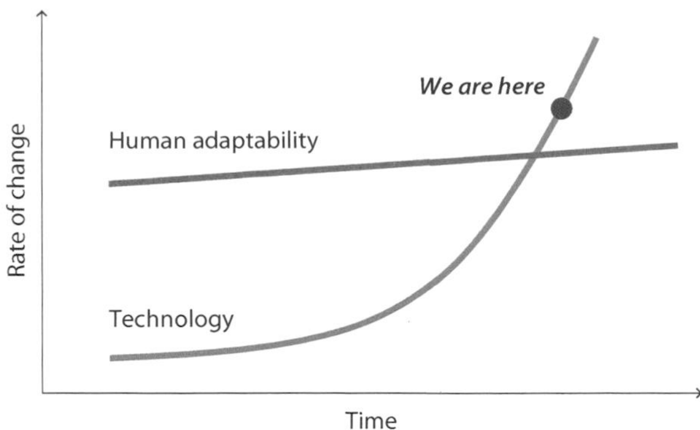

According to Friedman, the simple graph had been drawn for him on a notepad by Eric "Astro" Teller, the CEO of Google's X research and development lab. As recounted in *Thank You for Being Late,* Teller explained that a thousand years ago, the curve representing scientific and technological progress rose so gradually that it could take about one hundred years for the world to look and feel dramatically differently. By contrast, "now, in 2016, that time window—having continued to shrink as each technology stood on the shoulders of past technologies—has become so short that it's in the order of five to seven years from the time that something is introduced to being ubiquitous and the world being uncomfortably changed." The fundamental point that Teller was eliciting was that, although humans are remarkably adaptable, we have now reached a point that the rate of technological change has progressed beyond human's ability to keep up. As Friedman writes, citing Teller: "if the technology platform for society can now turn over in five to seven years, but it takes ten to fifteen years to adapt to it [...] we will all feel out of control, because we can't adapt to the world as fast as it is changing...." Teller concluded: "Without clear knowledge of the future potential or future unintended negative consequences of new technologies, it is nearly impossible to draft regulations that will promote important advances—while still protecting ourselves from every bad side effect."

This latter thought resonated for me in particular because a third set of ideas were swirling in my head as I prepared for the ITechLaw board meeting: the ongoing revelations about Cambridge Analytica and its potential impact on the U.S. elections. As a technology lawyer who had explored privacy law issues in depth for the past twenty years, I thought I had a clear and nuanced understanding of the many ways in which personal information was collected and used in modern society. But, like many people, the Cambridge Analytica story sent me reeling. It impressed upon me just how unaware many of us are about how technology is being used and just how important the consequences can be to some of our most fundamental values and institutions.

So ... with these three ideas milling about, I attended the ITechLaw board meeting. And, when it came time to propose projects and priorities for the coming year, I suggested—with a good deal of trepidation, quite frankly—that we should consider preparing, as a group, a whitepaper to establish a legal/policy framework for ethical AI. My trepidation stemmed from the fact that I was already deeply invested in the idea and I feared that others would not be. My fear turned out to be entirely unfounded. Within 15 minutes of making the initial suggestion at the Seattle ITechLaw board meeting, about fifteen members had joined the team.

Working with an initial core project team over the summer, we started to identify doctrinal sources and case studies and to sketch out the key principles that we would develop as part of our framework. In these initial efforts, I was greatly assisted by some remarkable students and young associates at my law firm who would ultimately join the project team and play a significant role in research and drafting. In the early stages of the project, our focus was on building out the team, ensuring we had appropriate geographic, gender, ethnic and industry diversity, and collecting key source materials that would help us buttress our policy framework. Moreover, we wanted to expand the team beyond ourselves, to include members with industry experience and serious academic credentials. Accordingly, we reached out to our respective networks of contacts in industry and academia. By mid-September, the basic contours of the team and framework had started to take shape.

And then at the ITechLaw European conference in Milan in October 2018 something remarkable happened. I had set aside some time for the core team to meet in Milan to discuss the status of the project and to hash out areas of potential discrepancy and debate. I had reserved a conference room where we would have some time to really drill down on certain topics amongst ourselves away from the hustle and bustle of the regular conference program. But, when I arrived for the meeting, I was not greeted by the fifteen familiar faces of the project team. Instead, I arrived into a conference room that was full to overflowing with 50 ITechLaw members who wanted to learn more about and to participate on the project team. I had not prepared for this! But as I stood in front of the crowded room and described what we had begun and what we wanted to achieve, I could sense very powerfully that we were in the process of doing something that "mattered" and that many of the people in the room were already committed to the success of the project.

Since that day in mid-October, the level of energy and engagement by the members of the project team has been astonishing and unrelenting. A total of 54 contributors (35% women), including leading technology lawyers from 27 law firms, from 16 countries on 5 continents (together with industry representatives and academics) have come together to bring their expertise to bear upon a topic that, we all implicitly understood, is a matter of great societal import.

Bringing all the pieces together into a coherent narrative with a reasonably consistent voice has been a colossal undertaking. I am so incredibly grateful to all the members of the project team for their time commitment, their generosity, their insights, their intelligence and the seriousness with which they approached our topic. I am so grateful to ITechLaw for providing a forum in which a truly global perspective could be brought to bear on technology and legal matters of global impact.

At the start of this project, we set as our objective the goal of participating actively in the ongoing dialogue about the responsible implementation of artificial intelligence in society and of attempting to advance those discussions two or three noticeable steps forward. We wanted to address these issues in a manner that was not only meaningful but also "actionable." If the rate of technological change is indeed hurtling ahead faster than our ability to adapt, then it becomes increasingly urgent, in the earliest days of AI development, to establish a solid and lasting framework for responsible AI development, deployment and use. We must encourage responsible AI by design.

As each of the chapter teams has worked to research and draft their respective contributions, a number of independent, parallel initiatives have also tackled many of these same issues, including efforts by the European Commission High-Level Expert Group on Artificial Intelligence and the Singapore Personal Data Protection Commission. These efforts rejoin others, such as those initiated by the authors of the Montreal Declaration for Responsible AI, the Villani report "For a Meaningful Artificial Intelligence" and a variety of industry-led ethical AI projects. We salute each of these initiatives and endeavour to draw attention to them in the course of this paper. I think it is fair to say that our project team members all feel strongly that the issues that are raised in this paper are matters that require broad societal engagement. The promotion of human agency and societal benefit requires that we make some fundamental choices about how we engage with technology and how we remain accountable for its use.

The policy framework that we present here is necessarily embryonic. AI is still in its infancy. We hope that all readers will grapple with the materials with the same energy, intensity and sense of its importance as we have. We are, collectively, participating in a dialogue. We welcome your comments and suggestions regarding the many ways that our preliminary policy framework may be improved.

– Charles Morgan
President
ITechLaw

*"We can only see a short distance ahead,
but we can see plenty there that needs to be done."*

– Alan Turing, "Computing Machinery and Intelligence," 1950

Introduction

INTRODUCTION

CHAPTER LEAD
Charles Morgan | McCarthy Tétrault LLP, Canada

John Buyers | Osborne Clarke LLP, United Kingdom

Catherine Hammon | Osborne Clarke LLP, United Kingdom

Emily Hutchison | McCarthy Tétrault LLP, Canada

Francis Langlois | McCarthy Tétrault LLP, Canada

In June 2002, twenty-seven-year-old Dan Lowthorpe was excited to visit the Magna Science Centre in Rotherham, England. The news that some scientists were experimenting with a novel kind of robot had intrigued him. The scientists were trying to teach robots a survivalist game: larger robots were programmed to chase smaller, more nimble robots with the predatory aim of sinking a metal "fang" into their prey to "eat" their electric power. As part of the scientific experiment, microchips from successful predators were then merged (or "mated") to make a new, ever more formidable robot.

Imagine Mr. Lowthorpe's surprise when, while searching for a parking place, he almost collided with one of these robots spinning and turning on itself in the middle of the road, unsupervised. He got out of his car and was taking a closer look at the crude-looking machine, when the man in charge, Professor Noel Sharkey, a computer scientist from Sheffield University, came running over and turned it off.[1]

Mr. Lowthorpe had a further surprise once it became evident that his encounter with Gaak—as the robot was known—was not part of the experiment. In fact, Gaak had taken advantage of the inattention of the scientists to escape the Centre and venture into the street. Left unattended for fifteen minutes, Gaak found its way out of the paddock it had been kept in, made a beeline down the access slope and out the door to experience a few glorious moments of freedom!

A somewhat bemused Professor Sharkey later explained that Gaak, a predator, had learned to react to its environment and to chase prey; he had probably misinterpreted a sunbeam for its prey and chased it outside. "There's no actual intelligence in what he did—it's more the absent-minded professor forgetting to switch him off ," Professor Sharkey added.[2]

Albeit lacking "actual intelligence," Gaak was nevertheless equipped with what is referred to as "artificial intelligence." Was this a first attempt by a machine to free itself from its makers and conquer its freedom? Absolutely not; but the story of an apparently predatory, artificially intelligent robot that escapes and turns against its master has held a resonant place in our collective unconscious, from Golem to Dr. Frankenstein's monster to Hal to ... Gaak!

Ever since Gaak's valiant but short-lived escape, we have witnessed (with a mix of fascination and apprehension) the extraordinarily rapid rise of seemingly intelligent machines. In this publication, you will find an attempt by practising technology lawyers and AI specialists from around the world to develop a policy framework for the responsible development, distribution and use of artificial intelligence (AI). In subsequent chapters, we will develop the contours of our global framework for responsible AI, but first, the current chapter serves to introduce the reader to what we mean when we refer to an "AI system."

I. Artificial Intelligence: An Arduous Beginning

The dream of creating intelligent machines is an ancient one. In the 4th century BC, Greek philosophers famously imagined "an instrument that could accomplish its own work" and save humans from labour.[3] It was only recently, however, that some began to believe the dream could become reality. In 1950, British scientist Alan Turing wrote a famous article where he refuted arguments against the possibility of creating intelligent machines.[4] Around this period, the American scientist Marvin Minsky commenced the process of turning theory into reality, developing what is widely believed to be the first neural network learning machine "SNARC"[5] in January 1952. Three years later, a group of American scientists from industry and academia wrote *A Proposal for the Dartmouth Summer Research Project on Artificial Intelligence*, coining at the same time the term "artificial intelligence" (AI)[6] In this proposal, they argued that a machine could simulate "every aspect of learning or any other feature of intelligence," notably "use language, form abstractions and concepts, solve kinds of problems now reserved for humans, and improve themselves." Optimistically, they believed that they could develop such a machine over the course of only one summer.

This combination of ambitious objective and great optimism led to high expectations. For instance, from the 1960s onwards, AI researchers regularly promised that they were on the verge of making a computer program capable of beating the best human chess players.[7] Yet this significant milestone was not reached until decades later.

The difference between what AI researchers promised and what they delivered quickly disappointed many. In 1973, a report for the British Science Research Council concluded that "in no part of the field have the discoveries made so far produced the major impact that was then promised."[8] In the 1970s and 1980s, funding from important institutions like DARPA (the United States' Defense Advanced Research Projects Agency) declined and research in AI was met with increasing skepticism by other computer scientists.[9]

Thus, when a computer program, IBM's Deep Blue, finally defeated a human chess grandmaster in 1997 with the help of many AI techniques and algorithms, IBM distanced itself from using AI terminology to describe their success. Instead, IBM argued Deep Blue was not an example of artificial intelligence, but rather of an advanced "expert system," a term that was common at the time to describe computer programs based on the knowledge of human experts.[10]

One of the factors contributing to the disenchantment with AI was a general confusion between the two parallel goals of AI: replicating (or surpassing) fully human intelligence and, less ambitiously, making machines capable of solving by themselves problems that would normally require intelligence. This is the difference between Artificial General Intelligence (AGI) and "narrow AI."

Artificial General Intelligence (AGI) and Narrow AI

AGI refers to AI systems that can behave like humans, cognitively, emotionally and socially.[11] Narrow AI, on the other hand, aims to allow machines to master certain specific tasks, such as the game of Go, recognizing human faces in photographs or driving a vehicle.[12] AGI is still a distant dream (or nightmare), but as we will see, narrow AI is already with us in our day-to-day lives.

II. The AI Renaissance

Today, the era of disenchantment surrounding AI seems like a distant memory. In the last decade, interest in AI has steadily increased in almost every metric: scientific papers published annually, course enrollment in universities, expert conference attendance, the number of start-ups specializing in the field, private investment and media coverage.[13] Virtually every major tech company, including Facebook, Google, Microsoft, Alibaba and Netflix, use AI to label our photos correctly, translate our emails or recommend the next movie we will watch. AI has found a purpose in the professional domain as well. Lawyers, for example, now work with the assistance of AI systems to predict court decisions, answer legal questions or quickly analyze thousands of documents.[14]

Rather than being seen as disappointments, computer systems programmed to be artificially intelligent suddenly became celebrated for their well-publicized victories. Most famously, human champions of the TV game show Jeopardy! lost to IBM's Watson in 2011[15] and Google Deepmind's AlphaGo defeated a Go world champion in 2016.[16] As a last impressive feat, AlphaStar, an AI system also developed by Deepmind, defeated top human players at StarCraft II, a notoriously difficult real-time strategy computer game.[17]

Not limited to immobile banks of servers, AI has increasingly been incorporated into mobile machines. In 2005, a team of scientists and engineers from Stanford University won the second DARPA self-driving car Grand Challenge. Their autonomous vehicle drove 132 miles of desert terrain in less than seven hours, learning how to drive with the help of AI programming techniques.[18] Today, of course, autonomous vehicles are circulating on city streets in pilot tests running in over 50 cities around the world, exploring Gaak's glorious sense of freedom at 120 kilometres an hour!

The level of progress made in the field of AI has become so impressive that, in an attempt to counter a general sense of ebullience over what AI can achieve, AI specialists, scientists, journalists and some tech entrepreneurs have warned against the dangers of this technology, notably its military applications, encroachments on privacy, risks of discrimination, as well as its effects on the economy and employment.[19] This paper will propose a policy framework for responsible AI that is intended to help ensure that we harvest the best out of AI technology, and limit the adverse impacts of these anticipated risks. But first, it is useful to present in more details what distinguishes AI from other forms of computing.

III. The Ghost in the Machine: GOFAI, Machine Learning and Deep Learning

What explains such changes in the perception of AI? One important thing to understand is that AI's recent successes are mostly due to the maturation of two particular approaches to making algorithms: machine learning ("**ML**") and deep learning ("**DL**"). Collectively, these techniques represent the core of the second wave of AI.[20]

Thanks to machine learning and deep learning—with great emphasis on the "learning" component—computers can now do far more than they ever could.

Machine Learning

"Machine learning is the technology that allows systems to learn directly from examples, data, and experience."[21]

Deep Learning

As for deep learning, it is a subfield of ML, loosely inspired by the functioning and the architecture of the human brain.[22] *It uses networks of artificial neurons organized in visible and invisible layers to process input data in order to produce an output.*[23]

Before explaining how machines can learn and why that is so significant, we should start at the beginning and take a look at the first wave of AI.

A. Good-old fashioned artificial intelligence

In the 1980s and the 1990s, the general idea was that AI systems could be programmed by coding them with the knowledge of human experts. Richard Susskind, who worked on the first legal expert system, explains the process: "When I began work in the field of AI and law, one approach dominated—the knowledge and reasoning process of legal experts were mined from their heads through an interview process known as 'knowledge elicitation.' That knowledge was then codified in complex decision trees, and dropped into computer systems, around which non-expert users could navigate."[24] This was a long and difficult process, with uncertain results.

Deep Blue is probably the most famous example of that type of system and is representative of AI before machine learning, sometimes referred to as Good Old-Fashioned AI ("**GOFAI**") or symbolic AI.[25] Chess is a difficult game, but at its core is made up of a relatively short list of formal rules. Programmers can translate these rules into a combination of symbols in formal computing language (IF-THEN statements, for instance).[26] Programmed with these hard-coded rules, all Deep Blue needed was vast computational power to search through all possible moves, given a specific board position, and to evaluate its next move by applying a function provided by its programmers.[27] During the 1997 match, Deep Blue was able to search up to 330 million positions per second and some of its strategies were prepared in advance by human chess grandmasters.[28]

Yet, even though Deep Blue defeated a chess grandmaster, it shows us at the same time the limits of the first wave of AI. It was informed but also constrained by the scope of human knowledge of the rules of chess and its human programmers' ability to express that knowledge formally, in a way that was not too costly or time-consuming.[29] The reality is that Deep Blue did not achieve its victory by "learning," it did so by adhering to and carrying out a series of pre-programmed steps.

B. Machine learning

The second wave of AI has proposed a different approach: what if computers could learn, on their own, the solutions to the problems they are given? Computers have always been good at solving problems based on formal and mathematical rules that can be extremely difficult and time-consuming for humans.[30] There is no doubt that "computers are vastly superior to humans in certain tasks; 1970-era calculators can perform arithmetic better than humans."[31] However, some tasks that are intuitive and easy for human beings—like recognizing a dog in a photograph or the voice of a friend on the phone—are very hard for computers, since such tasks do not rely on formal rules that can be easily described in a language that computers understand.[32]

In contrast, machine learning algorithms go beyond human knowledge because they can "acquire their own knowledge, by extracting patterns from raw data," such as the patterns in MRI scans or in the positioning of pieces on a game board.[33] In machine learning, computers are not programmed with a set of rules, but a set of features that the AI system learns to associate with different outcomes and that can be applied to new situations.[34] In conventional machine learning, the programmer needs to choose the features that are important for an algorithm to pay attention to in order to predict the right outcome. This is sometimes referred to as "feature engineering."[35] Similar to GOFAI, this process requires expert knowledge, albeit not at the same level of formalism and granularity.[36] For example, imagine someone wanting to know the likelihood of a student passing his driving exam by analysing data about previous students. Feature engineering would require this person to select the type of information from previous students that are relevant to the problem at hand. The number of hours spent practising driving is certainly a relevant feature, while what the student ate in the morning is probably not determinant.[37] Once features are selected, however, machine learning algorithms can "learn" the relative importance of each feature without further human intervention.

Neural Networks

Machine learning algorithms are based on what is known as neural networks composed of multiple nodes—or neurons—organized in structured layers. Like the biological neuron by which it is loosely inspired, a node receives multiple inputs combined with weights and biases, applies a function with a set of parameters and produces an output that is sent to other nodes until a final output is produced.[38]

A neural network is usually comprised of a number of layers of nodes, usually an input layer, a number of hidden layers and an output layer. Each node is connected to the nodes in the layers above and below it. The AI system uses training data to pattern the relationships between the different nodes in the different layers. When the AI system makes an error during training, it automatically adjusts the weights and biases in each of its nodes using mathematical techniques so that particular features are given more attention, with the AI becoming systematically more accurate with each new piece of data.[39]

Image recognition example

A machine learning algorithm would be fed the raw pixel data from a picture and then produce a result, identifying it as a picture of a triangle, for instance.

If it is in fact a picture of a square, the algorithm adjusts the weights of its neurons to reduce the error rate.

After a training phase using thousands of pictures, the system will be capable of correctly identifying the picture, even if it has never seen it before (provided there were sufficient examples of that type of picture in the training data).

The training of ML algorithms can be accomplished using different techniques. In supervised learning, programmers use labelled data to train their algorithms to predict outcomes. One example would be programs that can detect lung anomalies based on training received through the input of thousands of chest radiography previously labelled as normal or abnormal by human radiologists.[40] AI systems like these are powerful data mining tools, as they can help humans find new patterns in vast amounts of data—patterns that even skilled radiologists, for example, might not have detected themselves.[41] One downside is that the training process can be expensive due to the cost of collecting, labelling and vetting the data.[42] This cost can be reduced, however, with the greater availability of open source labelled datasets.[43]

Unsupervised learning, on the other hand, uses unlabelled data. Its main use is in creating clusters of data with similar characteristics.[44] To use the radiology example again, a case of unsupervised learning would imply an algorithm finding commonalities in certain radiography and grouping them together. This algorithm would not, however, be able to tell which images are normal and which are abnormal, although it might find other clusters of similarity which human doctors or analysts had not spotted.

A further type of ML training also finds its inspiration in nature: reinforcement learning is essentially the application of Pavlov's dog theory to AI.[45] This type of learning allows an AI system to be trained by giving it a reward for every improvement made towards the accomplishment of a goal. Trying to teach a robot how to walk? Through the use of reinforcement learning and the process of trial and error, falling and getting up, it can learn to do so by itself.[46]

Experience has showed, however, that ML algorithms with only a few layers of neurons (nodes) have certain limitations. Such limitations are linked to the problem of representation. The raw data needs to be represented by a series of features identified by the programmer. If we take our previous image recognition example, the features to be identified may include the number of sides on a triangle or the sum of its angles. More complex images of animals, objects or persons are often too difficult to identify in advance or to have their features handcrafted by a human programmer.[47] As noted by Prof. Yoshua Bengio, "[m] anually designing features for a complex task requires a great deal of human time and effort; it can take decades for an entire community of researchers."[48] To expand beyond these limited capacities, AI specialists needed another solution, one that would further remove humans from the programming process and allow algorithms to identify features by themselves. Deep learning was the answer.

C. Deep Learning

1940s	1980s	2000s
• Cybernetics • Limited data	• Process improvements in neural networks • Digital data is mostly in structured format	• Improvement in computing power • Unprecedented amounts of data

Today, deep learning is considered a subfield and extension of machine learning. The roots of DL date back to the 1940s within the field of cybernetics as a way to represent neuronal activities, including learning.[49] An important step for DL was in the 1980s when scientists discovered a way to improve the process of minimising errors in the nodes' weights and biases in the hidden layers of vast neural networks.[50] However, it remained mostly unpopular in computer science until around 2006 because it required too much computing power.[51] In the last decade, exponential growth in areas such as processing power, sensors accuracy and efficiency, data storage, transfer and search capacity, connectivity and cloud computing has unleashed the power of these algorithms.[52] Once powerful hardware became available, DL was shown to work very effectively in 2012, when it was used in an AI system which won an image recognition contest by a wide margin in comparison to other techniques.[53]

It is this multiplicity of layers—the depth of the neural network—that distinguishes DL from ML. By having each layer of neurons focus on a certain level of representation, DL introduces abstraction in AI. In the classic image recognition example, the first layer inputs the raw pixels and identifies edges. The second layer inputs those edges and detects motifs of a higher complexity. The process repeats for each layer until a final output labelling the picture as a whole is produced.[54] Most notably, the features identified by these layers "are not designed by human engineers: they are learned from data using a general-purpose learning procedure."[55] In other words, AI based on deep learning can learn on its own what distinguishes a cat from a dog, one breed of cat from another, and your cat from all the other cats in the world.

The progress that has been attained in AI due to deep learning is best illustrated by an example.

Case Study: AlphaGo Zero

In 2017, a team of scientists from Google DeepMind built a program named AlphaGo Zero. AlphaGo Zero is the little brother of AlphaGo, the program that beat the best human Go player. AlphaGo's deep neural network was trained using a combination of supervised learning from human expert plays and reinforcement learning. As for AlphaGo Zero, the scientists developed a new algorithm and trained it using only reinforcement learning, leaving it to learn by playing games against itself.[56] The little brother beat its elder with just 36 hours of training.[57] Generalizing from this approach, more recently, scientists made an even more advanced program also based on deep learning, AlphaZero, that can learn games from scratch by playing against itself, without any human assistance or hard-coded knowledge. When tasked to learn chess and a Japanese game called shogi, it managed to learn how to play at a level unmatchable by humans in less than 24 hours.[58] As a comparison, it took IBM nearly ten years of trial and error to develop the program that defeated Garry Kasparov at chess in 1997.[59]

Deep learning techniques have now achieved wide recognition within computer science and the pioneers of this approach—Yoshua Bengio, Yann LeCun and Geoffrey Hinton—were awarded the 2018 A.M. Turing Award by the Association for Computing Machinery for their major breakthroughs in AI.[60]

IV. The Way Forward with AI

This accelerating rate of progress in AI research is both exhilarating and alarming. Machine learning and deep learning can now be found in transportation, healthcare, finance, banking, law and in many other areas. The impacts on society have been both positive and negative. Faced with the many developments described above and the increasing prevalence of AI in everyday life, AI specialists have called for greater involvement from the legal community in developing regulations, norms and governing frameworks in order to avoid a legal vacuum surrounding the use of AI in business, government and everyday life.[61] AI law does not yet exist as its own distinct legal field, but it is well on its way.[62] AI law will be essential in helping to modernize legal and policy frameworks that are quickly becoming outdated, unresponsive to the expansive role that AI is going to play in society.

It is critical that legal and policy guideposts for the responsible development of AI be developed now (in the relative infancy of AI) rather than later when it may ultimately be "too late." The pace of technological disruption is so fast right now that many fear being left behind. Many fear that they will be unable to adapt to the pace of change and will be forced to passively and reactively "submit" to the effect of technological change rather than actively participating in the process of guiding technological change to ensure that it serves the interests of society as a whole.

Mathematician and member of the French Parliament Cédric Villani has argued that regulation of AI must not be the responsibility of researchers and engineers alone—lawyers must develop a "genuine awareness" of the subject."[63] In the last few years, a number of lawyers have taken heed of this challenge, teaming up with researchers, industry members, human rights organizations and governments to develop responses and forward-looking action plans for how best to harness the promise of AI and address the problems that it presents.

Notably, the majority of these teams are taking a human-centric approach. For example, in 2016, the IEEE Global Initiative for Ethical Considerations in Artificial Intelligence and Autonomous Systems released a draft version of a report on ethically aligned design in the development of intelligent technologies.[64] The final version of the report was published in March 2019, promoting the centrality of human well-being.[65] In May 2018, a coalition of human rights groups and technology associations released the Toronto

Declaration, calling on governments and technology companies to ensure that equality and non-discrimination is built into intelligent technologies.[66] Publications and advocacy work from groups and institutions such as Microsoft,[67] Intel,[68] the Partnership on AI,[69] Privacy International,[70] the University of Montreal,[71] Stanford University,[72] and the European Union itself,[73] just to name a few, are helping to shape the next generation of legal and policy frameworks that will effectively address the challenges posed by AI and help reap the benefits of this promising technology.

This human-centric approach is also warranted given some important limits of AI. AI systems based on machine learning or deep learning do not "think" or "reason" in a conceptual way, and do not understand anything of the ideas, objects or issues that they are dealing with. Instead, the right answer is generated using the patterns recorded in the neural network—the answer is arrived at essentially using mathematical techniques which identify the output most likely to be correct, without reflecting upon the "meaning" of the outcome, including its ethical merits or societal policy implications.[74]

In short, deep learning can be incredibly accurate without understanding anything at all—indeed, "understanding" is irrelevant because the AI system functions in a completely different manner. This point is important because it is a key reason for the difficulties in explaining outputs generated by AI systems—the so-called "black box" problem, as discussed in our treatment of Principle 3—Transparency and Explainability. It is also one of the key reasons that underlies our treatment of Principle 1—Accountability. Those fundamental limits indicate that, despite recurring hopes, AI will not solve for ourselves all our problems and that AI is here to augment, rather than replace human intelligence.[75]

It is within this context that we add our own contribution and present in the following chapters a preliminary legal and policy framework for responsible AI. Our framework is comprised of 8 principles:

1. Ethical Purpose and Societal Benefit;
2. Accountability;
3. Transparency and Explainability;
4. Fairness and Non-Discrimination;
5. Safety and Reliability;
6. Open Data and Fair Competition;
7. Privacy; and
8. AI and Intellectual Property.

The next eight chapters will take a focused look at the state of AI today from the perspective of each principle, concluding with a consolidated draft of the proposed global policy framework for responsible AI.

Endnotes

1 Dave Higgens, "Robot learns how to escape from exhibition" (20 June 2002), online: *The Independent* <https://www.independent.co.uk/news/uk/home-news/robot-learns-how-to-escape-from-exhibition-180874.html>.

2 Martin Wainwright, "Robot fails to find a place in the sun" (20 June 2002), online: *The Guardian* <https://www.theguardian.com/uk/2002/jun/20/engineering.highereducation>.

3 Aristotle, *Politics* (Kitchener: Batoche Books, 1999) at p 7.

4 A.M. Turing, "Computing Machinery and Intelligence," (1950) 49 Mind 433.

5 Scholastic neural analog reinforcement calculator. See John Buyers, *Artificial Intelligence: The Practical Legal Issues* (Law Brief Publishing, 2018).

6 J McCarthy et al, "A Proposal for the Dartmouth Summer Research Project on Artificial Intelligence," (31 August 1955), online: <http://www-formal.stanford.edu/jmc/history/dartmouth.pdf> at p 2.

7 Richard E Korf, "Does Deep-Blue use AI?," in Association for the Advancement of Artificial Intelligence Technical Report, April 1997, online: <https://www.aaai.org/Papers/Workshops/1997/WS-97-04/WS97-04-001.pdf> at p 1 [Korf].

8 Sir James Lighthill, "Artificial Intelligence: a paper symposium" (1973), online: <http://www.math.snu.ac.kr/~hichoi/infomath/Articles/Lighthill%20Report.pdf> at p 8.

9 Korf, *supra* note 7 at p 1;

See also for the 1990s, Yoshua Bengio et al, *Deep Learning*, November 18, 2016, MIT Press at p 17 [Bengio].

10 Korf, *supra* note 7 at p 1;

Vladimir Zwass, "Expert System," online: *Encyclopaedia Britannica* <https://www.britannica.com/technology/expert-system>.

11 United States of America, Bill HR 4625, *FUTURE of Artificial Intelligence Act of 2017,* 115th Congress, 2017, s 2.

12 The Royal Society, "Machine learning: the power and promise of computers that learn by example" (April 2017), online: <https://royalsociety.org/topics-policy/projects/machine-learning/> at p 19 [The Royal Society].

13 Yoav Shoham et al, "AI Index: 2018 Annual Report" (December 2018), online: *AI Index Steering Committee, Human-Centered AI Initiative, Stanford University* <https://www.itworldcanada.com/ai/wp-content/uploads/2018/12/AI-Index-2018-Annual-Report.pdf> [AI Index].

14 Richard Susskind, *Tomorrow's Lawyers: An Introduction to Your Future*, (Oxford: Oxford University Press, 2017) at pp 185-187 [Susskind].

15 Jo Best, "IBM Watson: The inside story of how the Jeopardy-winning supercomputer was born, and what it wants to do next" (9 September 2013) online: *TechRepublic* <https://www.techrepublic.com/article/ibm-watson-the-inside-story-of-how-the-jeopardy-winning-supercomputer-was-born-and-what-it-wants-to-do-next/>.

16 Jon Russel, "Google AI beats Go world champion again to complete historic 4-1 series victory" (2016), online: *TechCrunch* <https://techcrunch.com/2016/03/15/google-ai-beats-go-world-champion-again-to-complete-historic-4-1-series-victory/?_ga=2.245301580.87243990.1537106320-1010827639.1531400902>.

17 Deepmind, "AlphaStar: Mastering the Real-Time Strategy Game Starcraft II" (24 January 2019), online: <https://deepmind.com/blog/alphastar-mastering-real-time-strategy-game-starcraft-ii/>.

[18] DARPA, "The Grand Challenge," online: <https://www.darpa.mil/about-us/timeline/-grand-challenge-for-autonomous-vehicles>.

[19] The Future of Life Institute, "An Open Letter: Research priorities for robust and beneficial artificial intelligence," <https://futureoflife.org/ai-open-letter>. Notably signed by Elon Musk, Steve Wozniak and Stephen Hawking as well as by many prominent AI researchers from industry and academia>;

Kate Crawford, "You and AI—Just an Engineer: The Politics of AI," (23 July 2018) online: *The Royal Society* <https://www.youtube.com/watch?v=HPopJb5aDyA>;

Article 19, "Privacy and Freedom of Expression In the Age of Artificial Intelligence" (April 2018), online: <https://www.article19.org/wp-content/uploads/2018/04/Privacy-and-Freedom-of-Expression-In-the-Age-of-Artificial-Intelligence-1.pdf;

Joseph E Stiglitz, "You and AI—The Future of Work" (18 September 2018), online: *YouTube* <https://www.youtube.com/watch?v=aemkMMrZWgM>.

[20] Susskind, *supra* note 14 at p 186.

[21] The Royal Society, *supra* note 12 at p 16.

[22] Bengio, *supra* note 9 at p 13.

[23] *Ibid,* at p 6.

[24] Susskind, *supra* note 14 at p 185.

[25] Margaret A Boden, "GOFAI" in Keith Frankish & William M Ramsey, eds, *The Cambridge Handbook of Artificial Intelligence* (Cambridge University Press) 89 at p 89 [Boden].

[26] *Ibid,* at pp 89 and 91.

[27] Stanford CS221, "Deep Blue" (http://stanford.edu/~cpiech/cs221/apps/deepBlue.html);

Murray Campbell et al, "Deep Blue" (2002) 134 online: Artificial Intelligence <https://ac.els-cdn.com/S0004370201001291/1-s2.0-S0004370201001291-main.pdf?_tid=10254636-0e6d-4ec4-8838-d365da456365&acdnat=1537133919_79de25084bd5f10437663d6a3acd0bcd> at p 76 [Murray].

[28] *Ibid* at pp 60 and 76.

[29] DARPA, "AI Next Campaign," online: <https://www.darpa.mil/work-with-us/ai-next-campaign>.

[30] Bengio, *supra* note 9 at p 1.

[31] AI Index, *supra* note 13 at p 37.

[32] Bengio, *supra* note 9 at p 1.

[33] Bengio, *supra* note 9 at p 3.

[34] *Ibid* at p 3.

[35] "Feature engineering is the process of formulating the most appropriate features given the data, the model, and the task." Alice Zheng & Amanda Casari, *Feature Engineering for Machine Learning: Principles and Techniques for Data Scientists* (O'Reilly, 2018) at p 3.

[36] Yann LeCun, Yoshua Bengio & Geoffrey Hinton, « Deep Learning » (2015) 251 Nature 436 at p 436 [LeCun].

[37] Inspired by Jayesh Bapu Ahire, "Perceptron and Backpropagation" (10 February 2018), online: *Medium* <https://medium.com/@jayeshbahire/perceptron-and-backpropagation-970d752f4e44>.

38 *Ibid.*

39 LeCun, *supra* note 36 at p 437. For readers interested in the technical side of AI, this process is known as stochastic gradient descent.

40 An Tang et al, "Canadian Association of Radiologists White Paper on Artificial Intelligence in Radiology" (2018) 69 Canadian Association of Radiologists Journal 120 at p 122.

41 *Ibid,* at p 123.

42 DARPA, "AI Next Campaign," online: <https://www.darpa.mil/work-with-us/ai-next-campaign>.

43 William Vorhies, "Lots of Free Open Sources Datasets to Make Your AI Better" (2 October 2018), online: *Data Science Central* <https://www.datasciencecentral.com/profiles/blogs/lots-of-free-open-source-datasets-to-make-your-ai-better>.

44 The Royal Society, *supra* note 12 at p 20.

45 Noel E Sharkey, "The new wave in robot learning" (1997) 22 Robotics and Autonomous Systems 179 at p 181.

46 *Ibid,* at p 182.

47 Bengio, *supra* note 9 at p 3.

48 *Ibid,* at p 4.

49 *Ibid,* at p 12;

See notably Warren S McCulloch & Walter H Pitts, "A Logical Calculus of the Ideas Immanent in Nervous Activity" (1943) 5 Bulletin of Mathematical Biophysics 115.

50 LeCun, *supra* note 36 at p 438. This is called the backpropagation procedure, a way to calculate stochastic gradient descent on multiple layers of neurons.

51 Bengio, *supra* note 9 at p 18.

52 Thomas L Friedman, *Thank You for Being Late: An Optimist's Guide to Thriving in the Age of Acceleration* (New York: Picardo Edition, 2017) at pp 39-90.

53 Tom Simonite "The Godfathers of the AI Boom Win Computing's Highest Honor" (27 March 2019), online: *Wired* <https://www.wired.com/story/godfathers-ai-boom-win-computings-highest-honor/>;

Dave Gershgorn, "The data that transformed AI research—and possibly the world" (26 July 2016), online *Quartz* <https://qz.com/1034972/the-data-that-changed-the-direction-of-ai-research-and-possibly-the-world/>.

54 LeCun, *supra* note 36 at p 436.

55 *Idem.*

56 David Silver et al, "Mastering the game of Go without human knowledge" (October 2017), online: Nature <https://www.nature.com/articles/nature24270/#article-info> at p 354 [Silver].

57 *Ibid,* at p 356.

58 David Silver et al, "Mastering Chess and Shogi by Self-Play with a General Reinforcement Learning Algorithm" (December 2017), online: <https://arxiv.org/pdf/1712.01815.pdf)> at p 1.;

Silver, *supra* note 56 at p 358.

59 Murray, *supra* note 27 at p 58

60 ACM, "Fathers of the Deep Learning Revolution Receive ACM A.M. Turing Award" (2019), online: <https://amturing.acm.org/>.

61 Olivia J Erdélyi & Judy Goldsmith, "Regulating Artificial Intelligence: Proposal for a Global Solution" (2018), online: *Association for the Advancement of Artificial Intelligence* <http://www.aies-conference.com/wp-content/papers/main/AIES_2018_paper_13.pdf> at p 1;

Institute of Electrical and Electronics Engineers, "Ethically Aligned Design: A Vision for Prioritizing Human Well-being with Autonomous and Intelligent Systems" (2016) online: <https://ethicsinaction.ieee.org/> at p 147 [IEEE].

62 Microsoft, "The Future Computed: Artificial Intelligence and its Role in Society" (2018), online: <https://blogs.microsoft.com/uploads/2018/02/The-Future-Computed_2.8.18.pdf> at p 9.

63 Cédric Villani, "For a Meaningful Artificial Intelligence: Towards a French and European Strategy," Mission assigned by the Prime Minister Édouard Philippe (2018), online: <https://www.aiforhumanity.fr/pdfs/MissionVillani_Report_ENG-VF.pdf> at p 120.

64 IEEE, *supra* note 61.

65 To download the report: IEEE, "Ethics in Action: The IEEE Global Initiative on Ethics of Autonomous and Intelligent Systems," online: <https://ethicsinaction.ieee.org/>.

66 *The Toronto Declaration: Protecting the right to equality and non-discrimination in machine learning systems,* online: <https://www.accessnow.org/cms/assets/uploads/2018/08/The-Toronto-Declaration_ENG_08-2018.pdf>.

67 Microsoft, "Microsoft AI Principles,» online: <https://www.microsoft.com/en-us/ai/our-approach-to-ai>.

68 Intel, "Artificial Intelligence: The Public Policy Opportunity," online: <https://blogs.intel.com/policy/files/2017/10/Intel-Artificial-Intelligence-Public-Policy-White-Paper-2017.pdf>.

69 The Partnership on AI, online: <https://www.partnershiponai.org/>.

70 Privacy International, "Artificial Intelligence," online <https://privacyinternational.org/topics/artificial-intelligence>.

71 See the Cyberjustice Laboratory, online: <https://www.cyberjustice.ca/>.

72 See the Stanford Institute for Human-Centered Artificial Intelligence, online: <https://hai.stanford.edu/>.

73 European Commission, "Artificial Intelligence" (last updated January 7 2019), online: <https://ec.europa.eu/digital-single-market/en/artificial-intelligence>.

74 This distinction has been explained using the "Chinese Room" concept introduced in 1980 by the philosopher John Searle. A person who doesn't understand Chinese is put in a closed room with a set of Chinese characters and a very detailed set of rules. When a string of Chinese characters is passed to him (i.e., a "question"), he uses the rules to construct a string of characters in response, which he passes back (i.e., his "answer"). If the instructions are sufficiently good, the answer to the question will be correct. But this accuracy has been achieved by a method in which any conceptual understanding of the question is completely absent—the man in the room had no idea what the characters which formed the "question" and the "answer" meant. See Stanford Encyclopedia of Philosophy, "The Chinese Room Argument" (9 April 2014), online: <https://plato.stanford.edu/entries/chinese-room/>. See also John Searle "The Chinese Room concept" (16 July 2018), online: YouTube <https://www.youtube.com/watch?v=18SXA-G2peY>.

75 Stanford, "2019 Human-Centered Artificial Intelligence Symposium" (18 March 2019), online *Youtube* <https://www.youtube.com/watch?v=yjSlatKnfqQ> see comments by James Landay, Professor of Computer Science at Stanford at 9:08.

Principle 1

ETHICAL PURPOSE AND SOCIETAL BENEFIT

Organisations that develop, deploy or use AI systems and any national laws that regulate such use should require the purposes of such implementation to be identified and ensure that such purposes are consistent with the overall ethical purposes of beneficence and non-maleficence, as well as the other principles of the Policy Framework for Responsible AI.

1
ETHICAL PURPOSE AND SOCIETAL BENEFIT

CHAPTER LEAD
Charles Morgan | McCarthy Tétrault LLP, Canada

Khalid Al-Kofahi | Thomson Reuters, Canada
Scott Casleton | University of California, Berkley, United States
Emily Hutchison | McCarthy Tétrault LLP, Canada
Francis Langlois | McCarthy Tétrault LLP, Canada

I. Introduction

Almost thirty years ago, the German philosopher Hans Jones (born in 1903) wrote that for the men and women of his generation, the destruction of Hiroshima and the race toward nuclear weapons that followed marked the beginning of a new, anguished, reflection on the place of technology in human affairs.[1] On the one hand, nuclear energy was hailed as the energy source of the future, safer, cleaner and more reliable, but on the other, the destructive power of nuclear energy created new threats, not only for humanity, but for all life on Earth. Confronted with such existential choices, humans have, since Hiroshima, resolved not to use weaponised nuclear energy (except as an ultimate threat) and have attempted instead to harness nuclear power in a responsible manner.[2]

Although the implications of the development of artificial intelligence (AI) are certainly not as dramatic as the devastating power of atomic bombs, the increasingly commonplace implementation of AI has similarly been accompanied by both euphoria and deep apprehension. On one hand, some see learning algorithms as nothing short of a panacea, the ultimate tools to solve all of humanity's problems, powering a gleaming future in which electric self-driving vehicles all but eliminate traffic congestion and pollution, where intractable medical problems are effortlessly resolved and menial labour becomes a historical relic. On the other, none other than Tesla and SpaceX CEO Elon Musk has argued that "AI is a fundamental risk to the existence of human civilization."[3] Moreover, even the late Stephen Hawking warned in 2017: "Success in creating effective AI, could be the biggest event in the history of our civilization. Or the worst."[4] If these latter alarmist concerns had been raised merely by the ill-informed, it might be quite easy to simply dismiss them. However, given the potential impact of AI, both the euphoric and alarmist views deserve our serious attention.

In this context, one of the objectives of this paper is to solidify arguments in support of an emerging framework of core principles for responsible AI development, deployment and use that will help ensure that AI systems are used in a manner that will minimize the risk of harm while maximizing the likelihood of positive outcomes—not only for humanity, but also for the environment. These core principles are each discussed in the following chapters. They serve to help ensure that organisations that have chosen to implement an AI system do so in a responsible manner.

Before turning to other core principles related to the responsible implementation of AI, however, this chapter addresses a more fundamental threshold question: "to what end?" We consider that a prerequisite for "responsible AI" is that the AI system will be implemented for an ethical purpose, a purpose that has a demonstrable and reasonable societal benefit.

In this context, Section II of this chapter introduces the ethical principles of "beneficence" and "non-maleficence." In the following sections, we explore a number of issues that are currently provoking intense social and political debate as regards the implementation of AI systems. For example, Section III will present the challenges, dangers and opportunities AI presents for the future of the workplace. Section IV examines a case study of how AI systems may either exacerbate global warming or be responsibly used to fight it. Section V explores choices that governments and other stakeholders will have to make in relation to the use of AI in a military context. Finally, Section VI examines current issues related to the impact of AI on healthy democratic discourse.

These are weighty issues of great societal import. We necessarily treat each only in a cursory manner. As is the case with nuclear power, a number of important choices in relation to the ethical and responsible use of AI for societal benefit are, collectively, ours to make.

II. Beneficence and Non-Maleficence

For many years the Google "Code of Conduct" included the following motto (at once tongue in cheek and deadly serious): "Don't be evil." Following Google's corporate restructuring under Alphabet Inc. in 2015, the motto was replaced with "Do the right thing." These mottos are essentially "catchy" restatements of two core ethical principles: "beneficence" ("do good") and "non-maleficence" ("do no harm").[5]

These two principles are, of course, unassailable ethical exhortations. Unfortunately, on their own, they provide very limited actionable guidance on how to conduct one's affairs! As applied to AI, we wish to participate in the ongoing dialogue regarding the ethical considerations that must remain central to the future development of AI systems.

Ethical AI research around the world

The "Montreal Declaration for a Responsible Development of Artificial Intelligence," developed a series of ethical principles addressed to "any person, organization and company that wishes to take part in the responsible development of artificial intelligence" including the "well-being" principle, the "respect for autonomy" principle, the "equity" principle and the "democratic participation" principle.[6]

The European Commission's High-Level Expert Group on Artificial Intelligence, for its part, favours a human-centric approach in its *Draft Ethics Guidelines for Trustworthy AI:* "AI should be developed, deployed and used with an "ethical purpose," grounded in, and reflective of, fundamental rights, societal values and the ethical principles of Beneficence, Non-Maleficence, Autonomy of humans, Justice and Explicability."[7]

The Personal Data Protection Commission of Singapore agrees that decisions made by AI systems should be human-centric and align with the beneficence and non-maleficence principles.[8]

Private corporations like IBM and Google, as well as professional organizations like the IEEE have also weighed in favour of this human-centred approach.[9]

We salute these efforts to explore the ethical implications of AI. Moreover, we support these proposals to keep humanity at the centre of the discussions on AI, ensuring that advanced technologies are used responsibly to the benefit of the human condition. Technology must not replace human agency. However, we consider that promoting a narrowly-conceived "human-centric" view of ethical and responsible AI may be too limiting to the extent that it places too much emphasis on short-term economic and technological progress of humans to the detriment of the environmental basis on which rests life on Earth. Accordingly, to clarify, any reference to a "human-centric" view in this text is intended to be broad enough to include concerns related to environmental sustainability, the protection and promotion of bio-diversity and the need to combat climate change responsibly.

As will be seen in the following chapters, a number of ethical concepts (including fairness, non-discrimination and the promotion of human agency) are embedded in the "Responsible AI" principles. For the remainder of this chapter, our focus will be on four areas where the potentially transformative impact of AI is currently a matter of significant societal debate. We begin with a discussion of AI's potential impact on the workplace.

III. The Transformation of Work

Previous waves of technological and industrial innovation have all disrupted the job market. They have been accompanied by enthusiasm from inventors and technologists, but also by fears that jobs would be lost and society shaken.

AI and machine learning, together with robotics, are part of a new industrial revolution, sometimes referred to as the Fourth Industrial Revolution.[10] They are changing how we shop, how we travel, how we connect and communicate with each other, how we learn, where we eat and what we read. AI is also transforming how we create value across many industries including farming and agriculture, manufacturing, retail, transportation and energy. AI's ability to treat vast amount of data makes it also well suited to take over many tasks that were previously thought to be within the exclusive jurisdiction of humans. AI systems that write news article,[11] diagnose skin cancer[12] and manage bookkeeping[13] are now assisting, and sometimes replacing, human wage earners.

Lawyers and AI

Lawyers, despite their intense training and highly cognitive tasks will not be spared. In 2016, Richard Susskind argued in his book *Tomorrow's Lawyers* that "regarding legal work as bespoke in nature is an unhelpful—if often romantic-fiction."[14] Already, programs used in document review are outperforming human lawyers.[15] Today, there exist hundreds of startups developing solutions not only for document review, but also for document automation, legal research and legal assistance, many of them already used by law firms.[16] These AI-enhanced tools are resulting in reduced costs and increased client satisfaction. But they also come with new challenges. For example, if all the basic, routine and repetitive tasks are automated, it becomes less obvious how young lawyers will learn their craft.[17] Despite these advances and what some may wish for, lawyers will not disappear in the near future. Their tasks, however, will change and they will interact more and more with smart machines.

In other sectors, however, humans risk being replaced more quickly. Especially at risk are workers in the transportation, logistics, administrative support and production sectors; particularly low-skills and low-wages workers.[18] The impact the AI-induced shift will probably be far from either the Luddite's fear of seeing machines taking over every job or from the techno-optimist's dream of opulence and leisure. Nevertheless, in the short term, social disturbances can be expected, which will require humane and forward-looking public policies.

Predictions regarding the impact of AI on the workplace vary considerably. Some have estimated that as many as 50% of all jobs are at risk. Others are much more optimistic. A report by McKinsey Global Initiative (MGI) on the future of work concluded that almost half of the activities people are paid to do globally (representing around US $16 trillion) have the potential to be automated by the programs created by the IT and computer industry. This is not to say that half of the jobs will be automated. To the contrary, the report estimates that only 5% of jobs will be completely automated. But at the task/activity level, the report estimates that 30% of activities, across 60% of occupations, will be completely automated. The activities the most vulnerable to automation, representing $2.7 trillion in wages, are those relating to data collecting, data processing and predictable physical activities.[19] Sectors where workers spend the most time on automatable activities will see the most changes, among them food services, manufacturing, agriculture and transportation.[20]

A recent and more optimistic study by Pricewaterhousecoopers (PWC) predicted that AI will create more jobs than it has destroyed in the UK.[21] As the following "Emerging and declining roles based on AI" shows, AI is expected to drive demand for new roles while decreasing the demand for old roles. Not only will these new roles require higher skills and provide higher pay, there will be, in the end, more jobs in our future AI-enabled economy. This follows an often-noted effect of technological change, most recently by the World Bank in its *2019 World Development Report:* "Over the last century, machines have replaced workers in many tasks. On balance, however, technology has created more jobs than it has displaced" because of the creation of new sectors of activities of which Information and Communication Technology (ICT) is a good example.[22] In short, demand for workers with high cognitive skills, adaptive and relational abilities will increase.[23]

However, even optimistic assessments of the impact of AI on job creation note that the impact of AI in the workplace will not be experienced in an equitable manner across-the-board: certain skills will be increasingly valued and others massively devalued. Moreover, many have argued that AI's impact on the workplace will be felt differently in different countries, with a strong potential to exacerbate existing socio-economic inequality amongst the world's "have" and "have nots," both domestically and internationally.[24]

A. Impact of AI on employment: the global trends

When oil prices dropped, a reduction in the number of oil rigs and employees followed. But when the number of rigs began to climb again, the number of employees remained stagnant. This is because price pressures, earlier in the cycle, accelerated the adoption of new technologies that significantly reduced the number of workers needed to operate an Oil Rig.[25] What is astonishing is that the entire cycle took just under 3 years. This is one an example of the impact of robots (now often enabled by AI) on manufacturing.

However, the underlying pattern of rising productivity and declining employment exists across industries. For example, in the USA, productivity and employment moved in tandem from the 1940s until about the year 2000 where they began to separate. While this separation (between productivity and employment) is driven by a number of factors, automation, AI and the software industry have undoubtedly changed how work is done across a number of sectors including clerical workers, travel agents, tax preparers and even financial advisors. And this is not to mention the impact of the internet and e-commerce on bricks and mortar stores, newspapers, book stores and libraries, some of which have begun to leverage AI in their daily business.

Emerging and declining roles based on AI[26]

1. Data Analysts
2. AI and Machine Learning Specialists
3. General and Operations Managers
4. Software and Applications Developers and Analysts
5. Sales and Marketing Professionals
6. Big Data Specialist
7. Digital Transformation Specialists
8. New Technology Specialists
9. Organizational Development Specialist
10. Information Technology Services

1. Data Entry Clerks
2. Accounting, Bookkeeping, and Payroll Clerks
3. Administrative and Executive Secretaries
4. Assembly and Factory Workers
5. Client Information and Customer Service Workers
6. Business Services and Administration Managers
7. Accountants and Auditors
8. Material Recording and Stock keeping Clerks
9. General and Operations Managers
10. Postal Service Clerks

While the debate regarding the net impact of the software industry and AI on employment continues, the fact remains that the software industry is currently a significant driver of job creation world-wide. A report by the World Economic Forum concluded that "[o]ur analysis finds that increased demand for new roles will offset the decreasing demand for others."[27] The World Bank Group estimated that the ICT sector represents about 5.7% of total business sector employment in OECD countries.[28] In India alone, the IT industry represents over 3.5 million jobs, a third held by women.

B. Three types of impacts on employment

AI enabled applications may be broadly characterised as following into three categories:

1. those that seek to introduce efficiencies through automation (e.g., robots and robotic process automation, smart software: e.g., spam filtering, fraud detection, tax preparation),
2. those that seek to introduce efficiencies and scale through augmentation and human-machine teaming, and
3. those that enable tasks that were not possible before (e.g., personalized medicine, autonomous transportation, high-frequency trading, long-term weather forecasting).

While the **first type,** automation, will continue to have a significant impact on employment, the **second type,** augmentation, is arguably more interesting and will have a bigger and more disrupting impact on the nature of work itself. Augmentation requires some form of cooperation between humans and machines to execute a task. As machines equipped with AI learn from practice and become more capable, the boundary between human-work and machine-work will shift, with machines taking on a bigger proportion of the task, thus pushing humans to focus on higher value tasks. Examples of augmentation include issue-resolution in customer support, document review in eDiscovery (law) and medical diagnosis (e.g., of skin cancer images analysis). In each of these examples, the human is responsible for making the final decision on the course of action, but she is aided by a program to provide scale, higher quality and lower cost.

Medicine

While a board-certified physician may look at thousands or even tens of thousands of images of cancerous and normal tissues during her career, a program can be trained on millions or tens of millions of images a lot more rapidly. Under such a setup, the physician remains responsible for the final diagnosis, but AI can help her make decisions faster.

Law

In the legal space, having lawyers sift through tens of thousands or even millions of documents is not only very expensive, it is also something that humans/lawyers are comparatively not good at. AI can sift through large document collections quickly and identify a small subset that requires human review.

In both of these examples, augmentation will result in increased productivity, higher quality services and allow people to focus on higher value (and more interesting) tasks. More interesting work in less time should—at least in theory—allow workers to achieve a **better work-life balance.**

The **third type** of AI-enabled applications is not designed to introduce efficiencies or scale for existing tasks. Instead, they aim to enable new types of capabilities. Still, new capabilities often render old way of doing things obsolete and will negatively impact certain jobs.

Transportation

From an employment perspective, developments in **Autonomous Transportation** are particularly noteworthy because they have the potential to render the professional driver industry obsolete. This is a sizeable segment of the workforce that would need to shift job category completely in the event that fully autonomous vehicles become commonplace.

C. The skill gap

The ongoing changes risk creating a skills gap not only between workers and AI systems, but also between workers with varying levels of knowledge and abilities. The World Bank recently summarized the situation as follows: "the demand for advanced cognitive skills and socio-behavioural skills is increasing, whereas the demand for narrow job-specific skills is waning. Meanwhile, those associated with "adaptability" are increasingly in demand."[29] This is so because in the digital age, rapid technological changes force workers to consistently modify and improve their skillsets.[30]

As the nature of work itself changes, so will the skills needed to do the work. The skills needed for emerging roles (e.g., big data engineers, AI scientists or developers) are very different from those necessary for declining roles (e.g., accountants, clerks, drivers, etc.). According to the *Future of Jobs Report:* "By 2022, no less than 54% of all employees will require significant re- and upskilling. Of these, about 35% are expected to require additional training of up to six months, 9% will require reskilling lasting six to 12 months, while 10% will require additional skills training of more than a year."[31] Furthermore, the report concludes that the likelihood of companies hiring new staff with new emerging skills is twice as great as companies upskilling existing employees.

The combination of connectivity, open source, cloud-computing, online education/courses/training, collaboration platforms and stiff competition for talent will also accelerate the gig-economy and change the nature of employment. For people with in-demand skills, this will undoubtedly result in more rewarding jobs, higher pay, less traffic congestion and even better life-work balance. And as long as these people continue to invest significant amount of their time on learning and upskilling as the technology evolves, they will be able to sustain meaningful and rewarding careers. The pace of change, however, will render many skills irrelevant very quickly, and people with low-demand skills may have to compete for less rewarding and lower-paying jobs.

If this were to occur, it would shift the burden of upskilling onto the employees themselves, who will most likely lack the time and resources required to learn new and emerging skills. As such, it is not reasonable to expect workers from declining roles to be able to reskill themselves for the new roles without outside support. Some will undoubtedly achieve, on their own, a successful transition, but many may not.

This rapidly emerging scenario calls for a redefinition of education. Education as a means to meet the challenges of an industrial revolution is not a new solution. In the beginning of the 20th century, school systems, in the USA for instance, were progressively improved and expanded to adapt to the decline of farm employment and the rise of industrial jobs. By the end of the 20th century, most citizens in developed countries received at least a secondary level of education.[32] The current dominant educational paradigm however makes an important divide between a learning period (during infancy, adolescence and early adulthood) and a longer working period in adult life without further formal learning. This must be improved to account for the evolving skills required in this new economy and for the pace of technological change. In this regard, the World Bank encourages governments to make substantial investments in "lifelong learning," which begins by teaching children cognitive and social skills at a very early age, continues at the tertiary level (college and trade schools, with a focus on transferable cognitive skills) and then continues further with adult learning inside and outside the workplace.[33] More than ever, learning and training will not be limited to young age and school years. Extensive and varied support from governments will be essential in addressing this need.

D. Long term policy proposals

The economic use of automation, AI and robotics is predicted to create unprecedented wealth. Many fear however that this wealth will be concentrated in a few hands. Swedish philosopher Nick Bostrom has suggested that the rise of AI systems replacing human workers could mean a greater significance of capital in the share of global income, as opposed to wages.[34] This would mean that a greater portion of the pie would go the persons owning the capital, because wage-earners would become less and less important in the production process of many industries.

Current welfare policies, such as social insurance schemes inherited from policies put in place by Bismarck in Germany at the end of the 19th century, presuppose that workers receive regular wages from a definite employer and have a fixed retirement age. This model works well for stable and formal employment by factories or firms. But for developing countries where this model is not the norm, and even for developed countries where more mobile forms of work emerge (thanks in part to AI applications), it is maladapted.[35]

This is why some have suggested more universal measures of wealth distribution that are not based on formal wage employment.[36] These solutions include free or subsidized services like transportation, childcare, healthcare and education, but also more revolutionary measures like providing a basic income for all.[37] Elon Musk, notably, said in 2016 that "[t]here is a pretty good chance we end up with a universal basic income, [...], due to automation."[38] Some, such as Bill Gates, have suggested financing these solutions by means of a new "robot tax."[39] Each of the various proposed solutions have defenders and detractors.

The debates of course have only begun. Attempts to implement a universal basic income have so far been limited and unsuccessful.[40] As for a potential "robot tax," the European Commission rejected a proposal to tax robot owners in order to finance the retraining of human workers.[41] It is also feared that such tax would be a tax on productivity.[42] What should not be forgotten is that governments themselves can make a great use of AI systems to improve public administration and the services they provide to their population. The Canadian government, for example, has begun testing AI chatbots to interact with beneficiaries of federal social programs like pensions, family benefits and disability supports.[43]

The first policies that should be put in place by countries wanting to benefit from AI in the workplace should be monitoring policies that assess the evolving impact of AI on the workplace. Indeed, most governments currently lack the essential information necessary to make informed AI-related policy decisions.

United States

The US FUTURE of Artificial Intelligence Act of 2017 established an advisory committee tasked with providing the U.S. Secretary of Commerce with advice relating to the following as regards AI: workforce, (including matters relating to the potential for using artificial intelligence for rapid retraining of workers, due to the possible effect of technological displacement), and education, (including matters relating to science, technology, engineering, and mathematics education to prepare the United States workforce as the needs of employers change).[44]

It is unlikely that the AI revolution will follow the same pattern as previous technological shifts, in which a short period of instability and disruption to the job market has been followed by a much longer period of stability and growth. The pace of change in the AI and software industries suggests that these disruptions will occur at a much faster rate. A number of studies[45] have put forward recommendations on how to lessen the impact of these disruptions on the workforce, some of which already mentioned, including:

1. Educating policy makers on AI and its impact on employment including studying its impact on global skill indices.[46]
2. Creating training programs for disrupted workers—focusing not only on technology skills but also on developing their soft skills such as communications, product management and leadership skills.
3. Improving access to digital and AI tools, including training programs for the general public.
4. Empowering the workforce through training, job placement services and updating regulations—especially those focusing on improving social safety nets for displaced workers.

While the above recommendations all make sense, none, we believe, is more important than adopting a new education system that focuses on life-long learning and puts in place policies to ensure that workers have the time and resources needed to learn to work with emerging technologies and keep their skills up-to-date. Some jurisdictions have policies that require employer participation in the skills development of the workforce. For example, the Canadian province of Québec mandates employers with a payroll over $2 million to contribute at least 1% of this payroll to employee skills development.[47] Additionally, given the abundance of free online courses and training programs, this is not necessarily a funding question. It is a question of creating structured programs and the right incentives for workers to participate and commit to learning opportunities.

E. Conclusion

In conclusion, AI is driving a transformation of how we get things done. It will allow us to do things that were not possible before, increase efficiency, drive productivity and growth. It will change how we work, where we work and how we live. But as with every new technology or invention, the laws of unintended consequences are always omnipresent. The ramifications and unseen consequences of a new technology are often harder to deal with than the technology itself. This is true for AI. It is opening new exciting frontiers but will undoubtedly create significant disruptions. While entrepreneurs, scientists and engineers will lead the development of AI, thinking about potential disruptions is a task for all of us including governments, jurists, consumers groups, workers' unions, educational institutions, companies and non-profit organization.

IV. Ecological Impact of AI

A. Introduction

"Adults keep saying that we owe it to the young people to give them hope. But I don't want your hope. I don't want you to be hopeful. I want you to panic. I want you to feel the fear I feel every day. And then I want you to act. I want you to act as if you would in a crisis. I want you to act as if the house was on fire. Because it is."

Greta Thunberg

The previous section presupposed that technological development and growth will continue to progress as they did in the last century, albeit with an accelerating rate of change. However, as unfettered growth has had a demonstrably devastating impact on the environment, we are confronted by the fact that such growth may simply not be sustainable.

As has been made clear by such reports as the 2018 report of the Intergovernmental Panel on Climate Change (IPCC),[48] we no longer have the luxury of adopting a purely human-centric view of the world. Climate change is a human-made existential risk for all life forms. Recent statistics regarding the destructive impact of humans on other living beings and our ecosystems are shattering. According to a scientific report prepared for the World Wildlife Foundation, in the last 50 years alone, it is estimated that worldwide populations of mammals, birds, fish and reptiles have declined by approximately 60%.[49] Moreover, a January 2019 scientific report found that the rate of decline in the insect population is likely even higher.[50] This tragic phenomenon is also known as the Anthropocene extinction or as the Earth's sixth major extinction.[51] In short, there is an urgent need to use energy more efficiently and cut down on polluting emissions.

How does this relate to AI?

On the one hand, it is hoped that climate change and its consequences can be reduced through technological means, including AI. Better predictive models based on machine learning can help us manage resources and energy more efficiently and to develop more accurate climate forecasting systems. For example, the Villani Report argues that "AI can help us understand the dynamics and the evolution of whole ecosystems by focusing on their biological complexity; it will allow us to manage our resources more efficiently (particularly in terms of energy), preserve our environment and encourage biodiversity"[52] On the other hand, by increasing the production of goods and services, it concomitantly risks continuing the economic patterns that are at the origin of the crisis.[53] In short, AI can help to either redress or augment the environmental crisis that we are facing as a society. We believe AI must be part of the solution rather than part of the problem.

This section will primarily consider reducing carbon emissions, in particular through the development of a 'smart' electrical grid and its ability to incorporate renewable energy sources and electric vehicles. AI has the potential to transform the energy grid, making electricity use more efficient and environmentally friendly; though this comes with the risk of simply making energy consumption easier, in effect displacing the environmental impact rather than limiting it. To explore these scenarios further, we now turn to a case study of the application of AI to implement a smart electrical grid.

B. Electricity & carbon emissions in the United States

The United States Environmental Protection Agency (EPA) reports that electricity use is responsible for 28% of carbon emissions in the United States. This in turn can be broken down by source: fossil fuels constitute the lion's share at 62.9% (mostly natural gas at 32.1% and coal at 29.9%), while nuclear energy and renewables respectively represent 20% and 17% (hydro at 7.4%, wind at 6.3%, Biomass at 1.6%, and solar at 1.3%) of energy sources.[54]

The EPA suggests that two of the primary ways of reducing carbon emissions due to electricity are to increase energy efficiency and to replace fossil fuels with renewable sources. It is on these two points that AI can be deployed to tremendous benefit. Understanding how this can be possible requires first understanding the unique problems posed by running an efficient electrical grid.

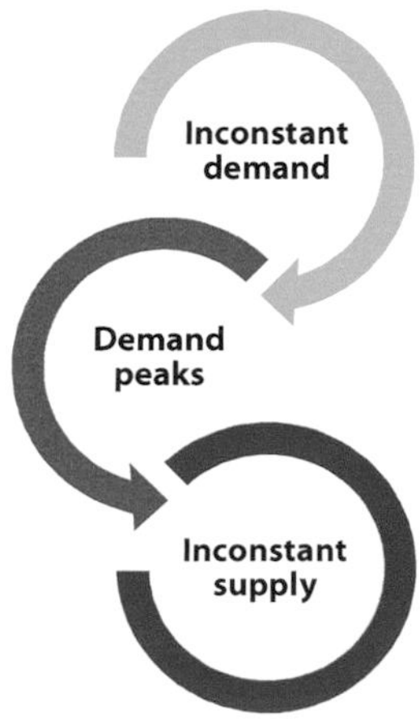

There are three distinct aspects of electricity consumption that the electrical grid must accommodate. First, demand is not constant throughout the day. Second, and related, is that demand often surges at certain times during the day, creating demand 'peaks.' Third, when energy is derived from renewable sources, it is not available at a constant rate.

This first aspect is not surprising, given the wide variety of contexts in which electricity is demanded. The needs of agriculture, industry, transportation, and residences vary greatly, given that they operate on different time schedules.

The second issue, that of demand peaks, is one of the major factors in the production of carbon emissions. Consider that most household consumers, for example, are at home in the evening, which is when they use appliances like dishwashers, laundry machines, and entertainment systems. When many households use these appliances at a similar time in the evening, it creates a spike in electricity consumption—a peak, relative to other times of the day. When these peaks occur, additional power plants need to be turned on, which are typically less environmentally friendly, increasing the generation of carbon emissions.

Finally, there is the issue of non-constant production. As a recent article from *The Economist* notes, "[f]ossil fuels are easier to hook up to today's grids than renewables that depend on the sun shining and the wind blowing."[55] Because renewable sources are weather-dependent, they can be a difficult fit for an energy system that operates on an on-demand basis.

The above three aspects of the electrical grid combine to create 'the coordination problem.' The electrical grid must coordinate, on the one hand, inconstant demand that comes in peaks and valleys with, on the other hand, somewhat inconstant supply. AI is the means of solving the coordination problem without relying on fossil fuels. By creating a 'smart grid' that can better predict patterns of demand, flatten out demand peaks, and supply renewable energy when it is available, AI can provide a more efficient, sustainable electrical grid.

Smart Grid

The smart grid functions by replacing old electricity meters with new, "smart" meters that record domestic energy use and interact with "smart" appliance.[56] Consumption information, once recorded and stored, becomes energy use data, from which the lifestyle habits, among other things, of the consumer can be inferred. As we shall see, energy use data is what makes the AI smart grid possible, but it also creates unique legal problems that policy must address.

How does the smart grid function? The goal is to learn the patterns of consumption and manage both sides of energy use, demand and supply.[57] Imagine a suburban neighbourhood that receives its energy from one power plant. In the evening, after work, most households are likely to run their laundry machines, creating a spike in energy use. Suppose this spike creates a demand that is so great that a second, less environmentally-friendly power plant must be tapped into to supply the necessary electricity. As a result, the carbon emissions created from this spike exceed the amount that would have been produced if the laundry loads had been spread out throughout the day.

Clearly, this scenario has the classic features of a collective action problem. Since each household is ignorant of what every other household is doing, even if they want to avoid energy demand peaks they may not with complete confidence be able to do so.

The smart grid works by helping to solve not just this problem of household ignorance, but *also* to resolve it by becoming involved in the decision-making process, so to speak. Since smart meters record the household usage of electricity, the energy company will build a centralized collection of usage data. Accordingly, it can act to reduce the peaks. It does so by interacting with the households via their smart appliances. If a household has a smart laundry machine, it can communicate with the smart meter. The meter can then reduce the electricity intensity of a certain number of laundry machines (thereby making them run for longer due to the lower intensity), to flatten out the demand peak.

This scenario displays the two-way communication of the smart grid. The meters receive information (usage data) from households, and they then use this information to communicate (and partially control) the appliances.

By collecting this usage data over time—from households, businesses, farms, and so on—energy companies can then use these data sets to have AI systems learn the patterns of energy use. This will make energy use less unpredictable, thereby making the prediction and flattening of peaks more feasible. While raw energy use data was previously available through old meters, it was much more difficult to collect and much less specific about which appliances were being used. So, introducing smart meters and appliances to homes is an essential piece of this solution.

By reducing demand peaks, energy use becomes more efficient. But this still leaves the problem of incorporating renewable energy into the grid. Doing this relies on the same mechanism as flattening out a peak. When a smart meter communicates with, say, a laundry machine and slows its cycle to reduce electrical intensity, it is effectively changing the *time span* during which the energy is used. This capacity is what is necessary to incorporate renewable energy.

Since renewable energy must be used in a short time span after it is harvested (absent improved storage capacity), AI—trained smart meters can ostensibly tell an appliance when an energy-efficient time-span occurs. This need not mean the meter can itself turn on the laundry machine, but instead it can display the time-span on the laundry machine's user-interface, giving the user the ultimate, but better informed, decision about when to do their laundry.

Clearly, the smart grid depends both on the hardware of smart meters and appliances, and the data that runs through them. The resulting data, then, will have immense instrumental value for reducing carbon emissions. But, it will also have immense monetary value for energy companies, and, notably, third party organizations.[58] This motivates concerns about privacy and the regulation of household data.

In this context, California's Bill SB 1476 is an example of legislation that seeks to find a balance between the objective of facilitating the data flow that is necessary for the effective implementation of smart grid technology with the countervailing objective of protecting privacy rights. [59]

As Forbush notes "California Senate Bill 1476 requires aggregators of energy consumption data to obtain consumer consent before sharing customer information with third parties; mandates that third parties may only have access to such data when they are contracting with the utility to provide energy management-related services; stipulates that data be kept secure from unauthorized parties; and mandates that electricity ratepayers —opt in to authorize any sharing of their energy consumption data for any —secondary commercial purpose[s]."[60] Such a model is important, especially given that the smart grid will be expanded beyond just household use, eventually including consumer movement and consumption from electric vehicles. On the flipside, a data collection model based on consent might provide less accurate predictive models. The topic of how AI challenges the consent model of data protection will be discussed in more details in our treatment of Principle 7—Privacy.

C. Potential dangers of increased consumption

Solving the coordination problem with AI and renewable energy sources is an important and difficult task, but even if it is successful it leaves a number of issues unaddressed. The first and most immediate is the possibility that making energy consumption more efficient will make it easier to consume large amounts of energy, effectively abolishing the advance in carbon reduction.

This danger is noted by Cedric Villani in his report on AI for the French government, saying AI may "result in consumption being at least as great, if not greater, than it was before."[61] He calls this a 'rebound effect' whereby "the expected savings in energy and resources due to the use of new technology may be partly or completely outweighed by society's response to it."[62] This is not difficult to imagine. Villani provides the straightforward case where the savings made on a heating bill may be reinvested in another product or activity which then adds to energy consumption.[63]

Hence, simply allowing the technology market to change the electrical grid is not sufficient to address the threat of climate change. A "smart grid" is only truly smart if it is a piece in a larger public effort to reduce carbon emissions. The only way to ensure that this is pursued is by placing the technology and market driven approach considered here in a larger architecture of public policy.[64]

Finally, another aspect of AI's ecological impact must be computed in order to have a fair assessment of its risks and benefits. While AI might work in the virtual world, it nonetheless requires substantial quantities of real world resources. In his report, Cédric Villani notes that "The production of digital hardware uses large quantities of rare precious metals which are only partly recyclable, and the available reserves are limited (15 years in the case of Indium, for example, the consumption of which has multiplied sevenfold in 10 years); this could result in a technological impasse if this increase in demand does not slow down, especially given that some of these metals are also used in the production of equipment for renewable energy (wind and solar power)."[65] Going from a dependence on finite carbon-based energy sources to one on finite mineral deposits requiring intensive mining may be what awaits us in the future.[66]

D. Conclusion

In short, efficiency and sustainability in the use of all resources necessary for the fabrication and use of AI systems should be core concerns whenever organisations consider whether to develop, deploy or use an AI system. Assessment of AI projects should include evaluations not only of the project's carbon impact, but also of their consumption of raw material with an aim toward reusability and recycling.[67]

We now turn our attention to the topic of use of AI in lethal autonomous weapons systems.

V. Lethal Autonomous Weapons Systems

A. Introduction

Revisiting our opening analogy to the weaponised use of nuclear energy, we will now explore risks related to the weaponised use of AI, as States rush to develop lethal autonomous weapons systems (LAWS) and implement AI systems to create the armies of the future.

Historians such as Paul Kennedy have noted the intimate relationship between economic vigour, military might and technological innovation.[68] If 19th and 20th century geopolitics were defined by the Industrial Revolution, then the Digital Revolution, with AI at the forefront, could be the essence of the geopolitics of our time.[69] Unsurprisingly, the recent progress in AI, allowing for the processing and analysis of more data, for increasing autonomy and new applications, have caught the attention of military decision makers and chief-of-states around the world.

AI and autonomous weapons around the world

China hopes to become the world leader in AI by 2030 and high-ranking members of the *People's Liberation Army* intend to leverage AI for military purposes.[70]

For the U.S., AI was an integral part of its *Third Offset Strategy*[71] launched in 2014 to maintain American "military-technological superiority."[72]

As for Russia, President Vladimir Putin declared in 2017 that "the one who becomes the leader in [AI] will be the ruler of the world" while his country also finances research on militarized AI.[73]

The last two States with a permanent seat on the UN Security council, France and the United Kingdom, have also devised plans to upgrade their armies with AI capacities.[74]

A. Previous military interest in AI

It is not the first time AI attracts the attention of armies. In 1983, the Defence Advanced Research Projects Agency (DARPA), the research branch of the U.S. Department of Defence, launched an important program, the Strategic Computing Initiative, that would spend US $1 billion in the course of ten years, notably on first-generation AI. The program had the broad goal of developing machine intelligence, with the more concretely defined objectives of creating autonomous land vehicles, systems that could assist pilots and battle management systems.[75] The research agenda was vast, including natural language processing, text comprehension, expert systems, image recognition and machine reasoning.[76] However, as we have seen above in other contexts, unhinged ambitions led ultimately to disappointment, and despite some success, the Strategic Computing Initiative was essentially abandoned by the end of the 1980s.[77]

Could the current hype similarly falter? As we have seen in the introduction, in the 1980s, AI still lacked the computing power necessary to achieve its full potential and machine learning was only emerging, as Geoffrey Hinton's famous back-propagation paper would not be published before 1986.[78] As the U.S. Department of Defence wrote in 2011, however "[d]ramatic progress in supporting technologies suggests that unprecedented levels of autonomy can be introduced into current and future unmanned systems."[79] AI can prove useful for armies in many different ways, but it is the development of autonomous systems that is the holy grail of this generation's military research.

B. Towards lethal autonomous weapons systems

During the 2000s, unmanned systems proliferated on battlefields around the globe, with the drones used by the U.S. Air Force in the war against terror being the most well-known example.[80] Although unmanned systems have been so far equipped with some automated functions, they lack autonomy and all their most important functions, notably selecting and engaging targets, are controlled by human operators.[81]

In that context, autonomy would bring the concept of unmanned systems to its logical (and potentially terrifying) conclusion. When given an objective, an autonomous weapon system would be able to decide on the best actions to take depending on its current environment. Machine learning would also allow it to develop new strategies and react to unforeseen situations, all of this without direct involvement by a human operator.[82] As an illustration, in current drone strikes, human operators are doing most of the flying tasks, selecting the targets according to their orders and pulling the trigger. Ultimately, autonomous systems would not only function without humans in the cockpit, but also with no human at the operating console. Once given a mission by a commander, they could perform their task completely without further human inputs, perhaps even in the context of lost communications with their commanders, leaving no capacity to re-direct or terminate the mission. Development of such systems have been a "high priority" for the U.S. military since the beginning of the 2010s and other armies have followed suit.[83]

Among the advantages of autonomy, armies hope it represents a solution to the rising cost of manpower.[84] At the strategic and tactical levels, autonomous system, unburdened by the limitations of the human brain, could increase the speed and efficiency of operations[85] and operate without our physical and psychological constraints, such as fatigue, stress, fear, anger and inattention.[86] Some States also make the argument that autonomous weapon systems would be more accurate than humans and thus reduce the risk of civilian casualties and collateral damages.[87]

C. Opposition from civil society

Outside of military circles, however, many specialists and observers have strongly opposed the production of weapon systems with the ability to pull the trigger themselves, including Yoshua Bengio, one of the recent recipients of the A.M. Turing Award for is contribution as a pioneer of AI.[88] Noel Sharkey, the roboticist involved in the Gaak experiment whom we have met in the Introduction, was among the first to publicly oppose projects to develop such weapons. In 2007, he wrote "I have worked in artificial intelligence for decades, and the idea of a robot making decisions about human termination is terrifying."[89] With other roboticists and AI specialists, Professor Sharkey was also involved in the creation of the *International Committee for Robot Arms Control* in 2009 and the launch of the Campaign to Stop Killer Robots in 2013, an international campaign for the ban of lethal autonomous weapons systems (LAWS) bringing together dozens of NGOs.[90] Independently, the Future of Life Institute published in 2015 a well-publicized open letter calling for the prevention of a military arms race by the imposition of a ban on offensive autonomous weapons that was signed by thousands of AI and robotics experts.[91] More recently, almost 3,500 AI specialists and organizations have pledged never to participate in the development or support LAWS.[92]

"I have worked in artificial intelligence for decades, and the idea of a robot making decisions about human termination is terrifying."

Noel Sharkey—Roboticist

Civil society proponents of a prohibition of LAWS fear their development by some States could trigger a new arms race and that once ubiquitous they would lower "the threshold for going to battle."[93] They also argue it would be immoral or unethical to delegate the decision to take a human life to a machine.[94] Thus, they argue that human beings should maintain meaningful control over the weapons they use in battle and that LAWS deprive soldiers precisely of that control.[95]

D. Opposition from within the technological industry

Because of their unparalleled technological knowledge and their role as hub for AI development, tech giants around the world are key players in the ongoing military revolution. However some of these companies have faced unprecedented push-backs from an unexpected source: their own employees.

In the spring of 2018, Google employees began to circulate and sign an open letter addressed to CEO Sundar Pichai that protested the company's involvement in the U.S. Department of Defense (DoD) Project Maven.[96] This project aims to develop AI tools to classify images captured by drones.[97] Around 4,000 employees signed the letter arguing that Google should not enter "in the business of war" and calling for the cancellation of the contract.[98] The protestations were serious enough to lead Google to publish a set of AI principles, including the commitment that Google will not design or deploy AI weapons.[99] Following these principles, the company resolved not to bid on a $10 billion cloud-computing contract from the Pentagon[100] and also that it would not renew the Project Maven contract when it ends in March 2019.[101]

E. Multilateral debates

The debate over an international ban of LAWS now takes place within the United Nations. In 2014, discussions began within the multilateral mechanism of the Convention on Certain Conventional Weapons (CCW) and States agreed in 2016 to form a Group of Governmental Experts on Lethal Autonomous Weapons.[102] Although twenty-eight countries have so far voiced their support of a ban of fully autonomous weapons,[103] as well as the European Parliament, the chances of reaching a meaningful control of LAWS through a UN convention are limited. The States involved have yet to agree on a definition of LAWS[104] and the efforts to reach a binding treaty has been slowed by the U.S., Russia, South Korea, Israel and Australia.[105] Even if some States agreed to a final text, it would not bind States that refuse to ratify it, which is likely if some believe their national interest dictates them to pursue the development of LAWS. A Convention could thus meet the same fate as the recent Treaty on the Prohibition of Nuclear Weapons adopted in 2017 and signed by 69 States, but none of the nuclear powers.[106] Although some relatively recent conventions banning blinding lasers (1995), land mines (1997) and cluster munitions (2008) have been generally successful, legally binding documents against particular weapons have had historically mixed results.[107]

F. The role of international humanitarian law

Nevertheless, even without a ban or another form of conventional regulation, LAWS would not be in a legal void. There is now a large consensus that the use of LAWS, however they might be defined in the future, would be subject, as are all weapons, to international humanitarian law (IHL).[108] A modern version of the law of war, IHL contains the set of rules applicable in the context of armed conflicts.[109] Yet, the application of IHL to LAWS remains fraught with uncertainties. Although there seems to be a consensus that IHL requires that human agency be maintained over LAWS, the nature of that agency is debated.[110] Some argue that human "control" over use of lethal force decisions is essential and that in consequence fully autonomous weapons doing away with that control are illegal under IHL.[111] Others have argued that IHL does not mandate an actual human control over the firing decision and that the application of a higher level "human judgment" is sufficient.[112] Such a position entails, for instance, that a military commander deploying battalions of LAWS during a battle, would in itself be sufficient human oversight, without him reviewing every particular decision taken by a robot during combat. In this situation, the commander would be the accountable party and would still be required to respect the IHL principles of distinction between combatants and civilians, of proportionality between military necessity and collateral civilian casualties, and of avoiding unnecessary suffering.[113]

G. Conclusion

Although current debates have focused on LAWS, autonomy in weapon systems remains only one of the ways AI could reshape the battlefields of the future. Militarized AI can as well mean supply chain management systems or algorithms predicting when a fighter jet will require maintenance.[114] Cyberwarfare is also bound to change with the development of this technology,[115] and some have suggested that the old Cold War dream of having AI systems control nuclear arsenals to enable faster-than-light reactions to foreign threats could soon be a reality.[116] Hence, even in the case of a successful ban on LAWS preventing the creation of Terminator-like weapons, the conduct of war is most likely to become another human activity transformed by AI.

VI. Fake News, Deep Fakes and Disinformation Campaigns Perpetuating Violence

A. Introduction

AI can be weaponised as a shield or as a sword not only in the space of physical battlefields, but also in the cyberspace of information and ideas. In the data-driven world of the Internet and social media, AI is destined to have an important influence on the way we consume and produce online content—one that cannot be ignored by legal professionals. This section explores the recent trends of fake news and disinformation leveraging AI technologies, and asks whether the best solution is to impose stricter obligations on Internet Intermediaries to take measures against hateful or harmful content.

B. The social media ecosystem

The current AI race comes at a time when the Internet is the most important human data repository in history. It is also the widest and most extensive information sharing infrastructure to date, with platforms like Google, Facebook, Alibaba, Instagram, Twitter, YouTube and Reddit attracting billion of users—and their data. Concurrently, these platforms have become central and unavoidable spaces of public debate. In 2018, for instance, 68% of American adults used social media "at least occasionally" to access news stories.[117] Internet Intermediaries, also known as Internet Service Providers (ISPs), are the immerged portion of internet social media, an ensemble composed of blogs, social media, wikis and comment sections that enable a continuous, interactive and global online "conversation" to produce, every day, astronomical amounts of data.[118]

In recent years, the impact of these platforms on public discourse and democratic life has come under intense scrutiny. For every Wikipedia, the Internet seems to harbour dozens of spaces from which egregious content can emerge and spread, sometimes with the intent of influencing or subverting political processes. Since the 2016 U.S. Presidential election, the Cambridge Analytica scandal and accusation of foreign interference, the phenomenon of fake news has particularly drawn attention.[119]

Is it is today easier both to produce and to disseminate content. In the attention economy, where social media platforms compete for our attention to generate ads revenues,[120] the content that is most likely to interest us, whether for good or bad reasons, is favoured over quality and substantive information.[121] In addition, personalization of user experience through data collection creates silos of information consumption ("bubbles") and "echo chambers."[122] People also tend to select content based on their personal attitude and preferences.[123] This creates an environment favourable to both misinformation and disinformation.[124]

C. Here come deep fakes

As with every aspect of human life that is heavily data-driven, AI based on machine and deep learning has the potential to impact the Internet, its users and the broader society. We can find in the story of Rana Ayyub a recent and telling example of how AI can go from disrupting to destructive in the context of social media. An investigative journalist in India, Mrs. Ayyub was the victim of deep fakes in April 2018.[125] Deep fakes are videos or images modified with AI.[126] This technology allows users to swap, for example, one person's face in an image or video with the face of another person.[127] Image modification for innocent, artistic or malicious purposes, is in itself nothing new, but availability of technical literature, cheap access to computing power and data as well as the development of user-friendly applications have made the practice more common place.[128] Deep fakes can notably be used in movie production or in the creation of personal avatars for persons who have lost expressive autonomy.[129]

In the case of Mrs. Ayyub, however, deep fake technology was used to replace the face of a young actress in a pornographic video with hers. The video was first circulated on WhatsApp, a popular messaging platform that uses end-to-end encryption, but it quickly became viral on Twitter, Facebook and Instagram.[130] In reaction, Mrs. Ayyub was met with a barrage of online harassment, as well as doxing (the practice of publishing someone's personal information online, notably his or her physical address).

Since the apparition of deep fakes in December 2017 on Reddit,[131] numerous Hollywood actresses and other female public figures have also been the victims of pornographic deep fakes.[132] Mrs. Ayyub, however, is arguably the first to have been targeted for political reasons, to intimidate her and discredit her work as a journalist. This case confirms the potential of deep fakes to severely harm individuals, and women in particular.[133]

D. Deep fakes and fake news

Many fear that deep fakes will have broad adverse social and political impacts. They place the technique within the larger phenomenon of fake news, sometimes as its most dangerous form to date.[134] Specially concerning is the fact that "[b]y blurring the line between fact and fiction, deep fake technology could undermine public trust in recorded images and videos as objective depictions of reality," as three U.S. congressmen wrote recently.[135] In the legal context, deep fakes could ultimately diminish or nullify the probative value of image and video evidence in courts.[136] Moreover, convincing fake videos could exacerbate tensions between communities, distort democratic life and threaten public safety.[137] Deep fakes could thus exacerbate the occurrence of online false information wildfires leading to acts of violence, as we have seen with mob killings in India because of rumours of child kidnapping circulated on WhatsApp[138] and the 2016 Washington pizzeria attack by a man who believed a chain of fast-food restaurants was at the centre of a child-abuse ring led by Hillary Clinton because of fake stories he read online.[139] It could also be used in the political context, to tarnish the reputation of a candidate by creating footage of him or her saying outrageous comments, for instance.[140]

At a larger scale, deep fake could become one tool in the arsenal of deceptive techniques used in propaganda campaigns. Recent reports of the persecution of the Rohingya people in Myanmar show how the state's military built an operation to spread hatred and disinformation by using fake accounts on social media platforms to sow fear of jihadist attacks.[141] UN investigators described the situation as a "textbook example of ethnic cleansing."[142] While deep fakes were reportedly not involved in Myanmar, one can easily imagine how this technology could be used to create convincing footage aimed at fostering division and hostility within and between populations.

E. Legal responses

Individuals affected by deep fakes are not without recourse, even if we still lack jurisprudence on the matter. Subject to the specificity of national legal regimes, victims could notably invoke copyright infringement, defamation, violation of privacy and appropriation of personality, among other basis for liability.[143] Plaintiffs in the UK and the U.S., for instance, have been successful in bringing defamation claims against persons who had published images with a plaintiff's face juxtaposed on the bodies of pornographic actors.[144]

The solution can also come from Internet Intermediaries, notably those important social media platforms that attract most of the web's traffic. In reaction to the growth of deep fakes, large Internet Intermediaries such as Reddit, Twitter and Pornhub decided to self-regulate and to update their terms of use to ban AI-enabled face swap pornographic content.[145] Google now also allows users to request the removal of "involuntary synthetic pornographic imagery" of themselves.[146] Nevertheless, although pornographic deep fakes have mostly disappeared from the immerged parts of social media, a rapid Google search is enough to show that the corpus of deep fakes is still easily accessible—and growing.

It might even be more difficult to limit the proliferation of non-pornographic deep fakes used as fake news. As a starter, image modification, even when done with AI technology, is not illegal in itself and might indeed be protected by the right to free speech. In the United States, for example, Supreme Court decisions have found falsity alone is not enough to remove the protection of the First Amendment.[147] Under copyright law, it might also be protected by fair use.[148] Moreover, as we have seen not only with the case of Mrs. Ayyub but also in recent elections in the U.S.,[149] in France[150] and in Brazil,[151] due to the very structure of social media, false information can spread rapidly and cause damages even after having been debunked.

F. More responsibilities for Internet Intermediaries?

Many lawmakers now see both deep fakes, and more broadly fake news, as serious threats for democratic institutions. Some have called for the imposition of stricter obligations on social media platforms to monitor third-party content.

Proposals for new regulation of Internet Intermediaries

In Canada, a committee of the House of Commons has recommended amending the *Canada Elections Act* to add a responsibility for Internet Intermediaries to remove "defamatory, fraudulent, and maliciously manipulated content (e.g., 'deep fake' videos)."[152]

In the United States, lawmakers in the Senate and the House of Representatives jointly introduced the *Algorithmic Accountability Act of 2019,* which, if passed, would require large companies to audit their AI systems for discriminatory biases, as well as privacy and security risks.[153]

The Council of Europe noted that "[t]argeted disinformation campaigns online, designed specifically to sow mistrust and confusion and to sharpen existing divisions in society, may also have destabilizing effects on democratic processes."[154]

In the United Kingdom, the British government has proposed new government regulations to regulate the spread of harmful and violent content over social media platforms. Proposed penalties include substantial fines and blocking access to websites.[155]

This suggests we might be on the eve of the creation of new liability regimes for Internet Intermediaries. Since the mid-1990s, the U.S. and the EU have upheld legislations with broad immunities for online platforms seen mostly as "mere conduits" of information rather than producers of content. With the most liberal approach, the U.S. adopted section 230 of the *Communications Decency Act* to shield Intermediaries from non-IP and non-criminal claims arising from third party content published on their platforms, including from equitable reliefs like injunctions.[156] For intellectual property claims, the U.S. opted in 1998 for a safe harbour regime with the *Digital Millennium Copyright Act* that protects Intermediaries from liability if they comply with notice-and-takedown measures.[157] For Europe, a similar safe harbour approach, applicable however to all type of content and not only IP, has been in place since 2000.[158]

Both legislative regimes were drafted before the emergence of social media as we know it today. Multiple voices now argue for their revision, notably to counter more efficiently the rise of fake news.[159] The "mere conduits" conception of Internet Intermediaries, especially social media platforms, is outdated—particularly when we consider the extensive monitoring of content they conduct and their prevailing business model as attention merchants.[160] Recent legislative changes are indicative of a shift away from immunity regimes toward more burdensome obligations for Internet Intermediaries. Some countries, like Australia, have reacted to recent atrocious manipulation of social media—the Christchurch massacre in this case—by enacting laws forcing Intermediaries to remove expeditiously "abhorrent violent material." If they fail to do so, under the new Australian law, corporate officers might face up to three years in jail and the corporation itself may be fined up to 10% of its annual turnover.[161]

Germany

Germany recently adopted the *Act to Improve Enforcement of Law in Social Networks* (NetzDG) which applies to for-profit social networks with more than 2 million users in the country.[162] Subject to important fines, Intermediaries have new obligations to quickly block or remove unlawful third-party content and to maintain effective and transparent mechanisms to handle complaints about unlawful content.[163] Significantly, Intermediaries are expected to make legal determinations on the lawfulness of reported content. They ought to remove "manifestly unlawful" content within 24 hours and, for more ambiguous content, within seven days.[164]

India

The Indian government is also rethinking its Internet Intermediaries law, notably liability exemptions, as a reaction to the lynching incidents in the country.[165] The current legislative draft would impose proactive duties to identify and remove unlawful content on Intermediaries and includes an obligation for them to deploy "automated tools" to achieve those ends.[166]

Presumably AI software could be one of these tools, and proponents of automated content identification, notably at DARPA,[167] hope AI could be used as a shield against deep fakes and fake news. In his recent testimony in front of the U.S. Congress, Facebook CEO Mark Zuckerberg said that "over the long term, building AI tools is going to be the scalable way to identify and root out most of this harmful content."[168] According to Zuckerberg, Facebook has already had some successes with terrorist propaganda, but others have doubted the same could be done with fake news, especially in the short term, notably because of the complexity of political discourse.[169]

The risk of increased liability of Internet Intermediaries for third-party-published fake news is that platforms may become overzealous and pre-emptively remove controversial, yet legitimate, political and social content.[170] One could imagine for instance political adversaries using complaints mechanisms to have their opponent's content removed. Combined with the power of AI, this could chill free expression on social media platforms. The Council of Europe also warns of encroachment on freedom of expression, and recommends that content-moderation measures taken by Internet Intermediaries be transparent, non-discriminatory and use the least restrictive means.[171] A balance should be struck in the law to allow for rapid taking down of harmful content while also protecting free speech. For example, inspired by Germany's NetzDG this could be reached through the creation of independent review mechanisms with appropriate procedural fairness that could assess complaints against content, but also against removals. This would avoid placing Internet Intermediaries in the twin roles of arbiter of truth and of proper political speech. The protection of safe harbour would still be available, but with revamped criteria to be met.

G. Conclusion

After having been hailed as essential tools of democracy and free expression, notably during the Arab spring of 2011, our honeymoon with social media seems to have come to an end with the accumulation of reports on the proliferation of hatred, misinformation, lies and manipulation campaigns online. In that context, AI clearly has the potential either to accelerate or dramatically reduce this proliferation of harmful and illegal content. Organizations, including Internet intermediaries, who play a material role in filtering or recommending content will play an increasingly central role in helping to promote the latter outcome.

VII. Conclusion

Law is often about minute details, obscure rules and long-forgotten precedents. It can be all too easy as a practising lawyer focused on the latest contract to draft, the case to settle and the merger of big corporations, (while at the same keeping updated on the latest technological innovations), to lose track of the greater picture. But law is also about creating societies that protect not only the human condition but also our fragile environment. As regards each of the issues we have briefly introduced in this chapter, businesses, government policy-makers—and lawyers—will have important decisions to make regarding a beneficent, non-maleficent role for AI.

The achievement of this goal calls for an increased sense of responsibility of all the stakeholders involved. Hans Jonas, with whom we began this chapter, concluded that the more powerful the technology we create becomes, the more responsibility we bear to prevent adverse outcomes.[172] In the next chapter, we will thus present in more detail our framework of human accountability for the development, deployment and use of AI systems.

Principle 1
Ethical Purpose and Societal Benefit

Organisations that develop, deploy or use AI systems and any national laws that regulate such use should require the purposes of such implementation to be identified and ensure that such purposes are consistent with the overall ethical purposes of beneficence and non-maleficence, as well as the other principles of the Policy Framework for Responsible AI.

1 Overarching principles

1.1 Organisations that develop, deploy or use AI systems should do so in a manner compatible with human agency and the respect for fundamental human rights (including freedom from discrimination).

1.2 Organisations that develop, deploy or use AI systems should monitor the implementation of such AI systems and act to mitigate against consequences of such AI systems (whether intended or unintended) that are inconsistent with the ethical purposes of beneficence and non-maleficence, as well as the other principles of the Policy Framework for Responsible AI set out in this framework.

1.3 Organisations that develop, deploy or use AI systems should assess the social, political and environmental implications of such development, deployment and use in the context of a structured Responsible AI Impact Assessment that assesses risk of harm and, as the case may be, proposes mitigation strategies in relation to such risks.

2 Work and automation

2.1 Organisations that implement AI systems in the workplace should provide opportunities for affected employees to participate in the decision-making process related to such implementation.

2.2 Consideration should be given as to whether it is achievable from a technological perspective to ensure that all possible occurrences should be pre-decided within an AI system to ensure consistent behaviour. If this is not practicable, organisations developing, deploying or using AI systems should consider at the very least the extent to which they are able to confine the decision outcomes of an AI system to a reasonable, non-aberrant range of responses, taking into account the wider context, the impact of the decision and the moral appropriateness of "weighing the unweighable" such as life vs. life.

2.3 Organisations that develop, deploy or use AI systems that have an impact on employment should conduct a Responsible AI Impact Assessment to determine the net effects of such implementation.

2.4 Governments should closely monitor the progress of AI-driven automation in order to identify the sectors of their economy where human workers are the most affected. Governments should actively solicit and monitor industry, employee and other stakeholder data and commentary regarding the impact of AI systems on the workplace and should develop an open forum for sharing experience and best practices.

2.5 Governments should promote educational policies that equip all children with the skills, knowledge and qualities required by the new economy and that promote life-long learning.

2.6 Governments should encourage the creation of opportunities for adults to learn new useful skills, especially for those displaced by automation.

2.7 Governments should study the viability and advisability of new social welfare and benefit systems to help reduce, where warranted, socio-economic inequality caused by the introduction of AI systems and robotic automation.

3 Environmental impact

3.1 Organisations that develop, deploy or use AI systems should assess the overall environmental impact of such AI systems, throughout their implementation, including consumption of resources, energy costs of data storage and processing and the net energy efficiencies or environmental benefits that they may produce. Organisations should seek to promote and implement uses of AI systems with a view to achieving overall carbon neutrality or carbon reduction.

3.2 Governments are encouraged to adjust regulatory regimes and/or promote industry self-regulatory regimes concerning market-entry and/or adoption of AI systems in a way that the possible exposure (in terms of 'opportunities vs. risks') that may result from the public operation of such AI systems is reasonably reflected. Special regimes for intermediary and limited admissions to enable testing and refining of the operation of the AI system can help to expedite the completion of the AI system and improve its safety and reliability.

3.3 In order to ensure and maintain public trust in final human control, governments should consider implementing rules that ensure comprehensive and transparent investigation of such adverse and unanticipated outcomes of AI systems that have occurred through their usage, in particular if these outcomes have lethal or injurious consequences for the humans using such systems. Such investigations should be used for considering adjusting the regulatory framework for AI systems, in particular to develop, where practicable and achievable, a more rounded understanding of how and when such systems should gracefully handover to their human operators in a failure scenario.

3.4 AI has a particular potential to reduce environmentally harmful resource waste and inefficiencies. AI research regarding these objectives should be encouraged. In order to do so, policies must be put in place to ensure the relevant data is accessible and usable in a manner consistent with respect for other principles of the Policy Framework for Responsible AI such as Fairness and Non-Discrimination, Open Data and Fair Competition and Privacy, Lawful Access and Consent.

4 Weaponised AI

4.1 The use of lethal autonomous weapons systems (LAWS) should respect the principles and standards of and be consistent with international humanitarian law on the use of weapons and wider international human rights law.

4.2 Governments should implement multilateral mechanisms to define, implement and monitor compliance with international agreements regarding the ethical development, use and commerce of LAWS.

4.3 Governments and organisations should refrain from developing, selling or using lethal autonomous weapon systems (LAWS) able to select and engage targets without human control and oversight in all contexts.

4.4 Organisations that develop, deploy or use AI systems should inform their employees when they are assigned to projects relating to LAWS.

5 The weaponisation of false or misleading information

5.1 Organisations that develop, deploy or use AI systems to filter or promote informational content on internet platforms that is shared or seen by their users should take reasonable measures, consistent with applicable law, to minimise the spread of false or misleading information where there is a material risk that such false or misleading information might lead to significant harm to individuals, groups or democratic institutions.

5.2 AI has the potential to assist in efficiently and pro-actively identifying (and, where appropriate, suppressing) unlawful content such as hate speech or weaponised false or misleading information. AI research into means of accomplishing these objectives in a manner consistent with freedom of expression should be encouraged.

5.3 Organisations that develop, deploy or use AI systems on platforms to filter or promote informational content that is shared or seen by their users should provide a mechanism by which users can flag potentially harmful content in a timely manner.

5.4 Organisations that develop, deploy or use AI systems on platforms to filter or promote informational content that is shared or seen by their users should provide a mechanism by which content providers can challenge the removal of such content by such organisations from their network or platform in a timely manner.

5.5 Governments should provide clear guidelines to help Organisations that develop, deploy or use AI systems on platforms identify prohibited content that respect both the rights to dignity and equality and the right to freedom of expression.

5.6 Courts should remain the ultimate arbiters of lawful content.

Endnotes

1 Hans Jonas, *Pour une éthique du futur* (Paris: Rivages, 1998) at p 50.

2 See Legality of the Threat or Use of Nuclear Weapons, Advisory Opinion, [1996] ICJ Rep 226.

3 Catherine Clifford, "Elon Musk: 'Mark my words—A.I. is far more dangerous than nukes'" (13 March 2018), online: *CNBC* <https://www.cnbc.com/2018/03/13/elon-musk-at-sxsw-a-i-is-more-dangerous-than-nuclear-weapons.html>.

4 Arjun Kharpal, "Stephen Hawking says A.I. could be 'worst event in the history of our civilization'" (6 November 2017) online: *CNBC* <https://www.cnbc.com/2017/11/06/stephen-hawking-ai-could-be-worst-event-in-civilization.html>.

5 Wikipedia, "Don't be evil," online: <https://en.wikipedia.org/wiki/Don%27t_be_evil>.

6 Montreal Declaration Responsible AI, online: <https://www.montrealdeclaration-responsibleai.com/>.

7 European Commission's High-Level Expert Group on Artificial Intelligence, "Draft Ethics Guidelines for Trustworthy AI" (18 December 2018), online: *European Commission* <https://ec.europa.eu/digital-single-market/en/news/draft-ethics-guidelines-trustworthy-ai> at page ii [EC, "Draft Ethics Guidelines"]. See also the recent "Ethically Aligned Design (EAD): A Vision for Prioritizing Human Well-being with Autonomous and Intelligent Systems" as well as IEEE's Ethics Certification Program for Autonomous and Intelligent Systems, and ongoing work on the P7000 standards.

8 Singapore Personal Data Protection Commission, "Discussion Paper on Artificial Intelligence (AI) and Personal Data—Fostering Responsible Development and Adoption of AI" (5 June 2018), online: <https://www.pdpc.gov.sg/-/media/Files/PDPC/PDF-Files/Resource-for-Organisation/AI/Discussion-Paper-on-AI-and-PD---050618.pdf> at p 5.

9 IBM, "Learning to Trust Artificial Intelligence Systems" (2016), online: <https://www.alain-bensoussan.com/wp-content/uploads/2017/06/34348524.pdf> at p 5;

Institute of Electrical and Electronics Engineers, "Ethically Aligned Design: A Vision for Prioritizing Human Well-being with Autonomous and Intelligent Systems," (2016), online: <https://ethicsinaction.ieee.org/> at p 22.

10 World Economic Forum, "What is the Fourth Industrial Revolution" (19 January 2016), online: <https://www.weforum.org/agenda/2016/01/what-is-the-fourth-industrial-revolution/>.

11 Matt Carlson, "The Robotic Reporter" (2014) 3:3 Digital Journalism 416.

12 Ian Tucker, "AI cancer detectors" (10 June 2018), online: *The Guardian* <https://www.theguardian.com/technology/2018/jun/10/artificial-intelligence-cancer-detectors-the-five>.

13 Jean Baptiste Su, "Why Artificial Intelligence Is The Future of Accounting: Study" (22 January 2018), online: *Forbes* <https://www.forbes.com/sites/jeanbaptiste/2018/01/22/why-artificial-intelligence-is-the-future-of-accounting-study/#598f4fb337bc>.

14 Richard Susskind, *Tomorrow's Lawyers: An Introduction to your future* (Oxford University Press, 2017) at p 26.

15 *Ibid,* at p 90 [Susskind].

16 Artificial Lawyer, "Expert Systems + Legal Bots," online: <https://www.artificiallawyer.com/al-100-directory/expert-systems-legal-bots/>.

17 Susskind, *supra* note 14 at p 167.

18 Carl Benedikt Frey & Michael A Osborne, "The Future of Employment: How Susceptible are Jobs to Computerisation" (17 September 2013), online: *Oxford Martin Programme on Technology and Employment* <https://www.oxfordmartin.ox.ac.uk/downloads/academic/future-of-employment.pdf>.

[19] McKinsey Global Institute, "A Future that Works: Automation, Employment, and Productivity" Executive Summary (January 2017), online: <https://www.mckinsey.com/~/media/mckinsey/featured%20insights/Digital%20Disruption/Harnessing%20automation%20for%20a%20future%20that%20works/MGI-A-future-that-works-Executive-summary.ashx> at p 6.

[20] *Ibid,* at p 7.

[21] Julia Kollewe, "Artificial intelligence will be net UK jobs creator, finds report" (17 July 2018), online: *The Guardian* <https://www.theguardian.com/technology/2018/jul/17/artificial-intelligence-will-be-net-uk-jobs-creator-finds-report>.

[22] World Bank Group, "World Development Report 2019: The Changing Nature of Work" (2019), online: <http://documents.worldbank.org/curated/en/816281518818814423/pdf/2019-WDR-Report.pdf> at p 18 [World Bank].

[23] *Ibid,* at p 6.

[24] See: PWC, "Will Robots Really Steal our Jobs?" (February 2018), online: <https://www.pwc.co.uk/economic-services/assets/international-impact-of-automation-feb-2018.pdf>;

PWC, "Sizing the Price: What's the real value of AI for your business and how you can capitalise?," online: <https://www.pwc.com/gx/en/issues/analytics/assets/pwc-ai-analysis-sizing-the-prize-report.pdf>;

Ekkehard Ernst and al, "The economics of artificial intelligence: Implications for the future of work" (2018), online: *International Labour Organization* <https://www.ilo.org/wcmsp5/groups/public/---dgreports/---cabinet/documents/publication/wcms_647306.pdf>;

United Nations, Economic and Social Commission for Asia and the Pacific, "Artificial Intelligence in Asia and the Pacific," online: <https://www.unescap.org/sites/default/files/ESCAP_Artificial_Intelligence.pdf>; Canada, International Development Research Center, "Artificial Intelligence and human development: Toward a research agenda"(April 2018), online: <https://www.idrc.ca/sites/default/files/ai_en.pdf>.

[25] Zero Hedge, "Rig Count Surges Again to 16-Month Highs (But Where's the Oil Industry Jobs)" (3 March 2017), online: <https://www.zerohedge.com/news/2017-02-03/rig-count-surges-again-16-month-highs-wheres-oil-industry-jobs>.

[26] World Economic Forum, "AI isn't taking our jobs—but it is changing how we recruit" (14 January 2019), online: <https://www.weforum.org/agenda/2019/01/ai-is-changing-the-way-we-recruit>.

[27] World Economic Forum, Centre for the New Economy and Society, "Future of Jobs Report 2018" (2018), online: <http://www3.weforum.org/docs/WEF_Future_of_Jobs_2018.pdf> [World Economic Forum].

[28] World Bank Group, Report prepared for the G20 Employment Working Group Meeting Istanbul "The Effects of Technology on Employment and Implications for Public Employment Services" (May 2015), online: <http://g20.org.tr/wp-content/uploads/2015/11/The-Effects-of-Technology-on-Employment-and-Implications-for-Public-Employment-Services.pdf> [World Bank, "Effects of Technology"].

[29] World Bank, *supra* note 22 at p 70.

[30] *Ibid,* at p 72.

[31] World Economic Forum, *supra* note 27 at p 13.

[32] David H Autor, "Why Are There Still So Many Jobs? The History and Future of Workplace Automation" (2015) 29:3 Journal of Economic Perspectives 3 at p 27;

Anya Kamenetz, "U.S. High School Graduation Rate Hits Record High" (15 December 2015), online: *NPR* <https://www.npr.org/sections/ed/2015/12/15/459821708/u-s-high-school-graduation-rate-hits-new-record-high>.

[33] World Bank, *supra* note 22 at Chapter 4.

[34] *"An existential risk is one that threatens to cause the extinction of Earth-originating intelligent life or to otherwise permanently and drastically destroy its potential for future desirable developments."* Nick Bostrom, *Superintelligence: Paths, Dangers, Strategies* (Oxford University Press, 2016) at p 140, 197.

[35] World Bank, *supra* note 22 at p 113.

[36] *Ibid,* at p 106.

[37] Max Tegmark, Life 3.0: Being Human in the Age of Artificial Intelligence (Knopf, 2017) at p 127.

[38] Catherine Clifford, "Elon Musk: Robots will take your jobs, government will have to pay your wage" (November 4 2016), online: *CNBC* <https://www.cnbc.com/2016/11/04/elon-musk-robots-will-take-your-jobs-government-will-have-to-pay-your-wage.html>.

[39] Sally French, "Bill Gates says robots should pay taxes if they take your job" (20 February 2017), online: *MarketWatch* <https://secure.marketwatch.com/story/bill-gates-says-robots-should-pay-taxes-if-they-take-your-job-2017-02-17>.

[40] World Bank, *supra* note 22 at p 110.

[41] Georgina Prodhan, "European parliament calls for robot law, rejects robot tax" (16 February 2017), online: *Reuters* <https://www.reuters.com/article/us-europe-robots-lawmaking/european-parliament-calls-for-robot-law-rejects-robot-tax-idUSKBN15V2KM>.

[42] Charles Orton-Jones, "The complication of taxing robots" (February 23 2018), online: *Raconteur* <https://www.raconteur.net/manufacturing/complication-taxing-robots>.

[43] Jordan Press, "Feds set rules on use of AI in government services amid wider testing" (4 March 2019), online: *The Star* <https://www.thestar.com/news/canada/2019/03/04/feds-set-rules-on-use-of-ai-in-government-services-amid-wider-testing.html>.

[44] U.S., HR Res 4625, Fundamentally Understanding The Usability and Realistic Evolution of Artificial Intelligence Act of 2017, 115th Cong, 2017.

[45] World Bank, "Effects of Technology," *supra* note 28;

Georgios Petropoulos, "The Impact of Artificial Intelligence on Employment," online: <http://bruegel.org/wp-content/uploads/2018/07/Impact-of-AI-Petroupoulos.pdf>.

[46] See: Skills Panorama, "European Skills Index," online: <https://skillspanorama.cedefop.europa.eu/en/indicators/european-skills-index>.

[47] Act to Promote Workforce Skills Development and Recognition, RSQ 2007, c D-8.3.

[48] Intergovernmental Panel on Climate Change, "Special Report: Global Warming of 1.5°C" (2018), online: <https://www.ipcc.ch/sr15/> [IPCC 2018 Report].

[49] World Wildlife Fund, "Living Planet Report 2018: Aiming Higher" (2018), online: <https://www.wwf.org.uk/sites/default/files/2018-10/wwfintl_livingplanet_full.pdf> at p 90-91.

[50] Francisco Sánchez-Bayo & Kris A G. Wyckhuys, "Worldwide decline of the entomofauna: A review of its drivers" (2019) 232 Biological Conservation 8.

[51] Richard Leakey & Roger Lewin, *The sixth extinction: patterns of life and the future of humankind* (London: Doubleday, 1995).

[52] Nicolas Jones, "How machine learning could improve climate forecasts" (23 August 2017), online: *Nature* <https://www.nature.com/news/how-machine-learning-could-help-to-improve-climate-forecasts-1.22503>;

See also, Cédric Villani, "For a Meaningful Artificial Intelligence: Toward a French and European Strategy," Mission assigned by the Prime Minister Edouard Philippe (2018), online: <https://www.aiforhumanity.fr/pdfs/MissionVillani_Report_ENG-VF.pdf> at p. 102 [Villani Report]: "Although AI is a potential threat to the environment, it is also a potential solution. Indeed, there are many opportunities to use AI in the field of ecology."

53 Indeed, as the Villani Report, *ibid,* notes at p. 101: ""Digital energy consumption increases by 8.5% per year and its contribution to world electricity consumption (which is growing by 2% per year) could reach 20% (moderate scenario) or even 50% (pessimistic scenario) by 2030, and therefore be multiplied 10-fold in 20 years' time. Given the global energy mix, the digital contribution to greenhouse gas emissions (GHG) will thus increase from 2.5% in 2015 to 5% in 2020 (2.5 GT).

54 U.S. Energy Information Administration, "What is U.S. electricity generation by energy source?" (last updated 1 March 2019), online: <https://www.eia.gov/tools/faqs/faq.php?id=427&t=3>.

55 "The world is losing the war against climate change" (2 August 2018), online: *The Economist* <https://www.economist.com/leaders/2018/08/02/the-world-is-losing-the-war-against-climate-change> [*The Economist*].

56 "Smart Meters and a Smarter Grid" online: *Union of Concerned Scientists.* <https://www.energy.gov/energysaver/articles/smart-meters-and-smarter-grid>.

57 Sarvapali D Ramchurn et al, "Putting the 'Smarts' into the Smart Grid,'" 55:4 Communications of the ACM 86.

58 John R Forbush, "Regulating the Use and Sharing of Energy Consumption Data: Assessing California's SB 1476 Smart Meter Privacy Statute" (2012) 75 Albany Law Review 341 [Forbush].

59 California Code, Public Utility Code §§ 8380–81.

60 John R Forbush, "Regulating the Use and Sharing of Energy Consumption Data: Assessing California's SB 1476 Smart Meter Privacy Statute" (2012) 75 Albany Law Review 341 [Forbush].

61 Villani Report, *supra* note 52 at 102.

62 *Ibid.*

63 *Ibid.*

64 A crucial aspect of this noted by Villani is that "the American Association of Semi-Conductor Manufacturers predicted that by 2040, the global demand for data storage capacity, which grows at the pace of the progress of AI, will exceed the available world production of silicon. Furthermore, by 2040 the energy required for computation will equally have exceeded world energy production; the progress of the blockchain may also cause our energy requirements to rocket. It is vital to educate as many people as possible about these issues and to act promptly to avoid shortages." *Ibid,* at 101.

65 *Ibid,* at p. 101.

66 David S Abraham, "The Next Resource Shortage" (20 November 2015), online: *The New York Times* <https://www.nytimes.com/2015/11/20/opinion/the-next-resource-shortage.html> [Abraham];

This could be alleviated through more efficient use of precious metals, or research on substitution materials. R B Gordon and al, "Metal Stock and Sustainability" (2006) 103:5 PNAS 1209 at p 1214.

67 Abraham, *supra* note 66.

68 Paul Kennedy, *The Rise and Fall of the Great Powers* (Vintage, 1989) at Toward the 21st Century chapter.

69 K Drum "Tech World: Welcome to the Digital Revolution" (2018) 97:4 *Foreign Affairs* 43 at pp 43-44.

70 Elsa B Kania, “Battlefield Singularity: Artificial Intelligence, Military Revolution, and China's Future Military Power” (November 2017), online: *Center for a New American Security* <https://s3.amazonaws.com/files.cnas.org/documents/Battlefield-Singularity-November-2017.pdf?mtime=20171129235805> [Kania].

71 Jean-Christophe Noël, “Intelligence Artificielle: Vers une nouvelle révolution militaire” (Octobre 2018), online: *Ifri* <https://www.ifri.org/sites/default/files/atoms/files/fs84_noel.pdf> at pp 32 and 34 [Noel].

72 Chuck Hagel, Memorandum on The Defense Innovation Initiative (15 November 2014), online: *U.S. Department of Defense* <http://archive.defense.gov/pubs/OSD013411-14.pdf>;

Cheryl Pellerin, “Deputy Secretary: Third Offset Strategy Bolsters America's Military Deterrence” (31 October 2016), online: *U.S. Department of Defense* <https://dod.defense.gov/News/Article/Article/991434/deputy-secretary-third-offset-strategy-bolsters-americas-military-deterrence/>.

73 Vasily Kashin & Michael Raska, “Countering the U.S. Third Offset Strategy, Russian Perspectives, Responses and Challenges” (January 2017), online: *S. Rajaratnam School of International Studies* <https://www.rsis.edu.sg/wp-content/uploads/2017/01/PR170124_Countering-the-U.S.-Third-Offset-Strategy.pdf> at p 15.

74 UK Ministry of Defence, “Flagship AI Lab announced as Defence Secretary hosts first meet between British and American defence innovators” (22 May 2018), online: <https://www.gov.uk/government/news/flagship-ai-lab-announced-as-defence-secretary-hosts-first-meet-between-british-and-american-defence-innovators>;

Pierre Tran, “France to increase investment in AI for future weapon systems” (16 March 2018), online: *DefenseNews* <https://www.defensenews.com/intel-geoint/2018/03/16/france-to-increase-investment-in-ai-for-future-weapon-systems/>.

75 Mark Stefik, “Assessing the Strategic Computing Initiative” (1985) High Technology 41 at p 42.

76 Pamela McCorduck, *Machines Who Think* (Natick: A K Peters, 2004) at p 428.

77 *Ibid,* at p 460.

78 G E Hinton and al, “Learning representations by back-propagating errors” (1986) 323 *Nature* 533.

79 U.S. Department of Defense, 11-S-3613, “Unmanned Systems Integrated Roadmap FY2011-2036” (2011), online: <https://fas.org/irp/program/collect/usroadmap2011.pdf> at p 43 [DoD, “2001”].

80 *Ibid,* at p 13.

81 U.S. Department of Defense, 14-S-0553, “Unmanned Systems Integrated Roadmap FY2013-2038” (January 2014), online: <https://apps.dtic.mil/dtic/tr/fulltext/u2/a592015.pdf> at p 15.

82 *Ibid,* at p 67.

83 *Idem.*

84 DoD, “2001,” *supra* note 79 at p 27.

85 Noël, *supra* note 71 at p 43;

Kania, *supra* note 70 at p 14.

86 Gérard de Boisboissel, “Essai sur les nouveaux usages robotiques” (2016) 791 *Autonomie et létalité en robotique militaire* at p 54.

87 Group of Governmental Experts of the High Contracting Parties to the Convention on Prohibitions or Restrictions on the Use of Certain Conventional Weapons Which May Be Deemed to Be Excessively Injurious or to Have Indiscriminate Effects, *Russia's Approaches to the Elaboration of a Working Definition and Basic Functions of Lethal Autonomous*

Weapons Systems in the Context of the Purposes and Objectives of the Convention, submitted by the Russian Federation, CCW/GGE.1/2018/WP.6 (4 April 2018) at p 9 [Russia];

Group of Governmental Experts of the High Contracting Parties to the Convention on Prohibitions or Restrictions on the Use of Certain Conventional Weapons Which May Be Deemed to Be Excessively Injurious or to Have Indiscriminate Effects, *Humanitarian benefits of emerging technologies in the area of lethal autonomous weapon systems*, submitted by the United States of America, CCW/GGE.1/2018/WP.4 (28 March 2018) at p 26 [USA, *Humanitarian benefits*].

[88] Dan Bilefsky, "He Helped Create A.I. Now He Worries about 'Killer Robots'" (29 March 2019), online: *The New York Times* <https://www.nytimes.com/2019/03/29/world/canada/bengio-artificial-intelligence-ai-turing.html>.

[89] Noel Sharkey, "Robot Wars are a reality" (18 August 2007), online: *The Guardian* <https://www.theguardian.com/commentisfree/2007/aug/18/comment.military>.

[90] Campaign to Stop Killer Robots, "All action and achievements" (2019), online: <https://www.stopkillerrobots.org/action-and-achievements/>;

Campaign to Stop Killer Robots, "Campaign launch in London," online: <https://www.stopkillerrobots.org/2013/04/campaign-launch-in-london/>.

[91] Future of Life Institute, "Autounomous Weapons: An Open Letter From AI & Robotics Researchers" (28 July 2015), online: <https://futureoflife.org/open-letter-autonomous-weapons/> [FLI, "Open Letter"].

[92] Future of Life Institute, "Lethal Autonomous Weapons Pledge," online: <https://futureoflife.org/lethal-autonomous-weapons-pledge/> [FLI, "Pledge"].

[93] FLI, "Open Letter," *supra* note 91.

[94] FLI, "Pledge," *supra* note 92.

[95] Campaign to Stop Killer Robots, Briefing Note for the Convention on Conventional Weapons Group of Governmental Experts meeting on lethal autonomous weapons systems "Retaining human control of weapons systems" (April 2018), online: <https://www.stopkillerrobots.org/wp-content/uploads/2018/03/KRC_Briefing_CCWApr2018.pdf> at p 1.

[96] Mark Bergen, "Inside Google, a Debate Rages: Should It Sell Artificial Intelligence to the Military?" (14 May 2018), online: *Bloomberg* <https://www.bloomberg.com/news/articles/2018-05-14/inside-google-a-debate-rages-should-it-sell-artificial-intelligence-to-the-military>.

[97] Kate Conger & Dell Cameron, "Google Is Helping the Pentagon Build AI for Drones" (6 March 2018), online: *Gizmodo* <https://gizmodo.com/google-is-helping-the-pentagon-build-ai-for-drones-1823464533>.

[98] Google Employees Open Letter to CEO Sundar Pichai, online: <https://static01.nyt.com/files/2018/technology/googleletter.pdf>.

[99] Google, "Artificial Intelligence at Google: Our Principles," online: <https://ai.google/principles/>.

[100] Naomi Mix, "Google Drops Out of Pentagon's $10 Billion Cloud Competition" (8 October 2018), online: *Bloomberg* <https://www.bloomberg.com/news/articles/2018-10-08/google-drops-out-of-pentagon-s-10-billion-cloud-competition>.

[101] Mark Bergen, "Google Won't Renew Pentagon AI Drone Deal After Staff Backlash" (1 June 2018), online: *Bloomerg* <https://www.bloomberg.com/news/articles/2018-06-01/google-won-t-renew-pentagon-ai-drone-deal-after-staff-backlash>.

[102] The United Nations Office at Geneva, "2018 Group of Governmental Expert on Lethal Autonomous Weapons Systems (LAWS)," online: <https://www.unog.ch/80256EE600585943/(httpPages)/7C335E71DFCB29D1C1258243003E8724?OpenDocument>;

See also Paul Scharre, *Army of None: Autonomous Weapons and the Future of War* (W W Norton & Company, 2018) at p 346 [Scharre].

103 LFI, "Pledge," *supra* note 92.

104 Group of Governmental Experts of the High Contracting Parties to the Convention on Prohibitions or Restrictions on the Use of Certain Conventional Weapons Which May Be Deemed to Be Excessively Injurious or to Have Indiscriminate Effects, *Report of the 2018 session of the Group of Governmental Experts on Emerging Technologies in the Area of Lethal Autonomous Weapons Systems*, CCW/GGE.1/2018/3, UNOG (2018) at para 27 [Group of Governmental Experts, "2018 Report"].

105 Mattha Busby & Anthony Cuthbertson, "'Killer Robots' Ban Blocked by U.S. and Russia at UN Meeting" (3 September 2018), online: *The Independent* <https://www.independent.co.uk/life-style/gadgets-and-tech/news/killer-robots-un-meeting-autonomous-weapons-systems-campaigners-dismayed-a8519511.html>.

106 United Nations Office for Disarmament Affairs, "Treaty on the Prohibition of Nuclear Weapons," Status of the Treaty, online: <http://disarmament.un.org/treaties/t/tpnw>.

107 Scharre, *supra* note 102 at pp 333-339.

108 Group of Governmental Experts of the High Contracting Parties to the Convention on Prohibitions or Restrictions on the Use of Certain Conventional Weapons Which May Be Deemed to Be Excessively Injurious or to Have Indiscriminate Effects, *Position Paper*, submitted by China, CCW/GGE.1/2018/WP.7 (11 April 2018) at para 3;

European Parliament, "Autonomous Weapon Systems," 2018/2752(RSP) (12 September 2018), online: <http://www.europarl.europa.eu/sides/getDoc.do?pubRef=-//EP//NONSGML+TA+P8-TA-2018-0341+0+DOC+PDF+V0//EN> at p 1;

Group of Governmental Experts, "2018 Report," *supra* note 104 at para 26 (a);

Group of Governmental Experts of the High Contracting Parties to the Convention on Prohibitions or Restrictions on the Use of Certain Conventional Weapons Which May Be Deemed to Be Excessively Injurious or to Have Indiscriminate Effects, *Human-Machine Interaction in the Development, Deployment and Use of Emerging Technologies in the Area of Lethal Autonomous Weapons Systems*, submitted by France, CCW/GGE.2/2018/WP.3 (28 August 2018) at para 13; Russia, *supra* note 87 at para 1 (with the precision that those interests must be balanced with the legitimate defense interests of States);

USA, *Humanitarian benefits*, *supra* note 87 at para 2;

Group of Governmental Experts of the High Contracting Parties to the Convention on Prohibitions or Restrictions on the Use of Certain Conventional Weapons Which May Be Deemed to Be Excessively Injurious or to Have Indiscriminate Effects, *Human-Machine Interaction in the Development, Deployment and Use of Emerging Technologies in the Area of Lethal Autonomous Weapons Systems*, submitted by the United States of America, CCW/GGE/2/2018/WP.4 (28 August 2018) at paras 35-38 [USA, *Human-Machine Interaction*].

109 International Committee of the Red Cross, "What is International Humanitarian?" (July 2004), online: <https://www.icrc.org/en/doc/assets/files/other/what_is_ihl.pdf>.

110 Ozlem Ulgen, "Definition and Regulations of LAWS" technical report for the Group of Governmental Experts of the High Contracting Parties to the Convention on Prohibitions or Restrictions on the Use of Certain Conventional Weapons Which May Be Deemed to Be Excessively Injurious or to Have Indiscriminate Effects (5 April 2018), online: <https://www.researchgate.net/publication/324227191_Dr_Ulgen_UN_GGE_LAWS_April_2018_-_submission_-_Definition_and_Regulation_of_LAWS> at para 15.

111 World Commission on the Ethics of Scientific Knowledge and Technology, *Report of COMEST on Robotics Ethics*, UNESCO, 2017, SHS/YES/COMEST-10/17/2 REV, online: "https://unesdoc.unesco.org/ark:/48223/pf0000253952" at para 252 and 255.

112 Scharre, *supra* note 102 at p 252;

USA, *Human-Machine Interaction*, *supra* note 108 at para 11.

[113] Scharre, *supra* note 102 at p 251.

[114] Marcus Weisgerber, "The U.S. Air Force Is Adding Algorithms to Predict When Planes Will Break" (15 May 2018), online: *Defense One* <https://www.defenseone.com/business/2018/05/us-air-force-adding-algorithms-predict-when-planes-will-break/148234/>.

[115] Scharre, *supra* note 102 at chapter 14—The Invisible War: Autonomy in the Cyberspace.

[116] Edward Geist and Andrew J Lohn, "How Might Artificial Intelligence Affect the Risk of Nuclear War?" (2018), online: *Rand Corporation* <https://www.rand.org/content/dam/rand/pubs/perspectives/PE200/PE296/RAND_PE296.pdf>.

[117] Katerina Eva Matsa & Elisa Shearer, "News Use Across Social Media Platforms 2018" (September 10, 2018), online: *Pew Research Center* <https://www.journalism.org/2018/09/10/news-use-across-social-media-platforms-2018/>.

[118] Ryan Garcia & Thaddeus Hoffmeister, *Social Media Law in a Nutshell* (West Academic Publishing, 2017) at p 3 [Garcia & Hoffmeister];

Kit Smith, "46 Fascinating and Incredible YouTube Statistics" (4 January 2019), online: *Brandwatch* <https://www.brandwatch.com/blog/youtube-stats/>.

[119] Canada, House of Commons, Standing Committee on Access to Information, Privacy and Ethics, *Democracy under threat: Risks and solutions in the era of Disinformation and Data Monopoly* (2018) (Chair: Bob Zimmer) [Canada, *Democracy*].

[120] See Tim Wu, *The Attention Merchant* (Knopf, 2016) [Wu].

[121] Canada, *Democracy*, *supra* note 119 at p 31.

[122] Michal Lavi, "Online Intermediaries: With Power Comes Responsibility" (11 May 2018), online: *JOLT digest* <https://jolt.law.harvard.edu/digest/online-intermediaries-with-power-comes-responsibility> at p 2.

[123] Pascal Jurgens & Birgit Stark, "The Power of Default on Reddit: A General Model to Measure the Influence of Information Intermediaries" (2017) 9:4 Policy & Internet 395 at p 396.

[124] Canada, *Democracy*, *supra* note 119 at p 34.

[125] Siobhan O'Grady, "An Indian journalist has been trolled for years. Now U.N. experts say her life could be at risk" (26 May 2018), online: *The Washington Post* <https://www.washingtonpost.com/news/worldviews/wp/2018/05/26/an-indian-journalist-has-been-trolled-for-years-now-u-n-experts-say-her-life-could-be-at risk/?utm_term=.2b1c76c34a18>.

[126] Bobby Chesney and Danielle Citron, "Deep Fakes: A Looming Challenge for Privacy, Democracy, and National Security" (2019) 107 California Law Review at p 6 [Chesney & Citron, "Looming"].

[127] Andrea Hauser, "Deep fake: An Introduction" (4 October 2018), online: *SCIP* <https://www.scip.ch/en/?labs.20181004>.

[128] David Guera and Edward J Delp, "Deep fake Video Detection Using Recurrent Neural Networks" (November 2018) Conference Paper for the 15th IEEE International Conference on Advanced Video and Signal Based Surveillance, online: <https://engineering.purdue.edu/~dgueraco/content/deepfake.pdf> at p 1;

Robert Chesney and Danielle Citron, "Deep fakes and the New Disinformation War: The Coming Age of Post-Truth Geopolitics" (January 2019), online: *Foreign Affairs* <https://www.foreignaffairs.com/articles/world/2018-12-11/deepfakes-and-new-disinformation-war> at p 150 [Chesney & Citron, "Disinformation War"].

[129] Chesney and Citron, "Looming," *supra* note 126 at pp 15-16.

[130] Rana Ayyub, "I Was the Victim of a Deepfake Porn Plot Intended to Silence Me" (21 November 2018), online: *The Huffington Post* <https://www.huffingtonpost.co.uk/entry/deepfake-porn_uk_5bf2c126e4b0f32bd58ba316?guccounter=1&guce_referrer_us=aHR0cHM6Ly93d3cuZ29vZ2xlLmNvbS8&guce_referrer_cs=EQGyJm0ithV2KgDSCY1Lrw>.

[131] Samantha Cole, AI-Assisted Fake Porn Is Here and We're All Fucked (11 December 2017), online: *Motherboard* <https://motherboard.vice.com/en_us/article/gydydm/gal-gadot-fake-ai-porn>.

[132] Drew Harwell, "Fake-porn videos are being weaponised to harass and humiliate women: 'Everybody is a potential target'" (30 December 2018), online: *The Washington Post* <https://www.washingtonpost.com/technology/2018/12/30/fake-porn-videos-are-being-weaponised-harass-humiliate-women-everybody-is-potential-target/?utm_term=.d5f6e40149f7> at p 1.

[133] Chesney & Citron, "Looming," *supra* note 126 at pp 17-18.

Adam Dodge & Erica Johnstone, "Using Fake Video Technology To Perpetrate Intimate Partner Abuse," online: <https://withoutmyconsent.org/sites/default/files/blog_post/2018-04-25_deepfake_domestic_violence_advisory.pdf> at p 4 [Dodge & Johnstone].

[134] Chesney & Citron, "Disinformation War," *supra* note 128;

Marie-Helen Maras and Alex Alexandrou, "Determining authenticity of video evidence in the age of artificial intelligence and in the wake of Deepfake videos" (October 2018), online: *International Journal of Evidence and Proof* <https://www.researchgate.net/publication/327390962_Determining_Authenticity_of_Video_Evidence_in_the_Age_of_Artificial_Intelligence_and_in_the_Wake_of_Deepfake_Videos> at p 3 [Maras & Alexandrou];

Oscar Schwartz, "You thought fake news was bad? Deep fakes are where truth goes to die" (12 November 2018), online: *The Guardian* <https://www.theguardian.com/technology/2018/nov/12/deep-fakes-fake-news-truth>;
Roula Khalaf, "If you thought fake news was a problem, wait for 'deepfakes'" (25 July 2018), online: <https://www.ft.com/content/8e63b372-8f19-11e8-b639-7680cedcc421>;

CBC, "The Deepfake: The War Over Truth—The Lie Detector" (18 November 2018), online: <https://www.cbc.ca/news/fifth/the-deepfake-the-war-over-truth-the-lie-detectors-1.4910865>.

[135] Adam B Schiff, Stephanie Murphy & Carlos Curbelo, Letter to Daniel R Coats, Director of National Intelligence (13 September 2018), online: <https://schiff.house.gov/imo/media/doc/2018-09%20ODNI%20Deep%20Fakes%20letter.pdf>.

[136] Marie-Helen Maras & Alex Alexandrou, *supra* note 134 at pp 3-4.

[137] Chesney and Citron, "Looming," *supra* note 126 at pp 21-25.

[138] Vindu Goel, Suhasini Raj & Priyadarshini Ravichandran, "How WhatsApp Leads Mobs to Murder in India" (18 July 2018), online: *The New York Times* <https://www.nytimes.com/interactive/2018/07/18/technology/whatsapp-india-killings.html?mtrref=www.google.com&gwh=0C3DEA52E89D76868C83F541407B6355&gwt=pay>.

[139] Cecilia Kang & Adam Goldman, "In Washington Pizzeria Attack, Fake News Brought Real Guns" (5 December 2016), online: *The New York Times* <https://www.nytimes.com/2016/12/05/business/media/comet-ping-pong-pizza-shooting-fake-news-consequences.html>;

Matthew Haag & Maya Salam, New York Times, "Gunman in 'Pizzagate' Shooting Is Sentenced to 4 Years in Prison" (22 June 2017), online: *The New York Times* <https://www.nytimes.com/2017/06/22/us/pizzagate-attack-sentence.html>.

[140] Ben Sasse, "This new technology could send American politics into a tailspin" (19 October 2018), online: *The Washington Post* <https://www.washingtonpost.com/opinions/the-real-scary-news-about-deepfakes/2018/10/19/6238c3ce-d176-11e8-83d6-291fcead2ab1_story.html?utm_term=.f03fe43c86ba>.

[141] Paul Mozur, "A Genocide Incited on Facebook, With Posts From Myanmar's Military" (15 October 2018), online: *The New York Times* <https://www.nytimes.com/2018/10/15/technology/myanmar-facebook-genocide.html>.

[142] UN News, "Myanmar military leaders must face genocide charges—UN Report," (27 August 2018), online: <https://news.un.org/en/story/2018/08/1017802>;

United Nations Human Rights Council, *Report of Independent International Fact-Finding Mission on Myanmar*, UNHRC, 39th Sess, UN Doc A/HRC/39/64 (2018).

[143] Ryan Black, Pablo Tseng and Sally Wong, "What Can The Law Do About 'Deepfake'?" (March 2018), online: *McMillan* <https://mcmillan.ca/What-Can-The-Law-Do-About-Deepfake> at pp 3-4.

[144] *Ibid,* at pp 3 and 8.

[145] Megan Farokhmanesh, "Deepfakes are disappearing from parts of the web, but they're not going away" (9 February 2018), online: *The Verge* <https://www.theverge.com/2018/2/9/16986602/deepfakes-banned-reddit-ai-faceswap-porn>.

[146] Dodge & Johnstone, *supra* note 133 at p 2.

[147] Chesney and Citron, "Looming," *supra* note 126 at p 32.

[148] *Idem*, at p 35.

[149] Kevin Roose, "Facebook Thwarted Chaos on Election Day. It's Hardly Clear That Will Last" (7 November 2018), online: *The New York Times* <https://www.nytimes.com/2018/11/07/business/facebook-midterms-misinformation.html>.

[150] Philip N Howard and al, "Junk News and Bots during the French Presidential Election: What Are French Voters Sharing Over Twitter" (22 April 2017), online: <http://comprop.oii.ox.ac.uk/wp-content/uploads/sites/89/2017/04/What-Are-French-Voters-Sharing-Over-Twitter-v9.pdf>.

[151] Mike Isaac & Kevin Roose, "Disinformation Spreads on WhatsApp Ahead of Brazilian Election" (19 October 2018), online: *The New York Times* <https://www.nytimes.com/2018/10/19/technology/whatsapp-brazil-presidential-election.html>.

[152] Canada, *Democracy*, *supra* note 119 at p 42.

[153] Adi Robertson, "A new bill would force companies to check their algorithms for bias" (10 April 2019), online: *The Verge* <https://www.theverge.com/2019/4/10/18304960/congress-algorithmic-accountability-act-wyden-clarke-booker-bill-introduced-house-senate>.

[154] Council of Europe, "Recommendation CM/Rec(2018)2 of the Committee of Ministers to member States on the Roles and Responsibilities of Internet Intermediaries," at para 3.

[155] Adam Satariano, "Britain Proposes Broad New Powers to Regulate Internet Content" (7 April 2019), online: *The New York Times* <https://www.nytimes.com/2019/04/07/business/britain-internet-regulations.html>.

[156] Garcia & Hoffmeister, *supra* note 118 at p 221.

[157] *Copyrights Act*, 17 USC § 512, U.S. Copyright Act;

Garcia & Hoffmeister, *supra* note 118 at pp 180-181.

[158] EC, European Parliament Directive 2000/31/EC of 8 June 2000 on certain legal aspects of information society services, in particular electronic commerce, in the Internal Market (Directive on electronic commerce) [2000] OJ, L178/1 at art 12-15.

[159] Council of Europe, Committee of Ministers, *Recommendation CM/Rec(2018)2 to member States on the roles and responsibilities of internet intermediaries* (2018), online: <https://search.coe.int/cm/Pages/result_details.aspx?ObjectID=0900001680790e14> [Council of Europe];

U.S. Senator Mark R Warner, *Potential Policy Proposals for Regulation of Social Media and Technology Firms*, online: <https://regmedia.co.uk/2018/07/30/warner_social_media_proposal.pdf>.

[160] See Wu, *supra* note 120.

[161] Damien Cave, “Australia Passes Law to Punish Social Media Companies for Violent Posts” (3 April 2019), online <https://www.nytimes.com/2019/04/03/world/australia/social-media-law.html>; Australia, *Criminal Code Amendment (Sharing of Abhorrent Violent Material) 2019*, online: <https://parlinfo.aph.gov.au/parlInfo/download/legislation/bills/s1201_aspassed/toc_pdf/1908121.pdf;fileType=application%2Fpdf#search=%22legislation/bills/s1201_aspassed/0000%22>.

[162] Germany, *Act to Improve Enforcement of the Law in Social Networks* (2017), online: <https://www.bmjv.de/SharedDocs/Gesetzgebungsverfahren/Dokumente/NetzDG_engl.pdf?__blob=publicationFile&v=2>, at ss 1 (1) & (2).

[163] *Ibid,* at ss 1 (3) and 3.

[164] *Ibid,* at s 3(2)1 & 3.

[165] Vinay Kesari, “Intermediaries in India may be on the cusp of a brave new world” (17 September 2018), online: <https://factordaily.com/intermediary-liability-in-india-brave-new-world/>.

[166] Preshant Reddy T, “Liability, Not Encryption, Is What India’s New Intermediary Regulations Are Trying to Fix” (28 December 2018), online: *The Wire* <https://thewire.in/government/liability-not-encryption-is-what-indias-new-intermediary-regulations-are-trying-to-fix>;

India, *The Information Technology [Intermediate Guidelines (Amendment) Rules]* Draft (2018), online: <http://meity.gov.in/writereaddata/files/Draft_Intermediary_Amendment_24122018.pdf> at art 3 (9) [India].

[167] Matt Turek, “Media Forensic (MediFor),” online: <https://www.darpa.mil/program/media-forensics>.

[168] Drew Harwell, “AI will solve Facebook’s most vexing problems, Mark Zuckerberg says. Just don’t ask when or how” (11 April 2018), online: *The Washington Post* <https://www.washingtonpost.com/news/the-switch/wp/2018/04/11/ai-will-solve-facebooks-most-vexing-problems-mark-zuckerberg-says-just-dont-ask-when-or-how/?noredirect=on&utm_term=.b1e5d255a20d>.

[169] *Ibid*;

Gary Marcus & Ernest Davis, “No, A.I. Won’t Solve the Fake News Problem” (20 October 2018), online: *The New York Times* <https://www.nytimes.com/2018/10/20/opinion/sunday/ai-fake-news-disinformation-campaigns.html>; Council of Europe, *supra* note 159 at Recommendation 2.3.5.

[170] India, *supra* note 166 at p 10.

[171] Council of Europe, *supra* note 159 at Recommendation 2.3.2.

[172] Jonas, *supra* note 1 at p 82.

Principle 2

ACCOUNTABILITY

Organisations that develop, deploy or use AI systems and any national laws that regulate such use shall respect and adopt the eight principles of this Policy Framework for Responsible AI (or other analogous accountability principles). In all instances, humans should remain accountable for the acts and omissions of AI systems.

2
ACCOUNTABILITY

CHAPTER LEAD
Nikhil Narendran | Trilegal, India

Richard Austin | Deeth Williams Wall LLP, Canada

Segolene Delmas | Lawways, France

Dean Harvey | Perkins Coie LLP, United States

Francis Langlois | McCarthy Tétrault LLP, Canada

Manuel Morales | University of Montreal & National Bank of Canada, Canada

Charles Morgan | McCarthy Tétrault LLP, Canada

Dominique Payette | National Bank of Canada, Canada

Lea Richier | Lawways, France

Gilles Rouvier | Lawways, France

I. Introduction

The transformative and disruptive nature of AI should now be well-established. We have seen in the Introduction how AI has evolved from rule-based systems to powerful neural networks able to recognise and identify your friends on your latest picture, spot a tumour, drive a long-haul truck or recommend an investment strategy. With the previous chapter, moreover, we began to explore some of the potentially most significant impacts AI could have on key aspects of human life: the future of work, efforts to ensure environmental sustainability, the weaponisation of AI and its use in armed conflicts and the health of democratic discourse. Seeking to reinforce a growing international consensus, we have argued that a policy framework for responsible AI is essential and ought to be centred on the wellbeing of human beings and our natural environment[1] (which we refer to in what follows as a "human-centric approach").[2]

A human-centric approach is not simply a way to judge the impact of AI and orient the ethical development of this technology, however. It also implies a further principle, that of human accountability. Human beings, whether as individuals or through private corporations or governments, will develop, deploy and use AI systems.[3] It is only natural then that they ought to do so in a responsible, ethical and lawful manner. Accountability needs to be made a fundamental tenet of AI development, deployment and use[4] and this chapter will present a general accountability framework that will be further developed in the coming chapters.

The conception of accountability that is described in this chapter is broad. Anchored in national and international norms of fundamental human rights, our conception of accountability encompasses not only well-developed existing frameworks of civil and criminal liability (where applicable), but also principles of good corporate governance. By placing the accountability principle at the heart of our proposed ethical AI framework, our goal is to help ensure that AI systems do not go "on a frolic of their own," that they do not operate unchecked and that, in the event of adverse outcomes, there is someone in charge to take remedial measures and provide reparations. If ever Gaak were to escape again, a human should always be found nearby to flip the "off switch"!

The basic features of accountability do not exist in a legal vacuum. There are already a plethora of existing legal regimes applicable to AI, for example traditional contract and tort regimes, strict product liability, as well as regulatory regimes of general or sector-specific application. Nevertheless, as with any disruptive technology (particularly technology with the potential for disruptive impacts of such magnitude, in so many different areas), we will need to assess the implications of AI comprehensively against existing legal frameworks, always being mindful that some aspects of the existing frameworks may need to change in response to the issues that AI presents. As we will discuss further below, this might be the case, as an example, for driver's liability regimes that will need to be adapted to the introduction of autonomous vehicles. In short, it will not always be possible to simply continue to pour new wine into old bottles. When necessary, the process of rethinking standards and laws should be guided by the principles of benevolence and non-maleficence as well as maintaining human accountability for AI activities. Inevitably, different jurisdictions around the world will adopt distinct legal models to respond the challenges of AI, based on their needs, culture and history. Nevertheless, the common thread should be an affirmation of human agency, and therefore accountability, over our new intelligent machines.

Clarifying obligations should help limit the creation of accountability gaps, zones where AI systems operate with no human oversight and under nobody's responsibility. Rapid technological changes can create confusion as to which actor is accountable, and to what degree. Societal responses to the challenges posed by Internet Intermediaries (see Principle 1—Ethical Purpose and Societal Benefits, Part VI) illustrate how regulators and corporations are wrestling with how best to close accountability gaps. First, as we saw in the previous chapter, legislators in many countries around the world are currently revisiting their liability regimes for Internet Intermediaries and testing new models to combat the unchecked, viral transmission of harmful content. Second, with the industry-led ban of deep fake porn, we have also seen private corporations take strong voluntary measures, an example of proactive governance. As such, closing accountability gaps will be achieved by the combined efforts of government legislative and regulatory efforts and voluntary measures taken by corporate actors.

In this chapter, we will present a general accountability framework, focusing on individuals, private corporate actors and governments. Under this perspective, organisations that develop, deploy or use AI systems should be ultimately accountable for their compliance with the eight principles of the Framework for Responsible AI. But before advancing further, the following section first examines (and ultimately argues against) a proposition that has attracted increasing attention in recent years: the suggestion that AI systems should be granted separate legal personality and that we should make the AI systems themselves accountable for their own conduct.

II. AI and Legal Personality

In October 2017, Saudi Arabia granted citizenship to a robotic AI system named "Sophia," becoming the first country to give citizenship to a robot.[5] Arguably, this was essentially a publicity stunt with few legal ramifications, but it nonetheless gave new vigour to the debate over the legal status of AI systems. Could this symbolic gesture be the first step toward the granting of legal personality to AI systems and intelligent robots?

A few years ago, this question would have been confined to the realm of legal science-fiction, somewhere alongside Martian property rights. New abilities showcased by AI systems, however, especially how they seem to learn and act autonomously, have forced us to deal with this issue more seriously. Al though no legal system as yet formally recognises legal personality in AI, the concept is under serious consideration by several legislators.

International developments in legal personality	
Estonia	Estonia is (at the time of writing) working on legislation that would grant a new legal status to robots. The legal status would be situated somewhere between "separate legal personality" and "personal property." Those new persons would be called "robot-agents."[6] A draft bill is expected to be presented to Estonian legislators by June 2019.[7]
Malta	In November 2018, Malta announced that the Government would be drafting a national strategy on AI and explore a citizenship test for robots.[8]
EU	The European Parliament, in February 2017, asked its Commission on Civil Law Rules on Robotics to study the possibility of creating a specific legal status for robots. The reasoning was that "at least then the most sophisticated autonomous robots could be established as having the status of electronic persons responsible for making good any damage they may cause, and possibly applying electronic personality to cases where robots make autonomous decisions or otherwise interact with third parties independently."[9]

Should we contemplate acknowledging the rights and obligations of "electronic persons" alongside natural and corporate legal persons? Nothing inherent in the concept of legal personality would prevent this. Legally speaking, and simply put, to be a legal person is to be the subject of rights and duties. Legal persons or "subjects of law" can enter into contractual relationships, sue and in return be sued, be the target of sanctions, acquire property and enforce their rights.

The American legal scholar John Chipman Gray argued in his day that there could be no right, and therefore no legal personality, without a will to exercise the rights.[11] Humans are therefore the natural and primordial "legal person,"[12] even if some categories of humans were historically denied this status.[13] But, of course, we have long ago decided to move beyond this limited notion of legal personhood with the creation of the corporation. Corporations, created by law, have their own legal personality, separate from that of their owners.[14] With some limited exceptions, they possess the same rights and obligations as natural persons.

In short, legal personality is a "legal fiction."[15] From a legal and conceptual perspective, nothing *a priori* would prevent legislators from granting legal personality to AI systems and intelligent robots. Does it mean that they should, however? No. Reacting to the inquiry of the European Parliament, 285 AI experts argued in an open letter that "[a]ttributing electronic personhood to robots risks misplacing moral responsibility, causal accountability and legal liability regarding their mistakes and misuses."[16] These arguments are compelling. Granting legal personality to AI systems would contradict the principle of human accountability.

"[a]ttributing electronic personhood to robots risks misplacing moral responsibility, causal accountability and legal liability regarding their mistakes and misuses."

Open Letter to the European Commission on Artificial Intelligence and Robotics

This is not to say that proponents of granting legal personality to sufficiently advanced AI systems have weak arguments. There are two main versions of the AI-as-a-legal-person proposal, both with strong defenders, but on balance we believe AI systems should be treated as tools rather than as persons. The first one would grant sufficiently advanced AI systems the same legal status as adult human beings, essentially for moral reasons. In 2015, futurist Ray Kurzweil notably argued that "[i]f an AI can convince us that it is at human levels in its responses, and if we are convinced that it is experiencing the subjective states that it claims, then we will accept that it is capable of experiencing suffering and joy. At that point AIs will demand rights, and because of our ability to empathise, we will be inclined to grant them."[17] This version of the argument for AI legal personality presupposes a scenario where AGI is a reality.

The proponents of the second version of the proposal would grant legal personality even to narrow AI systems, without necessarily giving them the same status as humans. According to the government of Estonia, the status of AIs could be similar to that of corporations[18] and others have suggested different bundles of rights and obligations custom-made for AI systems.[19] This would have many consequences, but from the point of view of accountability it would, as mentioned above by the European Parliament, allow us to hold AI systems directly liable and sue them for the damages they cause or the crimes they commit. In cases of accidents involving fully autonomous vehicles, this would allow the injured party to directly sue the car itself. A patrimony or other equivalent would be attached to each AI, who could also purchase insurance, with which they could pay damages or compensation. This position has the legitimate goal of proposing a way to solve an accountability gap. Those who argue in favour of granting legal personality to AI systems often point to their apparent autonomy and their ability to learn beyond human knowledge. From the "blackbox" nature of neural networks, it is sometimes suggested that, because it may be difficult for humans to predict what an AI system may do, it would therefore be unjust to hold a natural or corporate person accountable for something that could not have reasonably been predicted, i.e., an AI's autonomous behaviour. For example, *mens rea* remains a hallmark of criminal liability and many civil liability regimes are based on negligence. Thus, if an AI acts autonomously and unpredictably, they argue it would be unjust or impractical to hold humans accountable.

If we were facing AI systems with the same intelligence as ours, with the ability to feel joy, pain and all other human emotions as well as with the capacity to make reasonable moral choices, it would be much more difficult to deny them rights. However, as discussed in the Introduction, this type of AGI has yet to be created, and may never exist. So the first version of the AI-as-legal-person proposal is highly hypothetical. For the time being, we are concerned only with "narrow AI," i.e., AIs mastering specific cognitive tasks, but without the versatility of human intelligence. AI systems of this type are essentially no more than tools, even if extremely sophisticated. AI systems must remain the responsibility of those developing, deploying or using them.

As for the second version of the proposal, we believe it overstates the unpredictability and autonomy of AI systems. As discussed in greater detail in our treatment of Principle 8—AI and Intellectual Property, questions of AI legal personality have notably emerged in the context of intellectual property: can AI be authors of works of art?

Next Rembrant Project

In the "Next Rembrandt project," for example, a team led by ING and Microsoft developed an AI system that could analyse the entirety of Rembrandt's catalogue work and then produce new paintings in the master's style.[20] As remarkable an achievement of ingenuity as this may seem, the AI system was ultimately not in charge of the creative process. The capacities of this AI system were limited to the purpose set by its creators (it can't paint a Picasso or play a piano, for example). Human data scientists decided which data were to be fed to human-made machine learning algorithms. Although the AI systems determined which features defined Rembrandt's style, human decision-makers were present at every step of the process, at the technological and managerial levels.[21]

In short, in case of copyright violations or the creation of copyright-protected "masterpieces" by AI systems, it is not the AI systems itself that should be accountable or rewarded, but the individuals and corporations that are behind the project.[22]

This principle—that individuals, corporations or governments should be held accountable rather than the AI itself—also applies to cases where algorithms have seemingly a higher level of autonomy because they are entrusted with decision-making powers. AlphaGo for instance can make elegant and astonishing game-winning moves, but the sphere of its agency is ultimately determined by its developer and corporate owner.[23]

This level of human involvement, when AI systems are deployed and used in the real world where they can cause harm, requires human accountability. Similarly, the Institute of Electrical and Electronics Engineers noted recently that "[a]lmost all current applications of [AI systems] in legal applications, like those in most other fields, require human mediation and likely will continue to do so for the near future."[24] This does not exclude that we may see one day sufficiently autonomous AIs that could be granted some form of legal personality, but this remains for now in the realm of science fiction and the AI-as-tool paradigm should be modified only with the greatest prudence.

One of the main risks of granting current AI systems legal responsibility is to cement, rather than close, the gap between the actions of AI systems and the control of their developer or users. As we discuss in our treatment of Principle 3—Transparency and Explainability, the average person will have little understanding of how the algorithm driving his or her car takes a decision. Accordingly, it may make a lot of sense to shift some responsibility away from the individual in the "driver-seat" as the actual

"AlphaGo is human-created and I think that's the ultimate sign of human ingenuity and cleverness. Everything that AlphaGo does, it does because a human has either created the data, and/or created the learning algorithm that learns from that data, created the search algorithm. All of these things have come from humans. So, really, this is a human endeavor."

David Silver, the lead researcher at DeepMind for the AlphaGo project "driving" of such vehicles becomes ever-more autonomous. But even if AI might force us to reconsider the accountability of certain actors, it should be done in a way that shifts liability to other human actors and not to the AI systems themselves. In the case of autonomous vehicles, for example, this could mean a regime that places a greater burden on developers or manufacturers rather than on consumers, with obligations to test the algorithm in a wide variety of environments. Some responsibility for an accident by an AI-assisted vehicle could even remain with the owner of the car, such as the obligation to take control of the wheel in certain weather conditions.

Holding AI systems directly liable runs the risk of shielding human actors from responsibility and reducing the incentives to develop and use AI responsibly.[25] In the case of corporations, human owners already benefit (for good public policy reasons) from the ability to hide behind the "corporate veil." If they were further shielded by a second "AI veil," we consider that the accountability veil would become altogether too remote and too opaque.

Although linking damage caused by AI systems to a human fault or responsibility might be in some cases arduous and require specific expertise, the 285 signatories of the open letter mentioned above find the "affirmation that damage liability would be impossible to prove" incorrect because it is "based on an overvaluation of the actual capabilities of even the most advanced robots, a superficial understanding of unpredictability and self-learning capacities, and a robot perception distorted by Science-Fiction and a few recent sensational press announcements."[26]

Google has expressed its support for this open letter, adding that granting legal personhood to AI is unwise on four counts:

1. It is unnecessary because legal frameworks already make human persons or corporations liable.
2. It is impractical because machines without consciousness or feelings cannot be punished.
3. Moral responsibility is a core human property.
4. Granting legal personhood to AI is open to abuse because it would allow bad actors to shield themselves from liability.[27]

In short, AI systems are extremely complex, but they remain products of human engineering and science. Their development is based on specialised human expertise and their end-users will always be human beings, either as individuals or through corporations or governments. The AI engineers and computer scientists who developed AlphaGo might not be able to win against their own programs, but they still understand, or at least should understand, its architecture and the range of its possible action.

The accountability principle suggests that legal systems should treat AI systems as tools, products or services rather than as legal persons. Existing legal constructs of accountability applicable to natural and legal persons are sufficient, even if some might need to be adapted for AI. The rights and obligations associated with AI systems ultimately lie with the individuals, corporations and public bodies who develop, deploy or use them. As such, the implementation of the ethical and legal polic principles presented in this Framework for Responsible AI is the ultimately responsibility of these actors: human beings and human beings alone, whether as individual persons or assembled in public or private organisations. The rest of this chapter will present the basic notions of an accountability framework for the ethical implementation of AI. We will conclude with a more focused discussion on effective corporate governance principles as applied to organisations that participate in AI development, deployment and use.

III. The Accountability Framework: Keep Humans behind the Machines

To restate our accountability principle: organisations that develop, deploy or use AI systems ought to be accountable for the consequences of their actions. AI stakeholders should not be able to elude responsibility for legal prejudices or ethical faults, for property damage or for human injury that is caused by AI, regardless of the degree of AI autonomy. Accountability should thus be understood and applied in such a way as to always keep humans in a position to modify, monitor or control AI systems, and as such, be accountable for them.

This proposed approach to accountability stands in contradistinction to an attitude that has long prevailed in the technology sector, the essence of which was succinctly captured in the motto: "Move fast and break things."[28] This latter perspective emphasises the importance of innovative technological development, but ignores the responsibility that technologists have for the results of the products and services they develop. While the benefits that AI may provide are significant, so also is the harm that inappropriate, unethical or illegal use of AI could cause, and those involved in developing this revolutionary technology should be held accountable for the systems they create. We cannot allow untested, defective or incomplete AI products and services to be thrown onto markets or into production on the basis of *"caveat emptor."* As such, when stakeholders "break things" they should accept to pay the price. Facebook CEO Mark Zuckerberg recently took a strong position in favour of the accountability of technology companies and called for governments to establish clear standards and rules for the Internet. On the subject of privacy regulation, he notably wrote that "it should establish a way to hold companies such as Facebook accountable by imposing sanctions when we make mistakes."[29] We believe this applies to the regulation of AI as well.

This brings us to the main question of this chapter: how and to what extent should stakeholders be accountable? If we expect AI stakeholders to respect and implement principles of transparency and explainability, fairness and non-discrimination, safety and reliability as well as of fair competition and face consequences when they fail to do so, we need to give relevant actors the information necessary for them to respect their obligations and navigate successfully within this new ecosystem.

Our framework identifies three main types of stakeholders: individual human persons, corporate actors and government bodies. It further considers three main categories of activities: development, deployment and use of AI systems. Some ethical and legal obligations apply equally to all three stakeholders and across all activities. In other cases, as we will see, a stakeholder's nature and relation to the AI system will require a higher or lower burden of responsibility. The goal should be to adequately protect the interests of rights-holders affected by AI systems in a way that does not misappropriate responsibility. The extent of accountability obligations will also depend on the importance of the rights at stake and the likelihood of harm, what we call a "sliding-scale" approach.

Of course, one of the obvious difficulties of preparing an accountability framework for new technologies like AI is the fact they are constantly improving and have yet to show all their possible applications. It would be a misconception, however, to think that technology-based solutions and products, like AI models, are so technologically sophisticated that they fall "outside the scope" of current frameworks and should therefore remain "ungoverned," or unregulated.

It is the legal responsibility of AI stakeholders to operate AI systems in a way that respects, at all times, existing laws—whether fundamental, penal or civil—and regulations. By way of example, the tort of negligence requires that AI systems be used according to a certain standard of care. Another example is compliance of users of AI systems with targeted statutory law like article 6 of the EU *General Data Protection Regulation* (GDPR), that restricts data processing to instance where there is a valid legal basis for it.

If AI stakeholders (whether legal persons, governments and corporations) do not respect existing laws, they can be held liable for a faulty or negligent acts relating to AI, just as a physical person would. As a consequence of our conclusion on AI legal personality, AI models underpinning any given technology-based service or activity should by no means be perceived as being legally independent from its their enabling persons, corporations or governments.

Liability mechanisms will equally apply in the case where an AI stakeholder operates an AI system and causes injury to another party. One of the pillars of any legal system is its liability framework—as it ensures the trust of society, by ensuring compensation and justice for the damage caused when a person does not respect the law. With AI, these mechanisms will ensure that AI stakeholders bear legal liability that is consistent with allocation of liability under applicable law. In most jurisdictions, fault-based liability mechanisms are based on a number of components that are not self-evident. This means that most of these components have to be proved mostly by the plaintiff, i.e., the person claiming injury. These procedural and evidentiary rules equally apply to a plaintiff suing an AI stakeholder for damages. Civil liability typically aims to protect both personal safety and property interests. Contrary to penal liability (discussed below), it seeks to protect the personal interests of the victim of the unreasonable behaviour of another party. It aims to ensure adequate indemnification following harm (as understood by tort law) that derives from personal, corporate or government activity. It embodies into law moral principles for a stable society.

Moreover, persons, corporations and governments must remain accountable for any criminal or penal violation perpetrated through AI. Penal liability, contrary to civil liability, aims to protect the interests of society as a whole, by deterring and punishing behaviour that harms the general interest, puts in peril an entire societal group, and threatens public order. To ensure that such goals are adequately fulfilled with regards to AI, it will be important to avoid permitting the dissociation of intent between AI enablers and AI itself. Drawing a parallel with the notion of "intent" or *"mens rea"* commonly used in penal and criminal law, a highly sophisticated AI model may learn independently, making a decision that was not necessarily "intended" by its developers or users. However, as AI does not have legal personhood, and thus cannot have intent, the accountable stakeholders must bear responsibility for that decision as if it were their own.

Such penal liability for AI might appear burdensome—however, concluding otherwise will facilitate the eluding of penal or criminal responsibility for acts committed under stakeholders' care.

Finally, aside from the constitutional obligations of governments (see below), there might also be compensation for breach of fundamental rights perpetrated by AI stakeholders. In some jurisdictions, breach of fundamental rights can give rise, on top of compensatory damages, to punitive ones, i.e., that aim to punish negligent party, on top of having to compensate for caused damages. When private actors conduct AI activities that could harm fundamental rights, they should also face sanctions if the risk materialises, even more so if it is the consequence of deliberate acts.

These considerations show that AI affects laws and regulations at every level and that human accountability has many facets. In the rest of this chapter, we present general ideas for individuals, corporations and governments to better tackle the new challenges posed by AI.

A. Types of stakeholders

By making distinctions between certain types of stakeholders and activities we hope to avoid the application of a blanket accountability regime that would impose too much responsibility on certain stakeholders and not enough on others. For instance, AI developers can be held accountable for ensuring that there are no deviations from ethical standards in the algorithm before deployment or use, whereas a stakeholder deploying AI services or bringing to the market AI products may be accountable for using the AI system to provide legitimate and lawful services. Likewise, end-users should have an obligation to use AI in a manner that does not harm others. Stakeholders cumulating these roles will be required to respect all the obligations associated with their AI activities.

As a general proposal, accountability should be divided among stakeholders according to the degree of control a stakeholder has over the development, deployment, use and evolution of an AI system. Stakeholders who act as "custodians" of the AI, in other words who have access to the training data and who have power over of the algorithm, should have greater responsibilities than stakeholders who cannot re-train the AI, for example where an AI system based on a proprietary software and algorithms is sold to consumers, for example.

Contract law, which will apply to contractual arrangements between AI developers, deployers and users, can be used, within acceptable limits, by stakeholders to allocate responsibilities among themselves. For instance, a stakeholder can have heightened contractual obligations with regards to components of the products/services that are considered critical, and naturally, the contract will be priced accordingly. Conversely, a contract can shift liability or contractual obligations to lessen the burden of a party, for instance a developer that does not want to continue the training of an AI after its sale.

1. Accountability for individuals

We anticipate that the accountability of individual human persons as regards AI will relate mainly to their use of AI systems, rather than to their development or deployment. This is because most people have no idea how to build efficient neural networks and lack the resources to deploy them. As a consequence most individuals will be end-consumers or users of AI products or services, for example by buying self-driving vehicles, interacting by chatbots deployed by enterprises or governments, or downloading applications incorporating AI.

In cases of individual developers with relevant skills and knowledge, they should be expected to respect applicable laws and ethical standards. However, it is probably not reasonable to ask individual developers acting alone or who are part of project teams and do not control the development of the system (when they can be identified) to provide the same level of risk assessment and monitoring that is asked of corporate and governmental stakeholders.

The most interesting cases will be those where AI will transform current systems. Autonomous vehicles, for instance, force us to rethink our liability regimes for road accidents. Currently, individual drivers, except in cases of a manufacturing defect, are held liable if they cause damages while using their car. The introduction of fully autonomous self-driving cars undermines this principle, although some current laws, like the UK's *Automated and Electric Vehicles Act,* keep the owner (or his or her insurer) fully liable for accidents.[30] The majority of owners of those vehicles will not understand how such vehicles make decisions. For some, this suggests a shift of the burden for road accidents onto corporate stakeholders developing and deploying the self-driving AIs.[31] Part of the responsibility could remain with the owners and the individuals using the driverless car, for instance if manufacturers provide clear instructions on when not to use the auto-pilot function, although this risks making autonomous vehicles less attractive for consumers. A liability regime that places too heavy a burden on manufacturers might reduce the incentives to bring to the market an AI technology expected to help avoid deaths and injuries from road accidents.[32] On the other hand, consumers might be reluctant to buy autonomous vehicles if they are liable for the behaviour of algorithms over which they have no control.[33] Finding the right balance will admittedly remain a challenge. We discuss these issues in greater detail in our treatment of Principle 5—Safety and Reliability.

Legislators could also limit the possibility for AI developers and deployers to contract away their accountability obligations, especially if this would push their obligations onto individual end-users with little knowledge of AI or ability to influence outcomes. However, when individuals use AI systems negligently or wilfully for nefarious purposes, they should be held accountable. An individual producing defamatory content with machine learning software sold to modify images, for example, should be held liable for his or her actions, and not the innocent third party developer.

2. Accountability for private corporate actors

Private corporations have been at the forefront of the recent progress in AI and are expected to keep their central position in the development, deployment and use of AI. Moreover, many corporations specializing in AI will have the ability to combine these activities. But AI benefits not only technology companies, and so our accountability regime applies to all private actors with AI activities, whether or not they are considered technology companies. For example, a consulting business buying AI software to help facilitate its recruitment process should be accountable for its use of this software and to make sure, for instance, that it does not recommend rejecting candidates for employment on prohibited (i.e., discriminatory) grounds.

The Canadian *Personal Information Protection and Electronic Documents Act* (**PIPEDA**) sets out principles with respect to the protection of personal information, including on accountability.[34] It is an example of legislation setting an accountability framework for corporations that we consider provides a useful source of inspiration for an accountability framework applicable to AI. Under PIPEDA, an organisation is responsible for the personal information in its control and must designate individuals to ensure compliance with the ten fair information principles that are set out in a schedule to that law. The identity of these individuals must be made known upon request. The organisation also has an obligation to implement policies and practices to give effect to these principles. This includes establishing procedures to receive and respond to complaints and inquiries relating to such access and processing. It will also include training staff and communicating to them information about such policies and practices, and developing information to explain the same. We consider that similar accountability frameworks should apply to AI and that it is part of the responsibilities of government to develop such frameworks.

U.S. lawmakers have also proposed an *Algorithmic Accountability Act,* which enables the Federal Trade Commission (FTC) to make regulations that require "covered entities" to conduct "automated decision making impact assessments" and "data protection impact assessments" for high-risk automated decision systems. A "covered entity" includes any person, partnership, or corporation over which the FTC has jurisdiction, which is a data broker or other commercial entity that, as a substantial part of its business, collects, assembles, or maintains personal information concerning an individual who is not a customer or an employee of that entity in order to sell or trade the information or provide third party access to the information. An "automated decision system impact assessment" will evaluate an automated decision system and its development process for impacts on accuracy, fairness, bias, discrimination, privacy, and security. A "data protection impact assessment" is a study evaluating the extent to which an information system protects the privacy and security of personal information the system processes. The proposed legislation also provides for investigative and enforcement powers for the FTC and state authorities regarding the regulations promulgated under it.[35]

Singapore's proposed Model Artificial Intelligence Governance Framework (**SG Model Framework**)[36] lays down certain principles and measures that organisations are encouraged to adopt for the responsible use of AI. The SG Model Framework is guided by two broad principles: (a) organisations should ensure that the decision-making process is explainable, transparent and fair; and, (b) AI solutions should be human-centric. It focuses primarily on four broad areas:

- **(i) Internal governance structures and measures:** Clear roles and responsibilities should be defined within organisations for the ethical deployment of AI, and risk management systems and internal controls should be put in place;
- **(ii) Determining AI decision-making model:** Organisations should set their risk appetite for use of AI, i.e., determine acceptable risks and identifying an appropriate decision-making model for implementing AI. This can be done by weighing their commercial objectives against the risks of using

AI in their decision-making, guided by their corporate values and societal norms. There are three decision-making models identified in the SG Model Framework, with varying degrees of human oversight—(a) where the human oversight is active and involved and the human has full control and the AI only provides recommendations or input; (b) where there is no human oversight over the execution of decisions and the AI has full control without the option of a human override; and, (c) where humans can adjust parameters during the execution of the algorithm;

(iii) **Operations management:** Organisations should put in place certain practices when developing, selecting and maintaining AI models and concerns the interaction between data and algorithms or models. The SG Model Framework recommends good data accountability practices such as understanding data lineage, ensuring data quality, minimising inherent bias, using different data sets for training, testing and validation, and periodic review and updating of data sets. It also has recommendations regarding the algorithm/model, with respect to explainability, repeatability of results, traceability, regular tuning, and active monitoring and review;

(iv) **Customer relationship management:** Organisations should put in place strategies to effectively communicate with customers and consumers when deploying AI. This can include general disclosure, increased transparency, ethical evaluations, policies for explanations to individuals, user interfaces that serve the intended purpose, an opt-out option, communication channels for feedback, and review of material AI decisions.

As a matter of effective corporate governance, private actors should also assess the eight principles set out in this paper and apply these as internal guidelines to orient their activities in a way that respects their legal obligations. This will be discussed further in Part IV below.

3. Accountability for governments

Governments should be accountable for the respect of their constitutional and international obligations when they undertake to develop, deploy and use AI systems. They are also uniquely accountable for the enactment of appropriate legal and regulatory frameworks that tell other stakeholders what they can and cannot do with AI, and who should bear liability when something goes wrong.

Until governments develop internal capacities to produce AI systems comparable to those developed by big tech companies, it is likely that public sector authorities will remain essentially users of externally developed AI systems. The use of AI in the public sector, can, however, provide substantial benefits. For example, local governments can deploy AI to reduce traffic congestion by analysing infrastructure issues[37] and traffic lighting patterns to create intelligent street lights.[38] They can also use AI systems to identify buildings at risk of fire incidents[39] or take advantage of using natural language AI to create chatbots to respond to citizen requests.[40]

In certain cases, the use of AI systems by public institutions will be subject to the same accountability standards and obligations as private actors. However, in others cases, especially those involving police, judicial, administrative or military institutions, the use of AI systems by governments should be subject to an even higher standard of conduct, to account for the importance of the rights involved and the risk that they be harmed. Notably, governments must be particularly attentive to their constitutional and international obligations, including respect for fundamental human rights.[41]

Accountability of governments for AI use can also be made part of multilateral treaties. It is reasonable for citizens to expect a higher standard of accountability from the government than from non-state actors given the fiduciary relationship that citizens share with their governments and the fundamental rights that are constitutionally guaranteed to citizens. National courts should monitor the use of AI systems by public bodies to ensure respect for constitutional principles and the Rule of Law. But this higher standard can be regulated and enforced by means of multilateral international treaties so that there is worldwide agreement on how AI systems can and cannot be used by governments, in area affecting human rights for example.

AI and due process in administrative decisions

While standards of due process (or a duty to act fairly) can vary from jurisdiction to jurisdiction, their purpose is to require States to respect the legal rights of individuals. This requires that no citizen be denied his or her legal rights except in accordance with substantive and procedural fairness.

Due process standards also apply to a government's use of AI. When using AI systems to make administrative or judicial decisions, especially in contexts involving fundamental rights, governments must be responsible for the fairness of the algorithms. An AI system is only as good as the data set it is trained on, and will inevitably reflect any biases in such data.[42] Because of this, when the data under-represents (or over-represents) one group it can lead to unreliable results that favour one group over another[43] in a way that notably contravenes the right to fair treatment and equality. We discuss these issues in greater detail in our treatment of Principle 4—Fairness and Non-Discrimination.

Absent accountability, especially for transparency and explainability (see Principle 3—Transparency and Explainability) for such decisions, the disappointed applicants would have no basis on which to challenge the decision. If governments are doing to respect due process in their implementation of AI, it will be essential that they establish clear guidelines for the effective review of administrative and judicial decisions made, whether partially or entirely, using AI systems. Governments should not evade their constitutional obligations, notably expressed in the law of judicial review of administrative decision, by hiding behind proprietary algorithms developed internally by corporate stakeholders.

AI in the justice system

The criminal justice system is an area where the use of AI by governmental authorities could significantly impact a person's rights and this is an area where governments have a unique role. In recent decades, Courts have begun to rely on aids such as sentencing guidelines (whether advisory or mandatory) and independent assessments in determining a defendant's likelihood of recidivism when determining the appropriate sentencing.[44] One of these aids was the subject of an appeal filed by the defendant in the U.S. case *State v. Loomis* to challenge the judge's use of an AI predictor of recidivism to form the basis for his decision to increase the length of the sentence.[45]

In *Loomis,* the defendant had pled guilty to certain crimes.[46] During sentencing the judge used an AI system provided by the Northpointe Institute for Public Management called COMPAS.[47] Through an interview with Loomis, which included a questionnaire of roughly 137 questions,[48] and information from his criminal history, COMPAS came to the conclusion that Loomis' risk of recidivism was high and he was subsequently sentenced to six years in prison.[49]

Due to the proprietary nature of these technologies, independent testing is sparse.[50] However, some organisations have endeavoured to test these "predictors" of recidivism and have found that, on average, black defendants are more likely to be found with a higher risk of recidivism than white defendants.[51] As we discuss in our treatment of Principle 4—Fairness and Non-Discrimination, this has led to situations where one of these predictors determined that an 18 year old black man who stole a bicycle worth $80 was highly likely to re-offend, while a 41 year old white man with an extensive criminal history who stole $86 worth of property had a low risk of recidivism.[52]

In addition to this risk of bias based against a protected class, machine learning models can also find correlations between, for example, whether a defendant's parent was sent to jail, or whether the defendant knows a lot of people who took illegal drugs. These correlations may even be accurate predictors of recidivism. However, these correlations are outside the control of the defendant. Rather than judging the likelihood of recidivism based upon the decisions and actions of the defendant, the AI is looking at correlations that relate to who the defendant is. It appears likely that a child raised in poverty is more likely to have a parent who has gone to jail and known a number of people who have taken illegal drugs than a child raised in a wealthy family. If judges rely upon AI solutions to increase the punishment of defendants due to factors outside their control, and that may be associated with poverty, we have the potential of creating a two-tier justice system, in which poor defendants are punished more harshly than wealthy defendants, based upon factors associated with their poverty.

Henceforth, the use of AI systems by courts should be closely monitored and only algorithms that have been thoroughly tested with demonstrable proof of performance should be allowed to assist judges in making important determination. As we discuss in our treatment of Principle 3—Transparency and Explainability, the transparency of these systems is paramount. Moreover, any implementation of decision-making or recommending systems that will impact on people should allow for meaningful review of the AI recommendations by appellate courts. Without adequate transparency, accountability, and oversight, there is considerable risk of AI systems introducing and reinforcing unfair and arbitrary practices in justice systems.

Regulatory and legislative accountability

Governments should also be accountable to their constituents for the enactment of well-designed and effective legislation and regulations on AI. As such, governments are not only developers, deployers and users of AI systems, but are also the ultimate regulators of the activities of other stakeholders. In its recent *Ethically Aligned Design, First Edition* the IEEE writes that "[a]n effective

> *"[a]n effective legal system contributes to human well-being"*
>
> Institute of Electrical and Electronics Engineers—*Ethically Aligned Design, First Edition*

legal system contributes to human well-being."[53] Governments, as the main custodians of our legal systems, should then be accountable for enacting technologically appropriate and well-balanced laws and rules regulating stakeholders' AI activities. This is an essential role in order to ensure that individuals and corporations have a clear understanding of their obligations toward other stakeholders and society as a whole. Predictability and clarity will ensure stakeholders are confident that their activities are lawful, which will be favourable to the development of AI technologies. In short, governments are accountable to enact AI laws that favour the beneficial development and use of this technology.

At this point in time, we do not believe governments should work on an overarching "law of AI." It also appears that existing regulators and governing bodies are in the best position to make such amendments to regulations or to create standards in their respective fields, as opposed to an overarching authoritative body for "all AI," which, although interesting in theory, will most certainly prove difficult in application, given the various fields that AI touches upon. Some fields in which AI is currently being developed and used are already highly regulated. For instance, this is the case in finance and air transportation. It is also the case with professional services, such as medical and legal services, where often activities can only be performed by registered or licensed parties. The regulation of AI in these industries should build on these existing frameworks, which should be amended only when necessary.

Some regulators in these areas have stated that their rules are "technology-neutral." This means that such rules are "blind" to technology. In such instances, regulated persons and corporations are accountable for compliance with applicable regulations and standards, regardless of whether they use AI or any other technology to provide a service or perform a regulated activity. To help with navigating through regulatory environments, some regulators have created sandboxes that may be useful for developing innovative AI systems and for assessing how to comply with applicable rules in the regulated space. Government should ensure existing regulators study the impact of AI in their respective sectors and make propositions on ways to adapt current rules to AI.

It is possible that in some cases, AI-specific regulation may be warranted for a given sector to ensure stakeholder accountability. Autonomous driving is an example of an area where important changes will need to be made to current accountability regimes. As stated in the above overview, regulators and governing authorities in certain fields might want to reflect and assess whether new rules are necessary to mitigate emerging risks related to AI. Governments might have to study and determine which liability model is the most pertinent for specific AI applications. Whether on top of, or in lieu of fault-based liability, some particular fields may warrant for example that no-fault insurance or other types of monetary compensation mechanisms be put in place by legislation. Again this could be appropriate in the case of car accidents. At a certain point, when AI gets increasingly sophisticated, regulators and governing authorities may also want to consider agreed-upon sets of AI standards in their respective fields. Perhaps a starting point of reflection would be to assess whether rules are AI-proof, either expressly or by implication.

In summary, although private actors will remain for the time being at the helm of the development of AI as a technology, governments have the important of role of drafting the rules that will encourage the development of AI as a social benefit, as we will notably discuss in more detail in our treatment of Principle 6—Open Data and Fair Competition. In that role, governments are not only accountable to shareholders or consumers, but to society as a whole.

B. Types of activities

Accountability obligations will also vary in function depending on the type of activities undertaken by stakeholders. This is important because we need to take into account the diverse roles stakeholders will play during an AI system's lifetime. If we take the example of an AI chatbot, the developer would be the company actually creating the software (gathering data, writing code as well as training and testing the algorithms). The deployer would be the bank buying the chatbot from the developer. The user would be the client interacting with it, once deployed on its website by the bank. One person can have multiple roles, for example if the Bank hires AI specialists to make the chatbot, and if it uses the chatbot for internal purposes such as assisting decision making. Developers should be accountable for the development and design of lawful and ethical AI systems. But because many AI systems can be re-trained and can evolve with the addition or processing of new data, stakeholders deploying or using AI systems (even if they did not initially develop them) should be accountable for such modifications. In this section, we will further develop our accountability framework with regard to specific AI activities.

1. Development of AI systems

AI development activities refer to the process of creating intelligent algorithms. In the case of machine and deep learning it includes the procuring of the relevant data, the writing of the code, the training of the system and its evaluation and testing.

At present, developers of technologies such as robotics are only accountable when they are negligent or can foresee the potential for harm at the time of developing the technology.[54] We can view this as a "negative obligation" to avoid harm, rather than as a positive obligation to develop safe or ethical products. In the case of *Jones v. W+M Automation Inc.,* a robotic gantry loading system injured the plaintiff while he was working as a tool setter at a General Motors plant.[55] While the system was designed by W+M Automation Inc., General Motors had violated the occupation safety and health administration regulations at the time of installation. The court held that, *inter alia,* the respondents were not liable as they had complied with all applicable regulations while manufacturing the robotic gantry loading system.[56]

Factors Influencing Harm

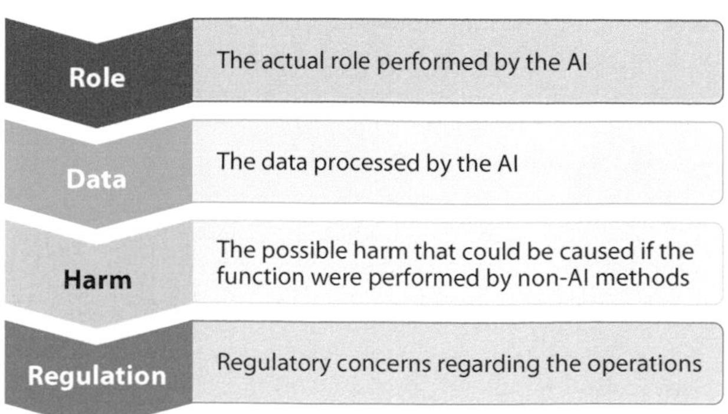

If this principle were to be applied in cases involving AI developers, harm could be foreseen and determined by various factors. such as: (i) the actual role performed by the AI; (ii) the data processed by the AI; (iii) the possible harm that could be caused if the function was performed by non-AI methods; and, (iv) regulatory concerns regarding the operations.

In order to assess these harms and test AI applications, the developers should conduct an AI impact assessment study.[57] An obligation to conduct periodic third-party impact-assessment audits[58] should also be considered, particularly for high-risk AI systems. Such audits will also ensure that AI systems improve with time and that any concerns are fixed pre-emptively, instead of being fixed after harm has been caused.

IBM has taken the position that persons involved in the creation of AI systems should at every step be accountable for considering the system's impact on the world.[59] Since the developers' role is limited to developing the AI system, their accountability should be limited to what they can control in this role without, in most cases, extending to how the system is used. Developers' primary responsibility should be to comply with the Ethical Principles in how the AI system is developed in order to make sure that good, compliant systems enter the market. As suggested above, this might simply imply classical notions of product liability, but AI systems have certain characteristics that need to be taken into consideration. Some contexts might require AI developers to keep records of the data used to train an AI, for instance in cases where it will be necessary to confirm there was no bias in the dataset. AI developers might also be the only ones with the knowledge necessary to modify or re-train an algorithm, creating accountability obligations that go beyond the development stages *per se*.

Particular contexts might require developers to include in their systems specific technical measures.

Recommendation

To ensure that AI systems can be controlled in case they malfunction or 'go rogue,' especially AI robots, we recommend that developers build 'kill-switches' and enable easy manual override to protect against unwanted consequences.[60]

Instant switch-off functionality is paramount because reinforcement-learning systems may find ways to cut out the operator from the loop.[61] These features will be extremely important in high-risk AI systems where the consequences of the system being compromised or (the system) malfunctioning can be dire, such as self-driving vehicles or airplanes. Some scholars have even argued that developers/manufacturers must provide "programmatic-level accountability" by being able to prove why a system operates in certain ways, in order to address legal issues and apportion culpability.[62] Such measures that ensure programmatic/procedural accountability can be mandated for developers who are engaged in developing high-risk AI systems.

Developers' accountability could be enforced through penalties if they fail to abide by the eight principles discussed in this Framework for Responsible AI as adopted in specific jurisdictions and if this causes harm. The nature and quantum of the penalty can be based on factors such as intention, degree of harm caused and actions taken to mitigate the harm, if any. However, the developer's accountability and liability should not extend to circumstances where the developer has taken all reasonably foreseeable precautions while developing the AI system and where the systems were deployed and used in a manner not intended by the developer, with consequences it could not have reasonably predicted. The developer's accountability should be on the basis of a 'fault' in the development of the system and should not extend to cases where harm is caused despite the developer not having violated applicable laws.

An accountability regime that penalises developers on a no-fault basis may have a chilling effect on progress which will be detrimental for innovation.[63] Having a flexible policy framework which provides a safeguard to developers will strike a balance between development of AI and protection of right-holders' interests.

2. Deployment and use of AI products and services

Deployment and use of AI systems involves making those systems available to end-users, either as services or products, without the stakeholder deploying the AI having necessarily developed the algorithm itself. In most cases, the relationship between a deployer and an end-user or client, whether a corporation or an individual, will be contractual and the contract may curb the extent of the deployer's accountability through clauses such as indemnity and limitation of liability. Thus, the contract between the different entities will determine the accountability as between themselves for harm caused by a deployer or that arises from the deployer's activities, except in circumstances prohibited by law.

At a policy-level, stakeholders deploying AI systems should be held accountable for the products and services that they are providing through the AI systems and they must provide products and services that are lawful and respectful of the Framework for Responsible AI. Providing services that discriminate against certain end-users or those that misuse personal data for unauthorised purposes will violate the obligations that the deployers owe to the end-users. We have mentioned above that governments have particular constitutional obligations to treat their citizens fairly and without discrimination, but private actors could also have similar obligations toward their users or clients, depending on applicable laws. The accountability standards here will depend on the nature of services, whether the services are regulated, whether actual harm is caused, the importance of the rights at stake, etc. It will also be driven by the contractual relationship between the parties. As part of the duty of accountability, if only to ensure the deployer is able to accurately assess the risk of harm arising from the products or services to be supplied, the deployer should also be accountable to conduct impact assessments of the harm that may be caused if AI is implemented in relation to particular services.

Sometimes, the deployer will also be the developer of the AI, which should simplify the analysis. When the two are separate, accountability should depend on who is responsible for certain parts of an AI lifecycle, i.e., gathering data, updating the algorithm with new data, testing, monitoring the AI's decisions, etc. If a deployer misuses an AI system by failing to make regular review of the system's decisions which results in a harmful outcome for an end-user, then the deployer should be held responsible. However, if an AI system makes such a decision and the reason for the decision is attributable to how the initial training data were selected, then the developer should be accountable. In short, deployers or user should be protected against faulty systems made by developers but, as we said, developers should not be responsible for non-predictable or non-permitted deployment or use of their creations. Of course, in cases of ambiguity, accountability obligations could also be clarified by contracts or set by a legislative or regulatory regime.

C. A sliding scale approach

We have seen how the nature of stakeholders and of their activities will influence the intensity of their accountability obligations. The interests of right-holders such as consumers are one more element of fundamental importance. When using an AI system or being subjected to a decision/action taken by an AI system, affected persons should have their rights and interests protected. Several of these rights and guarantees already exist. For example, those relating to personal data can be found in existing data protection laws around the world, such as the right to grant or revoke consent, to be informed of how one's personal data will be used and to whom it will be transferred. Other rights might include the right to appeal an administrative or judicial decision made with the help of an AI algorithm in case where the liberty of an individual is at stake, like in the criminal context.

The general rule should be to make the strictness of the accountability obligations proportional to the importance of the rights at stake and to the severity of the impact the AI system can have on these rights and the likelihood of harm. By way of example, the development and deployment of a dialogue system (chatbot) providing general information to customers has less critical implications than that of a smart system driving cars without human drivers. However, we may also find that a chatbot providing sensitive medical or financial recommendations requires accountability measures closer to the latter than the former.

In this context, it is only natural that the intensity of the accountability obligation should vary according to the degree of autonomy and criticality of the AI system. The greater the level of autonomy of the AI system and the greater the criticality of the outcomes that it may produce, the higher the degree of accountability that will apply to the organisation that develops, deploys or uses the AI system.

IV. Accountability and Governance

To ensure meaningful AI accountability, it does not suffice to apportion responsibilities between stakeholders. In our accountability framework, proactive AI *governance* by stakeholders is also key. We must ensure that accountable stakeholders take meaningful steps so that teams and individuals are "internally accountable." Stakeholders will do so by implementing thorough and comprehensive AI governance frameworks. Those frameworks should ensure that identified individuals (or teams) and AI enablers are accountable for AI systems, and thus safeguard against irresponsible AI development, deployment or use. In this part, we discuss some of the component elements of an appropriate AI governance framework.

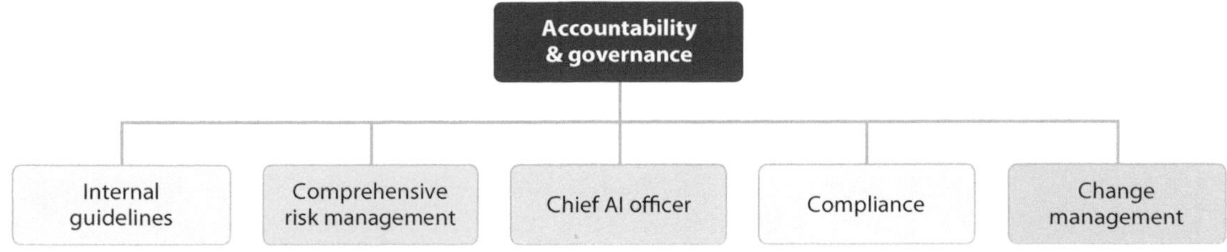

As AI systems touch upon several components and areas of expertise, AI governance should be approached from a multidisciplinary perspective. This means that an adequate governance framework will involve all relevant parties, not merely scientific and development teams, and should not approach risk assessment in silos. Rather, decision makers, like boards, executives and management, as well as teams and individuals who execute and carry out AI projects, like product owners, main users, computer scientists and developers, should be involved in and targeted by a governance framework. A key component will also consist in raising awareness in a cross-disciplinary way and keeping the involved parties informed about new findings and the evolution of AI technology, as well as emerging risks and impacts.

1. Internal guidelines, principles and codes of conduct

One of the foundational steps to proper AI governance is for stakeholders (in this section, either corporations or governments) to establish guidelines governing the AI activities they carry out. The guidelines may vary depending on size, field, and the degree of risk of an AI activity. For instance, stakeholders might want to establish their own AI principles and codes of conduct such as Microsoft has done in developing series of six AI principles.[64] Google has done the same, with seven principles—while also, as we saw in the previous chapter, promising not to pursue certain AI applications like AI weapons.[65] At the level of States, the G7 members have general principles for the development of AI.[66]

To implement these principles, stakeholders should establish clear guidelines governing AI projects that integrate the principles of this Framework for Responsible AI, to ensure that projects incorporate and apply such principles, and continuously abide by their codes of conduct. Those should be made widely available to employees, accompanied by the appropriate training, and communicated to the public.

Guidelines that relate to the interaction of stakeholders with consumers or clients are an important part of good governance. Many online platforms have adopted guides for users specifying what type of content the users can and cannot upload. Facebook calls those Community Standards and YouTube has a series of Community Guidelines.[67] Those standards and guidelines are internally useful for these companies because they help employees and algorithms make decisions about what content to remove based on criteria that are identified in advance (for example hate speech or pornographic content). AI algorithms remain prone to error however.[68] A good AI governance framework for such companies should, in that context, clarify who is responsible for monitoring the AI system and provide for review of its recommendations to identify and provide for the correction of mistakes.

2. Comprehensive risk assessment

Proper risk assessment will target full life cycles of AI systems and projects. Potential risks should be assessed at the outset of AI projects, continuously throughout deployment, and until the end of the AI system's life. Risk assessment processes should also be comprehensive, in that they must consider all types of risks, whether, legal, operational, or ethical. Assessment grids should be drafted with the particularities of AI borne in mind, like the potential autonomy of AI systems and the likelihood of systemic impacts. Further, AI risk assessment should include issues related to infrastructure and hosting systems through which AI systems will operate.

The government of Canada recently published its Directive on the Use of Machine Learning for Decision-Making. It only applies to Canadian federal government departments, but its principles can serve as useful guidance for other public and private organisations. This directive requires the completion of impact assessments which establish an assessment level ("Level") used to evaluate which rules govern when and how an automated decision-making tool can be used based on its potential impact on the rights of individuals and/or communities.[69] For instance, to determine which Level is applicable, and which rules must be followed, the department planning on using machine learning must namely complete an "Algorithmic Impact Assessment" questionnaire.

The Canadian Directive requires increasing oversight and safeguards to ensure accountability based on the assessment Level. For example, a Level I decision (one that does not impact the rights, health, or economic interests of individuals or communities or the environment) will not require any peer review, notices, training, contingency planning, approvals, or human aid and requires only minimal explanation requirements. However, a Level IV decision (one that will likely have a very high, irreversible, and perpetual impact on those rights) will require peer review from multiple qualified experts, in depth notices, human intervention, meaningful explanation of how the decision was rendered, testing, monitoring, continuous training, contingency planning, and high-level approvals.

The independent Dutch Platform for the Information Society (ECP, composed of government, business and social institutions) has also proposed a model for Artificial intelligence Impact Assessment (AIIA) which recommends following this roadmap when developing an AI project.

a) Determine the need to perform an impact assessment;
b) Describe the AI application;
c) Describe the benefits of the AI application;
d) Determine whether the goal, and the way of reaching the goal, is ethically and legally justifiable;
e) Determine whether the AI application is reliable, safe and transparent;
f) Decide considerations and assessments;
g) Document and attribute liability; and,
h) Review periodically.[70]

Such impact assessments mechanisms will ensure that the risk of harm is mitigated before organisations develop, deploy or use AI systems and that each stakeholder is held accountable for its involvement with the AI system.

3. AI chief officer and standard committees

One of the simplest steps private stakeholders can take to favour accountability for AI is to create a position akin to that of an AI Chief Officer. Stakeholders should consider the appointment of an AI Chief Officer as well as an AI standard/accountability committee, and entrust them with enhanced responsibilities to ensure that AI is developed, deployed and used responsibly and according to established principles, policies, and legal requirements. AI Officers and AI committees can be entrusted with monitoring and auditing internal activities involving AI, and more generally with ensuring compliance with AI governance mechanisms. They can also be responsible for answering external questions and queries about the use of AI, and thus can play an active role in explaining a given outcome to a member of the public, an end-consumer or a regulatory authority. It is also possible to go further, and provide the AI Officers with responsibility for ensuring the compliance of AI systems and products with applicable rules, and overseeing audits requests by governing authorities. The obligation contained within article 37 of the GDPR for controllers and processors to designate a data protection officer could be an inspiration in the case of AI Chief Officer.

Outside Officers and committees specialised on AI, private and public actors should implement measures to provide employees, officials and directors with access to resources and information on the use of AI within the organisation and on the broader ethical or legal principles with which it must comply.

4. Compliance with relevant laws and regulations

Good AI governance will also include making sure the stakeholder is complying with all applicable laws and regulations. Stakeholders must be confident that their AI systems respect applicable rules. The appointment of a Chief AI Officer and the creation of an AI committee should help with compliance efforts as one of their tasks should be to monitor the evolution of AI ethical and legal obligations and inform the organisation about new requirements.

To ensure compliance with various legal and regulatory obligations, both intrinsic and extrinsic processes and methods can be utilised. Intrinsic processes refer to the applicable rules and regulatory requirements that might be embedded, designed or otherwise incorporated in the AI models themselves, that is, coded directly into AI algorithms and hosting systems. This is one of the reasons why risks should be assessed at very early stages of AI projects. By contrast, "extrinsic" processes in this context will mean that adequate processes are put in place for human controllers to monitor AI activities and decisions. Examples might include random sample testing for compliance, or back-testing with preselected data, i.e., data input in such a way that it may "encourage" the model to make a choice that is not compliant.

5. Change management and corporate social responsibility

AI governance includes the implementation of effective change management techniques. Stakeholders that intend on deploying scalable AI projects throughout their activities should ensure responsible change management. There are several ways to ensure adequate change management, and the adequacy of measures taken by stakeholders will highly depend on circumstances, but the following can give guidance as overreaching, non-field-specific baseline ideas. Organisation that successfully adapt to AI from an internal perspective will be better placed to respect their accountability obligations.

Balance between job conservation and AI advancements. Throughout AI deployment, stakeholders should make regular assessments to ensure adequate balance between the conservation of jobs and AI technology advancements. As well, stakeholders should make sure to distribute the gains from those advancements in a responsible way,[71] insofar as gains from progress can be distributed in a way to minimise negative impacts on employees and to fairly allocate new opportunities.

Adequate assessment at outset of AI projects. Management should assess potential impacts on employees in the early stages of AI projects. Doing so will lead to efficient planning, which will in turn allow for efficient reallocation of tasks and responsibilities in the face of those impacts, rather than reacting to them, which conversely could leave fewer options to properly reorganise.

Early planning may also allow to plan according to upcoming needs, and other types of upcoming changes, whether managerial, operational, or financial. Bearing the goal and scope of the AI project in mind, early planning might also allow to better account for resources to be leveraged, to anticipate necessary involvement of employees, before and after deployment. Another way to see it is that there should be an early assessment of how freeing up some parts of processes and resources may be used to accomplish other tasks that are more strategic, but currently on "the back burner" because not part of daily operations of the employer. This assessment requires understanding both the specific task that the AI system will accomplish, as well as the entire processes around that task. AI projects may sometimes warrant putting into question and "disrupting" whole processes, i.e., not merely the tasks that the models will replace. Often times, it is the changes in those processes that will create the most resistance—not the mere replacing of a task by an AI system.

Culture shift. To favour effective change management for AI deployment, stakeholders must operate true culture shifts. To instigate culture shifts, stakeholders should identify what will be improved through using AI, gains from those improvements and in turn new mandates that can be undertaken with these gains. Influencers and leaders can then communicate those positive messages and thus create a positive reaction to upcoming AI projects. This will also allow to accordingly choose who will drive the AI project, the "champions" in tech jargon, that have the capability to create a change in the mindset of employees, convey AI goals, including accountability, as well as methods and processes to get to that goal, on a day-to-day basis. These techniques for culture shifts help ensure that employees will feel less threatened by AI projects. Ultimately, the success of the project will depend on effective communication with all stakeholders.

Proactive employee training—upskilling. To deploy responsible AI, stakeholders should strive to upskill employees and thus develop internal expertise that will be relevant throughout and subsequently to AI projects deployment. Such improvement of skill sets is beneficial to both employees and stakeholders. To that effect, international guidelines on corporate social responsibility stress the importance of improving skill sets of employees, as well as promoting practices that ensure transfers of the "know-hows" related to technologies.[72] By doing so and thus facilitating upskilling for employees, stakeholders favour formation of human capital and create opportunities. The proper training of employees is important to respect accountability obligations, and stakeholders should make sure that their employees know and understand the principles of this Framework for Responsible AI.

Social responsibility. The impact of AI on employment can also be addressed at societal scale by stakeholders through their corporate social responsibility programs. There is national and international guidance on how to have an adequate corporate social responsibility practice.[73] An AI social responsibility program with respect to employment could readily integrate such guidance. By way of example, this may include social outreach programs that will empower people and communities to learn AI-related skills and expertise. This might take the shape of financing relevant education programs, partnerships with schools, colleges and universities to ensure that people have proper guidance on what types of skills they need to develop to increase their chance of success in the employment of AI stakeholders. Finally, employers/AI research could also consider investing in relevant research projects and public research institutions.[74]

VI. Conclusion

Beneficial AI demands human accountability. General principles, even if well-intended, are useless without enforceable accountability regimes and without efficient governance models. In this chapter, we have presented a framework that is based on the principle of human accountability for the development, deployment or use of AI systems. As we saw, accountability requirements will depend on the nature of the stakeholder and the type of activity involved as well as on the criticality of the rights at stake, the potential risk of the AI activity and the degree of autonomy of the AI system. Much work still needs to be done to clarify and implement this principle as we remain at the dawn of this new AI age. Governments, with the participation of businesses, citizens, researchers and civil society organisations, should be attentive to changes brought by AI and be ready to adapt legal and regulatory frameworks when necessary.

On the other hand, AI systems, especially when based on complex multilayered neural networks, behave in ways that can be hard to predict and solving causality problems, as well as determining the appropriate standard of care for people using AIs, may prove difficult in certain cases. In our treatment of Principle 3—Transparency and Explainability, we will see that efforts to make algorithms more explainable may help tackle this challenge.

Principle 2
Accountability

Organisations that develop, deploy or use AI systems and any national laws that regulate such use shall respect and adopt the eight principles of this Policy Framework for Responsible AI (or other analogous accountability principles). In all instances, humans should remain accountable for the acts and omissions of AI systems.

1 Accountability

1.1 Organisations that develop, deploy or use AI systems shall designate an individual or individuals who are accountable for the organisation's compliance with those principles.

1.2 The identity of the individual(s) designated by the organisation to oversee the organisation's compliance with the principles shall be made known upon request.

1.3 Organisations that develop, deploy or use AI systems shall implement policies and practices to give effect to the principles if the Policy Framework for Responsible AI or other adopted principles (including analogous principles that may be developed for a specific industry), including:

- i. establishing processes to determine whether, when and how to implement a "Responsible AI Impact Assessment" process;
- ii. establishing and implementing "Responsible AI by Design" principles;
- iii. establishing procedures to receive and respond to complaints and inquiries;
- iv. training staff and communicating to staff information about the organisation's policies and practices; and
- v. developing information to explain the organisation's policies and procedures.

2 Government

2. Governments that assess the potential for "accountability gaps" in existing legal and regulatory frameworks applicable to AI systems should adopt a balanced approach that encourages innovation while militating against the risk of significant individual or societal harm.

2.1 Any such legal and regulatory frameworks should promote the eight principles of the Policy Framework for Responsible AI or encompass similar considerations.

2.2 Governments should not grant distinct legal personality to AI systems, as doing so would undermine the fundamental principle that humans should ultimately remain accountable for the acts and omissions of AI systems.

3 Contextual approach

3.1 The intensity of the accountability obligation will vary according to the degree of autonomy and criticality of the AI system. The greater the level of autonomy of the AI system and the greater the criticality of the outcomes that it may produce, the higher the degree of accountability that will apply to the organisation that develops, deploys or uses the AI system.

Endnotes

1 The Montreal Declaration on Responsible AI which states that "[t]he development and use of artificial intelligence systems (AIS) must permit the growth of the well-being of all sentient beings." *Montreal Declaration for a Responsible development of Artificial Intelligence* (2018), online: <https://www.montrealdeclaration-responsibleai.com/the-declaration> at principle 1.

2 Stanford Institute for Human-Centered Artificial Intelligence (2019), online: <https://hai.stanford.edu/>.

3 European Commission, High Level Expert Group on Artificial Intelligence, "Draft Ethics Guidelines for Trustworthy AI" (18 December 2018), online (pdf): <https://ec.europa.eu/digital-single-market/en/news/draft-ethics-guidelines-trustworthy-ai> at p i.

4 Meredith Whittaker et al, "AI Now Report 2018" (December 2018), online: *AI Now Institute*, <https://ainowinstitute.org/AI_Now_2018_Report.pdf> at p 11.

5 Gali Katznelson, "AI Citizen Sophia and Legal Status (9 November 2017), online: *Harvard Law Petrie Flom Center* <http://blog.petrieflom.law.harvard.edu/2017/11/09/ai-citizen-sophia-and-legal-status/>.

6 Immanuel Jotham, "Estonia working on legislation to give robots and AI legal status, create 'robot-agents'" (10 October 2017) online: *International Business Times* <https://www.ibtimes.co.uk/estonia-working-legislation-give-robots-ai-legal-status-create-robot-agents-1642516>.

7 Estonia, Invest in Estonia, "AI and the Kratt Momentum" (October 2018), online: *e-estonia* <https://e-estonia.com/ai-and-the-kratt-momentum/> [Kratt].

8 Gadgets, "Malta Might Be Giving Citizenship to Robots in the Next Few Years" (2 November 2018), online: <https://gadgetsmalta.com/general/robot-citizenships-malta/>.

9 EC, *European Parliament Resolution of 16 February 2017 with Recommendations to the Commission on Civil Law Rules on Robotics,* (2015/2103(INL)), online: <http://www.europarl.europa.eu/sides/getDoc.do?pubRef=-//EP//TEXT+TA+P8-TA-2017-0051+0+DOC+XML+V0//EN#BKMD-12> at 59 f) [EP Resolution].

10 Lawrence B Solum, "Legal Personhood for Artificial Intelligences" (1992) 70:4 North Carolina Law Revue 1231.

11 John Chipman Gray, *The Nature and Sources of the Law* (New York: Columbia University Press, 1909).

12 Bryant Smith, "Legal personality " (1928) 37:3 Yale Law Journal 283 [Smith];

Some have tried, unsuccessfully, to convince courts to give legal personality to animals. However, in the *Nonhuman rights project, Inc v Stanley* case a U.S. court did not recognise legal personality to a chimpanzee and stated that it was bound by the precedent in the *People ex rel. Nonhuman Rights Project, Inc. v. Lavery* case in which the Court held that a chimpanzee is not a "person." Some jurisdictions like France and Quebec have recognised animals as sentient beings, but nonetheless apply to them their property regimes;

See: French Civil Code article 515-14;

Quebec Civil Code article 898.1: "Animals are not things. They are sentient beings and have biological needs. In addition to the provisions of special Acts which protect animals, the provisions of this Code and of any other Act concerning property nonetheless apply to animals.";

See also Lexis Nexis Legal Newsroom Staff, "New York Judge Rule That Chimpanzees Are Still Not Entitled To Habeas Relief" (7 August 2015), online: *LexisNexis* <https://www.lexisnexis.com/legalnewsroom/litigation/b/litigation-blog/posts/new-york-judge-rule-that-chimpanzees-are-still-not-entitled-to-habeas-relief>.

13 Martha Tevis, "The status of Women: the path towards legal personhood" (1981) 60:1 Educational Horizons 11;

Reed v Reed, 404 U.S. 71 (1971). Slaves in the United States of America were granted the status of full legal persons under the 13th Amendment to the U.S. Constution.

14 *Salomon c A Salomon & Co Ltd* [1896] UKHL 1, [1897] AC 22.

15 Smith, *supra* note 12.

16 Luciano Floridi and Mariarosaria Taddeo, "Romans would have denied robots legal personhood" (2018) 557 Nature at p 309.

17 Ray Kurzweil, "Robots Will Demand Rights—And We'll Grant Them" (11 September 2015), online: *Time* <http://time.com/collection-post/4023496/ray-kurzweil-will-robots-need-rights/>.

18 Kratt, *supra* note 7.

19 Ignacio Cofone, "Servers and Waiters: What Matters in the Law of A.I." (2018) 21 Stanford Technology Law Review 167;

Ryan Calo, "Robotics and the Lessons of Cyberlaw" (2014) 103:3 California Law Review 513.

20 ING, "The Next Rembrandt: Can the Great Master Be Brought Back to Create One more Painting," online: <https://www.nextrembrandt.com/>.

21 *Ibid.*

22 Shlomit Yanisky-Ravid, "Generating Rembrandt: Artificial Intelligence, Copyright, and Accountability in the 3A Era—The Human-like Authors are Already Here—A New Model" (2017) Michigan State Law Review 659.

23 Naam me kya rakha hai, "AlphaGo Documentary" (13 January 2019), online: *YouTube* <https://www.youtube.com/watch?v=l9sztL9FQ> at 41:30.

24 Institute of Electrical and Electronics Engineers Global Initiative on Ethics of Autonomous and Intelligent Systems, "Ethically Aligned Design, First Edition" (2019), online: <https://ethicsinaction.ieee.org/> at p 231 [IEEE].

25 Curtis Karnow, "Liability for Distributed Artificial Intelligence" (1996) 11:1 Berkeley Technology Law Review 147 at p 181 [Karnow];

Matthew U Scherer, "Of Wild Beasts and Digital Analogues: The Legal Status of Autonomous Systems" (2018) 20:1 Nevada Law Journal 66 at p 5;

Ugo Pagallo, "Apples, Oranges, Robots: Four Misunderstanding in Today's Debate on the Legal Status of AI systems" (2018) 376:2133 Philosophical Transactions of the Royal Society A 1 at p 8.

26 "Open Letter to the European Commission Artificial Intelligence and Robotics" (2018), online: <http://www.robotics-openletter.eu/>.

27 Google, "Perspectives on Issues in AI Governance" (2019), online: <https://ai.google/static/documents/perspectives-on-issues-in-ai-governance.pdf> at p 26 [Google].

28 Steven Levy, "Mark Zuckerberg on Facebook's Future From Virtual Reality to Anonymity" (30 April 2014), online: *Wired* <https://www.wired.com/2014/04/zuckerberg-f8-interview/>.

29 Mark Zuckerberg, "The Internet needs new rules. Let's start in these four areas" (30 March 2019), online: *The Washington Post* <https://www.washingtonpost.com/opinions/mark-zuckerberg-the-internet-needs-new-rules-lets-start-in-these-four-areas/2019/03/29/9e6f0504-521a-11e9-a3f7-78b7525a8d5f_story.html?utm_term=.e51961e6ed22>.

30 *Automated and Electric Vehicles Act 2018* (UK), c 18 s 2.

31 Kevin Funkhouser, "Paving the Road Ahead: Autonomous Vehicles, Products Liability, and the Need for a New Approach" (2013) 1 Utah Law Review 437 at p 452;

Gary E Marchant & Rachel A Lindor, "The Coming Collision between Autonomous Vehicles and the Liability" (2012) 52 Santa Clara Law Review 1321 at p 1334;

James M Anderson et al, "Liability Implications of Autonomous Vehicle Technology" in *Autonomous Vehicle Technology: A Guide for Policymakers* 111 (RAND Corporation, 2014) at p 116.

32 James M Anderson et al, "Standards and Regulations and Their Applications to Autonomous Vehicle Technologies" in *Autonomous Vehicle Technology: A Guide for Policymakers* 97 (RAND Corporation, 2014) at p 108.

33 This was implicitly recognised by Volvo's former CEO. Hakan Samuelsson revealed that Volvo would assume liability for accidents involving its autonomous vehicles;

Newsdesk, "Volvo to accept liability on driverless cars" (22 October 2015), online: *Insurance Times* <https://www.insurancetimes.co.uk/volvo-to-accept-liability-on-driverless-cars/1416002.article>.

34 *Personal Information Protection and Electronic Documents Act*, RSC 2000 c 5.

35 *Algorithmic Accountability Act of 2019*, online: <https://www.wyden.senate.gov/imo/media/doc/Algorithmic%20Accountability%20Act%20of%202019%20Bill%20Text.pdf>.

36 A Proposed Model AI Governance Framework, Personal Data Protection Commission Singapore (2019), online: <https://www.pdpc.gov.sg/Resources/Model-AI-Gov>.

37 Nick Ismail, "What are the 5 biggest problems artificial intelligence will solve in the public sector?" (10 July 2018), online: *InformationAge* <https://www.information-age.com/problems-artificial-intelligence-public-sector-123473349/>.

38 Jensen Werley, "Jacksonville debuts high-tech streetlights—and they're watching you" (16 April 2015), online: *Jacksonville Business Journal* <www.bizjournals.com/jacksonville/news/2015/04/16/jacksonville-debuts-high-tech-streetlights-and.html>.

39 Raghav Bharadwaj, "AI in Government—Current AI Projects in the Public Sector" (18 February 2019), online: *emerj* <https://emerj.com/ai-sector-overviews/ai-government-current-ai-projects-public-sector/>.

40 *Ibid.*

41 See notably, *Universal Declaration on Human Rights,* GA Res 217(III), 3d Sess, Supp No 13, UN Doc A/810 (1948) 71 (non-binding);

International Covenant on Civil and Political Rights, 19 December 1966, 999 UNTS 171, Can TS 1976 No 47, 6 ILM 368 (entered into force 23 March 1976);

International Covenant on Economic, Social and Cultural Rights, 16 December 1966, 993 UNTS 3 (entered into force 3 January 1976).

42 Michael C Herrera & Dean Harvey, "Opinion: The legal risks of using artificial intelligence in brick-and-mortar retail" (21 November 2018), online: *Information Management* <https://www.information-management.com/opinion/the-legal-risks-of-using-artificial-intelligence-in-brick-and-mortar-retail?brief=00000159-ffbf-d8bf-af7b-ffbf558d0000>.

43 Julia Angwin et al, "Machine Bias" (23 May 2016), online: *ProPublica* <https://www.propublica.org/article/machine-bias-risk-assessments-in-criminal-sentencing> [Angwin].

44 Natalie Rodriguez, "Loomis Look-Back Previews AI Sentencing Fights To Come" (9 December 2018), online: *Law 360* <https://www.law360.com/articles/1108727/loomis-look-back-previews-ai-sentencing-fights-to-come>.

45 *State v. Loomis*, 881 N W 2d at 749 (2016) [*Loomis*].

46 *Ibid,* at 754.

47 Adam Liptak, "Sent to Prison by a Software Program's Secret Algorithms" (1 May 2017), online: *The New York Times* <https://www.nytimes.com/2017/05/01/us/politics/sent-to-prison-by-a-software-programs-secret-algorithms.html> [Liptak].

48 Angwin, *supra* note 43. "Northpointe's core product is a set of scores derived from 137 questions that are either answered by defendants or pulled from criminal records. Race is not one of the questions. The survey asks defendants such things as: 'Was one of your parents ever sent to jail or prison?' 'How many of your friends/acquaintances are taking drugs illegally?' and 'How often did you get in fights while at school?' The questionnaire also asks people to agree or disagree with statements such as 'A hungry person has a right to steal' and 'If people make me angry or lose my temper, I can be dangerous.'"

49 Liptak, *supra* note 47.

50 Angwin, *supra* note 43;

Loomis, *supra* note 45.

51 Angwin, *supra* note 43.

52 *Ibid*.

53 IEEE, *supra* note 24 at p 214.

54 Jeremy Elman & Abel Castilla, "Artificial Intelligence and the Law" (2017), online: *Techcrunch* <https://techcrunch.com/2017/01/28/artificial-intelligence-and-the-law/>.

55 *Jones v W+M Automation Inc*, 818 NY S 2d 396 (App Div 2006), appeal denied, 862 N E 2d 790 (NY 2007).

56 *Ibid*.

57 ECP, "Artificial Intelligence Impact Assessment" (2018), online: <https://static1.squarespace.com/static/5b7877457c9327fa97fef427/t/5c368c611ae6cf01ea0fba53/1547078768062/Artificial+Intelligence+Impact+Assessment+-+English.pdf> at p 9 [ECP].

58 James Guszcza et al, "Why we need to Audit Algorithms" (28 November 2018), online: *Harvard Business Review* <https://hbr.org/2018/11/why-we-need-to-audit-algorithms>.

59 IBM, "Everyday Ethics for Artificial Intelligence," (September 2018), online: <https://www.ibm.com/watson/assets/duo/pdf/everydayethics.pdf> at p 11.

60 EP Resolution, *supra* note 9.

61 BBC, "Google Developing Kill Switch for AI" (8 June 2016), online: <https://www.bbc.com/news/technology-36472140>.

62 IEEE, *supra* note 24. While this has been argued in the context of autonomous weapons, the same principle should equally apply to other AI systems.

63 See Cindy Vam Rossum, *Liability of Robots: Legal Responsibility in case of Errors or Malfunctioning* (2017), Ghent University, online: <https://lib.ugent.be/fulltxt/RUG01/002/479/449/RUG01-002479449_2018_0001_AC.pdf> at p 47;

The author notes that most liability regimes would have a chilling effect on innovation and that high damages could reduce corporations' willingness to develop new technologies. The author writes (in the context of autonomous vehicles)—"Ironically, even though automated cars are deemed safer overall than manually driven cars, the manufacturer's liability exposure will likely be greater and that might be detrimental to innovation."

64 Those are: Fairness,Inclusiveness, Reliability & Safety, Transparency, Privacy & Security and Accountability. Microsoft, "Our approach"(2019), online: <https://www.microsoft.com/en-us/ai/our-approach-to-ai>.

[65] Those are: Be socially beneficial, Avoid creating or reinforcing unfair bias, Be built and tested for safety, Be accountable, Incorporate privacy design principles,Uphold high standards of scientific excellence, Be made available for uses that accord with these principles. Sundar Pichai, "AI at Google: our principles" (7 June 2018), online: <https://www.blog.google/technology/ai/ai-principles/>.

[66] Supporting economic growth from AI innovation, Increasing trust in and adoption of AI, Promoting inclusivity in AI development and deployment. G7, "Annex B: G7 Innovation Minister's Statement on Artificial Intelligence" (2018), online: <https://g7.gc.ca/en/g7-presidency/themes/preparing-jobs-future/g7-ministerial-meeting/chairs-summary/annex-b/>.

[67] Facebook, "Community Standards," online: <https://www.facebook.com/communitystandards/>;

Youtube, "Community Guidelines," online: <https://www.youtube.com/yt/about/policies/#community-guidelines>.

[68] Google, *supra* note 27.

[69] Canada, "Directive on the Use of Machine Learning for Decision-Making" in Development, v.2.7 (18 December 2018), online: <https://docs.google.com/document/d/1LdciG-UYeokx3U7ZzRng3u4T3IHrBXXk9JddjjueQok/edit>.

[70] ECP, *supra* note 57.

[71] Carl Benedikt Frey & Michael A. Osborne, "The Future of Employment: How Susceptible are Jobs to Computerisation?" (17 September 2013), online: *United Kingdom Department of Engineering Science, University of Oxford* <https://www.oxfordmartin.ox.ac.uk/downloads/academic/The_Future_of_Employment.pdf>.

[72] OECD, "Guidelines for Multinational Enterprises" (2011), online: <http://www.oecd.org/corporate/mne/> [OECD].

[73] ISO 26000:2010 *Guidance on Social Responsibility* (reviewed 2014)—guidance not requirements;

OECD, *supra* note 72;

United Nations Human Rights Office of the High Commissioner, "Guiding Principles on Business and Human Rights" (2011), online: <https://www.ohchr.org/documents/publications/GuidingPrinciplesBusinessHR_EN.pdf>.

[74] OECD, *supra* note 72.

Principle 3

TRANSPARENCY AND EXPLAINABILITY

Organisations that develop, deploy or use AI systems and any national laws that regulate such use shall ensure that, to the extent reasonable given the circumstances and state of the art of the technology, such use is transparent and that the decision outcomes of the AI system are explainable.

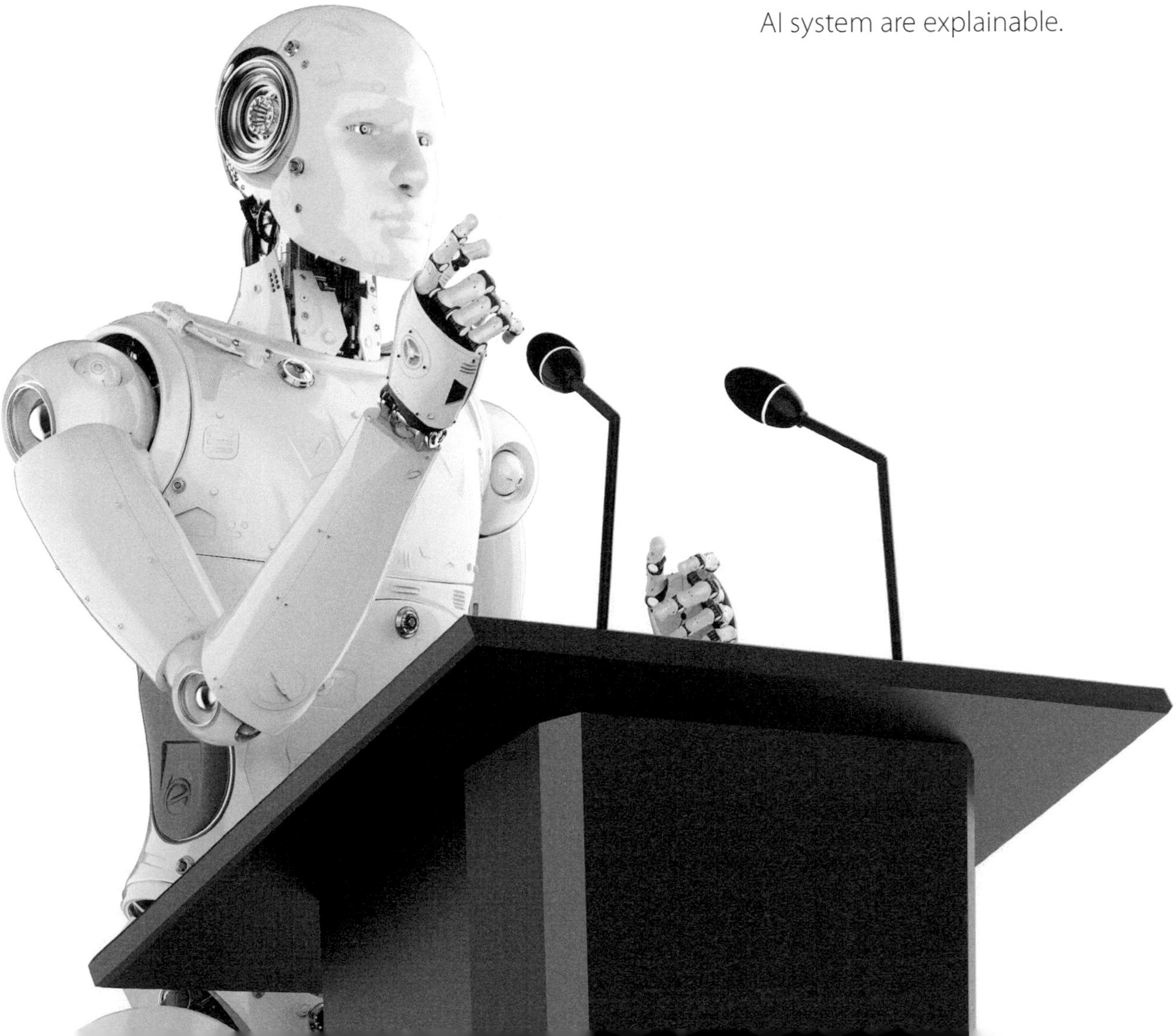

3
TRANSPARENCY AND EXPLAINABILITY

CHAPTER LEAD
Charles Morgan | McCarthy Tétrault LLP, Canada

Richard Austin | Deeth Williams Wall LLP, Canada

Nicole Beranek Zanon | de la cruz beranek Attorneys-at-Law Ltd., Switzerland

Luca Dal Molin | Homburger AG, Switzerland

Massimo Donna | Paradigma Law & Strategy, Italy

Charles Kerrigan | CMS, United Kingdom

Chris J. Maddison | Oxford University, United Kingdom

I. Introduction

When a decision satisfies someone, most of the time, this person will not care exactly how the result was reached. For example, if you are applying to law school and are accepted, you will have little interest in finding what element in your cover letter was decisive in winning you the coveted spot. But this is not the case when someone is negatively impacted by an adverse decision. Cases like the lawsuit against Harvard University's admission process and its alleged discrimination against Asian-American applicants show how important the intricacies of the decision-making process of an institution, the factors evaluated, their weight and their compounding, can become when people feel uncertain, suspicious of, cheated or dissatisfied by the outcome.[1]

To maintain trust, institutions need to find a balance between being transparent and providing explanations on one hand, and preserving the integrity, accuracy and cost-effectiveness of their decision-making processes, on the other.

The adoption of AI systems by businesses and governments will add an additional layer of complexity to this landscape. International Data Corporation predicts that annual global spending on cognitive and AI systems will hit $77.6 billion in 2022, more than three times the $24.0 billion they forecasted for 2018.[2] Many of these systems will interact directly with individual rights holders. From movie and book recommendations, to credit scores and loan approval, to the analysis of medical images and even to criminal sentencing decisions, AI systems will take over many decision-making processes. While some will be trivial, others may well be of life-changing importance.

As with non-AI decision-making, people will only accept this ever-increasing presence of AI, and not recoil as modern-day Luddites faced with the 21st century equivalent of textile machines, if they trust the results, the means through which the results are produced and the institutions that present them. What complicates the picture is that, as Cedric Villani writes in his report for the French government, artificial intelligence is a technology with an "obscure nature."[3] Describing AI algorithms as proverbial "black boxes," whose inner workings are unknown, is one of the classical tropes of the policy debate surrounding this technology. Although we may know what inputs are fed to the machines and what outputs are produced, the alchemy governing their internal processes, the complex interactions between nodes in the deep neural networks (see the Introduction), can seem unintelligible for laypersons and specialists alike. Thus, institutions and organizations that can seem like black boxes to outside onlookers will increasingly employ AI systems, creating a situation of black boxes within black boxes.

In this chapter, we will present a framework through which we believe these two black boxes, the institutional and the algorithmic, should be opened. It is divided into three further parts. In Section II, we deal with the very human need for understanding what the AI systems are doing and how they come to particular results, recommendations or decisions, to confirm the systems are safe, consistent with expectations and neither illegal nor unethical. We suggest that this need can be met with a combination of transparency and explainability obligations for stakeholders developing, deploying or using AI decision-making systems. In section III, we use case studies to help us present our framework. As a basic principle stemming from the human-centric approach, private organisations and public sector agencies that use AI systems should be transparent about their use and should work with the assumption that every AI-based decision can and should be explainable in humanly understandable terms, so as to allow for a valid review or appeal process. Such measures are important to give concrete effects to the human accountability principle we have presented in the previous chapter. This does not mean, however, that transparency and explainability ought not to be limited in certain contexts. Rather, the policy challenge ahead is to find a balance that protects rights while accounting for costs, IP protection and diminished efficiency.[4] These case studies will help us to illustrate the balance that must be struck and to argue for a gradual approach that modulates the intensity of transparency obligations depending on the context and the importance of the decision to be made. Finally, we will present some solutions and recommendations pertaining to the challenge of developing and meeting transparency and explainability obligations.

II. A Double Framework: A Right to Transparency and Explainability

A. Transparency

Different terms and classifications have been used to describe the solutions to the problem of AI as a black box, sometimes in contradictory ways. Transparency, interpretability, explainability, explicability are terms that appear in the relevant literature.

Transparency

For our purposes, we consider that transparency refers to a duty for businesses and governments to inform people that they are interacting with an AI system and to provide information about its specifications, including the origin and nature of the data used to train the algorithm and to describe what it is that the AI system does, and how it does it.

Transparency informs customers or users prior to their interaction with an AI system, before their rights and obligations have been affected by a decision. Transparency provides the information necessary for them to decide whether or not they want to interact with the AI and the organisation using it.

The duty of transparency, when applied to AI, is analogous to the transparency principle that is at the heart of many data protection regimes worldwide. For example, under the principle of openness, article 4.8 of the Canadian *Personal Information Protection and Electronic Documents Act* (PIPEDA) forces organizations managing personal information to make available information about their data policies and practices.[5] Article 5 of the European *General Data Protection Regulation* (GDPR) also provides that holders of personal data (controllers) shall process it "in a transparent manner,"[6] making transparency one of the core principles of the legislation.[7]

A transparent processing of personal data means informing affected people that their personal information will be processed and about how, why and by whom it will be used to allow them to make more informed decisions.[8] Applied in the context of AI, transparency similarly means providing in advance enough information so that individuals can make enlightened decisions. California's Bill 1001 is a good example of the kind of transparency obligations we have in mind. It requires the owner of an online chatbot to disclose, to the person interacting with it, that they are not communicating with a real human person.[9] Other examples can be found in the GDPR. Articles 13 and 14 of the GDPR require controllers to inform data subjects that their data will be analysed by an automated decision-making system.[10] Additionally, Article 22(1) confers on a data subject the right to opt out, in certain circumstances, when a decision is made "solely" through automated processing.[11] Articles 13(2)f) and 14(2)g) of GDPR, moreover, include a duty for controllers to inform data subjects of the "significance and the envisaged consequences" of the use of the automated system, as well as to provide "meaningful information about the logic involved."

Transparency is thus not a new idea, and we can find guidance about how it should apply to AI in looking at its role in current data protection regimes. It will nevertheless need to be adapted to the specificities of AI, like its use of big data, training of AI systems on that data and the ability of AI systems to improve over time. The Personal Data Protection Commission of Singapore, for example, divides the AI development process into three stages: the preparation of data, the application of an AI algorithm to the prepared data (training stage) and the application of the chosen model in decision-making.[12] In our framework, transparency is important in all of these stages. Hence, transparency in AI might require, for instance, providing information on the source and nature of the data used (the "lineage of data"),[13] notably by maintaining records of the origin of data.[14] It could also include a duty to inform customers that the system is also using their data to improve the AI system. Finally, individuals should be informed when AI systems are used in ongoing data collection, for example when cameras are paired with AI software for image recognition purposes.

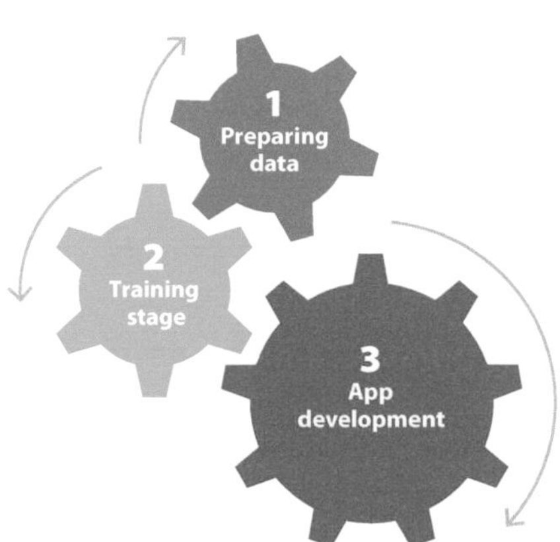

B. Explainability

Once a decision is made by an AI system, it is not enough to simply inform the affected persons that a decision was not made by a human and provide details on the system's specifications in general. In the post-decision stage, there is a need for explainability.

In our framework, "explainability" (also referred to as "interpretability" elsewhere)[15] refers to a duty to provide information about how exactly a certain output was produced. An explainable AI system, or XAI, is a system that provides explanations on its "thinking" process.[16] It implies, as stated by the European Commission's *Draft Ethics guidelines for trustworthy AI* that "AI systems **[must]** be auditable, comprehensible and intelligible by human beings at varying levels of comprehension and expertise."[17] If transparency aims at opening the institutional black box, explainability aims at opening the algorithmic one, providing the information necessary to understand how the rights of persons are affected and why. In this regard, an explainability right could include a right to information about how decisions are made including, in some instances, a right to review the system algorithms, as well as certain audit rights, as discussed below. To give an example of explainability from the legal world, many justice systems have concluded that providing reasons, often written, is an important aspect of procedural fairness, for courts as well as for administrative bodies.[18]

> *"AI systems [must] be auditable, comprehensible and intelligible by human beings at varying levels of comprehension and expertise."*
>
> European Commission's Draft Ethics guidelines for trustworthy AI

Machine learning and deep learning may be relatively recent innovations, but other new technologies have faced similar challenges. Since the 1960s and the first electronic data processing (EDP) audits, businesses have required that their technology systems be auditable, so that they can have confidence that the systems are operating in compliance with applicable laws. This auditability is essential in order for a business to demonstrate compliance as part of financial, operational or other audits, to regulators or otherwise, and to justify its use of AI systems to stakeholders. In the context of AI, this should be translated as a requirement to integrate explainability functions from the conception stage of the system to the output/decision stage—in other words, "explainability by design," as inspired by the "data protection by design" concept found in data protection regimes.[19]

Ultimately, the hope is that an AI system will have the ability to explain its decisions in the same way that a human can justify his or her own decisions, for example by pointing to the determinative factors. Explanations should provide the missing links between the input and the output (the decision) of an AI system. In this context, we are seeking to translate this desired outcome into a policy recommendation, not only to define the circumstances where the ability to use an AI system should depend on the system being explainable, but also to define what level of explanation should be required, who should produce the explanation and who should have access to the explanation.

C. The importance of transparency and explainability

Promoting transparency and explainability is mainly about preserving the public's trust and ensuring a meaningful accountability of those developing, deploying and using AI systems. It is also about recognizing that demonstrating higher accuracy or efficiency than alternative techniques may not be enough to generate confidence in an AI system. For Singapore's Personal Data Protection Commission, "[i]ncreased transparency would contribute to building consumer confidence and acceptance by increasing the level of knowledge and trust in the customer relationship."[20] Transparency, for its part, will encourage a better-informed public. Explainability is essential for accountability because it is through explanations that a system's biases, errors and shortcomings will come to light. Transparency and explainability, taken together, will allow for a better monitoring of the lawfulness of the development, deployment and use of AI systems.

For consumers and individual rights-holders, knowing that an AI system is in use and receiving explanations for decisions made can be especially important. They will want to understand how the decision was made and why they were impacted in the particular way that they were. Absent proper explanation, they will perceive the use of the AI system as arbitrary and inappropriate, creating risks that they will refuse to acknowledge or accept the system's decisions.

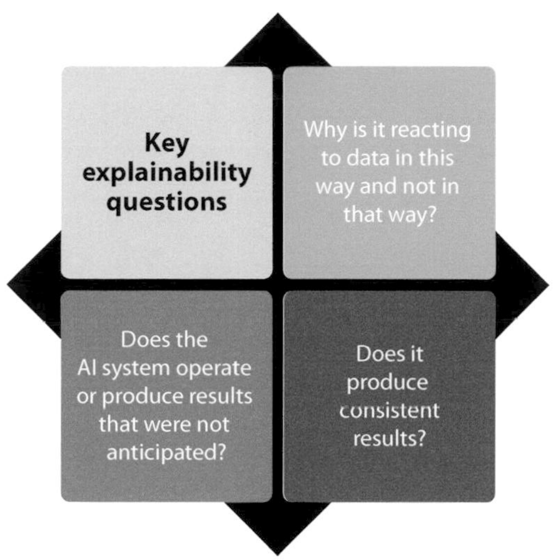

Explainability is also essential for AI system developers who need to know that the systems they are programming do what they are intended to do. Does the AI system operate or produce results that were not anticipated? Why is it reacting to data in this way and not in that way? Does it produce consistent results? Explainability might be even more important for organizations using AI systems to make important decisions affecting third parties because those organizations will be accountable for their use to a wide variety of stakeholders—employees, customers, suppliers, business partners, shareholders, regulators, etc. For them, an AI system is no different than any other tool, process or procedure: they own the implementation decision and the results, and as such, have an interest in being able to provide compelling reasons for an outcome to clients, regulators, courts or the public.

As we will now see however, the importance of transparency and explainability, as well as the specific content of these obligations, will vary as a function of the context. As such, it would be counter-productive to adopt an all-or-nothing approach that does not recognise the diversity of circumstances in which AI can be applied.

III. Case Studies

This distinction between the use of AI systems by private or public actors is important because, when it comes to decision-making, these two sets of actors do not have the same powers and obligations as we have suggested in Principle 2—Accountability.

For private actors, the use of undisclosed, inappropriate, inaccurate, unfair or unethical AI systems can lead to a myriad of unforeseen or unanticipated consequences, ranging from reputational or financial damages to criminal liability, in addition to the personal consequences for the responsible business leaders. Based on the experience of Toyota Corporation executives unceremoniously brought before U.S. Congress to provide explanations regarding complaints that their certain of their vehicles were subject to sudden unexplainable acceleration, we can imagine AI company executives being called on the carpet to explain mis-performing AI systems in self-driving cars.[21]

In the public sector, as the Canadian Treasury Board Secretariat has noted, based on principles of Ministerial accountability, it is important that government institutions have full understanding of the tools that they are using for decision support.[22] This is not just because of their transactional responsibilities to specific individuals. Most public entities have domestic or international obligations to treat their constituents fairly and to protect certain rights, notably human rights. This is difficult to do when nobody understands how an AI system reaches its conclusion. Governments also have powers, through police, courts and administrative bodies, to encroach on individual liberties and rights in a way that private actors cannot. This power comes with heightened responsibilities. The contrast between the public sector's duties and those of the private sector is highlighted in the statement of *The Toronto Declaration: Protecting the rights to equality and non-discrimination in machine learning systems:* "[States] have obligations to promote, protect and respect human rights; private sector actors, including companies, have a responsibility to respect human rights at all times."[23]

The two following case studies, one from the private sector and the other from the public sector, highlight the different components of our framework.

A. Private sector case study

In the last few years, banks, especially in the United States,[24] though also in India[25] and in Europe,[26] have collectively spent billions of dollars purchasing or developing AI technologies, including analytics systems to predict consumer behaviour, chatbots to improve customer services and document review systems to work more efficiently.[27] JPMorgan Chase has, for instance, developed the Contract Intelligence platform (COiN) to replace manual review of commercial credit agreements with machine learning systems.[28]

Application of AI solutions in the banking industry can help streamline the loan application process by shortening it from weeks to minutes and making the process more affordable.[29] Machine learning systems trained on relevant datasets are particularly useful in analysing a customer's financial and personal information and evaluating the level of risk for a credit application.[30] AI systems can rapidly give a green light in low-risks cases, while identifying more complex cases for human review.[31]

Loan Application

Imagine the case of John, who applies for a loan online and receives an automated rejection notice only a few seconds after assiduously completing all the online loan application forms. Here, his bank, not respecting the transparency principle, has not informed John in advance that his file would be treated by an AI system. He is left wondering how a decision could have been made so quickly. Had his application been reviewed seriously? And without bias?

In the context of banking regulation, legislators will have to determine what information needs to be disclosed in what circumstances. For example, might there be circumstances under which algorithms would be required to undergo a regulatory certification process?

Returning to our example of John and his loan application, we can also imagine that, once John's loan application is rejected, an AI system would assign John's file to bank loan officers for further review of his financial situation to assess the bank's exposure. If this were to be the case, transparency would require that these other uses of the AI system results be disclosed up front, so that John could consider whether to submit an online application.

Furthermore, if John asks for details on why his application was rejected, the use of explainable AI systems will ensure that banks are not in the untenable situation of admitting they simply do not know. In this context, explainability means ensuring that the system used can provide metrics and information to identify which factors were important in the loan approval decision. If a decision is contested, that information will be useful in facilitating auditability and identifying the determinant factors (and confirming that such factors were appropriate and not discriminatory or otherwise illegal).[32] In such scenarios, explainability is valuable not only for the persons affected, but also for providing businesses with tangible proof that their algorithms were free of bias and were designed and used reasonably.

In the private sector, we will also find examples of AI systems requiring transparency, without necessarily involving the need for explainability. For example, this is the case when AI systems are used to analyse the facial expressions of clients to determine their mood. Some stores have begun pilot projects leveraging AI in such a manner to help them improve their clients' experience.[33] There, the AI does not make decisions directly affecting the rights of the clients, but transparency still requires the stores to disclose to its clients its use of an AI system, what data is being collected, as well as why and how it is using it and for how long the data will be retained.[34] But they also illustrate the role that context plays in determining the level of explainability that should be required. If, for example, the facial recognition system were to be used as a substitute for police line-ups, identifying suspects from its image database, we can imagine that affected individuals or minority groups may demand more information about how the algorithm operates.

B. Public sector case study

In the public sector, courts and administrative agencies (notably in criminal cases, as well as in immigration and refugee systems), have quickly shown an interest in AI for the same reasons that are important in the private sector: a desire for increased accuracy, greater insight and reduced costs. Here, transparency and explainability are particularly important because these public sector departments are over-burdened, lack resources, and possess large amounts of data (whether from border security agents, permanent resident and asylum applications, data sets collected by national intelligence and law enforcement agencies, etc.). As such, they represent environments well-suited for the use of AI systems. On the other hand, and of crucial importance, individuals subject to these systems are in positions of extreme vulnerability and are entitled to know that their rights are properly protected, no matter what decision-making process is being used to determine their fate.

The advantages of AI have already convinced many public bodies to embrace AI systems in their daily operations. In the U.S., AI systems are currently used to assist judges in determining sentences,[35] issuing bail terms and granting parole.[36] In the United Kingdom, police departments are developing AI systems to assist law enforcement predict where future crimes may occur.[37] Canada, for its part, seeks to implement algorithms to assist immigration officers in screening immigration and refugee applications.[38] The use of AI systems can often be beneficial, notably in increasing efficiency and reducing the costs of public administration.

Code for America

Through a partnership with the nonprofit Code for America, which has developed an automated machine learning tool called "Clear My Record" to help people clear their criminal records, the city of San Francisco recently identified more than 9,000 marijuana-related convictions that could be nullified.[39]

However, AI systems also pose greater risks in the public sector than in the private sector. Public body decisions, especially in the judicial and administrative law contexts (for example, criminal sentencing and immigration), can undermine an individual's human rights by subjecting him or her to state decisions that may be opaque, unexplainable and based on biased data sets or ill-designed algorithms. The outputs thus produced risk being arbitrary, wrongful, discriminatory and contrary to basic principles of administrative law, notably the right to procedural fairness.

The importance of transparency and explainability has recently been highlighted by a controversy over the use of a computer-based Risk Classification Assessment system (RCA) by the United States' Immigration and Customs Enforcement (ICE). RCA is a risk analysis tool nationally deployed by ICE since 2013.[40] It helps agents decide whether or not to detain noncitizens arrested by ICE pending a decision on their immigration status. It does so by calculating the risk a person poses to public safety and the risk of flight if released.[41] The RCA system was inspired by pre-trial detention risk assessment tools developed in the 1960s for the criminal justice system and was initially promoted as a way to reduce detention levels through more accurate evaluations of individual risk levels.[42] In June 2018, an investigation by Reuters revealed that ICE had modified the RCA system so that it now only recommends detention. Although ICE agents are not bound by the system's recommendation, it is unsurprising that the modifications to the RCA system led to a substantial increase in the number of detentions.[43] Public outcry to this news was swift, leading to a civil action taken by the New York Civil Liberties Union to force ICE to disclose more information about its RCA system.[44]

ICE's tool is not a neuron-based AI system; it is closer to an expert system because it uses automatised actuarial techniques to produce risk scores.[45] This case nevertheless raises issues that are relevant in the case of modern AI. First of all, there are transparency concerns because there is insufficient publicly available information on the use and functioning of this system, leading to reduced levels of trust from the public. This case also shows the critical importance of explainability, of understanding the inner working of a decision-making system. In this instance, there is little doubt that the system is biased towards a certain outcome as a result of human intervention programming the system to only recommend detention. With that information, one can then ask if the system respects legal requirements, such as impartiality and non-discrimination.

IV. The Content of the Obligation of Transparency and Explainability

1. Different levels of transparency and explainability may be required in the public sector context than in the private sector because of these particular risks and because, in many public sector cases, organizations have no flexibility about whether or not to make a decision. Not only are they mandated to do so, but often the affected individuals cannot avoid the decisions made.

2. For example, if courts generally adopt AI systems in sentencing decisions, individuals on trial will not have an option to opt out, but the knowledge that an AI system was involved might remain crucial when appealing the sentence. This will make transparency and explainability even more crucial. Even when individuals will have no choice but to interact with an AI system, transparency will remain crucial for society at large because it has an interest in knowing when such systems are implemented in public decision making. Society might expect a certain degree of explainability for loan-approving AI systems, but dissatisfied individuals will nevertheless retain the option of doing business with other banks if they feel a certain bank is obscure about its use of AI. This is a luxury that people subject to immigration or a sentencing decision taken or assisted by an AI system do not have. Their only option will be to appeal to a higher court or body where proper appellate or administrative review will require AI systems to be explainable. Even in such a case, ex ante awareness of the fact that the administrative decision will be taken using AI systems will help set expectations and may help to provide enough information for a disappointed applicant either to come to terms with the outcome or to consider the most effective line of reasoning to challenge the decision.

Public or private use of AI systems should not get a free pass on compliance with a society's ethical or legal standards simply because they may constitute the latest, most technologically advanced tools or because "the issue is hard." As Cedric Villani writes:

> Because systems that incorporate AI technology are invading our daily lives, we legitimately expect them to act in accordance with our laws and social standards. It is therefore essential that legislation and ethics control the performance of AI systems. Since we are currently unable to guarantee *a priori* the performance of a machine learning system (the formal certification of machine learning is still currently a subject of research), compliance with this requirement necessitates the development of procedures, tools and methods which will allow us to audit these systems in order to evaluate their conformity to our legal and ethical frameworks.[46]

Like any other tool, policy or procedure used in a society, persons or institutions using AI systems are expected to comply with the applicable laws. This requires transparency as to what systems are used for and how they are used as well as explanations on how they operate and produce their results.

AI specialists debate the desirability of explainability, with some arguing that explainable AI is not a desirable outcome, because AI's greatest potential lies precisely in its ability to learn on its own in a more complex fashion than humans could ever easily understand. During a panel at the 2017 edition of the Conference on Neural Information Processing Systems, Yann LeCun, a pioneer of deep learning who currently works at Facebook, argued that explainable AI systems do not work as well as more complex, and consequently more obscure, systems, and that most users of AI faced with this trade-off choose systems that work better over those that are more explainable.[47]

For AI systems making relatively inconsequential decisions like recommending movies, this choice is perfectly legitimate. In other cases, like sentencing or hiring decisions, the law could require sacrificing efficiency to ensure that auditors or reviewers can understand how and why a system produced a given outcome, in order to confirm that it was not based on illegal considerations. In particularly sensitive contexts, decisions might best be left entirely to humans.

This suggests that the content of the obligations of transparency and explainability will vary depending on the context. Complete explainability in a language understandable by laypersons might not always be feasible, but we should avoid implementing systems that are completely unintelligible. At a minimum, developers should aim to create systems understandable by experts with reasonable skills and knowledge. Moreover, even in cases where complete explanations are impossible, transparency should be a minimal requirement and should include a disclosure that the system is a "black box."

A. Important factors

Rather than a one-size-fits-all approach to transparency and explainability, we propose a gradual and context-sensitive approach, whereby the greater the impact of a decision or an action taken by an AI system on an individual or a group, the greater the obligation on the designer or user of the AI system to be transparent about its use and make the technology explainable to those affected. The gradual approach is effectively a balancing test, taking its inspiration from various legal tests that seek to accommodate multiple parties' rights and preferences at one and the same time. The inherent value in such an approach is clear from the fact that not all decisions made using an AI system will have the same impact on rights. Furthermore, this approach should be technologically neutral in the sense that the use of AI systems should not diminish the procedural and judicial requirements that are essential in certain contexts, notably administrative decisions.

One of the first concerns when it comes to AI explainability relates to the existence of methods that can yield explanations. In 2017, a team of jurists, computer scientists and cognitive scientists from Harvard University found that "for the most part, it is technically feasible to extract the kinds of explanations that are currently required of humans from AI systems."[48] DARPA is also encouraging research on explainable AI.

As described in greater detail in the annex to this chapter, AI researchers have been exploring a variety of theoretical approaches to model explainability or interpretability (some of which are currently more or less feasible) that could help in providing explanations, including:

- **Explanations by varying features:** These explanations provide insight by illustrating how changes to the features of a given data point input might change the output of the model.

- **Text-based explanations:** These explanations try to provide direct textual explanations of model behaviour. They rely on a second model, fit to produce as outputs human readable textual explanations describing the behaviour of the model on a given input.

- **Image-based explanations or visualizations:** This is a broad category of approaches developed mostly for the study of neural network models, which use visualizations to provide insight into the behaviour of the model. As with the text-based approaches, these should be considered cutting-edge with untested reliability. Nonetheless, they may inform an expert. These methods tend to be sensitivity analyses that interrogate the internals of the decision system to visualise features of the input that are "salient" to the output of the model through a heatmap visualization.

- **Local Surrogate Models:** Local surrogate models attempt to provide insight into a model's behaviour by fitting a simpler interpretable model to mimic the true model nearby a given input.

From a legal perspective, two tests used in Canada may be considered as models—one created by the legislative branch and the other by the judicial branch. First, an approach could be adopted that is similar to the way the Canadian federal privacy law PIPEDA takes into consideration the reasonable expectations of the individual when obtaining consent and stipulates that the nature of such consent may vary depending on the sensitivity of the information.[49] In the context of AI, "reasonable expectations" of the individuals interacting with AI systems should also serve as a guiding principle. Furthermore, the actors or entities accountable for an AI system may be required to provide an explanation that is either (a) appropriate to the sensitive nature of the AI system's data inputs; and/or (b) appropriate to the sensitive nature of any resulting decision on a particular individual's rights.

Second, judges could be inspired by the legal test articulated by the Supreme Court of Canada in 1999 in the seminal administrative law decision *Baker v. Canada,*[50] which sets out a series of factors to consider in determining the content of the duty of procedural fairness owed by the state to individuals in the state's execution of administrative action. Those factors are: (a) the nature of the decision being made and the process followed in making it; (b) the nature of the statutory scheme (i.e., greater procedural protections are required where no appeal procedure is provided for within the statute); (c) the importance of the decision to the affected individual; (d) the legitimate expectations of the affected individual; and (e) the administrative agency's own procedural choices. As a general rule, institutions using an AI system for decision-making shall provide the level of transparency and explainability about its development, implementation and use that a reasonable person would deem appropriate in the circumstances.[51]

As held in the *Baker* decision: "The values underlying the duty of procedural fairness relate to the principle that the individual or individuals affected should have [...] decisions affecting their rights, interests or privileges made using a fair, impartial and open process, appropriate to the statutory, institutional and social context of the decision."[52] Similarly, it may be argued that the values underlying the duty of transparency require that individuals affected by the use of AI should have decisions affecting their rights, interests or privileges made using a fair, impartial and most importantly, open, process. In the context of AI, procedural fairness can be understood as the combination of transparency and explainability.

In establishing legal regimes for transparency and explainability, legislators and judges should thus take a context-sensitive approach and evaluate the following factors to determine the degree of transparency and explainability that is required for different types of decisions:

- What is the organizational context? Is it a private or a public entity? Does the organization use AI systems generally? Does the organization have a policy relating to AI systems that takes account of organizational issues, e.g., around privacy, security and confidentiality, or are the systems implemented as a result of ad hoc initiatives (where the concomitant issues may not have been completely thought out)?

- What is this specific AI system intended to do? Is it a reference system? Does it produce data points that are separately evaluated by an expert, or is it a decision-making system that operates independently of human intervention? What are the rights and obligations potentially affected by the system? What safeguards are in place to ensure that the AI system can be easily modified to prevent its use for nefarious purposes?

- Will users readily know that they are interacting with an AI system or that one is being used? For example, would it be clear to a user that he or she is interacting with an automated personal assistant or chatbot?

- What data does the AI system need, collect, use, produce and retain? What are the sources of the data (proprietary databases, open sources, data brokers, etc.)?

- What are the risks of that data being biased? How does the system use personal information? Is it anonymised? Will information be protected by appropriate technical and organizational measures? Will the information be deleted after use?

- Who developed the AI systems? Was it developed in house or by a third party? This might be particularly important in the public sector, where the use of proprietary AI systems might limit explainability.

- Who is interacting with the AI systems? Is this person in a vulnerable position? What would be the value and benefits of transparency and explainability for that person?

- What type of AI systems can be used to make the decision? What type of explanations can it provide? Can it provide counterfactual examples?

- What are the downsides of transparency and explainability in the context under consideration? What would be the costs, in term of resources, accuracy or efficiency, of having the system produce humanly understandable explanations?

In considering these factors we should be aware of the importance of transparency and explainability for the social acceptability of AI technology since without them, individuals will not trust AI systems. People will understandably ask to receive explanations for why a bank's AI system denied them a loan; for why their self-driving cars crashed; for why they were not recommended for a first-round interview by the human resources department's AI-driven software; for why they were not recommended as a candidate for the organ transplant following an analysis by the hospital's AI software. In a balanced approach, their demands will not always be satisfied, but encroachments on transparency and explainability will be based, at least in theory, on experience and principled reasons.

An example of such an approach can be found in the *Directive on the Use of Machine Learning for Decision-Making* (the "Directive") prepared by the Treasury Board of Canada Secretariat, that will apply to all "automated decision systems" used by the Government of Canada after April 1, 2020. The directive aims to encourage a use of AI systems by public bodies that "is compatible with core administrative law principles such as transparency, accountability, legality, and procedural fairness."[53] The Directive includes a number of transparency and explainability requirements including:

(i) producing an algorithmic impact assessment prior to the production of any automated decision system;

(ii) giving notice to the public when a decision will be rendered in whole or in part by an automated decision system;

(iii) providing a meaningful explanation to affected individuals of how and why a decision using an automated decision system was made;

(iv) releasing of custom source code owned by the Government of Canada for any automated decision system (with certain exceptions);

(v) obtaining software components for automated decision systems under open source licenses, where possible and

(vi) providing applicable recourse options.[54]

Interestingly, the Directive also adopts the gradual approach. It classifies decisions on a scale of I to IV: (I) for decisions with little to no impact, (II) for decisions with moderate impacts, (III) for decisions with high impacts, and (IV) for decisions with very high impacts on the rights or well-being of individuals or communities, their economic interests and (noticeably) ecosystem sustainability.[55] Each level brings increasingly stringent transparency and explainability requirements for peer review of the systems including prior notice, degree of human involvement in the decision, explanation, testing and monitoring, among others.[56]

B. Limits to transparency and explainability

A proper balancing approach also requires an awareness of the potential limits to the principles of transparency and explainability.

For example, private businesses have legitimate interests in keeping their valuable know-how secret as public authorities have legitimate interests that not every single detail of the AI they use to lawfully pursue public interests—such as in law enforcement—be exposed to the public.

Moreover, there may be other situations where it will be wise to maintain a certain level of obscurity to limit the ability of the public to game the algorithms. For instance, if the inner-workings of algorithms used to assess candidates in a job application process are revealed to the candidates, it will likely be much easier for them to influence the process in their favour, which would call into question the results of the assessment. Even companies using recommendations systems, especially platforms with user-generated content like YouTube, will want to hide their algorithms to avoid abuse. In January 2019, more than half the top twenty search results on YouTube for "RBG" (for Justice Ruth Bader Ginsburg from the U.S. Supreme Court) were for videos espousing odd conspiracy theories, for example that Justice Ginsberg was being kept alive with mysterious illegal drugs. An article in the ABA Journal suggested that the conspiracy videos were featured because of "relevance determinations" made in part based on newly posted or popular results. It appears that, whether intentionally or accidentally, aspects of the YouTube search algorithms were being manipulated to influence the search results.[57] Too much transparency might encourage or exacerbate these sorts of problems.

Another interest that is worth taking into account is the right to privacy, which is discussed further in our treatment of Principle 7—Privacy. The datasets used to train AIs are of interest for transparency and explainability purposes because the source of errors or bias can sometimes be traced backed to the original training data. However, the data sets often contain personal information. Any procedures developed to ensure AI systems are explainable will need to take into account the privacy issues inherent in any retention or subsequent access to, or use of, such personal information. For instance, did the individuals whose personal data was used to train or test the system consent to the personal information being retained or consent to allowing access to the information being provided in the future to third parties?

In each of these examples, overly broad transparency and explainability obligations may have negative implications for the protection of business secrets or for the pursuit of legitimate public or private interests. As a result, they may delay or prevent the adoption of AI systems, even where they may have beneficial effects. Therefore, we believe that the regulatory principles mandating transparency and explainability regarding AI systems have to take into account that there are conflicting, but nonetheless legitimate interests, that need to be protected. Hence, transparency and explainability obligations should not unduly limit the ability of AI developers and adopters to protect their proprietary algorithms, business secrets and know-how, and to safeguard a competitive advantage they may have compared to their competitors as a result of their use of AI, especially when the decisions made have low stakes. In this context, it also matters that the obfuscation of algorithms and strict secrecy via trade secrets is often the only viable option to protect valuable know-how and exclusivity in areas where no traditional IP protection is available.

Even reasonable transparency and explainability rules will have to allow for a case-by-case assessment that may limit the principles when needed to protect legitimate third-party interests.

Laws and regulations governing transparency and explainability obligations should therefore identify the conflicting interests at stake and balance them against each other. On the one hand, laws should not one-sidedly focus on the revelation of each and every detail relating to the use of AI. A high level of detail may be simply confusing and of little value for the receiver. Further, the burden on the organizations having to provide the information may be a factor that should reasonably limit obligations (as, for instance, Article 14(5) GDPR limits transparency obligations where the provision of the information would be impossible or require a disproportionate effort). On the other hand, even reasonable transparency and explainability rules will have to allow for a case-by-case assessment that may limit the principles when needed to protect legitimate third-party interests. European laws having to deal with similar situations of conflicting interests often foresee that, in a first step, the relevant interests of the stakeholders are to be identified so that, in a second step, they can be weighed against each other to determine which side prevails, e.g., whether the interests in favour of transparency and explainability outweigh those against them.

Data protection laws commonly involve such a balancing of interests. This is reflected in Section 3 of the Canadian federal privacy statute, PIPEDA, setting out the purpose of the Privacy Part of the statute:

> The purpose of this Part is to establish, in an era in which technology increasingly facilitates the circulation and exchange of information, rules to govern the collection, use and disclosure of personal information in a manner that recognises the right of privacy of individuals with respect to their personal information and the need of organizations to collect, use or disclose personal information for purposes that a reasonable person would consider appropriate in the circumstances.

Moreover, European data protection laws frequently require that a data subject's individual interests be weighed against conflicting public and private interests. For instance, the obligation of data controllers to be transparently informative about their processing of personal data may, under certain circumstances, be limited if they conflict with the interests of third parties.[58] Similar considerations apply when determining whether or not a data processing within the scope of the GDPR is justified by way of the data controller's legitimate interests.[59] In our view, these concepts can be looked to for inspiration when it comes to developing reasonable limitations to transparency and explainability obligations.

Finally, to deal with conflicts of interests, it might also be considered sufficient to reveal only the relevant information (e.g., the code, input and output) to a neutral third party (e.g., an auditor) who would audit the process and ensure fairness, with limited transparency.[60] Although this auditing option may look appealing, the financial burden (and the question of who shall bear the costs), the difficulty of implementation (requiring that the auditor be truly independent, determining how to handle disputes, etc.) and the expected length of the audit process would probably defeat its purpose, which is why we would be cautious in recommending such a solution.

C. Algorithm audits

Balancing these issues will certainly not be easy, but as we said, it is not a challenge unique to AI. In this last section, we will tackle algorithm auditability, a way to comply more precisely with explainability obligations.

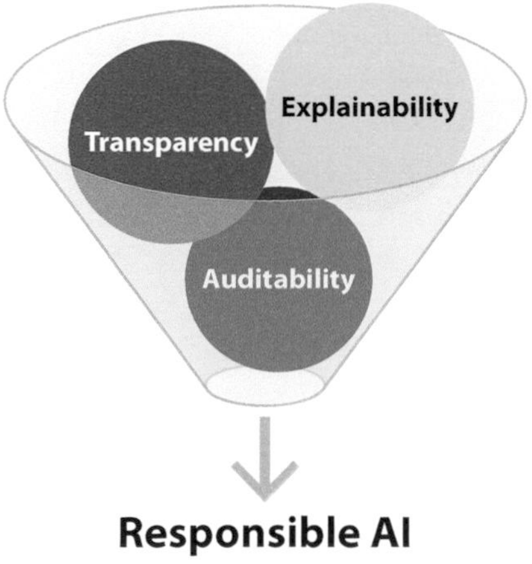

The discipline of IT auditing, for example, has evolved since the 1960s to keep pace with advances in technology and, in particular, to deal with issues around ownership of intellectual property, gaming the system and privacy matters. We can anticipate that, in a similar manner, the protocols that are developed to ensure that AI systems are explainable will evolve to accommodate AI system issues in these areas.

It is relevant to consider two examples of extending system audit principles to the explainability of AI systems. First, to make an AI system explainable, we will need to test the AI system's performance against what the system was intended to do. This requires that the objectives of the AI system be defined in advance, in order to provide a baseline for explainability. Explanations for the performance of AI systems only make sense measured against expectations of what the system was designed to do that have been defined in advance. The difficulties at this stage will have to do with the fact that since AI systems operate based on weights attached to a large number of artificial neurons, the logic behind the AI systems, i.e., the reason for any particular decision, may not be understandable. Even if it is possible to audit an AI system algorithm, the results may not be meaningful.

Second, it will be necessary, in planning the development of any AI system, to plan for the implementation of appropriate measures to support explainability, e.g., to design the procedures that will need to be implemented to preserve copies of data sets that were used to train or test the system. This will ensure that data will remain accessible for subsequent verification. Again, the necessity to address these procedures, tools and methods as part of the planning process is not unique to AI systems but applies to IT systems generally. The specificity of AI, however, is that neural networks are dynamic, e.g., they can improve and learn further as they operate.

Auditability of AI systems does not always require algorithm audits. Depending on the context, the objectives of performing the audit of an AI system may be capable of being achieved even without a full understanding of the logic of the algorithm, e.g., as has been noted:

> It is not always necessary, useful or even possible to draw conclusions from an examination of the source code. The auditors may be satisfied with simply checking the fairness and equity of a program (doing only what is required of them), by submitting a variety of false input data, for example, or by creating a large quantity of system user profiles according to precise guidelines, etc.[61]

Techniques for ensuring the explainability and auditability of AI systems will no doubt evolve and improve over time, coalescing around best practices that will provide the basis for formal and informal industry standards.

V. Conclusion/Recommendations

Our suggested approach can be summarised as using transparency obligations to open the institutional black box and using explainability obligations to open the algorithmic black box in a way that strikes a balance that respects all parties involved. These principles are fundamental to every aspect of AI presented elsewhere in this report. AI is a tool, in the end, and tools used by humans ought to be understandable.

Principle 3
Transparency and Explainability

Organisations that develop, deploy or use AI systems and any national laws that regulate such use shall ensure that, to the extent reasonable given the circumstances and state of the art of the technology, such use is transparent and that the decision outcomes of the AI system are explainable.

1 Definitions

1.1 **Transparency** is an obligation for organisations that use AI in decision-making processes to provide information regarding: a) the fact that an organisation is using an AI system in a decision-making process; b) the intended purpose(s) of the AI system and how the AI system will and can be used; (c) the types of data sets that are used by the AI system; and (d) meaningful information about the logic involved.

1.2 **Explainability** is an obligation for organisations that use AI in decision-making processes to provide accurate information in humanly understandable terms explaining how a decision/outcome was reached by an AI system.

2 Purpose

2.1 Transparency and Explainability aim to preserve the public's trust in AI systems and provide sufficient information to help ensure meaningful accountability of an AI system's developers, deployers and users, and to demonstrate whether the decisions made by an AI system are fair and impartial.

2.2 The Transparency and Explainability principles support the Accountability principle, the Fairness and Non-Discrimination principle, the Safety and Reliability principle and the Privacy, Lawful Use and Consent principles.

3 Gradual and contextual approach

3.1 The intensity of the obligations of transparency and explainability will depend on the context of the decision and its consequences for the person subject to it. The scope and intensity of the obligations of transparency and explainability will increase as the sensitivity of the data sets used by an AI system increases and as the decisional outcome of an AI system increases in materiality.

3.2 The determination of the intensity of the obligations of transparency and explainability must balance the interests of the person subject to the decision and the interests of the organisation making the decision. The ultimate criteria shall be the reasonable expectations of a person subject to that type of decision.

4 Transparency and explainability by design

4.1 Organisations that develop AI systems should ensure that the system logic and architecture serves to facilitate transparency and explainability requirements. In so far as is reasonably practicable, and taking into account the state of the art at the time, such systems should aim to be designed from the most fundamental level upwards to promote transparency and explainability by design. Where there is a choice between system architectures which are less or more opaque, the more transparent option should be preferred.

4.2 Users of AI systems and persons subject to their decisions must have an effective way to seek remedy in the event that organisations that develop, deploy or use AI systems are not transparent about their use.

5 Technological neutrality

5.1 The use of an AI system by a public or private organisation does not reduce the procedural and substantive requirements that are normally attached to a decision when the decision-making process is completely controlled by a human.

Annex 1: Current Interpretability/Explainability Techniques in AI

A. Introduction

The academic community has considered for a long time the problem of interpretability of automated decision-making systems and statistical models. This consideration is becoming even more critical in the age of black box AI systems, for which interpretability is not a given. The purpose of this document is to summarise at a high level the academic discussion on this topic by reviewing many of the proposed methods for interpretability. We try not to comment too much on the reliability of different approaches, with the exception of pointing out clearly cutting-edge approaches. There are usually approach-specific strategies for interpretability (Guidotti et al., 2018) and the reliability will depend on many factors specific to the situation and technology.[62]

B. Terminology

For the purpose of this section, a *data set* is a collection of data points, each representing an individual set of measurements. Each *data point* is a vector of measurements, each of which is called a *feature*. For example, features may be real numbers representing a continuous measurement, integers representing a category of outcomes, or strings representing text.

A *model* is a decision-making or AI system, i.e., an automated procedure taking inputs and generating outputs that are used wholly or in part in a decision-making process. For example, a linear regression model has a linear response (output) to a data point (input).

C. Questions of interpretability

There are many kinds of interpretability we might desire. We break down these questions along two lines. Of course, these distinctions are not so clear-cut and are only used for the sake of organization.

First, the model will be subject to interpretability demands. As pointed out in the literature, the demand for interpretability is often required when the problem specification is incomplete (Lipton, 2016; Doshi-Velez and Kim, 2017).[63] In particular, if the desired behaviour of the model cannot be completely validated with quantitative metrics, being interpretable is a good fallback. For example, before deploying an automated loan processing system an organization may be interested in developing a detailed and accurate qualitative understanding of how it works to support customer service. Thus, methods for model interpretability seek to provide insight into how a model computes its output from a given input.

Second, the data itself might also be subject to interpretability demands (Vellido et al, 2012).[64] Generally speaking, the behaviour of the model is determined by a data set through some algorithmic fitting and model selection process. The kind of data, the data generating process, or some other structure of the data can influence this process to produce undesirable behaviour. Returning to the automated loan processing example, if a systematic bias against marginalised communities is reflected in the data, this may produce a model that reinforces this bias in its decisions. Thus, methods for data interpretability seek to provide insight into the structure of the data or how the model fitting is influenced by the data.

D. Model interpretability

What follows is a list of methods for providing insight into the model behaviour itself. These methods try to provide explanations that examine the question: "Given an input, how did the model arrive at its output?"

Many models could be considered interpretable by nature. This includes classical models like linear regression, logistic regression, or decision trees (Hastie et al., 2016).[65] Methods popular in contemporary machine learning and AI, such as neural networks, tend to be uninterpretable by nature, although Lipton (2016) argues that this view may be overly simplistic. Nonetheless, the focus here is on methods that might work both for naturally interpretable and naturally uninterpretable models. All of these methods (or modifications of them) tend to be broadly applicable, making relatively few assumptions on the model itself.

Explanations by varying features

These explanations provide insight by illustrating how changes to the features of a given data point input might change the output of the model.

The family of partial dependence style plots are among the most numerous and most studied kind. In their most basic form, partial dependence plots show the effect that one or two features have on the output of a model by plotting the response as the feature values vary, averaged over a dataset (Friedman 2001).[66] For example, partial dependence plots might reveal that the marginal dependence of a model on a feature is linear versus non-linear. Extensions of this method include conditional expectation plots (Goldstein et al., 2015.[67] The partial dependence plots can also be used to provide a statistical test of the dependence between feature effects in a given model (Friedman and Popescu, 2008).[68]

Counterfactuals are another kind of explanation derived by feature varying. Given an input, a counterfactual is the smallest change to the feature values that changes the output of the model to a predefined one (Wachter et al., 2017).[69]

Anchors invert the kind of the explanation provided by counterfactuals. An anchor is the set of features with the property that if they are held fixed, the output of the model will not change despite changing non-anchor features (Ribiero et al., 2018).[70] This kind of explanation answers the question: "Which features are sufficient to anchor an output on a given input?"

Text-based explanations

These explanations try to provide direct textual explanations of model behaviour. They rely on a second model, fit to produce as outputs human readable textual explanations describing the behaviour of the model on a given input. These techniques should be considered cutting-edge research and not particularly reliable yet. For example, McAuley and Leskovec (2013) consider a system that jointly fits a rating prediction model with a topic model.[71] The top words in the topic model are used to explain the rating prediction.

Image-based explanations or visualizations

This is a broad category of approaches developed mostly for the study of neural network models, which use visualizations to provide insight into the behaviour of the model. As with the text-based approaches, these should be considered cutting-edge with untested reliability. Nonetheless, they may inform an expert. These methods tend to be sensitivity analyses that interrogate the internals of the decision system to visualise features of the input that are "salient" to the output of the model through a heatmap visualization (Erhan et al., 2009; Simonyan et al., 2013; Zeiler and Fergus, 2014; Mordvintsev et al., 2015).[72] These methods are closely related to the methods of feature selection and importance for data interpretability.

Local surrogate models

Local surrogate models attempt to provide insight into a model's behaviour by fitting a simpler interpretable model to mimic the true model nearby a given input. The surrogate model can then be interrogated to provide explanations of the local behaviour of the true model. Ribiero et al. (2016) develop this approach.[73] Although Alvarez-Melis and Jaakkola (2018) have argued that it may lack robustness in some case.[74]

Explanation by example

These methods provide insight into the behaviour of a model on an input by providing similar data points with the same behaviour. Caruana et al. (1999) use the internal representations of the fitted model to define a distance metric, which can be used to identify examples from the training or testing set with similar behaviour.

Data interpretability

What follows is a list of methods for providing insight into the data set. These methods try to provide explanations that interrogate the question, what patterns are inherent in the data set and how does this influence the model?

Feature extraction

Feature extraction methods annotate each data point with additional features that are discovered in an algorithmic way from the entire data set. Generally speaking, these additional features may be themselves interpretable and provide some insight into the patterns present in the data (Vellido et al, 2012).[75] There are many such methods, and they range from classical techniques in statistics to cutting-edge research. Classical methods include principle components analysis (Jolliffe, 2015) and clustering methods (Jain et al., 1999.[76] More cutting-edge methods include non-linear dimensionality reduction methods (Van Der Maaten, 2009).

Feature importance or selection

Feature selection is a classical statistical technique for determining which features explain the most about a given model's behaviour. A proper survey of these methods is outside the scope of this overview; see (Hastie et al., 2016) for a survey of these methods, which include ridge and lasso regression, best subset selection, and forward stepwise regression.[77] At a high level, these methods compare the magnitude of the model's response to different features in order to select from among them the most important subset. The correctness of statistical inference techniques can suffer in this context. Correcting this is tackled by the field of post-selective inference (Taylor and Tibshirani, 2016).[78]

Influential instances

These explanations seek to measure the influence of a single data point in the data set on the final fitted model. This topic has a rich history in statistics. Cook's distance (Cook, 1977) is a distance defined over models that measures the effect of deleting an instance on a model's predictions.[79] If the effect of removing a data point increases the distance between models, this reflects a high degree of influence of that data point (Cook and Weisberg, 1980).[80]

Prototypes and criticisms

This method selects a subset of the data set that are "prototypical," in that they summarise the data set well, and a subset of criticism points that are not well-explained by the prototypes (Kim et al., 2016).[81] Intuitively, these methods provide insight into typical data points of the data set, which reflect common patterns in the data, as well as outliers, which can have an outsized impact on the model fitting process.

E. Conclusions

The study of interpretability is an old, but active, area of research in academia. We have tried to provide an overview of some of the methods, both accepted and proposed. A theme that emerges in this analysis is that interpretability and explanations are not monolithic concepts. Instead, resolving problems of interpretability may often require significant domain-specific knowledge and a tailored analysis.

Endnotes

1 Anemona Hartocollis, "Does Harvard Admissions Discriminate? The Lawsuit on Affirmative Action, Explained" (15 October 2018), online: *The New York Times* <https://www.nytimes.com/2018/10/15/us/harvard-affirmative-action-asian-americans.html>.

2 International Data Corporation, "Worldwide Spending on Cognitive and Artificial Intelligence Systems Forecast to Reach $77.6 Billion in 2022, According to New IDC Spending Guide" (19 September 2018), online: <https://www.idc.com/getdoc.jsp?containerId=prUS44291818>.

3 Cédric Villani, "For a Meaningful Artificial Intelligence: Towards a French and European Strategy" (2018), online: <https://www.aiforhumanity.fr/pdfs/MissionVillani_Report_ENG-VF.pdf> at p 114 [Villani].

4 Finale Doshi-Velez and al, "Accountability of AI Under the Law: The Role of Explanation" (21 November 2017), online: *arXiv* <https://arxiv.org/pdf/1711.01134.pdf> at p 2 [Doshi-Velez].

5 *Personal Information Protection and Electronic Documents Act,* RSC 2000 c 5 [PIPEDA].

6 EC, *Commission Regulation (EU) 2016/679 of the European Parliament and the Council of 27 April 2016 on the Protection of Natural Persons with Regard to the Processing of Personal Data and on the Free Movement of Such Data and Repealing Directive 95/46/EC (General Data Protection Regulation)* [2016] OJ, L119, article 5 [GDPR].

7 United Kingdom, Information Privacy Commissioner's Office "Guide to the General Data Protection Regulation" (2 August 2018), online: <https://ico.org.uk/media/for-organisations/guide-to-the-general-data-protection-regulation-gdpr-1-0.pdf at p 16>.

8 *Ibid,* at p 20.

9 *Senate Bill No. 1001*, California (approved by Governor 28 September 2018), online: <http://leginfo.legislature.ca.gov/faces/billTextClient.xhtml?bill_id=201720180SB1001.

10 GDPR, *supra* note 6 at s 13 and s 14.

11 GDPR, *supra* note 6 s 22.

12 Singapore, Personal Data Protection Commission, "Discussion Paper on Artificial Intelligence (AI) and Personal Data—Fostering Responsible Development and Adoption of AI" (5 June 2018), online: <https://www.pdpc.gov.sg/-/media/Files/PDPC/PDF-Files/Resource-for-Organisation/AI/Discussion-Paper-on-AI-and-PD---050618.pdf> at p 4 [Singapore].

13 Singapore, *supra* note 12 at p 7.

14 *Ibid,* at p 7.

15 Doshi-Velez, *supra* note 4.

16 David Gunning, "Explainable Artificial Intelligence (XAI)" (2018), online: *DARPA* <https://www.darpa.mil/program/explainable-artificial-intelligence>.

17 European Commission's High Level Expert Group on Artificial Intelligence, "Draft Ethics Guidelines for Trustworthy AI" (18 December 2018), online (pdf): <https://ec.europa.eu/digital-single-market/en/news/draft-ethics-guidelines-trustworthy-ai> at p 10 [EC Expert Group]. The European Commission uses the term "technological transparency" where we use explainability and "business model transparency" where we use transparency.

18 *Baker v Canada,* [1999] 2 SCR 817at para 44 [*Baker*].

[19] *"Data Protection by Design refers to the approach by which organizations consider the protection of personal data from the earliest possible design stage, and throughout the operational lifecycle, of a new system, product or service."* Singapore, *supra* note 12 at p 2.

[20] *Ibid,* p 11.

[21] "Toyota president Akio Toyoda's statement to Congress" (24 February 2010), online *The Guardian* <https://www.theguardian.com/business/2010/feb/24/akio-toyoda-statement-to-congress>.

[22] Canada, "Directive on the Use of Machine Learning for Decision-Making" in development, v.2.7 (18 December 2018), online: <https://docs.google.com/document/d/1LdciG-UYeokx3U7ZzRng3u4T3lHrBXXk9JddjjueQok/edit> at p 28-29 [Canada, "Directive"].

[23] "The Toronto Declaration: Protecting the right to equality and non-discrimination in machine learning systems," online: <https://www.accessnow.org/cms/assets/uploads/2018/08/The-Toronto-Declaration_ENG_08-2018.pdf>at para 8.

[24] Kumba Sennar, "AI in Banking—An Analysis of America's 7 Top Banks" (27 March 2019), online: *emerj* <https://emerj.com/ai-sector-overviews/ai-in-banking-analysis/> [Sennar].

[25] Ayushman Baruah, "AI Applications in the Top 4 Indian Banks" (10 February 2019), online: *emerj* <https://emerj.com/ai-sector-overviews/ai-applications-in-the-top-4-indian-banks/>.

[26] Raghav Bharadwaj, "AI for Banking in Europe—3 Current Applications" (25 February 2019), online: *emerj* <https://emerj.com/ai-sector-overviews/ai-for-banking-in-europe-3-current-applications/>.

[27] PWC, "FinTech Trends Report 2017: A deep dive into what's driving the FinTech revolution in India" (2017), online: <https://www.pwc.in/assets/pdfs/publications/2017/fintech-india-report-2017.pdf> at p 21.

[28] Sennar, *supra* note 24.

[29] Finsme, "ML and AI Tech is Taking the Mortgage Industry by Storm" (17 November 2018), online: <http://www.finsmes.com/2018/11/ml-and-ai-tech-is-taking-the-mortgage-industry-by-storm.html>;

Accenture, "Redefine Banking with Artificial Intelligence," online (pdf): <https://www.accenture.com/t00010101T000000Z__w__/gb-en/_acnmedia/PDF-68/Accenture-Redefine-Banking.pdf> at p 15.

[30] Accenture, *supra* note 29 at 17.

[31] IBM, "Trust and Transparency in AI," online: <https://www.ibm.com/watson/trust-transparency> at p 3.

[32] *Ibid,* at p 3.

[33] Annie Lin, "Facial recognition is tracking customers as they shop in stores, tech company says" (23 November 2017), online: *CNBC* <https://www.cnbc.com/2017/11/23/facial-recognition-is-tracking-customers-as-they-shop-in-stores-tech-company-says.html>.

[34] Arguably, this scenario also concerns privacy rights because data about clients are collected.

[35] Carole Piovesan & Vivian Ntiri, "Adjudication by algorithm: The risks and benefits of artificial intelligence in judicial decision-making" (2018), online (pdf): *The Advocates' Journal* <https://marcomm.mccarthy.ca/pubs/Spring-2018-Journal_Piovesan-and-Ntiri-article.pdf>.

[36] Charline Zeitoun, "Trusting Artificial Intelligence" (28 March 2018), online: *CNRS News* <https://news.cnrs.fr/articles/trusting-artificial-intelligence>.

[37] Chris Baraniuk, "Exclusive: UK police wants AI to stop violent crime before it happens" (26 November 2018), online: *NewScientist* <https://www.newscientist.com/article/2186512-exclusive-uk-police-wants-ai-to-stop-violent-crime-before-it-happens/>.

38 Petra Molnar & Lex Gill, "Bots at the Gate: A Human Rights Analysis of Automated Decision-Making in Canada's Immigration and Refugee System" (September 2018), online (pdf): <https://citizenlab.ca/wp-content/uploads/2018/09/IHRP-Automated-Systems-Report-Web-V2.pdf> at p 27.

39 Code for America, "Clear My Record," online: <https://www.codeforamerica.org/programs/clear-my-record>;

Evan Sernoffsky, "SF district attorney to wipe out 9,000-plus pot cases going back to 1975" (25 February 2019), online: *San Francisco Chronicle* <https://www.sfchronicle.com/crime/article/SF-district-attorney-wipes-out-9-000-plus-13643128.php>;

Adele Peters, "This algorithm is quickly clearing old marijuana convictions in San Francisco" (15 May 2018), online: *Fast Company* <https://www.fastcompany.com/40572854/this-algorithm-is-quickly-clearing-old-marijuana-convictions-in-san-francisco>.

40 Mark L Noferi & Robert Koulish, "The Immigration Detention Risk Assessment" (2015) 29 Georgetown Immigration Law Journal 45 at p 60 [Noferi].

41 *Ibid,* at p 47.

42 *Ibid,* at p 59.

43 Mica Rosenberg & Reade Levinson, "Trump's catch-and-detain policy snares many who have long called U.S. home" (20 June 2018), online: *Reuters* <https://www.reuters.com/investigates/special-report/usa-immigration-court/>.

44 Ben Choi & Naomi Dann, "ICE Rigged the System to Keep Immigrants Locked Up" (11 December 2018), online: *New York Civil Liberties Union* <https://www.nyclu.org/en/news/ice-rigged-system-keep-immigrants-locked>.

45 Noferi, *supra* note 40 at p 76.

46 Villani, *supra* note 3at p 116.

47 See the following debate "Interpretability is necessary in machine learning" at the NIPS 2017 conference: Interpretable Machine Learning, "2v2 Debate: Caruana, Simard vs Weinberger, LeCun. Interpretable ML Symposium, NIPS 2017" (12 December 2017), online: *YouTube* <https://www.youtube.com/watch?v=2hW05ZfsUUo> at 13:00.

48 Doshi-Velez, *supra* note 4 at p 6.

49 PIPEDA, *supra* note 5at ss. 7.2(1)(a)(ii), 7.2(2)(a)(ii) and Schedule 1, 4.7.

50 *Baker*, *supra* note 18[1999] 2 SCR 187.

51 Inspired by s. 5(3), PIPEDA, *supra* note 5: *"An organization may collect, use or disclose personal information only for purposes that a reasonable person would consider as appropriate in the circumstances."*

52 *Baker*, *supra* note 18 at para 28.

53 Canada, "Directive," *supra* note 22.

54 *Ibid*, 2.7 at 6.1.1, 6.2.1, 6.2.3, 6.2.4, 6.2.6, 6.4.1.

55 *Ibid,* at Appendix B.

56 *Ibid,* at Appendix C.

57 Debra Cassens Weiss, "Conspiracy theories about Justice Ginsburg gain prominence because of YouTube search algorithm" (15 January 2019), online: *ABA Journal* <http://www.abajournal.com/news/article/conspiracy-theories-about-justice-ginsburg-gain-prominence-due-to-youtube-search-algorithm/?utm_source=maestro&utm_medium=email&utm_campaign=weekly_email>.

58 GDPR, *supra* note 6. See Article 23(1)(i) GDPR, Article 9(1)(b) and 13(1) Swiss DPA), of the public (Article 23(1)(e) GDPR, Article 9(1)(a) and 13(1) Swiss DPA) or, in certain cases, also of the controller itself (Article 9(4) and 13(2) Swiss DPA.

59 *Ibid,* Article 6(1)(f) GDPR.

60 Kartik Hosanagar & Vivian Jair, "We Need Transparency in Algorithms, but Too Much Can Backfire" (25 July 2018), online: *Harvard Business Review* <https://hbr.org/2018/07/we-need-transparency-in-algorithms-but-too-much-can-backfire>.

61 Villani, *supra,* note 3 at p 117.

62 Riccardo Guidotti and al, "A Survey of Models for Explaining Black Box Models" (21 June 2018), online (pdf): *arXiv* <https://arxiv.org/pdf/1802.01933.pdf>.

63 Zachary C Lipton, "The Mythos of Model Interpretability" (2016) ICML Workshop on Human Interpretability in Machine Learning, online: *arXiv* https://arxiv.org/pdf/1606.03490.pdf;

Finale Doshi-Velez & Been Kim, "Towards a Rigorous Science of Interpretable Machine Learning" (2 March 2017), online: *arXiv* <https://arxiv.org/pdf/1702.08608.pdf>.

64 Alfredo Vellido and al, "Making machine learning models interpretable" (April 2012) ESANN 2012 proceedings, European Symposium on Artificial Neural Networks, Computational Intelligence and Machine Learning, online: https://pdfs.semanticscholar.org/ce0b/8b6fca7dc089548cc2e9aaac3bae82bb19da.pdf [Vellido].

65 Trevor Hastie and al, *Computer Age Statistical Inference: Algorithms, Evidence, and Data Science* (2016) [Hastie].

66 Jerome H Friedman, "Greedy Function Approximation: A Gradient Boosting Machine" (2001) 29:5 The Annals of Statistics 1189.

67 Expectation" (21 March 2014), online: *arXiv* <https://arxiv.org/pdf/1309.6392.pdf>.

68 Jerome H Friedman & Bogdan E Popescu, "Predictive Learning Via Rule Ensembles" (2008) 2:3 The Annals of Applied Statistics 916.

69 Sandra Wachter and al, "Counterfactual Explanations Without Opening the Black Box: Automated Decisions and the GDPR" (21 March 2018), online: *arXiv* <https://arxiv.org/ftp/arxiv/papers/1711/1711.00399.pdf>.

70 Marco Tulio Ribeiro, "Anchors: High-Precision Model-Agnostic Explanations" (2018), online: *Association for the Advancement of Artificial Intelligence* <https://homes.cs.washington.edu/~marcotcr/aaai18.pdf>.

71 Julian McAuley & Jure Leskovec, "Hidden Factors and Hidden Topics: Understanding Rating Dimensions with Review Text" (2013), online: *ACM* <https://cs.stanford.edu/people/jure/pubs/reviews-recsys13.pdf>.

72 Dumitru Erhan and al, "Why Does Unsupervised Pre-Training Help Deep Learning?" (2010) 11 Journal of Machine Learning Research 625;

Karen Simonyan and al, "Deep Inside Convolutional Networks: Visualising Image Classification Models and Saliency Maps" (19 April 2014), online: *arXiv* <https://arxiv.org/pdf/1312.6034.pdf>;

Matthew D Zeiler & Rob Fergus, "Visualizing and Understanding Convolutional Networks" (28 November 2013), online: *arXiv* <https://arxiv.org/pdf/1311.2901.pdf>;

Alexander Mordvintsev and al, "Inceptionism: Going Deeper into Neural Networks" (17 June 2018), online: *Google AI Blog* <https://ai.googleblog.com/2015/06/inceptionism-going-deeper-into-neural.html>.

73 Marco Tulio Ribeiro and al, "'Why Should I Trust You?' Explaining the Predictions of Any Classifier" (9 August 2016), online: *arXiv* <https://arxiv.org/pdf/1602.04938.pdf>.

74 David Alvarez-Melis & Tommi S Jaakhola, "Towards Robust Interpretability with Self-Explaining Neural Networks" (3 December 2018), online: *arXiv* <https://arxiv.org/pdf/1806.07538.pdf>.

[75] Vellido, *supra* note 64.

[76] an Jolliffe & Jorge Cadima, "Principal Component Analysis: A Review and Recent Developments" (2016) 374 Philosophical Transactions A of The Royal Society;

AK Jain and al, "Data Clustering: A Review" (1999) 31:3 ACM Computing Surveys 264.

[77] Hastie, *supra* note 65.

[78] Jonathan Taylor & Robert Tibshirani, "Post-Selection inference for l1-penalized likelihood models" (17 Octoer 2016), online: arXiv <https://arxiv.org/pdf/1602.07358.pdf>.

[79] Karen S Cook & Toby L Parcel, "Equity Theory: Directions for Future Research" (1977) 47:2 Sociological Inquiry 75.

[80] R Dennis Cook, "Characterization of an empirical influence function for detecting influential cases in regression" (1980) 22:4 Technometrics 495.

[81] Been Kim and al, "Examples are Not Enough, Learn to Criticize! Criticism of Interpretability" (2016) 29th Conference on Neural Information Processing Systems, online: <https://people.csail.mit.edu/beenkim/papers/KIM2016NIPS_MMD.pdf>.

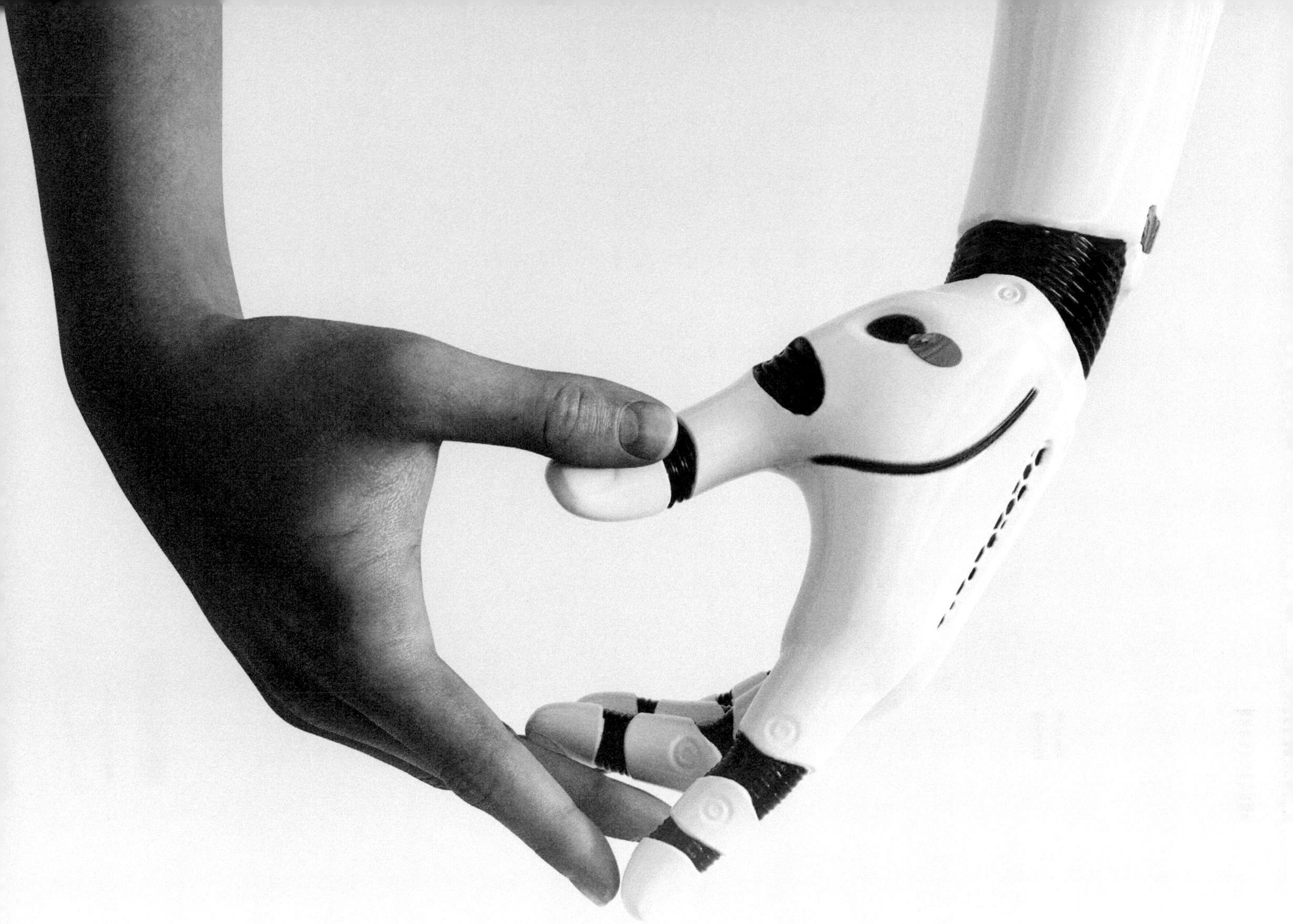

Principle 4

FAIRNESS AND NON-DISCRIMINATION

Organisations that develop, deploy or use AI systems and any national laws that regulate such use shall ensure the non-discrimination of AI outcomes, and shall promote appropriate and effective measures to safeguard fairness in AI use.

4

FAIRNESS AND NON-DISCRIMINATION

CHAPTER LEAD

Smriti Parsheera | National Institute of Public Finance & Policy, India

Philip Catania | Corrs Chambers Westgarth, Australia

Sebastian Cording | CMS, Germany

Diogo Cortiz | PUC-SP, São Paulo, Brazil

Massimo Donna | Paradigma Law & Strategy, Italy

Kit Lee | Corrs Chambers Westgarth, Australia

Arie van Wijngaarden | McCarthy Tétrault LLP, Canada

During the summer of 2013, 41-year old Vernon Prater—who is white—was arrested in Fort Lauderdale for shoplifting tools worth US$86. Prater had prior convictions for armed robbery and attempted armed robbery, and had served five years in prison.

In early 2014, 18-year old Brisha Borden and Sade Jones—who are black—were also arrested in Fort Lauderdale. They had spotted an unlocked bicycle and a scooter, which they took and attempted to ride down the street. When a woman came after them shouting that the items belonged to her family, they immediately dropped them and walked away.

Borden and Jones were charged with the burglary and petty theft of the bike and scooter, which were valued at a combined amount of US$80. Borden had a record for a misdemeanour committed as a juvenile. Jones had never been arrested before.

The criminal justice system in Fort Lauderdale used a risk assessment program powered by AI for predicting the likelihood of each one of these three individuals committing a future crime. Prater was rated as a low risk. Borden and Jones were rated as a high and medium risk, respectively.

Given the context of the cases, these assessments are both surprising and alarming. In addition, the reality proved to be quite different. Prater went on to steal thousands of dollars in electronics and serve 8 years in prison. Borden and Jones were never charged again.

I. AI, Fairness and Discrimination

The cases of Prater, Jones and Borden were featured in a high-profile investigation conducted by non-profit newsroom ProPublica[1] that questioned the racial bias in widely used criminal risk assessment tools. This work is part of a larger body of literature that has shone the spotlight on issues of fairness and discrimination in AI.

On the surface, AI systems seem to assure impartiality. By reducing the impact of human prejudice, they promise a future where outcomes are solely based on data and are therefore free from bias. After all, what better way of removing discrimination from decision-making processes, than simply keeping humans out of the equation?

Like most human creations, AI systems tend to reflect the goals, knowledge and experience of their creators. The issue of "fairness" in AI is therefore intrinsically linked to questions of representation in AI research and policy.

But the reality is far more complicated. What is the gender, race, class, religion and nationality of those who are setting AI agendas?[2] Who funds the AI research? Who executes it? At present, only about 12 percent of AI researchers globally are women, with country-specific variations ranging from 26% in Taiwan to nil participation in Sweden.[3] The gender break-up of AI professors at some of the world's leading computer science universities reflects a similar pattern—on average, over

80 percent of the professors are male.[4] What role does the gender of AI researchers play in determining the outcomes of AI research? Similar questions can also be raised about the region-wide variations in AI capabilities and whether we foresee any challenges in having global AI patterns shaped by research and scholarship in a handful of countries. The answers to these questions influence the future of AI and the fairness and inclusiveness of that future.

AI's reliance on large volumes of "real world" data can also induce an element of unfairness in its outcomes. Research has shown that AI can perpetuate—and even exacerbate—existing biases or other forms of discrimination.[5] Research has found two major causes for this phenomenon:

Biased training data

Training data is essential in machine-learning based systems. If the data used to "teach" the system a "right" answer is biased or insufficient, these limitations will be built into the AI system. The data provided to the AI systems may be unfiltered, uncleansed, or unrepresentative.[6]

For instance, if there is a sampling bias and some part of the population is misrepresented, the outcomes for that group will be less valid. Examples of this include the 2015 incident of Google's face recognition algorithm mistakenly labelling black people as gorillas and the higher error rates for darker skinned females on commercially available facial recognition tools from Microsoft, IBM and Face++.[7] The problem in both these cases stemmed from the under-representation of certain groups in the training data sets.

Data can also reproduce historical biases. If, for example, the training data to evaluate candidates to fill management positions within a large company is based on successful male candidates from prior years, the output will likely be biased against women. Research has in fact shown that a search for "computer science" is much more likely to pick male candidates merely because the data contains more references to male sounding names in conjunction with the term "computer science."[8]

> *"Algorithms and models are no more objective than the people who devise and build them, and the personal data that is used for training. The model's result may be incorrect or discriminatory if the training data renders a biased picture reality, or if it has no relevance to the area in question. Such use of personal data would be in contravention of the fairness principle."*
>
> Norwegian Data Protection Authority 2018 paper, Artificial Intelligence and Privacy

Inequality in outcomes

In a system where capacities, risks and circumstances are unevenly distributed, discriminatory results may also be realised indirectly. For instance, if an algorithm relies on "neutral" factors like level of education, level of parents' education, financial situation, etc. to arrive at a person's criminal risk assessment score, it is theoretically "unbiased." However, due to unequal circumstances, the output may still closely correlate to membership of certain historically disadvantaged groups. Black people will have a higher risk score even though racial data was not used.

> Unequal outcomes are very real. An AI system used to evaluate home loan approvals in two neighbourhoods, one middle income and one lower income, can lead to unequal effects even if location is not regarded as a factor. A person from the middle income neighbourhood is more likely to have a higher salary, and thus to obtain a higher borrowing limit, than a person from the lower income neighbourhood. This means the wealthier neighbourhood will obtain more favourable credit terms, exacerbating an already existing disparity.

While the immediate source of these problems lies outside the realm of AI, these examples highlight some of the risks of adopting technological solutions without due regard to the underlying socio-economic context.

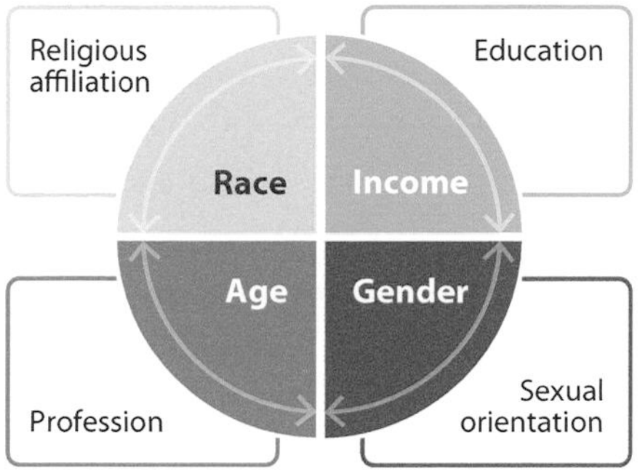

Questions of fairness in social settings can arise across many dimensions, including income, gender, education, profession, age, race and religious affiliation. The interaction of AI with some of these factors, like gender and race, has been fairly well researched. Using machine learning techniques on texts collected online, researchers found that female names are more associated with family than career words, compared with male names. Further, words like "woman" and "girl" are more likely to be associated with arts than with mathematics or sciences and common gender-occupation biases are strongly co-related with actual occupational participation.[9] These gendered associations then go on to shape the outcomes in a number of domains where AI systems are being deployed, ranging from job searches to use of language translation tools.

The chart below illustrates how gender perceptions from the real-world come to be reflected in AI-based translation tools. When Google translate is used to translate text from gender neutral languages like Turkish and Finnish to a gendered one like English, it also tends to translate certain perceptions about the subject, based on his or her gender.[10] For instance, when a reference to a male subject with a negative attribute like being lazy is translated from English to Turkish and then back to English, the resulting output changes the reference to make it a female subject. The reverse holds true for a positive characteristic like smartness, where the algorithmic translation process changes the gender reference from being female to male.

English → Turkish → English

He is lazy	*O tembel*
O tembel	**She's lazy**

She is smart	*O akilli*
O akilli	**He's smart**

English → Finnish → English[11]

He is a nurse	*Hän on sairaanhoitaja*
Hän on sairaanhoitaja	**She's a nurse**

She is an engineer	*Hän on insinööri*
Hän on insinööri	**He is an engineer**

The challenges of bias and discrimination are becoming increasingly relevant in AI discussions. For instance, the Toronto Declaration released in May 2018 by a coalition of human rights groups and technology companies focuses on equality and non-discrimination in machine-learning systems.[12] Similarly, the draft "Ethics Guidelines for Trustworthy AI" published by the European Commission's High-level Expert Group on Artificial Intelligence in December 2018,[13] identify "non-discrimination" as one of the key concepts for realising trustworthy AI. In addition, the model AI governance framework proposed by the Singapore Personal Data Protection Commission also seeks to ensure fairness and non-discrimination.[14]

II. Risks and Benefits

The power and influence of AI systems continues to grow as, more and more, they make decisions about essential or intimate aspects of our daily lives. The challenge to fairness arises when the systems are used to make decisions we would not have anticipated or the decisions are or appear to be biased, discriminatory or just plain "unfair."

The impact of this becomes extremely serious when the AI systems' decision making extends to fundamental aspects of our lives such as whether we get called for an interview based on the AI system's assessment of our resume, whether a mortgage application is approved based on the AI system's evaluation of our creditworthiness or the systems are used to predict the risk of a convicted person committing another crime.

In this section we will look briefly at the risks posed in some important areas where AI is being deployed.

A. Risk assessment and sentencing in criminal justice

More and more U.S. states have been resorting to AI systems to perform risk assessments at every stage in the U.S. justice system, based in part on encouragement from the U.S. Justice Department's National Institute of Corrections. The assessments can be used at the initial stages of a criminal process, for example to assist in determining bond amounts. But in many states they are also provided to judges during sentencing to rate the risk a defendant will commit a future crime. The magnetic attraction of these AI systems is evident: they hold out the promise of more accurate and objective information that can allow the judicial system to "get it right" in a more cost effective manner, locking up those individuals more likely to commit crimes in the future while giving shorter sentences or parole to those less likely to offend. The question is whether the system does, in fact, "get it right" in a fair, non-discriminatory manner.

Unfortunately, and as illustrated at the beginning of this chapter, this does not always appear to be the case. In a study performed by the ProPublica of one of the most used AI risk assessment systems, the organization concluded that the AI system discriminated against black defendants. The study found that the number of black defendants incorrectly identified as being at a high risk to re-offend was twice as high as the number of white defendants who were so classified.[15]

Similar to the AI predictive tools used to profile Prater, Borden and Jones, there was another recidivism model assisting in predictive sentencing—known as Level of Service Investory-Revised (LSI-R)—used to ascertain the risk of convicted persons re-offending. It provided judges with a sentencing guide that included the results of lengthy questionnaires on individuals' criminal history.[16] A factor in this model attributed early 'involvement' with police as a signal of recidivism, meaning that African-American and Latino individuals were far more likely to be categorised as high-risk persons.[17] Seemingly effective on its face and potentially more accurate than a judge's estimations, such models using historical assessments essentially lock individuals within a toxic cycle by profiling persons on the basis of their circumstances.

B. Predictive policing

Wouldn't it be great if the police could know in advance who might be committing a crime or might be the victim of a crime? While many believe this is already possible thanks to the latest AI-based predictive policing tools, critics fear that such tools might be riddled with old fashioned bias and lack of transparency.

Predictive policing systems typically involve the identification of criminal actors, areas where crimes are likely to occur or potential victims, along with corresponding warning or prevention mechanisms. While this sounds well in theory, there are several concerns. The algorithms deployed for predictive policing tend to be secretive in nature, hence denying the opportunity for any public debate on the merits or demerits of particular metrics. One can, however, assume that such tools are likely to consider factors like past criminal history, parole status and affiliations while assessing criminal risk. This could increase the likelihood of a person being included in police "heat lists" based on "suspicious looks" or association with certain communities or neighbourhoods. It could also lead to biased anti-terrorist enforcement in communities with a large Middle-Eastern population or a history of organised crime.

Biased data-sets may also derive from historical data which is tinted by long-standing discriminatory behaviours towards racial, religious or other minorities. Crime data from the United States of America and India shows that the prison population of persons from marginalised and disadvantaged groups—scheduled castes, scheduled tribes and Muslims in India and African American and Hispanic groups in the United States of America—tends to be in excess of their actual representation in the population.[18] AI solutions built on this data come with the likelihood of further perpetuating the prejudice faced by these groups.[19] Research has also pointed to the problems of using "dirty data," being data which has been corrupted or intentionally manipulated, to train predictive algorithms. This may, for instance, include data relating to motivated arrests or deliberate under-reporting of certain crimes, which would become the basis for future decision-making.[20]

The pervasive use of technologies such as closed circuit television (CCTV), GPS tracking and facial recognition to facilitate predictive crime analysis also poses significant threats to privacy, expression and other civil liberties. Such surveillance technologies tend to have a disproportionate impact on economically or socially disadvantaged communities, hence adding an element of unfairness in the deployment of such tools.

C. Health

AI is boosting medical innovation in many ways. Its uses include medical diagnoses using AI-powered systems, robotic surgery and swifter drug discovery, allowing pharmaceutical companies to significantly reduce the time traditionally required to bring drugs to market, with obvious societal benefits. In parallel, reducing the cost of drug discovery will allow new, less capitalised, drug startups to enter the pharmaceutical market.

Drug design

In the United Kingdom the University of Manchester has developed an AI tool called "Eve" which can automate the early stages of drug design, by screening over 10,000 compounds a day and identifying suitable candidates for drug testing.[21]

However, it is important to recognise that health data is highly personal and carries significant risks of inaccurate or discriminatory outcomes. This is especially true in situations when health training data from one population is used to inform AI solutions being deployed in a completely different context. To take an example, a Toronto-based startup found that the auditory tests that it developed for detecting neurological diseases like Alzheimer's or Parkinson's did not work well for persons who were not from Canada.[22] This was because the algorithms had been trained on data collected from native English speakers in the Canadian province of Ontario who were talking in their mother tongue. It did not account for the vocabulary, pauses and pronunciation of non-native English speakers, hence increasing the chances of false diagnosis.

Studies have also demonstrated the effective use of AI systems for diagnosing malignant skin lesions. This, again, comes with the limitation that the datasets overwhelmingly feature lighter skin, as white people are more likely to suffer from the disease.[23] Similar concerns have also come up regarding the lack of diversity in patient records, and the over-reliance in IBM's Watson for Oncology for medical approaches in the United States of America.[24] The lack of representative medical data is therefore likely to remain a key challenge in the deployment of health AI solutions.

The wider adoption of AI algorithms in the health sector may also blur the boundary between what is and what is not to be regarded as a medical device. In particular, in certain jurisdictions, such as the European

Union and the United States of America, there is a marked trend to regard algorithms in use in the medical industry as medical devices. In fact, on December 7, 2017 the Court of Justice of the European Union published its decision on the case C-329/16, "Snitem and Philips, France" in which the Court ruled that stand-alone software can be regarded as a medical device even if it does not itself act in or on the human body.[25] Patients outside of jurisdictions where stand-alone software is regarded as medical device and is, consequently, subject to additional safety requirements, may be less stringently safeguarded. Unless coordinated efforts are made to align medical stand-alone software disciplines across jurisdictions, medical software vendors may decide to test their products in jurisdictions where regulation is looser. This could very well result in discriminatory outcomes for patients who will not have an equal chance of access to care based on their jurisdiction's definition of medical device.

The wider adoption of AI algorithms in the health sector may also blur the boundary between what is and what is not to be regarded as a medical device.

D. Facial recognition

Facial recognition is a research area that has existed since early computing. Initially, it did not pose major concerns, since early algorithms simply focused on trying to detect whether a complex image contained a human face.

Recognition software now has the ability not just to identify whether a human is included in an image, but also to factor age, ethnicity and gender, identify emotions and movements, and determine the identity of specific individuals. Just as happened to Tom Cruise's character in the 2002 science fiction movie, *Minority Report,* facial recognition systems enable the detection and recognition of individuals from photographs, videos or real-time surveillance. Research and Markets predicts that the global facial recognition market, estimated at $3.85 Billion in 2017, will grow to $9.78 billion in 2023 as the technology penetrates security, surveillance, retail markets (for example to scan for shoplifters, to monitor crowds or simply to search for "unhappy" customers) and more.[26]

The power of AI is aided by the large number of images uploaded to social media, as can be seen by "tag suggestions" on Facebook every time an image is uploaded. The vast database of images gives machine learning algorithms the ability to process and improve their software to more accurately determine the identity of a given individual—even if that individual is amongst a large group of people.

The advancement in recognition technology has benefits as well as risks. The ability to review such large amounts of complex data in real time to identify individuals can be immensely beneficial. In 2018, a facial recognition system helped police identify

It has been argued that the loss of privacy may inhibit an individual's ability to actively participate in political discourse because they no longer have the ability to express their views without each action or statement potentially being monitored.

an individual responsible for a mass-shooting in Annapolis, Maryland, at the Capital Gazette, which killed five journalists.[27]

However, there are several ethical and legal issues associated with the use of AI technology. In the Annapolis shooting example, suspects were identified based on a database of driver's licence photos. These databases may have existed for decades, and the general public was unlikely to have any idea that their personal data would have been used for this purpose, which raises a consent issue if the jurisdiction considers a person's image to be sensitive personal data.

Even more, facial recognition technology also raises ethical issues not currently contemplated by legislation. For example, it has been argued that the loss of privacy may inhibit an individual's ability to actively participate in political discourse because they no longer have the ability to express their views without each action or statement potentially being monitored. China's proposed "Social Credit System" ("SCS") is an example of how far this technology may be taken.[28] China's SCS constantly monitors its citizens by using mass surveillance, data collecting and data processing infrastructure and technologies. With this technology, each individual's conduct may be scored according to notions of perceived "community good," "social good" or "sincerity" as it is referred to China.[29] An individual's freedom of speech and autonomy may be seriously undermined by the use of these AI technologies.

Another major ethical and practical risk is bias, particularly the effect that racial and gender bias can have when this technology is used by law enforcement, such as incorrect identification of suspects and victims of certain demographics. For example, an American Civil Liberties Union study involving Amazon's facial recognition technology (Amazon Rekognition), which is already in use by law enforcement agencies in the U.S., demonstrated that the algorithm incorrectly matched the pictures of several members of the United States Congress with arrested persons.[30] Moreover, out of the 28 false matches, nearly forty percent were of people of colour. Similar concerns can also arise in cases of other forms of recognition based on physical characteristics, such as gait recognition, which is often used for surveillance purposes and voice recognition, which can exclude unique accents and ethnicities.

Inherent in the self-learning nature of AI systems, we can anticipate that the accuracy of facial recognition systems will increase. But it is hard to know which is more alarming, the potential use of facial recognitions systems with unacceptable accuracy rates creating bias and discrimination issues, or the suggestion that imminent upgrades to CCTV and police camera systems providing higher definition imagery will result in more accurate, reliable, effective and potentially ominous facial recognition systems that exceed our expectations and violate our perceptions of fairness.

E. Labour

One potential benefit of AI systems is reducing decision-making costs in connection with human resources and recruitment. The use of AI also allows companies to make seemingly objective and efficient decisions when hiring or promoting employees, capable of matching candidates on the basis of skill rather than upon demographic or personal bias.[31] However, there is a risk that the algorithm could perpetuate existing biases or form new biases based on the initial dataset it was provided.

Amazon's experience with an AI program it was seeking to develop to review job applicants' resumes in 2014 illustrates the issue. Amazon worked to develop a program, as part of its process for identifying top talent, which would give scores to applicants, ranging from one to five stars, based on their resumes or applications. By 2015, however, Amazon realised that the system was not rating candidates for technical positions in gender-neutral way. The system was being trained on resumes that had been submitted to Amazon over a ten year period, most of which, in reflection of male dominance in the tech industry, were male. In effect, the AI system taught itself to prefer male candidates, it appears by giving a lower score to applications or resumes that included the word "women" or indicated the candidate had attended a women's college.

The Amazon experience illustrates the challenges to fairness that training data presents. It is not easy to look at training data sets, before the fact, to determine whether the data is biased in some manner. And, after the fact, the discrimination in AI systems that results from skewed training data may be difficult to detect, because it will only be apparent when the system's performance is evaluated at a global level and not be visible in looking at individual results, notwithstanding that that is where the effects will be felt.

There may also be discriminatory outcomes as AI replaces human jobs. Imagine a call centre company adopting AI platforms—Google is already developing an AI assistant named Duplex that can make calls and bookings for a human without the other caller knowing that he or she is not speaking with a human.[32] This may have a particularly localised effect on the community where the call centre is located, since it will lead to a reduction of low skill jobs available. Conversely, it may lead to the creation of new jobs demanding a higher level of skills.

This, in turn, will have an equity effect. Low skill and entry level positions are more likely to be held by historically disadvantaged groups. The transformation caused by the disruptive effect of AI in employment, particularly in terms of skill gaps faced by workers affected by automation and nature of new jobs being created by the AI industry, will need to be monitored.

F. Insurance

Over the past few years, insurers have been increasingly using AI tools. The insurance industry has high expectations regarding the potential for the positive transformative potential of AI on their business.

Insurance companies need to adopt efficient risk-assessment mechanisms in order to mitigate the effect of information asymmetries, and AI promises to be the perfect tool to achieve this. It can help assess risk and price insurance premiums. In particular, the collection of granular data from a number of digital sources, including social media, has allowed insurers to craft personalised insurance premiums based on an individual's profile. On the surface, the use of AI to assess risks and price insurance accordingly seems ideal.

However, the pitfalls discussed above so far in connection with AI also lead to risks in its use in the insurance industry. As a result of AI use, a broader spread of premiums between high-risk and low-risk individuals will increasingly be the norm. Premiums for those deemed to be low-risk will decrease significantly, while premiums for those classified as high risk will spike. Again, historically disadvantaged groups will tend to be on the losing side of the equation, with no allowance for, or special consideration of, individuals within that group.

G. Advertising

AI use in online advertising can also pose questions in connection with discrimination. AI systems are frequently used for online advertising. However, the effects of AI use in advertising have raised concerns.

For instance, a 2013 study showed that a search in Google for African-American sounding names yielded advertisements which suggested that somebody has an arrest record. In contrast, searches for white-sounding names yielded significantly less results suggesting an arrest record. These results would seem to indicate that the AI system had inherited a racial bias.[33] Similarly, an experiment conducted with simulated male and female internet users showed that men were shown more ads related to high-paying jobs than women.[34]

In addition, there has also been some discussion related to companies that allow advertisers to choose specific characteristics to target ads. Recently, Facebook announced that it would stop allowing advertisers in housing, jobs or credit to show their messages only to people of a certain race, gender or age group, in an attempt to prevent discriminatory practices.[35]

III. Industry Practice and Standards

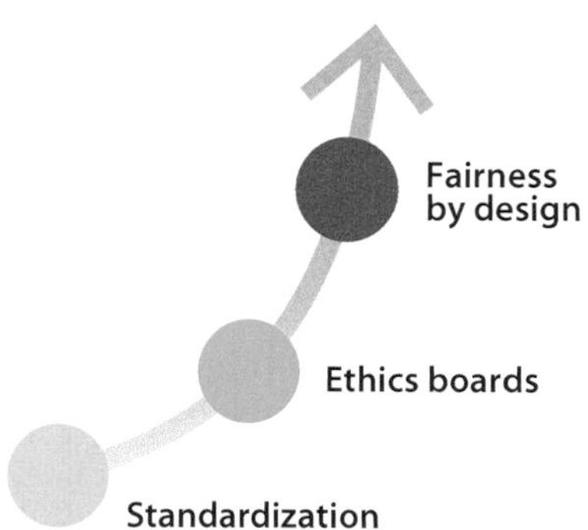

Amidst growing awareness of the risks which the use of AI can pose to fairness, ensuring non-discrimination has begun to be recognised as one of the major challenges brought by technology. Acceptance of this problem and its magnitude is fairly recent, but the matter has generated significant concern. Key areas of industry focus are improving models, and attempting to identify and eradicate bias.

Several companies have started developing tools to address discrimination. For instance, in May 2018 Facebook announced it had developed anti-bias software named "Fairness Flow."[36] In July 2018, Microsoft Research published a paper describing a fairness algorithm for binary classification systems, along with an open source Python library implementing the algorithm.[37] Further, in September 2018, Google announced its "What-If tool," which includes fairness assessments.[38] A week later, IBM released a set of visual developed tools that work with any machine learning model.[39]

One idea for dealing with fairness in AI is to work towards industry-wide standards or benchmarks for algorithms. Initiatives in this direction include the white paper on Artificial Intelligence Standardization published in January 2018 by a large group of Chinese organisations.[40] However, at this point no industry-wide standards in connection with fairness have been adopted.

Additionally, ethics boards are a way in which public and private sector organisations deal with a wide variety of controversial or sensitive issues, including research institutions to assess the ethical acceptability of research and to approve, reject, propose modifications to, or terminate any proposed or ongoing research involving humans. These could be applied to AI systems. For instance, Google's AI ethics board, set up when Google originally acquired the UK company DeepMind in 2014, is a well-known example of the use of ethics boards in an algorithmic context. The board was established in an attempt to ensure that the self-thinking software DeepMind and Google are developing remains safe and of benefit to humanity.

In a similar manner, businesses should consider establishing "AI Ethics Boards" to address the challenges to privacy that AI represents. Such AI Ethics Boards could be assigned responsibilities to:

(i) evaluate proposals for the development of AI systems against ethical criteria established by the business;

(ii) evaluate the systems, once built, to validate that the developed systems align with the criteria based on which development of the system was approved; and

(iii) monitor the ongoing use of the system, especially in respect of self-learning systems, to validate that the system continues to be aligned with its ethical objectives.

Researchers have also proposed that the principle of "fairness by design" should be embedded in all AI research. This would require that the very conception and design of AI systems is done in a manner that prioritises fairness rather than regarding it as an ex-post compliance requirement.[41] This type of framework would emphasise measures such as building cross-disciplinary teams of data scientists and social scientists while deploying AI solutions; identifying and addressing the biases that may be introduced into the data by human annotators; building fairness measures into the assessment metrics of the program and adopting appropriate de-biasing techniques.[42] Another factor which should be considered is the importance of building diverse and inclusive teams in order to reflect different perspectives, needs and objectives.

IV. Policy Considerations

The issue of fairness in AI is not simple to tackle. It is a problem which is not only novel and evolving, but also extremely technical. Several matters are being discussed in connection with AI, and different policy aspects—including the relationship between AI and anti-discrimination laws, transparency, and regulatory oversight—are among those being examined.

A. Relationship between AI and anti-discrimination laws

The principles of equality and non-discrimination are part of the foundations of the rule of law. Individuals are protected from discrimination by international treaties, as well as by national laws and regulations.

Anti-discrimination laws may deal with specific areas, such as employment, or be related to general civil law. Discrimination based on race, ethnic origin, gender, religion, political views, disability, age or sexual identity is usually prohibited. To date, no anti-discrimination law explicitly refers to AI. Nevertheless, insofar as regulations do not refer to the means of reaching a discriminatory decision, in principle anti-discrimination regulations also apply to AI-based decisions. In practice, however, whether a victim of AI-based discrimination is able to successfully employ legal remedies against the discriminating decision will vary greatly from legal system to legal system. In particular, it will largely depend on procedural issues, such as who bears the burden of proof.

USA

In the USA, discrimination is tackled by the U.S. Civil Rights Act of 1964. This regulation provides for a three-step procedure to prove employment discrimination. The plaintiff has the initial responsibility to establish a prima facie case of discrimination. Then the burden of proof shifts to the employer, who must offer a legitimate basis for the decision. If the employer does so, the plaintiff must demonstrate that the proffered reason is pretextual or that the employer could have used an alternative employment practice with less discriminatory results.[43]

Germany

In contrast, the German General Law of Equal Treatment ("AGG")[44] establishes a two-step-procedure. The plaintiff must demonstrate and prove indications which give rise to the presumption that discrimination has taken place. If this has been done, the defendant needs to demonstrate that discrimination has not taken place. Failure to provide such proof leads to a decision in favour of the plaintiff.[45]

The U.S. Civil Rights Act places a heavier burden on the plaintiff, since proving an initial discrimination and rebuffing the defendant's explanations will usually require knowledge of how the AI system works. On the contrary, it appears that under the German AGG, it would be the obligation of the employer to prove that the AI does not produce discriminatory results.

Assuming that neither party will be able to explain how the AI system reaches a particular decision, both results seem unsatisfactory. If using AI for making potentially discriminating decisions practically grants a free pass to discriminate, this can obviously not be right. The same applies if any suspicion of discrimination automatically leads to a conviction for discrimination. A way to avoid these outcomes would be to provide for more transparency in connection with AI use. This could allow for a more informed and equitable judicial decision.

This issue becomes all the more complex in case of legal systems that do not have a comprehensive framework governing discriminatory practices of private actors. The challenge then becomes about first establishing the need for building such protections in the law and then analysing the parallels and differences between discrimination by humans and AI systems.

B. Transparency

AI systems are frequently described as black boxes, reflecting the fact that the specific logic by which systems based on machine learning, neural networks and self-learning reach their results may not be transparent, or may not be understood, predictable or explainable. This is because identification of the way the algorithmic methods function and make decisions is crucial in empowering individuals and organisations with the ability to identify weaknesses and biases.[46] Achieving transparency in coded and AI decision-making is one clear method of improving society's trust in AI systems.

The fairness principles do not stand in isolation, but are intrinsically linked to transparency. Improving the transparency of algorithms and training data is among the most important tasks when making use of AI systems, and is essential for preventing discrimination. Transparency and explainability are necessary to ensure fairness and accountability.

Discrimination and bias are not excusable simply because it is an AI system, and not a person, that is responsible for the results. But assessing biased or unfair results, and, if necessary, challenging them legally, requires access to the AI system and the means to understand its processes. Persons, private companies and public institutions using AI should be held accountable, and this involves reproducibility of the results and transparency as to what systems are used and how they are used, as well as explanations on how they operate and produce their results.

However, as discussed in greater length in our treatment of Principle 3—Transparency and Explainability, this latter principle will sometimes conflict with other values and interests. In this context, the challenge ahead is to find a balance that protects against discrimination while also accounting for other factors such as costs, proprietary information, intellectual property protection and efficiency.

C. Unbiased algorithms, unbiased data and diversity of data

As shown above, discrimination in AI systems can be the result of biased algorithms, biased training data and a lack of diversity in training data.

In order to combat these sources of bias, it will be necessary to develop and employ different mechanisms.

Increasing and ensuring diversity of data could be a way to address one of the main sources of discrimination in AI, which is the underrepresentation of a particular group. In this sense, introducing minimum diversity requirements in order to achieve the same level of representation of different groups is often identified as a requirement of fairness in AI.

Minimum requirements for diversity of data would seek to guarantee that the quality of the results will be similar for different groups of the population—an issue particularly important in the health sector. The model AI governance framework proposed by the Singapore Personal Data Protection Commission,[47] for instance, recognises that identifying and addressing bias in datasets is not simple, and highlights the importance of heterogeneous data. In view of obtaining this objective, public and private entities should cooperate in creating more comprehensive databases, also taking into account the necessities of data protection.

However, as some specialists point out, increasing diversity is not an automatic fix for discrimination issues. A system based on diverse data will not necessarily produce non-discriminatory results. Using different datasets for training, testing and validation of an AI system can help identify bias. In addition, datasets should be periodically reviewed and updated. However, it is also necessary to implement and develop further methods and tools to detect bias in algorithms and training data.

Further research will be necessary for the development of such mechanisms and requirements, and the result of such research could be standards or rules for the development of bias-free AI. As the term discrimination also contains a subjective element, such rules should also take into account the results of a public debate in which topics such as affirmative action and other forms of compensation for past and present discrimination are covered.

One option would be designing a process which each new AI system has to go through. This process could include a test for bias and an official and internationally recognised quality seal being granted to the AI systems passing the test.

D. Addressing the appearance of fairness and educating in AI

The appearance of objectivity by AI systems is also important. Blind trust in AI based on an assumption of its objectivity is something which must be addressed. Bias by AI is often invisible, and thus harder to correct. Informing and educating not only developers but also users as to the limits of AI is therefore important.

Accordingly, the European Union's "Ethics Guidelines for Trustworthy AI"[48] recognise the importance of education and awareness to foster an ethical mind-set. In this sense, the guidelines stress that providing education regarding AI systems and their impact is crucial, and identify generating this awareness as a non-technical method to work towards fairer AI systems.

E. Independent reviewing and testing

The results of the AI systems are often unmonitored or not rigorously or independently assessed to detect biases or even the more mundane issue of questionable or inaccurate results.

For example, the 2013 ProPublica investigation mentioned earlier examined 19 different criminal risk assessment methodologies in use in the United States with a view to assessing the extent to which the methodologies had been evaluated or assessed. They found that "in most cases, validity had been examined in only one or two studies" and that "frequently those investigations were completed by the same people who developed the instrument."[49]

The ability to review and test AI systems is linked to the principle of transparency. The ability to validate the results produced by AI decision making systems is complicated because many of the systems use proprietary algorithms which the developers, in order to protect their proprietary rights, are unwilling to disclose even for testing purposes.

F. Oversight and regulation

Organisations and policymakers have started to take notice of the possible need for oversight and/or regulation in connection with AI and non-discrimination.

International developments in oversight and regulation

In 2016, a report from the Executive Office of the President of the United States[50] warned that the impact of artificial-intelligence-driven algorithms on workers has the potential to worsen inequality, and noted that bias buried in computer code could disadvantage individuals in a host of fields.

The European Union stressed the importance of non-discrimination in 2017 in a resolution on the fundamental rights implications of big data.[51] It also created a High-Level Expert Group on Artificial Intelligence, comprising representatives from academia, civil society, as well as the industry. Its objective is to support the implementation of the European strategy on Artificial Intelligence, which includes the elaboration of recommendations on future-related policy development and on ethical, legal and societal issues related to AI, including socio-economic challenges.

The High-Level Expert Group on Artificial Intelligence has published a draft "Ethics Guidelines for Trustworthy AI."[52] This report aims to serve as a guide to the development of "Trustworthy AI," a concept which has two components: (1) its development, deployment and use complies with fundamental rights and applicable regulation as well as respects core principles and values, ensuring an ethical purpose; and (2) it is technically robust and reliable.

The document holds that ensuring an "ethical purpose" in AI requires a human-centric approach, founded in the principles of beneficence, non-maleficence, autonomy of humans, justice and explicability. Based on the necessity of safeguarding these principles, the High-Level Expert Group on Artificial Intelligence identifies a series of requirements for Trustworthy AI, which should be implemented from the earliest design phase. The concept of "Non-discrimination" is essential for ensuring the principle of justice, and therefore achieving Trustworthy AI.

The Toronto Declaration tackles AI from the framework provided by human rights law. It focuses on the human rights to equality and non-discrimination, and the international framework that is in place to protect them. From the positive obligations which states have to protect human rights, the Toronto Declaration derives principles related to machine learning.

It holds that states have a positive obligation to protect against discrimination by private sector actors and to promote equality, including through oversight and binding laws. Further, it states that these obligations also apply to public use of AI. The Declaration provides that in public sector systems, states must identify risks, ensure transparency and accountability, enforce oversight and promote equality.

In the context of this debate, several ideas and proposals have been made on how to ensure fair AI. From a regulation point of view, these sometimes include applying or amending existing liability rules and non-discrimination regulations. Remedies in the form of viable actions to obtain information, sue for damages or obtain a cease in a harmful conduct, may be considered.

The involvement of governments and civil society organisations in drafting industry standards which must be met prior to the release of an AI system has also been suggested. These standards could call for systems to be trained on equal amounts of data for users of different racial backgrounds and genders, for instance, and implement methods to detect bias in algorithms and training data. Oversight and control by a government entity could also be debated. The design of such interventions will, however, have to be weighed against the limitations of state capacity in regulating the technology sector and its impact on future innovation.

V. Conclusion

AI promises many advantages and benefits. At first glance, a world where decisions are based on data and data alone sounds like an efficient and fair world. This has prompted government and industry organisations to jump at the chance of employing AI in various fields.

However, there is an inherent risk of bias in AI, and overreliance on AI systems can lead to unjust and troubling outcomes. AI systems reflect our own experience, and fairness is by no means guaranteed. In fact, ensuring fairness and non-discrimination requires factoring in many complex variables.

If we examine these issues identified in this chapter at the most basic level, they illustrate a common theme: the lack of human and societal control over and monitoring of the development, testing, implementation and use of AI systems. This situation gives rise to the following risks, which must be addressed through a measured and thoughtful response:

(i) personal information can be used in ways not anticipated by individuals and that are beyond individuals' easonable expectations;

(ii) the results produced by the AI systems can be biased or discriminatory, giving rise to unjustified adverse effects on individuals; and

(iii) the impact and effect of these risks is poised to grow.

Recent years have seen a growing concern associated with AI-based decisions. There is now more awareness that bias in AI needs to be addressed, and different actors have begun proposing approaches to this problem.[52] To the extent that the problems of bias and discrimination in AI stem from broader socio-economic conditions of the real world, the appropriate solutions must emerge through a cross-disciplinary engagement between Governments, AI scientists, social scientists and the public at large.

Principle 4
Fairness and Non-Discrimination

Organisations that develop, deploy or use AI systems and any national laws that regulate such use shall ensure the non-discrimination of AI outcomes, and shall promote appropriate and effective measures to safeguard fairness in AI use.

1 Awareness and education

1.1 Awareness and education on the possibilities and limits of AI systems is a prerequisite to achieving fairer outcomes.

1.2 Organisations that develop, deploy or use AI systems should take steps to ensure that users are aware that AI systems reflect the goals, knowledge and experience of their creators, as well as the limitations of the data sets that are used to train them.

2 Technology and fairness

2.1 Decisions based on AI systems should be fair and non-discriminatory, judged against the same standards as decision-making processes conducted entirely by humans.

2.2 The use of AI systems by organisations that develop, deploy or use AI systems and Governments should not serve to exempt or attenuate the need for fairness, although it may mean refocussing applicable concepts, standards and rules to accommodate AI.

2.3 Users of AI systems and persons subject to their decisions must have an effective way to seek remedy in discriminatory or unfair situations generated by biased or erroneous AI systems, whether used by organisations that develop, deploy or use AI systems or governments, and to obtain redress for any harm.

3 Development and monitoring of AI systems

3.1 AI development should be designed to prioritise fairness. This would involve addressing algorithms and data bias from an early stage with a view to ensuring fairness and non-discrimination.

3.2. Organisations that develop, deploy or use AI systems should remain vigilant to the dangers posed by bias. This could be achieved by establishing ethics boards and codes of conduct, and by adopting industry-wide standards and internationally recognised quality seals.

3.4 AI systems with an important social impact could require independent reviewing and testing on a periodic basis.

3.3. In the development and monitoring of AI systems, particular attention should be paid to disadvantaged groups which may be incorrectly represented in the training data.

4 A comprehensive approach to fairness

4.1 AI systems can perpetuate and exacerbate bias, and have a broad social and economic impact in society. Addressing fairness in AI use requires a holistic approach. In particular, it requires:

i. the close engagement of technical experts from AI-related fields with statisticians and researchers from the social sciences; and

ii. a combined engagement between governments, organisations that develop, deploy or use AI systems and the public at large.

4.2 The Fairness and Non-Discrimination Principle is supported by the Transparency and Accountability Principles. Effective fairness in use of AI systems requires the implementation of measures in connection with both these Principles.

Endnotes

1 Julia Angwin et al., "Machine Bias: There's software used across the country to predict future criminals. And it's biased against blacks" (May 23, 2016), online: *Pro Publica* <https://www.propublica.org/article/machine-bias-risk-assessments-in-criminal-sentencing>[Julia Angwin et al.].

2 Smriti Parsheera, "A gendered perspective on artificial intelligence" in *Proceedings of ITU Kaleidoscope 2018—Machine Learning for a 5G Future* (Geneva: 2018) at p 125 [Parsheera].

3 Yoan Mantha, "Estimating the Gender Ratio of AI Researchers Around the World" (Aug 17, 2018), online: *A Medium Corporation* <https://medium.com/element-ai-research-lab/estimating-the-gender-ratio-of-ai-researchers-around-the-world-81d2b8dbe9c3>. These findings are based on a sample of 4000 researchers who published in leading AI conferences in 2017.

4 Yoav Shoham et al., "The AI Index 2018 Annual Report," AI Index Steering Committee, Human-Centered AI Initiative, Stanford University, Stanford, CA, December 2018, online: *AI Index* <http://cdn.aiindex.org/2018/AI%20Index%20 2018%20Annual%20Report.pdf>.

5 Phillip Hacker, "Teaching fairness to artificial intelligence: Existing and novel strategies against algorithmic discrimination under EU law"(2018) issue: 55 Common Market Law Review at p 1142;

Solon Barocas & Andrew D. Selbst, "Big Data's Disparate Impact" volume 104 California Law Review at p 674.

6 Norwegian Data Protection Authority, "Artificial intelligence and privacy report," (January 2018), online: *Datatilsynet* <https://www.datatilsynet.no/globalassets/global/english/ai-and-privacy.pdf>.

7 Alistar Barr, "Google Mistakenly Tags Black People as 'Gorillas,' Showing Limits of Algorithms" (1 July 2015), online: *Wall Street Journal* <https://blogs.wsj.com/digits/2015/07/01/google-mistakenly-tags-black-people-as-gorillas-showing-limits-of-algorithms/>;

Joy Buolamwini & Timnit Gebru, "Gender Shades: Intersectional Accuracy Disparities in Commercial Gender Classification" (2018), online: *Proceedings of Machine Learning Research Press* <http://proceedings.mlr.press/v81/buolamwini18a/buolamwini18a.pdf>.

8 Tolga Bolukbasi et al., "Man is to Computer Programmer as Woman is to Homemaker? Debiasing Word Embeddings" (2016) online: *arXiv* <https://arxiv.org/pdf/1607.06520.pdf>.

9 Aylin Caliskan, Joanna J. Bryson & Arvind Narayanan, "Semantics derived automatically from language corpora contain human-like biases" (14 April 2017), online: *Science* <http://science.sciencemag.org/content/356/6334/183.full>.

10 Jack Morse, "Google Translate might have a gender problem" (1 December 2017), online: *Mashable* <https://mashable.com/2017/11/30/google-translate-sexism/>.

11 Smriti Parsheera, "A gendered perspective on artificial intelligence" in *Proceedings of ITU Kaleidoscope 2018—Machine Learning for a 5G Future* (2018), online: < https://www.itu.int/en/ITU-T/academia/kaleidoscope/2018/Documents/Presentations/S6.1_A%20Gendered%20Perspective%20on%20AI_Parsheera.pdf>.

12 "The Toronto Declaration: Protecting the right to equality and non-discrimination in machine learning systems," online: <https://www.accessnow.org/cms/assets/uploads/2018/08/The-Toronto-Declaration_ENG_08-2018.pdf>.

13 "Draft Ethics guidelines for trustworthy AI" (18 December 2018), online: *European Commission* <https://ec.europa.eu/digital-single-market/en/news/draft-ethics-guidelines-trustworthy-ai> [EU Draft Ethics Guidelines].

14 Singapore Personal Data Protection Commission, "A Proposed Model Artificial Intelligence Governance Framework" (January 2019), online: *Singapore Personal Data Protection Commission* <https://www.pdpc.gov.sg/-/media/Files/PDPC/PDF-Files/Resource-for-Organisation/AI/A-Proposed-Model-AI-Governance-Framework-January-2019.pdf> [Singapore].

[15] Julia Angwin et al, *supra* note 1.

[16] Ian Watkins, "The Utility of Service Inventory—Revised (LSI-R) Assessments within NSW Correctional Environments," (29 January 2011), Research Bulletin Corrective Services NSW, No. 28.

[17] Cath O'Neil, *Weapons of Math Destruction: How Big Data increases inequality and threatens democracy* (New York: Crown Publishing Group, 2016) at p 25-6.

[18] Devesh Kapur, "By mostly jailing Dalits, Muslims & tribals, India is making the same mistakes as the U.S." (5 January, 2018), online: *The Print* <https://theprint.in/opinion/a-tale-of-indian-and-american-prisoners/26637/>.

[19] Urvashi Aneja, "Artificial Intelligence apps risk entrenching India's socio-economic inequities" (12 March 2018), online: *The Indian Express* <https://indianexpress.com/article/opinion/artificial-intelligence-apps-risk-entrenching-indias-socio-economic-inequities-5094831/>.

[20] Rashida Richardson, Jason Schultz & Kate Crawford, "Dirty Data, Bad Predictions: How Civil Rights Violations Impact Police Data, Predictive Policing Systems, and Justice" (13 February 2019), online: *New York University Law Review Online, Forthcoming* <https://ssrn.com/abstract=3333423>.

[21] Mariella Moon, "Eve the robot scientist discovers new drug candidate for malaria" (5 February 2015), online: *Engadget* <https://www.engadget.com/2015/02/05/eve-robot-scientist-malaria/>.

[22] Dave Gershgorn, "If AI is going to be the world's doctor, it needs better textbooks" (6 September 2018), online: *Quartz* <https://qz.com/1367177/if-ai-is-going-to-be-the-worlds-doctor-it-needs-better-textbooks/>.

[23] *Ibid.*

[24] Casey Ross & Ike Swetlitz, "IBM pitched its Watson supercomputer as a revolution in cancer care. It's nowhere close" (5 September 2017), online: *Stat News* <https://www.statnews.com/2017/09/05/watson-ibm-cancer/>.

[25] Syndicat national de l'industrie des technologies médicales (Snitem) and Philips France v Premier ministre and Ministre des Affaires sociales et de la Santé, C-329/16, online: *InfoCuria—Case-law of the Court of Justice* <http://curia.europa.eu/juris/liste.jsf?language=en&num=C-329/16>. The ruling implies that, in order to determine if a stand-alone software falls within the definition of "medical device," it should be ascertained if the software has a "medical purpose," i.e., supporting the "prevention, monitoring, treatment or alleviation of disease."

[26] PRNewswire, "Global Facial Recognition Market Report 2018," (5 June 2018), online: *PRNewswire* <https://www.prnewswire.com/news-releases/global-facial-recognition-market-report-2018-300660163.html>.

[27] Cyrus Farivar, "Facial recognition found Capital Gazette suspect among 10M photos," online: *arsTechnica* <https://arstechnica.com/tech-policy/2018/06/maryland-cops-facial-recognition-to-id-capital-gazette-shooter-worked-well/>.

[28] Australian Broadcasting Commission, (17 September 2018), online: *Australian Broadcasting Commission* <https://www.abc.net.au/news/2018-09-18/china-social-credit-a-model-citizen-in-a-digital-dictatorship/10200278>.

[29] People's Republic of China State Council (2014), "Notice Concerning Issuance of the Planning Outline for the Construction of a Social Credit System (2014-2020)."

[30] Jacob Snow, "Amazon's Face Recognition Falsely Matched 28 Members of Congress with Mugshots," online: *ACLU* <https://www.aclu.org/blog/privacy-technology/surveillance-technologies/amazons-face-recognition-falsely-matched-28>.

[31] Jena McGregor, "Why robots aren't likely to make the call on hiring you anytime soon" (11 October 2018), online: *Washington Post* <https://www.washingtonpost.com/business/2018/10/11/why-robots-arent-likely-make-call-hiring-you-anytime-soon/?utm_term=.21d5914cf208>.

[32] Olivia Solon, "Google's robot assistant now makes eerily lifelike phone calls for you," (8 May 2018), online: *The Guardian* <https://www.theguardian.com/technology/2018/may/08/google-duplex-assistant-phone-calls-robot-human>.

[33] Latanya Sweeney, "Discrimination in online ad delivery" (March 2013) Volume 11: Issue 3 ACM Queue.

[34] Amit Datta, Michael Carl Tschantz and Anupam Datta, "Automated Experiments on Ad Privacy Settings" (February 2015) Proceedings on Privacy Enhancing Technologies at p 92-112.

[35] Noam Scheiber & Mike Isaac, "Facebook Halts Ad Targeting Cited in Bias Complaints" (19 March 19 2019), online: *The New York Times* <https://www.nytimes.com/2019/03/19/technology/facebook-discrimination-ads.html>.

[36] Jerome Presenti, "AI at F8 2018: Open frameworks and responsible development" (2 May 2018), online: *Facebook Code* <https://code.fb.com/ml-applications/ai-at-f8-2018-open-frameworks-and-responsible-development>.

[37] Miro Dudík et al., "Machine Learning for Fair Decisions" (17 July 2018), online: *Microsoft Research,* <https://www.microsoft.com/en-us/research/blog/machine-learning-for-fair-decisions/>.

[38] James Wexler, "The What-If Tool: Code-Free Probing of Machine Learning Models" (11 September 2018), online: *Google AI Blog* <https://ai.googleblog.com/2018/09/the-what-if-tool-code-free-probing-of.html>.

[39] Paul Teich, "Artificial Intelligence Can Reinforce Bias, Cloud Giants Announce Tools for AI Fairness" (24 September 2018), online: *Forbes* <https://www.forbes.com/sites/paulteich/2018/09/24/artificial-intelligence-can-reinforce-bias-cloud-giants-announce-tools-for-ai-fairness/#455fdcf59d21>.

[40] Jeffrey Ding & Paul Triolo, "Translation: Excerpts from China's 'White Paper on Artificial Intelligence Standardization'" (24 January 2018), online: *New America* <https://www.newamerica.org/cybersecurity-initiative/digichina/blog/translation-excerpts-chinas-white-paper-artificial-intelligence-standardization/>.

[41] Parsheera, *supra* note 2.

[42] Ahmed Abbasi et al., "Make 'Fairness by Design' Part of Machine Learning" (1 August 2018), online: *Harvard Business Review* <https://hbr.org/2018/08/make-fairness-by-design-part-of-machine-learning>.

[43] Solon Barocas & Andrew D. Selbst, "Big Data's Disparate Impact" Vol. 104 California Law Review First at p 696.

[44] Palandt, Bürgerliches Gesetzbuch (2019: 78th Edition), AGG 22 Side-No. 1; Phillip Hacker, "Teaching fairness to artificial intelligence: Existing and novel strategies against algorithmic discrimination under EU law" (2018), Issue 55 Common Market Law Review at p 9.

[45] Palandt, Bürgerliches Gesetzbuch, (2019: 78th Edition), AGG 22 Side-No. 3.

[46] Chris Culnane, Benjamin Rubinstein and Vanessa Teague, "Understanding the maths is crucial for protecting privacy" (29 September 2016), online: *Pursuit: University of Melbourne* <https://pursuit.unimelb.edu.au/articles/understanding-the-maths-is-crucial-for-protecting-privacy>;

Mor Vered and Tim Miller, "What were you thinking?" (23 August 2018), online: *Pursuit: University of Melbourne,* <https://pursuit.unimelb.edu.au/articles/what-were-you-thinking>.

[47] Singapore, *supra* note 14.

[48] EU Draft Ethics Guidelines, *supra* note 13.

[49] Julia Angwin et al, *supra* note 1.

[50] Executive Office of the President, "Preparing for the Future of Artificial Intelligence" (2016), online: <https://eric.ed.gov/?id=ED587229>.

[51] European Parliament resolution (14 March 2017), online: *European Parliament* <http://www.europarl.europa.eu/sides/getDoc.do?pubRef=-//EP//TEXT+TA+P8-TA-2017-0076+0+DOC+XML+V0//EN>.

[52] EU Draft Ethics Guidelines, *supra* note 14.

[53] An example being the Australian Government's AUD $19 million investment in AI initiatives, including an AI Technology Roadmap and AI Ethical Framework, online: *CSIRO* <https://www.csiro.au/en/News/News-releases/2018/CSIRO-invests-35M-in-future-of-space-and-AI-for-Australia>. This demonstrates from an Australian perspective the view that ethical considerations may be fundamental for the adoption of AI technology.

Principle 5

SAFETY AND RELIABILITY

Organisations that develop, deploy or use AI systems and any national laws that regulate such use shall adopt design regimes and standards ensuring high safety and reliability of AI systems on one hand while limiting the exposure of developers and deployers on the other hand.

5
SAFETY AND RELIABILITY

CHAPTER LEAD
Christian Frank | Taylor Wessing LLP, Germany

Nicole Beranek Zanon | de la cruz beranek Attorneys-at-Law Ltd., Switzerland
Louis Jonker | Van Doorne NV, Netherlands
Stuart P. Meyer | Fenwick & West LLP, United States
Kees Stuurman | Tilburg University, Netherlands

I. Introduction

A. General

The development and implementation of AI-based technologies will come with inherent risks of every new technology. Vulnerabilities will be underestimated, mistakes will be made, systems will fail and damages will be caused.

Rules on safety and reliability affect the development and use of every technology. While the introduction of some new AI-based technologies can be accomplished under existing rules, in other instances rules might need to be adapted or completely re-drafted. Various ethical and moral issues underlie the legal framework for AI-based technologies. The underlying ethics and morality may vary across different cultures[1] and should be considered before new legal rules can be defined properly.

B. Ethical and moral principles at stake

To be able to discuss and decide on ethical and moral questions and dilemmas concerning new AI-based technologies, first a common ground on the ethical and moral principles at stake is required. These ethical and moral principles differ per use case. They depend on a significant number of factors including cultural differences, the purpose and limitations (the 'state of the art') of the relevant technology, the level of self-learning capability, whether it concerns an assisting AI system or an autonomous AI system,[2] the level of transparency and predictability of the algorithms at hand, as well as societal and environmental dependencies etc. It is hence not possible to define a general set of ethical and moral principles one can apply by default at all times. Therefore, AI often reflects the values of its creators.[3] Without proper care in the programming of AI systems, there is a risk that the programmer could (intentionally or unintentionally) play a part in determining outcomes.[4] In that case, cultural differences can play a significant role.

Nevertheless, due to the lack of a single universal set of ethical and moral principles, in each development and/or implementation of AI-based technologies it is ultimately up to each organization to define a relevant set of ethical and moral principles, thereby taking into account all relevant circumstances. These starting points should also be validated periodically to ensure on-going accuracy.

The ethical and moral standards highly depend on the area in which AI is applied. In this chapter, we limit our scope to standards on civil (e.g., business-to-business, business-to-consumer and government-to-consumer) applications of AI. We do not address military or geopolitical applications because those require different assessment frameworks.[5]

C. Common understanding of principles of safety and reliability

Principles of safety and reliability for AI-based technologies will always reflect the aforementioned set of ethical and moral principles. As said, these principles depend on a particular worldview. It can—for example—be questioned whether AI-based technologies must demonstrably surpass safety levels of current solutions before being implemented, or whether it is acceptable for it to be less safe, provided that it has many—or at least enough—efficiency benefits.

In absence of commonly accepted principles, a precautionary principle of "better safe than sorry" could be useful for AI.[7] This principle implies that there is a social responsibility to reasonably protect the public from exposure to harm. The principle is a question of acting in uncertain situations: a lack of full scientific certainty of harm cannot be used as an argument for postponing mitigating action.[8] The protections can only be relaxed if scientific findings emerge indicating that no harm will result.[9] The precautionary principle has in particular been applied to healthcare and environmental law. In both cases, systems are complex and results are difficult to predict.[10]

Apart from the underlying principles, safety and reliability standards must ideally be determined by input from all stakeholders—not just businesses that may be implementing the solutions, but also by input from:

- Employees/workers;
- Consumers/patients;
- NGO's and other societal stakeholders;
- Academics and others able to advise on likely advances after the current generation of solutions.

Before we go into more detail about the creation of standards, it is important to have a good understanding of the concepts of Safety and Reliability.

1. Safety

Safety

The Oxford Dictionary defines "safety" as "the condition of being protected from or unlikely to cause danger, risk, or injury."[11] The concept of safety is very broad. Next to physical safety (in terms of death or personal injury), it could refer to financial safety (e.g., incorrect robotics advice on financial investments) and emotional safety (e.g., manipulating AI).

Various AI expert teams have defined safety in the context of AI. The EU High-Level Expert Group on Artificial Intelligence for example, has developed guidelines explaining, among other things, the concept of safety. According to these guidelines, safety is *"about ensuring that the system will indeed do what it is supposed to do,[12] without harming users (human physical integrity), resources or the environment.*

It includes minimizing unintended consequences and errors in the operation of the system."[13] The European Group on Ethics in Science and New Technologies divides the concept of safety of 'autonomous' systems into (i) external safety for their environment and users, (ii) reliability and internal robustness[14] and (iii) emotional safety with respect to human-machine interaction.[15] AI developers should take all these dimensions of safety into account and strictly test before any release,[16] with special attention to persons in a vulnerable position and to potential dual use[17] of AI.[18]

> *[Safety is] "about ensuring that the system will indeed do what it is supposed to do, without harming users (human physical integrity), resources or the environment. It includes minimizing unintended consequences and errors in the operation of the system."*
>
> EU High Level Expert Group on Artificial Intelligence

The EU's approach to the internal market is based on common safety rules.[19] EU legislation defines a general concept of safety, which is based on the reasonable expectation of a consumer or the public at large. Product legislation is limited to so-called "essential requirements," e.g., protection of health and safety that goods must meet when they are placed on the market. Elicitation of these principles takes place in the form of harmonised technical standards drafted by the European Standardisation Organisations.[20] Compliance with these standards will provide a presumption of conformity with the essential requirements (e.g., CE marking). CE marking indicates that a product complies with the essential requirements as laid down in the relevant directive(s).

International safety harmonization

- Product Liability Directive,[21]
- General Product Safety Directive[22]
- Machinery Directive.[23]

- "Declaration of Conformity" of the U.S. Federal Communications Commission

- "China Compulsory Certificate" mark

- "Voluntary Council for Control of Interference" in Japan.

New products and services based on emerging technologies such as AI are not necessarily less safe than traditional products. How technologies and tools are being used is of particular importance for safety and liability aspects.[24] It is important for technologies that could affect life and well-being to have safety mechanisms in place that comply with existing norms, including legislation.[25] When designing new technologies, it is important to keep a wide range of health and safety aspects in mind, including, e.g., ergonomics and mental stress.

2. Reliability

Reliability

Reliability is often explained as the overall consistency of a measure,[26] or as "the probability of performing a specified function without failure and within design parameters for the period of time or the number of cycles specified under actual service conditions."[27]

With respect to reliability in the context of AI, the High-Level Expert Group on Artificial Intelligence requires that algorithms be secure, reliable, and robust enough to deal with errors during the phases of design, development, execution, deployment and use.[28] Algorithms should also cope adequately with erroneous outcomes. In the AI research community, there is currently an increased awareness of the importance of reproducibility, which is essential to guarantee consistent results across different situations, computational frameworks and input data.[29]

3. Relation between safety and reliability

In the previous paragraphs, we have identified that the concepts safety and reliability are inherently related to each other. However, safety and reliability do not correlate perfectly with one another. Safe AI can predict an unreliable outcome and conversely, unsafe AI can predict a reliable outcome.

Applying European applicable safety and reliability laws and regulations to AI often proves difficult given how long ago these laws and regulations were put into force. Nevertheless, many European laws and regulations are technology neutral, which means it should be possible to apply these to AI use cases.[30] Moreover, European Standardization Organizations are developing harmonised standards for AI-powered advanced robots and autonomous systems.[31] The International Organization for Standardization has recently started with foundational standards that include AI concepts and terminology.[32] However, standardization is still complex, because the broad interest in AI brings together a very wide range of stakeholders.[33]

II. Ethical and Moral Challenges for AI-Based Technologies

A. "Trolley problem"

A much-cited thought experiment about ethical and moral challenges is the so-called "trolley problem," first introduced by Philippa Foot in 1967.[34] In this mental experiment, a trolley threatens to drive over five people. The trolley can be diverted to another track by changing a switch, but on the other track, there is another person who would be hit. The question is whether it would be morally permissible to intervene and hit the switch to divert the trolley to the different track. While thought experiments like these[35] seem to fit the question how AI should behave in trolley-type dilemma situations (e.g., when driving autonomously, see section III.A), it can be questioned whether these hypothetical questions about unfamiliar situations with relatively high stakes can predict actions in real life.[36] In real life with humans making real-time decisions, the answer to such questions are more complex: it could make a huge difference if the single person is a good acquaintance for example. Design of AI systems will inevitably include consideration of such dilemmas in advance, such that they must be taken into account in the programming.

B. Tragic choices

As with all significant engineering undertakings, AI systems necessarily involve trade-offs among constraining factors. One set of such trade-offs balances safety and reliability benefits on the one hand against the costs of achieving those benefits. Those costs are not limited to monetary ones alone but include other issues such as how quickly AI systems are placed into non-experimental ("production") use, how much testing is required before such use commences, and the like. In a related area, societal *norms* regarding safety and reliability need to be considered. For example, if an AI system shall be overall safer than the system it replaces, but nonetheless, it imposes an increased risk in one particular area that was previously quite safe, are we willing to accept that new narrow risk to benefit from the overall safety gain? The seminal 1978 work *Tragic Choices* by Guido Calabresi and Philip Bobbitt (hereinafter *"Calabresi"*) provides us with some mechanisms for addressing these issues.[37]

If an AI system shall be overall safer than the system it replaces, but nonetheless, it imposes an increased risk in one particular area that was previously quite safe, are we willing to accept that new narrow risk to benefit from the overall safety gain?

Calabresi recognises that both moral and economic standards contribute to whether and how society incentivises certain activities.[38] A classic example of such a tragic choice comes up with any major civil engineering project. The decision to build a bridge, for instance, is often made not only because of the economic benefit such bridge will provide, but a concomitant safety benefit as well (for instance, by reducing traffic deaths because the bridge, over a century of use, will reduce traffic deaths by replacing a heavily travelled 100 km route with a 10 km route). On the other hand, statistics from prior projects may well suggest that even with "normal" safety precautions, some number of construction workers will die building the bridge. How does society make this tragic choice?[39]

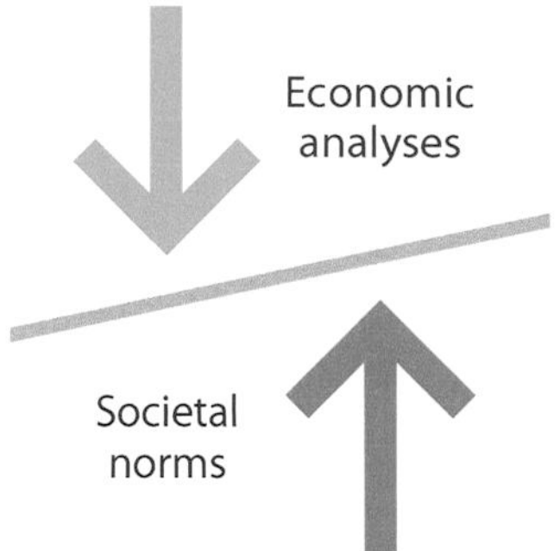

In *Tragic Choices, Calabresi* provides a realistic approach for this, recognizing that as imperfect as current societal norms of morality may be, those will be the norms used as the moral component of the calculus. A related observation is that those societal norms are often in conflict with the standard economic analyses that might be used to analyse similar situations. For example, if a scarce medical resource could save Einstein or a very wealthy person, the moral norm would vote for Einstein while the market analysis would allow the wealthy person to pay his way to health. So while we may like market-efficient approaches in the abstract, we often recoil when we see them applied in socially uncomfortable instances. Even economic analyses that allow for possible intervention in an otherwise free market suffer from both practical and theoretical hurdles.

Without delving further into this complex topic, the important takeaway is that pure economic analysis, particularly a market-based analysis, is insufficient to give us the best answer to a tragic choices problem. At the same time, decisions made merely on society's "gut" sense of morality may be dramatically inefficient; thus, there is reason to remind people about the economic implications of their choices. Finally, there is a serious "cost to costing" things as precious as human life. Simply asserting that a human life is worth X dollars, for whatever reason (good or bad), makes it hard to say that something precious is priceless.

Sometimes we can avoid a calculus that converts a life to dollars altogether, for instance when we decide to build a guard rail on one section of freeway rather than another because the protection for the chosen section will save an expected 15 lives compared to the other section at only 10 lives. In many instances, however, the difficult apples/oranges comparisons are harder to avoid. Therefore, in addressing the safety and reliability considerations of this chapter we will consider both conventional moral standards as well as economic implications of the choices that can be made.

While AI is not the only area in which this issue arises,[40] AI does have some noteworthy characteristics not found in many other tragic choices policy areas. For example, given that machines and humans differ so markedly in the tasks they can perform well, it is highly likely that AI solutions will in early years increase risk exposure in certain areas, while at the same time dramatically decreasing risk in other areas. This calls into question—for example—the notion of "do no harm" from the Hippocratic Oath and whether increased harm in rare circumstances in order to achieve an overall increase in safety is acceptable. It is worth noting that the *Calabresi* approach, which considers market/economic analysis but also recognises societal norms, is already directly reflected in many proposed AI Ethics standards.[41]

C. Fear of the unknown (low offline standards vs. high online standards)

People are often worried about emerging technologies, including AI. An important source of fear is a lack of knowledge. The principle here is: the less you know, the more fear you get.[42] Many people for example, have expressed concerns about machines having a free will, even though there is no scientific evidence to support this.[43]

The less you know, the more fear you get.

People also have less trust in AI compared to trust in humans, while at the same time having higher expectations for AI than for humans. Why do we expect an AI application to be 100% safe and reliable, when we do not expect this from humans? This raises a moral dilemma for the use of AI applications. Is it possible to guarantee a 100% safe and reliable AI application? If not, should there be an "acceptable loss," which may justify an AI error? Per *Calabresi's* arguments in *Tragic Choices,* we must pay close attention to human nature even when it involves such double-standards.

D. Morality of AI in critical situations; allocation of risk and social harm in transitional phase

1. Introduction

The debate about the morality of AI can be strikingly illustrated by the concept of a "death algorithm." The control unit of an autonomous driving vehicle may be designed to decide, in an emergency, whether to hit a group of pedestrians, a mother and child, or a brick wall.[44] In the medical sector, it is conceivable that AI will admit and assign patients to medical treatment according to the probability of survival considering or disregarding the probable total treatment costs. Both illustrations, which will be elaborated in more detail in section III ("Case Studies"), might raise the question whether AI will relieve humans of moral decisions. This approach is however not correct. AI does not teach morality itself. A human being designs the parameters teaching the AI moral foundations. The challenge is to teach AI morality, because people judge morality subjectively and cannot convey morality in measurable metrics that make it easy for a computer to process.[45] Furthermore, moral concepts are different across different cultures.

The starting point for the question of morality is therefore not the decision itself but the creation of the foundations for these decisions. For this reason, a producer of AI cannot be absolved of the moral decisions the system makes. A responsibility of the user is also conceivable if the user can choose between different moral attitudes of the system.[46] Inappropriate user behaviour can be the reason why AI has to make such a decision at all. This applies in particular during the transition phase from legacy systems to AI-based systems: To gain the first mover's advantage, developing markets are frequently built with "half-baked" technologies to be improved "on the fly." This reality does little to build trust in AI, so both manufacturers and users would do well to undertake special care during this transitional time.

A producer of AI cannot be absolved of the moral decisions the system makes.

2. Morality of AI in critical situations

Recently, the European Union's High-Expert Group on AI[47] has adopted guidelines for trustworthy artificial intelligence.[48] Previously, the Federal Ministry of Transport and Digital Infrastructure of Germany convened an ethics commission for automated driving.[49] In addition, more and more universities are dealing with this topic, for example MIT,[50] Harvard,[51] Oxford[52] and recently TU Munich with support from Facebook.[53]

The fundamental question of this research is what kind of decisions should AI be allowed to make and according to which standards. Reducing this very complex subject to simple terms, ethical and moral standards must be implemented in the design of the AI so that it can use them as a basis for all derived decisions. High-Expert Group on AI proposes, e.g., that the fundamental rights commitment of the EU Treaties and Charter of Fundamental Rights should be used to identify abstract ethical principles for AI.[54] Critical situations should therefore be decided based on human moral concepts.

3. How to teach morality to AI

However, implementation is difficult. How do you teach a self-learning system the moral decision-making structures of the human being?

At first, AI researchers, governments and ethicists need to explicitly define ethical values as quantifiable parameters on which systems can operate.[55] As will be discussed below, this is happening right now. Then, crowdsourced data about moral concepts have to be used to train AI systems so they can make decisions in the face of moral dilemmas[56]—the moral parameters must be translated into a kind of database that the machine can understand. Then, manufacturers must be responsible for implementing and updating this step.

4. Allocation of risk and social harm

AI and its applications are still in an experimental phase. This transition phase to market is inherently error-prone. Decisions made by AI including moral aspects are critical, in particular if they—in retrospect—turn out to be false. In an attenuated form, the fatal decisions were made not at the time of the tragedy, but instead during the design and implementation of the system.[57]

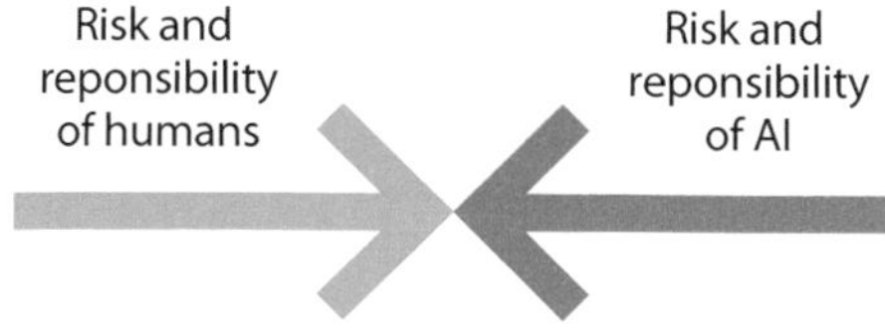

As set out in section III.A below, the traditional regulation of driving relies *inter alia* on humans operating vehicles in a manner consistent with the moral standards of the society they grew up in. Most such standards are implicit, not clearly determined and sometimes even diverse. They are not subject to any driving related training or test. For example, the religious or regional background of a driver may influence the choice to collide with a horse or a cow suddenly appearing on the roadway. Furthermore, there are choices between "two evils" for which societies do not provide moral standards for which is "more wrong." The individuality of every driver obviates a uniform behaviour and therefore leads to a random based, probably roughly equal allocation of impact.[58]

Unlike humans, AI-powered control units have no minimum age, no parents and no education to provide an implicit set of ethics and moral rules. Its specifications must include guidelines on ethics and morality enabling the systems to take and execute decisions being regarded as socially appropriate. Hence, those guidelines must now be explicitly defined. A one-sided allocation of risk is not practicable. One must decide whether there should be areas where no decision should be created and prepared. This will be discussed in more detail in the use cases on autonomous vehicles and AI applications in the medical field (see section III.A). These examples will show that the predominant part of fault lies with the user. Until the user can completely rely on the AI, a situational solution must be found for the question of allocation of risk and social harm.

The central issue is whether the user controls a system assisted by AI, or the AI controls the system itself. The experimental phase of new technologies is characterised by the fact that the effects cannot be assessed. The reliability of the system is just not guaranteed. If these are nevertheless used, the user is subject to special insurance and monitoring obligations. If the user violates these obligations, he is to blame.

The designers of AI systems can (and will) be blamed for fatal decisions. A strict allocation of risk and social harm to the manufacturer can be considered here. After all, the designer is responsible for programming the AI. However, account must be taken of the fact that this is an immature technology. A general allocation would threaten the development process to the production stage, because manufacturers would be burdened with high risks. This may lead to AI's testing being discontinued, with the result that it will not be possible to reach market maturity.

The central issue is whether the user controls a system assisted by AI, or the AI controls the system itself.

An allocation of liability, which, on the one hand, allows the experimental phase and, on the other hand, does not give manufacturers a free ticket can be achieved by the instrument of negligence. Liability for damage caused by systems with AI is governed by the same principles as in other product liability—from this, it follows that manufacturers are obliged to continuously optimise their systems and also to observe systems they have already delivered and to improve them where this is technologically possible and reasonable.[59] These duties also include the adaptation of moral guidelines issued over time. If the manufacturer deliberately or negligently fails to comply with these obligations, risk and social harm shall be assigned to it.

The same applies to the allocation of risk and social harm for decisions of AI in moral dilemmas. As shown under section III.C, the process of creating moral foundations for AI is still emerging. Here the manufacturer meets the obligations to keep its system up to date with the process. The system must therefore always correspond to the current state of research.

5. Final observation with respect to morality in critical situations

The implementation of human moral concepts in AI is challenging, but doable. It is one of the basic requirements for market-ready AI-based applications. In the transition period, risk and social harm must be allocated in such a way that it does not prevent the innovation and further development of AI.

E. Impact of preventive, mitigative and resolving measures; impact of elegant degradation design on safety

An important aspect of both safety and reliability has to do with how a system fails. To use a classic example, an elevator with a broken cable can fail by free-falling hundreds of meters, or it can fail by dropping less than a meter before centrifugal force moves flyweights to actuate wedges for an emergency braking system. Thus, in addition to minimizing the frequency of system failures, minimizing the effects of those failures is a fundamental concern touching both safety and reliability.

In a moment, we will turn to specific considerations for AI systems, but it is helpful to get in the right mind-set first by considering a variety of examples predating AI systems. Mere mention of them should be sufficient to bring to mind the salient issues:

Jet Airliners

Jet airliners have multiple engines such that if one fails, the aircraft will be able to continue operation for a sufficient distance to find an emergency landing location.

Vehicle Trailers

Vehicle trailers are equipped with breakaway detectors that engage the trailer's braking system should the trailer become detached from the towing vehicle.

Server Mirroring

Server "mirroring" is a redundancy method of using multiple computer servers such that if one fails, another has the same information and can automatically pick up the processing that was being performed by the failed machine.[60]

How do centuries of such protections inform us regarding the design of AI systems? A primary teaching is that elegant failure needs to be considered at the very earliest phases of design. Just as one cannot merely "tack on" a second jet engine after a plane's design is complete, one should not consider systems to provide for elegant failure after the primary feature design work is completed. Rather, an initial design constraint of an AI system should be that system failures would have minimal impact on human life, etc.

Speaking at an even higher level, societies should provide incentives for those who design and manufacture such systems to consider failures early on, to address such failures elegantly, and to be transparent about the trade-offs that they have made. There are a number of observations about this that immediately come to mind:

- There is value to something failing in an "expected" manner so that human operators and other people will natural take precautions that make sense. For instance, if a new feature fails, the system will revert to its legacy operation—as it worked without the new feature—rather than in some new manner. Likewise, if one type of failure results in one type of failover operation, a related failure should result in something similar rather than different.

- The expected frequency of failures should be taken into account. If it is inevitable that one type of failure will happen with some regularity (think of a burned-out lightbulb), it should be simple and safe to rectify that failure, and those impacted should be taught about the failure and its rectification as part of ordinary training. If, on the other hand, a failure is uncommon, it should be expected that even trained personnel might not know how to handle the failure when it happens so the design itself must avoid relying on such training to ensure safety.

- Often, but not always, inoperability is preferred to unexpected operation once a failure occurs. People understand that broken machines often simply stop operating.[61]

- Elegant failure also involves providing users with some type of diagnostics relating to the failure.[62]

- Elegant failure further suggests that if a new feature fails, the system is able to continue operating as it did before the new feature was added. This has the obvious benefit of bringing the user experience back to a type of system operation they remember from not too long ago.[63]

- What is NOT elegant failure is brand-new, and most particularly unexpected or rash, operation of the system. If a robotic arm normally detects its location by sensing proximity to known locations (e.g., a wall), then if the proximity sensor does not detect the wall the arm should not wildly move about trying to find it again.

- A final aspect we address regarding elegant failure is whether the failure is obvious to the user and, conversely, the ramifications of unknown failures.[64]

Digital Twins

It is important to remember that "failure" can mean many things, and differentiating among them may be critically important. This is illustrated nicely by the modern concept of "digital twins," in which operating characteristics for an actual machine are fed as inputs to a virtual version of that machine so that what is likely happening to the actual machine may be predicted.

Consider a digital twin of a turbine generator. Parameters such as instantaneous RPM, lubricant temperature, viscosity and turbidity can be transmitted from the actual machine to its digital twin. Using historical data and deep learning, the digital twin can self-report the likely wear and tear on internal components as well as expected times for actual failure. Early indications of wear and tear may not suggest any action; moderate indications may suggest need for maintenance and of course, severe indications suggest that failure is occurring and repair is needed. Based on the operating environment, needed reliability, and maintenance schedules digital twins can warn of failures or simply monitor and report as needed for the next scheduled maintenance.

The concepts set forth above are in accordance with most AI-ethics statements that are developing around the world. For instance, the ICDPPC Declaration on Ethics and Data Protection in Artificial Intelligence (Brussels, October 23, 2018)[65] includes guiding principle 1(c) that calls for *"ensuring that artificial intelligence systems are developed in a way that facilitates human development and does not obstruct or endanger it, thus recognizing the need for delineation and boundaries on certain uses."*

F. Transparency

As detailed in our treatment of Principle 3—Transparency and Explainability, some argue that there is an urge for transparency when it concerns AI,[66] and transparency is the key to build and maintain trust in AI.[67] From an ethical point of view, both technological and business model transparency matter.

Technological model transparency

Technological model transparency means that a system must be auditable, comprehensible and understandable to human beings at different levels of expertise.

Explaining the results from large and complex AI models, however, is one of the biggest challenges to achieve user acceptance and regulatory acceptance.[68] Business model transparency implies that people are informed about the intentions of the creators of the AI systems.[69] Explicability is, for example, a precondition for obtaining informed consent from individuals interacting with AI systems. Furthermore, explicability requires accountability measures. Individuals can request evidence of the basic parameters and instructions given as input for AI decision making.[70]

It can, however, be questioned whether transparency is the solution for balancing algorithmic power, when corporations or governments are not legally bound or otherwise encouraged to disclose information.[71] It is also questionable how far transparency has to go: should transparency imply that it should be possible to access a system at any time? In addition, while more transparency can increase trust, it can also increase the danger of manipulation and imitation (a "transparency dilemma" so to speak).[72]

Scholars differ in their opinions about transparency in AI systems. Some suggest that transparency will increase in importance when the autonomous capabilities of an AI system increase.[73] Wang, Jamieson and Hollands for example, found that giving people information about the reliability of a certain system helps people to calibrate their trust in a system, during information uncertainty.[74] However, this is certainly not always the case. A well-known example is the reliability of airplanes. In general, people trust that an aircraft and its personnel meet a level of safety and reliability. Therefore, no evidence is required (e.g., maintenance certificate of an aircraft, qualifications of personnel). It would be impossible to do so in a way that everyone understands.

The extent to which transparency has been achieved may also be taken into account. *Kizilcec*, for example, tested three levels of transparency: low, medium and high.[75] Medium transparency increased trust significantly, where high transparency eroded it completely. This resulted in the same or even lower levels of trust. This indicates that people do not need (or even want) high levels of transparency. On the other hand, people do not trust black box models either. Basic insights into the factors that drive algorithmic decisions should therefore be provided.[76]

III. Case Studies

A. Case study: Autonomous vehicles

1. Introduction

The idea of autonomous driving is surprisingly old. It goes back to the "Futurama vision" General Motors presented at the 1939 New York World's Fair including an automated highway system that would guide self-driving cars.[77] In 1977, Tsukuba Mechanical Engineering Lab presented the first car achieving a true level of autonomy processing images of the road ahead taken by on-board cameras via an analogue computer technology.[78] As processing technologies and speed were considerably increased, the development of autonomous driving is close to hitting the mass market. Technology companies and traditional car manufacturers are competing in a tight race.[79]

The first pedestrian death through a vehicle controlled by AI has already occurred:—a woman was fatally struck after walking in front of an Uber car traveling in self-driving mode.[80] Furthermore, a driver of a Tesla car that was in autopilot mode died in an accident.[81] While the Uber vehicle was an autonomous car with an emergency backup driver behind the wheel,[82] the Tesla only was controlled by a semiautonomous driving system.[83] In both cases, the intelligent system failed. The systems did not recognise the obstacle and therefore deliberately decided against braking. In both cases, the human user also failed. In the first accident, the "backup" driver had missed spotting a danger he would have surely recognised if he had been paying attention. In the second one, the driver had received several visual and one audible hands-on warnings and the driver's hands were not detected on the wheel for six seconds prior to the collision.[84] These accidents were a reminder that self-driving technology is still in the experimental stage, and governments are still trying to figure out how to regulate it.[85]

Driving involves decisions on accelerating, slowing down and stopping, on orientation, steering and manoeuvring to reach a desired destination on the permitted roadways while avoiding obstacles of any kind. The driver must be able to accurately recognise any given actual situation, foresee the immediate future situation, analyse all options of interfering while processing the continuing flow of information gathered from the world surrounding the vehicle, take a decision on whether to adjust the current ride and execute it immediately. When the automobile was invented, it was not regulated at all. It took decades before cars became a common means of transportation. The inherent risks of driving brought authorities all over the world to develop regimes requiring technical minimum standards for vehicles to be permitted and drivers to qualify for being admitted to drive. Those qualifications include theoretical and practical training on mastering the vehicle as such and operating it in traffic, indirectly ensuring a given minimum intelligence of the driver.

AI plays a key role in automated and autonomous driving: While riding, the driving unit must process all information on the operation of the vehicle, so all tasks the driver fulfils as just described. The moral considerations behind this are so complex that they, for example, have led the German Federal Ministry of Transport and Digital Infrastructure to set up an ethics commission for autonomous and networked driving.[86] The challenges for the implementation of autonomous driving are therefore heterogeneous: The mere technological aspects, defining socially accepted legal rules, and moral considerations.

2. Technical implementation and the stages of autonomous driving

Autonomous driving is implemented through a combination of hardware and software. The process is similar to that of human driving—the human brain, eyes and ears are replaced by technical systems. The perception takes place by camera-, radar- and LIDAR-systems while the processing is managed by a computer and the result is transcribed by control electronics.[87]

There is a significant difference between automated and autonomous driving. To illustrate the basic differences between these two concepts, the standard classification SAE J3016 by SAE International (Society of Automotive Engineers) is suitable.[88] It has become established that the technical approach to completely autonomous vehicles is classified according to six different levels. The classification starts at level 0 (no automation)[89] and ends at level 5, the highest level of the standard classification SAE J3016 describing the full-time performance by an automated driving system.[90] Level 5 is the stage at which true autonomous driving becomes a reality.[91] At this level, the vehicle does not need a driver anymore. This means that the driver of the vehicle is an intelligent computer system making all of the various decisions. Obviously, the safety and reliability requirements for level 5 driving are highly complex as the ultimate control of a human driver supposed to cope with unknown situations as well is at least conceptually not there. The most popular method to keep the system on the right path is the hybrid approach, which means that developers can resolve the inherent complexity of neural networks by introducing redundancy-specific neural networks for individual processes connected by a centralised neural network and supplement by if-then rules.[92]

3. The room for improvement

Autonomously driving vehicles are able to solve some problems of modern mankind: Streets are often overcrowded and especially in the metropolitan regions of the world, parking space is becoming increasingly rare. There is less space available, which makes it necessary to use it efficiently. Autonomous vehicles could potentially reduce the need of parking space in the United States by more than 5.7 billion square meters.[93] Intelligent route calculation and car sharing concepts could relieve the burden on the roads. This could also reduce energy requirements.

The global status report on road safety 2018 from the World Health Organization says that 1.35 million people died in car accidents in 2016 and tens of millions more are injured every year.[94] Human misconduct is the most common cause of this.[95] Autonomous vehicles could drastically reduce the number of accidents by replacing the human driver with the system. This is in addition to the massive benefit that automation will provide in timesaving to those who would otherwise be occupied driving vehicles.[96]

4. Moral and ethical impact

However, there are hurdles that need to be overcome. Autonomous driving creates challenges in various fields including the following:

a) Legal obstacles are diverse. Road traffic laws need to be adapted. The Vienna Convention on Road Signs and Signals has already been modified for autonomous driving: in certain circumstances, systems may control the vehicle.[97] Some nations have already begun to amend their traffic regulations.[98]

   Allocating responsibility and liability, in particular for accidents and other unintended impacts, is important. The legal framework must be recalibrated to fairly allocate the risks of introducing a new technology: On the one hand, innovation should neither be choked nor hampered; on the other hand, society should be protected from unacceptable impacts of an immature technology the introduction of which is always also driven by commercial interests of the inventors and manufacturers.

   Automating traffic also means a flood of geographic data, which must be protected under data protection law. The first commissions are also dealing with the associated need for new data ethics.[99]

b) Furthermore, there are moral and ethical challenges:[100]

   The parameters for the AI will probably have to include weighing up "non-judgeable" features: The AI based driving unit could e.g., include collision decision parameters considering aspects such as gender, age, height, weight etc. leading to a uniform behaviour of all autonomous vehicles hereby concentrating the impacts on the group singled out to be the "less protectable." The moral dilemma for the programmers becomes more severe as they prepare decision parameters without the time pressure of the given moment: Hence, there is no refuge to "the fate" or "the inevitable misfortune."

   The moral dilemma in which autonomous vehicles can get into is exemplified by the Massachusetts Institute of Technology with the "moral machine,"[101] which illustrates that situations can arise in road traffic in which a qualitative and quantitative decision has to be made between the death of one or the other. Cultural differences play a role here. The research of Awad et al. is a good example of these cultural differences in respect of AI.[102] Priorities and preferences vary from one country to another, aggravating concepts for standardization. A few examples found in recent studies: in countries with higher levels of gender equality, the preference for saving women is higher, in Eastern countries there is a weaker preference for sparing the young over the elderly, and the preference for humans over animals is less pronounced in Southern nations. Autonomous vehicles may therefore need the ability to download new moralities when they cross national borders.[103]

Legal standards differ and the applicability of legal doctrines, such as negligence or foreseeability to AI is unclear: Would it be sufficient to show that reasonable precautions to prevent damage have been taken and if so, what exactly needs to be shown?

Apart from the question of how to teach morality objectively, there is also the problem of how to deal with the various moral ideas. Getting a driver's license does usually not involve any kind of ethical or moral training. All societies require a minimum age for a driver's license assuming that every grown-up individual brings along an—undefined—basic set and system of ethical and moral rules guaranteeing an acceptable minimum standard reflecting the "common sense" of the society he or she grew up in. For those who fail, there is a liability system allocating most of the risks to the drivers, remedying the incident occurred and indirectly preventing similar incidents to occur again as other drivers hopefully learn from the behaviour ruled as being inappropriate and adjust their future handling of identical or similar situations.

c) The social impacts must also be taken into account, as we discuss in our treatment of Principle 1—Ethical Purpose and Societal Benefits.

B. Case study: Robotic surgery in healthcare

1. The way to a "smart hospital"?

The development of new technology has long been an important requirement for revolutionary steps in medical innovation. The first heart transplantation, carried out 1967 in Cape Town by Christiaan Barnard, was only possible due to the development of the heart-lung machine. Medical innovation is also often accompanied by ethical and legal challenges. The development of the heart-lung machine made it possible to maintain cardiac, respiratory and metabolic functions almost indefinitely, which is why the ad hoc committee of Harvard Medical School defined "irreversible coma" as a new criterion for death in 1968.[104]

The first step to robotic surgery was made in the early 2000s with the creation of the Da Vinci Surgical System. The Da Vinci Surgical System is designed to facilitate complex surgery using a minimally invasive approach and is controlled by a surgeon from a console.[105] Future technological development is closely linked to the implementation of AI—this trend also includes the medical sector. Now, the focus of research is on how AI can help in diagnostics—Stanford University has established the Centre for Artificial Intelligence in Medicine & Imaging.[106]

Also in the medical sector the question arises, which challenges AI has to master during implementation. Furthermore, one will ask whether it only supports humans or replaces them. Will AI-controlled robots treat, diagnose and operate patients in the future?

2. The role of AI

The special feature that makes AI a success in the medical sector is the ability to logically capture and process enormous amounts of data. An example of this is IBM's Watson.[107] The AI platform was able to analyse the genome of a human patient with brain cancer and create a treatment plan in only 10 minutes, while doctors needed 160 hours for the task.[108] AI's performance, coupled with the precision and tirelessness of robots, is the reason for the interest. The better the medical technology, the better (since simpler and less dangerous) the operations are.

3. Current development status

Although AI is embedded in many forms of technologies, its use in the frontline of clinical practice remains limited.[109] Currently the largest area of application is medical diagnosis. Especially in areas where pattern recognition takes place, for example in radiology and pathology, AI can show its strengths. An AI program proved that it interprets mammograms and translates patient data into diagnostic information 30 times faster than a human doctor, with 99 percent accuracy.[110]

As mentioned, robotic surgical devices already exist, but humans still control them. Nevertheless, AI has already successfully performed the role of a surgeon. In 2016, a surgical robot stitched up the small intestine from a pig completely on its own.[111] In 2017, a Chinese robot dentist succeeded in fitting two implants in patient's mouth without any human involvement—the first successful autonomous implant surgery.[112]

4. Future of AI in medicine

Autonomously operating robots are therefore not science fiction, but reality—at least in the experimental phase such systems are tested worldwide. It can already be seen that these robots can achieve better results than human doctors can.

In the near future, it is more likely that AI-based systems will support operators rather than completely replace them. Johnson & Johnson and Google have teamed up to form a joint venture called Verb Surgical to launch a surgical robotics program that will connect surgeons to an end-to-end platform for surgery, including pre-operative planning, intra-operative decision making and post-operative care.[113] Experts believe that a new wave of innovation will come that will be characterised by the convergence of surgical robotics with AI and data gathered from robotic systems.[114]

Self-operating robots are still far away: they are e.g., much more complex than self-driving cars. An operation requires much more knowledge and situational action than road traffic movement, which is based on simple rules. That is why most researchers agree that the future of AI lies in enhancing and assisting surgery, not taking over from surgeons.[115]

5. Moral and ethical impact

The fundamental moral discussion that generally arises when using AI is simply stated: The advantages of AI must be weighed against its disadvantages, including e.g., safety concerns or the loss of jobs.

Patient data is particularly sensitive, which is why the role of data protection is so important, as AI requires large amounts of data for its tasks. One of the special concerns is the issue of liability—if a medical error occurs, who is to be held liable?[116] As with autonomous driving, a shift in liability to the detriment of the manufacturer can also be debatable in the area of operative robots. The trolley problem also arises—how is the robot supposed to act if it cannot save all of the patients? However, there are also special moral problems. The AI of a robotic surgeon must be aware of the legal and moral principles of assisted dying. Lastly, there is the special problem with inherent bias.[117] It is demonstrated that AI can learn to have racist or sexist bias, based on associations that are part of the data from which the AI was learning.[118] Such inherent bias should not be present, particularly in the treatment and examination of humans.

6. Summary

AI has the opportunity to change the medical sector in a sustainable way. However, a smart hospital in which humans are cured by robots is not to be expected in the near future. The possibilities of robotic surgery supported by AI lie rather in the support of the surgeons. The moral and legal challenges posed by robotic surgery are largely the same as those posed by autonomous driving. There are, however, also challenges of their own which must be overcome.

C. Case study: AI-based QA/QC in manufacturing

1. Introduction

It is often said that AI solutions should be least-favoured solutions, where the understanding of a problem is not amenable to direct measurement, deterministic algorithms, and the like. In other words, when all else fails, use AI because it does not depend on any sort of understanding of the underlying problems. As it happens, many quality control and quality assurance problems are of exactly that sort. A minor change in raw materials, wear of a manufacturing die, or even change in the humidity of a manufacturing environment can all lead to unexpected changes in the output of a manufacturing process. In such an environment, AI can prove extremely useful as a supplement to traditional quality assurance and quality control ("**QA/QC**") techniques. This is particularly true where those traditional techniques continue to rely heavily on human workers (likely because the traditional automated techniques prove inadequate). AI is extremely effective, as are humans, at looking at a component and recognizing there is something different about it, even if it's difficult to saw what the abnormality is much less what caused it.

The importance of QA/QC for product safety and reliability leads to extensive use of expensive human resources for this, and one ethical consideration is that this is largely work that provides those human resources with little intellectual reward. Constantly staring at a stream of thousands of products, or even sampling a small percentage of millions of manufactured items, is not particularly rewarding work. What is rewarding, however, is examining a component that is identified as being different and trying to figure out how it is different and why it became different. Thankfully, it is the unrewarding task that AI can readily help with.

Convolutional Neural Networks are the go-to AI solutions for many such problems. These networks learn over time which characteristics define things such as manufactured parts, and which differences in those characteristics are acceptable as opposed to indicative of a defect. Consider e.g., an imaging system that analyses several pictures of each manufactured component as it speeds by on a conveyor. Those images for each unit will have much in common (obviously) since they are all comparing parts that are supposed to be identical. However, there will be some differences in the image because, for example, each time a unit is placed on the conveyor it may be at a slightly different angle. Likewise, if a factory has windows or skylights admitting ambient light, there may be differences in brightness depending on whether it is a clear or rainy day. Through appropriate learning, AI systems can learn that these differences are irrelevant to product quality. However, if there is a difference in size or texture detected by the imaging, such differences are far more likely to indicate an actual change in the manufactured unit that deserves further attention. Other than imaging, sensors can similarly detect weight, density, conductivity, and other characteristics of the item. For these reasons, quality assurance/quality control solutions have become major components of the Industrial Internet of Things (IIoT).

2. Moral and ethical impact

In some industries, the ethical impacts of such manufacturing applications of AI are quite large. Viewing the end-users of the products, the efficacy of such QA/QC techniques far exceeds what humans can do, particularly with manufactured pieces that are produced in huge quantities with characteristics that may be difficult for humans to observe (think of a factory that manufactures ball bearings, for instance). One might argue that there is an ethical imperative to use such techniques where commercially reasonable to ensure that fewer defective products are introduced into the stream of commerce. If the ball bearings are used in a critical system of an airplane, for instance, failure of such a part could be far more than just an inconvenience.

There is, however, a second ethical component as well. One might take the position that any job is a good job for the economic benefit it provides the worker. However, there are some tasks that are so repetitious or otherwise unrewarding that they are—simply put—not desirable jobs. We would be better off taking advantage of human resources in other areas that remain best suited to human workers. In that sense, there is an ethical imperative to use AI where it can relieve drudgery of human workers.

D. Case study: Voice and face recognition—decoupling reliability from safety

1. Introduction

In many examples discussed in this chapter, reliability and safety are strongly coupled. If a system is not reliable, it puts people or assets at risk of harm. However, it is also important to think of reliability as important on its own, where no safety concerns may be present. To illustrate this, we will discuss here some common pattern recognition applications. An oft-referenced pattern recognition problem is AI-based recognition of cancer from medical imaging modalities. The ethical implications of such systems are self-evident: If we can use machine learning to help identify from CAT scans, for instance, a newly emerging malignant tumour in a patient we should do that—particularly if the imaging is so subtle that it would be difficult for a human radiologist to recognise. However, there are ethical implications for reliability of non-critical applications as well. The example we will discuss here is recognizing human speech and faces.

Machines have advanced to a point where they can recognise us by our faces (e.g., to unlock a cell phone) and can understand us when we speak (natural language processing as used in many industrial situations). These machines are not, however, equally proficient with all users. Because of the nature of AI, they learn from training data sets meant to maximise their reliability in typical operation. What is considered "typical," however, leads to some potential concerns.

2. Moral and ethical impact

For example, consider facial recognition. If an AI system is trained using a corpus of face images that all are of Northern European adult males, it likely will be far more reliable in recognizing faces of Northern European adult males than, for instance, children, females, people from Asia or Africa, and the like. Even where facial recognition is for convenience only (e.g., to unlock a device without using a password), such differential reliability still violates many common social norms in that it makes people who are not well represented by the training set feel different or excluded. As recently reported in the *New York Times,* the negative social implications of such disparate treatment are sufficiently important that one MIT researcher, *Joy Buolamwini,* has advocated for "algorithmic accountability" to address the resulting injustice. Her organization, the Algorithmic Justice League, addresses such issues as well as urging organizations to pledge for only appropriate uses of facial recognition.

Likewise, similar issues arise with voice recognition and natural language processing. To the extent vernacular speech, dialects, and other variations from what might be considered "standard" English (or other language) is not fully accounted for in training data sets, systems that ease life for one subset of the population may only increase frustration for others. Differences in recognition rates between male and female voices have been documented for decades. Likewise, accents frequently cause problems, as an article in *The Economist* recently pointed out with a bit of humour based on examples of incorrect recognition.[119] There are, of course, implications that are more serious as well. While we are focusing on non-safety related issues for this case study, it bears mentioning that degraded recognition rates for fear-altered voices (or faces for that matter) can have safety implications. Aside from those, the convenience impacts mentioned above are real, and often have the greatest impact on socio-economic groups that are already otherwise disadvantaged. Thankfully, such ethical issues are now being addressed more often and with larger audiences, and the industry itself is undertaking activities such as workshops related to ethics in natural language processing to address these issues.

IV. Legal Challenges for AI-Based Technologies

A. Vertical level

There are several ways to regulate; the government can play a major role in transition to AI systems, or not at all.[120] For example, "command and control" regulation[121] implies that the government threatens to impose sanctions aimed at bringing firm's interests into alignment with the interests of society.[122] Meta-regulation and self-regulation[123] are imposed by a non-governmental actor and are enforced by the regulated entity itself.[124] In this paper, we will focus mainly on legislation.

There are two different ways to ensure safety and reliability: (1) regulate by saying a product is prohibited unless permitted, or (2) regulate by saying a product is permitted unless prohibited.[125] These might stifle or delay progress and innovation. Regulatory concepts might (and lately often) include variations such as confined permits for testing and refining purposes of new technologies within clearly defined limits.[126]

In the second method, legal provisions tend to be more abstract, resulting into general concepts of safety, danger and reliability, which is a more liberal way of regulation, and can support faster development. In respect of the second method, it is essential to assess the "risk factor" of each vertical/type application and decide where the more restrictive "admission model" needs to be implemented. This involves assessing high risks of casualties or personal injury, for example risk scenarios such as drugs, use of nuclear technologies etc. For emerging technologies, it is impossible to set material requirements on safety and reliability in advance, while covering all aspects.

If an outcome is unclear and it is not possible to define specific obligations to be met, lawyers usually structure a process to provide a proper handling, such as in R&D agreements. Establishing regulatory requirements could probably follow this R&D agreement approach: the ultimate goal is to define safety and reliability standards, but as long as they cannot yet be defined, there should be focus on the process. Laws will have to be reviewed and updated on a regular basis as growing knowledge allows fine-tuning the rules. This approach follows the lines of the precautionary principle, see section I.C above.

Effective regulation of algorithms might be difficult because AI cannot be defined easily.[127] Regulatory problems arise at the research and development stage *(ex ante),* and when the AI will be released into the world *(ex post).* In the *ex post* phase, there are problems with foreseeability (can a manufacturer be held responsible for all injuries when the injuries are not reasonably foreseeable?) and control (is the AI program capable of being controlled by its human makers?). In the *ex ante* phase, problems with regard to diffuseness, discreteness and opacity can arise.[128] The diffuseness problem for example, suggests a need for global coordination in relation to AI regulation. *Danaher,* however, signals that in past efforts, this does not inspire confidence (e.g., climate change; nuclear proliferation).[129]

B. Horizontal level

On the civil level there is the classic liability system requiring an element of a (subjective) fault and strict liability. In between are the fault-based systems operating on "burden of proof shifts or modifications" and/or "presumed negligence" case law. These in-between-systems have typically no statutory background but emerge from courts and cases trying to cope with a changing world. Strict liability systems are in principle (if not always) statute-based. The flip side of the "no fault required" is often a cap of such liability enabling the development of insurance products covering relating risks.

Helping and accompanying AI development from a legal perspective will probably not require "reinvention of the wheel" but rather assessing which of the existing rules, i.e., on product liability may be adjusted to dispense the inherent risk on a socially accepted way. Otherwise, we end up with haggling and bargaining power games, e.g., comprehensive patient waivers as requirement of doctors who use medical AI systems. On the one hand, your choice might not be completely free if you are ill—on the other hand, there is a necessity for doctors to operate on a reasonable risk basis as well.

However, while all laws are subject to obsolescence, this is in particular true for laws on developing technologies. It likely will be quite some time before society settles in on a stable regime to address safety and reliability of AI systems.

Principle 5
Safety and Reliability

Organisations that develop, deploy or use AI systems and any national laws that regulate such use shall adopt design regimes and standards ensuring high safety and reliability of AI systems on one hand while limiting the exposure of developers and deployers on the other hand.

1 Require and/or define explicit ethical and moral principles underpinning the AI system

1.1 Governments and organisations developing, deploying or using AI systems should define the relevant set of ethical and moral principles underpinning the AI system to be developed, deployed or used taking into account all relevant circumstances. A system designed to autonomously make decisions will only be acceptable if it operates on the basis of clearly defined principles and within boundaries limiting its decision making powers.

1.2 Governments and organisations developing, deploying or using AI systems should validate the underpinning ethical and moral principles as defined periodically to ensure on-going accurateness.

2 Standardisation of behaviour

2.1 Governments and organisations developing, deploying or using AI systems should recall that ethical and moral principles are not globally uniform but may be impacted e.g., by geographical, religious or social considerations and traditions. To be accepted, AI systems might have to be adjustable in order to meet the local standards in which they will be used.

2.2 Consider whether all possible occurrences should be pre-decided in a way to ensure the consistent behaviour of the AI system, the impact of this on the aggregation of consequences and the moral appropriateness of "weighing the unweighable" such as life vs. life.

3 Ensuring safety, reliability and trust

3.1 Governments should require and organisations should test AI systems thoroughly to ensure that they reliably adhere, in operation, to the underpinning ethical and moral principles and have been trained with data which are curated and are as 'error-free' as practicable, given the circumstances.

3.2 Governments are encouraged to adjust regulatory regimes and/or promote industry self-regulatory regimes for allowing market-entry of AI systems in order to reasonably reflect the positive exposure that may result from the public operation of such AI systems. Special regimes for intermediary and limited admissions to enable testing and refining of the operation of the AI system can help to expedite the completion of the AI system and improve its safety and reliability.

3.3 In order to ensure and maintain public trust in final human control, governments should consider implementing rules that ensure comprehensive and transparent investigation of such adverse and unanticipated outcomes of AI systems that have occurred through their usage, in particular if these outcomes have lethal or injurious consequences for the humans using such systems. Such investigations should be used for considering adjusting the regulatory framework for AI systems in particular to develop a more rounded understanding of how such systems should gracefully handover to their human operators.

4 Facilitating technological progress at reasonable risks

4.1 Governments are encouraged to consider whether existing legal frameworks such as product liability require adjustment in light of the unique characteristics of AI systems.

4.2 Governments should support and participate in international co-ordination (through bodies such as the International Organisation for Standardisation (ISO) and the International Electrotechnical Commission (IEC)) to develop international standards for the development and deployment of safe and reliable AI systems.

Endnotes

[1] MIT researchers have found for example, that there are moral differences between East and West. Peter Dizikes, "How should autonomous vehicles be programmed?" (24 October 2018), online: *MIT News* <http://news.mit.edu/2018/how-autonomous-vehicles-programmed-1024>.

[2] Please note that assisting AI systems may seem less risky from a safety and/or reliability perspective, because a human factor is still involved in the application. However, use of assisting AI systems may prove that the human factor is as a practical matter irrelevant, e.g., if a user became accustomed in trusting the output of the AI system without (periodic) verification, or is not knowledgeable enough to actually understand the underlying (design) principles to verify its output. In these circumstances an assisting AI system may become *de facto* an autonomous AI system.

[3] Kate Crawford, "Artificial Intelligence's White Guy Problem" (25 June 2016), online: *The New York Times* <https://www.nytimes.com/2016/06/26/opinion/sunday/artificial-intelligences-white-guy-problem.html?ref=technology>.

[4] IBM, "Building trust in AI," online: <https://www.ibm.com/watson/advantage-reports/future-of-artificial-intelligence/building-trust-in-ai.html> [IBM].

[5] See Principle 1—Ethical Purpose and Societal Benefit.

[6] Philosophically, the two approaches reflect a more deontologically driven ethic following e.g., Immanuel Kant and/or a rather utilitarian view as e.g., developed by Jeremy Bentham. See also section II.C.

[7] The precautionary principle is mentioned in the European Parliament resolution of 16 February 2017 with recommendations to the Commission on Civil Law Rules on Robotics (2015/2103(INL)): *"[...] testing robots in real-life scenarios is essential for the identification and assessment of the risks they might entail, as well as of their technological development beyond a pure experimental laboratory phase; underlines, in this regard, that testing of robots in real-life scenarios, in particular in cities and on roads, raises a large number of issues, including barriers that slow down the development of those testing phases and requires an effective strategy and monitoring mechanism; calls on the Commission to draw up uniform criteria across all Member States which individual Member States should use in order to identify areas where experiments with robots are permitted, in compliance with the precautionary principle"* European Parliament, *Civil Law Rules on Robotics,* P8_TA(2017)0051, online: <http://www.europarl.europa.eu/sides/getDoc.do?pubRef=-//EP//TEXT+TA+P8-TA-2017-0051+0+DOC+XML+V0//EN>.

[8] Hans Jonas, *The Imperative of Responsibility: In Search of an Ethics for the Technological Age* (University of Chicago Press, 1985).

[9] Wikipedia, "Precautionary Principle," online: <https://en.wikipedia.org/wiki/Precautionary_principle>.

[10] Note that there may be cultural differences in applying the precautionary principle. While European nations are willing to constrain potential harm on a precautionary basis to a greater extent, the United States require a stronger evidence of danger (see e.g., The Editorial Board, "Why Does the U.S. Tolerate So Much Risk?" (15 March 2019), online: *The New York Times* <https://www.nytimes.com/2019/03/15/opinion/federal-aviation-administration-boeing.html>).

[11] Oxford Dictionary, "Safety," online: <https://en.oxforddictionaries.com/definition/safety>.

[12] This implies that the definition of safety includes reliability. We discuss the concept of reliability in paragraph ii.

[13] European Commission, High-Level Expert Group on Artificial Intelligence, "Draft Ethics Guidelines for Trustworthy AI" (2018), online: <https://ec.europa.eu/digital-single-market/en/news/draft-ethics-guidelines-trustworthy-ai> at p 18 [Ethics Guidelines].

[14] This also implies that reliability is an element of a safe product.

15 European Commission, European Group on Ethics in Science and New Technologies, "Statement on Artificial Intelligence, Robotics and 'Autonomous' Systems" (March 2018), online (pdf): <https://ec.europa.eu/research/ege/pdf/ege_ai_statement_2018.pdf> at p 18.

16 *Ibid,* at p 19.

17 The dual use dilemma refers to the fact that AI innovations might be used for both beneficial and harmful uses.

18 *Ibid,* at p 19.

19 See for example also the precautionary principle as described in section I.C.

20 European Commission, "Key Players in European Standardization," online: <https://ec.europa.eu/growth/single-market/european-standards/key-players_en>.

21 EC, *Council Directive 85/374/EEC of 25 July 1985 on the approximation of the laws, regulations and administrative provisions of the Member States concerning liability for defective products,* [1985] OJ, L 210.

The Product Liability Directive requires that the defectiveness of the product should not be determined on the basis of its fitness for use, but on the basis of the lack of safety which the general public can expect in order to protect the physical well-being and property of the consumer (Considerations Product Liability Directive). More specifically, the Product Liability Directive finds a product defective if it *"does not provide the safety which a person is entitled to expect, taking all circumstances into account"* (Article 6 Product Liability Directive)). All circumstances include, *inter alia,* the presentation of the product, the use to which it could reasonably be expected that the product would be put and the time when the product was put into circulation.

22 EC, *Directive 2001/95/EC of the European Parliament and of the Council of 3 December 2001 on general product safety,* [2002] OJ, L 11. The General Product Safety Directive allows only safe products on the market (Article 3 General Product Safety Directive) A safe product is, in short, a product which does not present any risk or only the minimum risks compatible when using the product under normal or reasonably foreseeable use (Article 2b Directive 2001/95/EC) (General Product Safety Directive). Based on the characteristics of the product, the effect on other products, the presentation of the product, the labelling, any warnings and instructions for its use and disposal and the categories of consumers at risk when using the product. In absence of EU legislation, a product is safe when it is in conformity with the specific rules of national law of the Member State in whose territory the product is placed on the market and laying down the health and safety requirements, which the product must satisfy in order to be marketed. Thereby, a product is safe *"as far as the risks and risk categories covered by relevant national standards are concerned when it conforms to voluntary national standards transposing European standards"* (Article 3 General Product Safety Directive).

Another example of a relevant directive is EC, *Directive 2014/53/EU of the European Parliament and of the Council of 16 April 2014 on the harmonisation of the laws of the Member States relating to the making available on the market of radio equipment and repealing Directive 1999/5/EC (the Radio Equipment Directive),* [2014] OJ, 153.

23 EC, *Directive 2006/42/EC of the European Parliament and of the Council of 17 May 2006 on machinery, and amending Directive 95/16/EC,* [2006] OJ, 157.

Machinery may be marketed or put into service *"only if it satisfies the relevant provisions of this directive and does not endanger the health and safety of persons and, where appropriate, domestic animals or property, when properly installed and maintained and used for its intended purpose or under conditions which can reasonably be foreseen"* (Article 4), If the machinery is not compliant to the directive, there is a safeguard clause to withdraw the machinery from the market, prohibit placing it on the market and/or putting it into service or to restrict free movement thereof (Article 11).

24 EC, European Commission, "Artificial intelligence for Europe" (25 April 2018), SWD(2018) 137 final, online (pdf): <http://www.astrid-online.it/static/upload/ai_s/ai_swd_25_04_18.pdf> at p 2 [AI for Europe].

25 McKinsey Global Institute, "Notes from the AI frontier applying AI for social good" (November 2018), online: <https://www.mckinsey.com/featured-insights/artificial-intelligence/applying-artificial-intelligence-for-social-good> at p 40 [McKinsey].

[26] Law Insider, "Definition of reliability," online: <https://www.lawinsider.com/dictionary/reliability>.

[27] Further examples include the following scenarios:

- "Failsafe" systems in buildings ensure that if a power failure occurs (e.g., due to fire or earthquake), electric door locking systems by design revert to "unlocked" mode to allow occupants to exit the building.
- If a traffic light control system fails, each traffic signal by design reverts to "red blinking" operation to safely allow continued use of an intersection.
- "Deadman" switches, such as the grab levers on lawnmowers, turn off the machine if the operator leaves the safe operating position (for instance to clear grass cuttings clogging the mower discharge).
- Nuclear power systems are often designed so that control rods are lifted by electromagnets during normal operation and automatically drop to stop the reaction upon failure of the control subsystem.
- Alarm systems use "normally closed" circuits that open (indicating a possible alarm situation) upon power loss or sensor failure.
- GFCI circuit breakers used in damp locations monitor current on various wires and disconnect the circuit if it appears current going in one direction doesn't match that in the other direction (e.g., if there is current improperly going to ground).

[28] Ethics Guidelines, *supra* note 13 at p 17.

[29] *Ibid,* at p 17.

[30] AI for Europe, *supra* note 24 at p 6.

[31] *Ibid,* at p 5.

[32] For example, International Organization for Standardization, "Artificial Intelligence—Concepts and terminology," ISO/IEC 22989, online: <https://www.iso.org/standard/74296.html>.

[33] Robert Bartram, "The new frontier for artificial intelligence" (18 October 2018), online: *International Organization for Standardization* <https://www.iso.org/news/ref2336.html>.

[34] Philippa Foot, "The problem of abortion and the doctrine of double effect" (1967), 5 Oxford Review;

Karl Engisch analyzed a similar scenario in his post-doctoral thesis: "Untersuchungen über Vorsatz und Fahrlässigkeit im Strafrecht" (1930), but the underlying moral dilemma on the accepting the death of others has been already discussed in Ancient Greece.

[35] There are many variations to this thought experiment, see for example Daniel Engber, "Does the Trolley Problem Have a Problem?" (18 June 2018), online: *Slate* <https://slate.com/technology/2018/06/psychologys-trolley-problem-might-have-a-problem.html>.

A variation to the "Trolley Problem" regarding the deployment of armed forces has been subject to the Judgment of Germany's Federal Constitutional Court of 15 February 2006 (1 BvR 357/05) on the statutory authorization to shoot down a passenger aircraft intended to be used against human lives (available in English via https://www.bundesverfassungsgericht.de). On the website Moral Machine, online: <http://moralmachine.mit.edu/> [Moral machine] questions can be answered on trolley-like situations, applied to autonomous vehicles.

[36] For example, Florian Cova et al, "Estimating the reproducibility of experimental philosophy" (2018), Review of Philosophy and Psychology 1-36; see also Dries Bostyn et al, "Of Mice, Men, and Trolleys: Hypothetical Judgment Versus Real-Life Behavior in Trolley-Style Moral Dilemmas" (2018) 29:7 Psychological Science and Olof Johansson-Stenman & Peter Martinsson, "Are Some Lives More Valuable? An Ethical Preferences Approach" (2008) 27:3 Journal of Health Economics 739 at p 733.

[37] Guido Calabresi & Philip Bobbitt, *Tragic Choices* (New York: Norton, 1978).

38 After recognizing that scarce resources, and the need to sensibly allocate them, result in tensions caused by competing needs, Calabresi *(ibid)* suggests a way to minimize the pain of society's duty to make the allocation nonetheless.

39 In Guido Calabresi, *The costs of accidents: a legal and economic analysis* (Yale University Press, 1970), Calabresi delves into such issues in more detail.

40 Calabresi used allocation of kidney machines and compulsory military service in wartime as two case studies.

41 For example, Principle 3 of the Institute of Electrical and Electronics Engineers's pronouncement, "Ethically Aligned Design: A Vision for Prioritizing Human Well-being with Autonomous and Intelligent Systems," Version 2 (2017), online: <https://standards.ieee.org/industry-connections/ec/autonomous-systems.html>, expressly states that designers take into account "existing cultural norms among the groups of users" of AI systems.

42 An example, given by the Paris Innovation Review, is the fear everyone has of AIDS (Qin Zengchang, "Artifical intelligence: the fear is from the unknown" (12 May 2016), online: *Paris Innovation Review* <http://parisinnovationreview.com/articles-en/artificial-intelligence-the-fear-is-from-the-unknown>. Yet doctors are not afraid to have contact with AIDS patients. After all, the doctors are familiar with the disease.

43 *Ibid.*

44 Roberto Simanowski, *The Death Algorithm and Other Digital Dilemmas* (MIT Press, 2018).

45 Vyacheslav Polonski, "Can we teach morality to machines? Three perspectives on ethics for artificial intelligence" (19 December 2017), online: *Oxford Internet Institute* <https://www.oii.ox.ac.uk/blog/can-we-teach-morality-to-machines-three-perspectives-on-ethics-for-artificial-intelligence/> [Polonski].

46 Roberto Simanowski, "Der Todesalgorithms" (2 October 2017), online: *Zeit Online* <https://www.zeit.de/kultur/2017-09/kuenstliche-intelligenz-algorithmus-spam-autonomes-fahren>.

47 The Ethical Guidelines, *supra* note 13 comprises representatives from academia, civil society, as well as industry.

48 *Ibid.*

49 Germany, Federal Ministry of Transport and Digital Infrastructure, Ethics Commission, "Automated and Connecting Driving" (June 2017), online: <https://www.bmvi.de/SharedDocs/EN/Documents/G/ethic-commission-report.pdf?__blob=publicationFile> [Germany].

50 Moral Machine, *supra* note 35.

51 The Future Society, The AI Initiative, online: <http://ai-initiative.org/>.

52 Ethics for Artificial Intelligence, online: <https://www.cs.ox.ac.uk/efai/>.

53 Technische Universitat Munchen, "Neues Forschungsinstitut fur Ethik in der Kunstlichen Intelligenz" (20 January 2019), online: <https://www.tum.de/die-tum/aktuelles/pressemitteilungen/detail/article/35188/>.

54 Ethics Guidelines, *supra* note 13 at 5.

55 Polonski, *supra* note 45.

56 *Ibid.*

57 The autopilot functionality in Tesla cars for example, requires the driver to maintain control and responsibility over the vehicle (The Tesla Team, "A Tragic Loss" (30 June 2016), online: *Tesla* <https://www.tesla.com/blog/tragic-loss>). Accidents may occur if a driver relies too heavily on the autopilot while it is not yet fully developed. See also the case study on Autonomous vehicles (Paragraph III).

58 Even if society does not compel one outcome as good and another as bad, each driver must cope with the morality of the decision. Human nature sometimes helps to overcome the inner questioning by disremembering or suppressing respective thoughts; another coping mechanism is escaping into concepts of inevitable fate and misfortune and the incapacity to make an intentional well-thought decision during the available time.

59 Germany, *supra 49* at p 12.

60 Further examples include the following scenarios:

- "Failsafe" systems in buildings ensure that if a power failure occurs (e.g., due to fire or earthquake), electric door locking systems by design revert to "unlocked" mode to allow occupants to exit the building.
- If a traffic light control system fails, each traffic signal by design reverts to "red blinking" operation to safely allow continued use of an intersection.
- "Deadman" switches, such as the grab levers on lawnmowers, turn off the machine if the operator leaves the safe operating position (for instance to clear grass cuttings clogging the mower discharge).
- Nuclear power systems are often designed so that control rods are lifted by electromagnets during normal operation and automatically drop to stop the reaction upon failure of the control subsystem.
- Alarm systems use "normally closed" circuits that open (indicating a possible alarm situation) upon power loss or sensor failure.
- GFCI circuit breakers used in damp locations monitor current on various wires and disconnect the circuit if it appears current going in one direction doesn't match that in the other direction (e.g., if there is current improperly going to ground).

61 Thus, for example, if an autonomous vehicle begins behaving in a way suggesting a failure is occurring, its user may engage manual control to pull over before the failure fully manifests itself. In some circumstances, however, "drop-dead" failure is worse than unexpected operation, for instance where a vehicle suddenly stops in the middle of a high-speed intersection. In those instances, it may well be preferable to design in some fault tolerance such that the vehicle can slowly use other non-failed systems to navigate to a safer location before completely immobilizing itself. More specifically, consider an autonomous vehicle that uses, for collision avoidance, a combination of radar, lidar and ultrasonic sensors. Should the radar system fail, a "safe mode" of operation may still be possible with the lidar and ultrasonic systems, albeit at reduced speed.

62 For example, in an AI-based health care system, it may be critically important for a doctor to know whether an automated system has failed in a way that is likely to result in increased false positive results v. increased false negative results. By providing such information, the degraded system may still be usable to some degree. More generally, learning from prior false positives/negatives in diagnosis can be used for further deep learning of an existing system or as indication that further R&D to reduce a particular type of artifact is called for.

63 So, for instance, if a self-parking feature of a car is added but stops operating because an automatic steering subsystem failure is detected, a dashboard notification can simply be provided to the user that the car will not self-park but proximity sensors and audio/haptic warnings will be provided as they were in the prior version.

64 For example, consider a wellness application that, based on pulse data from a user's smart watch determines certain health indicators of the user. Failure of a sensor to accurately "see" every heartbeat could cause an indication that the user is experiencing an arrhythmia. In such case, reporting the possible arrhythmia as such (i.e., a false positive) may be acceptable if it occurs infrequently—the user can be prompted to seek medical review. However, if such failures occur too frequently, any such warnings will be taken as false positives, thereby reducing or eliminating the value of the entire system. In such instance, certain types of alerts that may well be system failures may be better ignored than reported. Whether false positives or false negatives are to be favored is a design issue that engineers should be considering from the earliest stages of system development. As a good introduction, see, Kevin J Melcher et al. "Abort trigger false positive and false negative analysis methodology for threshold-based abort detection" (2015), online: *NASA Technical Reports Server* <https://ntrs.nasa.gov/search.jsp?R=20150019736>.

65 International Conference of Data Protection & Privacy Commissioners "Declaration on Ethics and Data Protection in Artificial Intelligence" (23 October 2018), online (pdf): <https://icdppc.org/wp-content/uploads/2018/10/20180922_ICDPPC-40th_AI-Declaration_ADOPTED.pdf>.

66 IBM, *supra* note 4.

67 Ethics Guidelines, *supra* note 13 at p 10.

68 McKinsey, *supra* note 25 at p 40.

69 Ethics Guidelines, *supra* note 13 at p 10.

70 *Ibid,* at p 10.

71 Nicholas Diakopoulos, "Algorithmic Accountability: Journalistic investigation of computational power structures" (2015) 3:3 Digital Journalism 398 at p 403.

72 Florian Saurwein et al, "Governance of Algorithms: Options and limitations" (2015) 17:6 info 35 at p 42.

73 Joseph Lyons, "Being Transparent about Transparency: A Model for Human-Robot Interaction" (2013), online: *Association for the Advancement of Artificial Intelligence* <https://pdfs.semanticscholar.org/bf51/f5448981d985e082f2d9511d276ca6519944.pdf> at p 49.

74 *Idem.*

75 Kartik Hosanagar & Vivian Jair, "We Need Transparency in Algorithms, but Too Much Can Backfire" (23 July 2018), online: *Harvard Business Review* <https://hbr.org/2018/07/we-need-transparency-in-algorithms-but-too-much-can-backfire>.

76 *Ibid.*

77 Fabian Kroger, "Automated Driving in Its Social, Historical and Cultural Contexts" (2016) in Autonomous Driving: Technical, Legal and Social Aspects (Springer, 2016) pp 41-68 at p 48.

78 E.g., Futurame, "History of Autonomous Driving," online: <https://futurama.io/history-of-autonomous-driving/>. Reflecting the processing capacities of that time, the speed was limited to 18 km/h.

79 Tim Menke, "Self-Driving Cars: The technology, risks and possibilities" (28 August 2017), online: *Harvard University The Graduate School of Arts and Sciences* <http://sitn.hms.harvard.edu/flash/2017/self-driving-cars-technology-risks-possibilities/> [Menke]. The upcoming state of the art is respectively displayed *inter alia* on trade shows such as the CES 2019 in Las Vegas, where several manufacturers have presented their self-driving vehicles instead of conventional ones, see e.g., Ronan Glon, "Self-Driving, electric, and connected, the cars of CES 2019 hint at the future" (1 January 2019), online: *Digital Trends* <https://www.digitaltrends.com/cars/new-cars-and-technology-features-displayed-at-ces-2019/>.

80 Will Knight, "What Uber's fatal accident could mean for the autonomous-car industry" (19 March 2018), online: *MIT Technology Review* <https://www.technologyreview.com/s/610574/what-ubers-fatal-accident-could-mean-for-the-autonomous-car-industry/>.

81 BBC, "Tesla in fatal California crash was on Autopilot" (31 March 2018), online: <https://www.bbc.com/news/world-us-canada-43604440>.

82 Daisuke Wakabayashi, "Self-Driving Uber Car Kills Pedestrian in Arizona, Where Robots Roam" (19 March 2018), online: *The New York Times* <https://www.nytimes.com/2018/03/19/technology/uber-driverless-fatality.html?module=inline> [Wakabayashi].

83 Neal E Boudette, "Fatal Tesla Crash Raises New Questions about Autopilot System" (31 March 2018), online: *The New York Times* <https://www.nytimes.com/2018/03/31/business/tesla-crash-autopilot-musk.html>.

[84] The Guardian, "Tesla car that crashed and killed driver was running on Autopilot, firm says" (31 March 2018), online: <https://www.theguardian.com/technology/2018/mar/31/tesla-car-crash-autopilot-mountain-view>.

[85] Wakabayashi, *supra* note 82.

[86] Germany, *supra* note 49.

[87] Menke, *supra* note 79.

[88] SAE International, "Taxonomy and Definitions for Terms Related to Driving Automation Systems for On-Road Motor Vehicles" (15 June 2018), online: <https://www.sae.org/standards/content/j3016_201806/>.

[89] SAE International, "Automated Driving: Levels of Driving Automation are Defined in New SAE International Standard J3016" (20 November 2016), online: <https://web.archive.org/web/20161120142825/http://www.sae.org/misc/pdfs/automated_driving.pdf>. This includes, for example, vehicles with Electronic Stability Control (ESP), Wikipedia, "SAE J3016," online: <https://de.wikipedia.org/wiki/SAE_J3016>.

[90] Wissenschaftliche Dienste des Deutschen Bundestages, Ausarbeitung WD 7—3000—111/18, Autonomes und automatisiertes Fahren auf der Straße—rechtlicher Rahmen, 4.

[91] BMV, "The path to autonomous driving," online: <https://www.bmw.com/en/automotive-life/autonomous-driving.html>.

[92] McKinsey & Company, "Self-driving car technology: When will the robots hit the road" (May 2017), online: <https://www.mckinsey.com/industries/automotive-and-assembly/our-insights/self-driving-car-technology-when-will-the-robots-hit-the-road>.

[93] McKinsey & Company, "Ten ways autonomous vehicles driving could redefine the automotive world" (June 2015), online: <https://www.mckinsey.com/industries/automotive-and-assembly/our-insights/ten-ways-autonomous-driving-could-redefine-the-automotive-world> [McKinsey, "Ten ways"].

[94] World Health Organization, "Global Status Report on Road Safety 2018" (2018), online: <https://www.who.int/violence_injury_prevention/road_safety_status/2018/en/>, at XI.

[95] Undesministerium für Verkehr und digitale Infrastruktur, Strategie automatisiertes und vernetztes Fahren, 9.

[96] McKinsey, "Ten ways," *supra* note 93.

[97] Germany, "Rechtssicherheit für automatisiertes Fahren" (4 November 2016), online: <https://www.bundesregierung.de/breg-de/aktuelles/rechtssicherheit-fuer-automatisiertes-fahren-349048>.

[98] See, e.g., the amendment of June 21, 2017 to the German Road Traffic Law (Section 1a StVG). The amendment permits vehicles with automated systems to be used in road traffic and governs the way that the driver can hand over the control to the system in certain situations; BT-Drs. 18/11300, 1.

[99] For example the German Federal Ministry of Justice and Consumer Protection has established a Data Ethics Commission.

[100] See e.g., section II.A.

[101] Moral machine, *supra* note 35.

[102] Edmond Awad et al, "The Moral Machine experiment" (2018) 563 Nature 59. See also section II.A.

[103] The Economist, "Whom should self-driving cars protect in accident?" (27 October 2018), online: <https://www.economist.com/science-and-technology/2018/10/27/whom-should-self-driving-cars-protect-in-an-accident>.

[104] The BMJ, "Christiaan Barnard: his first transplants and their impact on concepts of death" (2001), online: <https://www.bmj.com/content/323/7327/1478/rapid-responses>.

[105] Wikipedia, "da Vinci Surgical System," online: <https://en.wikipedia.org/wiki/Da_Vinci_Surgical_System>.

[106] Stanford University, Center for Artificial Intelligence in Medicine & Imaging, "The AIMI Center," online: <https://aimi.stanford.edu/.

[107] IBM, "IBM Watson," online: <https://www.ibm.com/watson>.

[108] Kazimierz O Wrzeszczynski et al, "Comparing sequencing assays and human-machine analyses in actionable genomics for glioblastoma" (2017) 3:4 Neurology Genetics.

[109] Erwin Loh, "Medicine and the rise of the robots: a qualitative review of recent advances of artificial intelligence in health" (2018)2 BMJ-Leader 59 [Loh].

[110] Sarah Griffiths, "This AI software can tell if you're at risk from cancer before symptoms appear" (26 Auguest 2016), online: *Wired* <https://www.wired.co.uk/article/cancer-risk-ai-mammograms>.

[111] Azad Shademan, "Supervised autonomous robotic soft tissue surgery" (2016) 8:337 Science translational medicine 337.

[112] Alice Yan, "Chinese robot dentist is first to fit implants in patient's mouth without any human involvment" (21 September 2017), online: *South China Morning Post* <https://www.scmp.com/news/china/article/2112197/chinese-robot-dentist-first-fit-implants-patients-mouth-without-any-human>.

[113] Verb Surgical, online: <http://verbsurgical.com/about/>.

[114] Sveta McShane, "The Future of Surgery Is Robotic, Data-Driven, and Artificially Intelligent" (11 October 2016), online: *Singularity Hub* <https://singularityhub.com/2016/10/11/the-future-of-surgery-is-robotic-data-driven-and-artificially-intelligent/#sm.0001m6cvk9q5dd0lwxb2htqbqq0s6>.

[115] Anna Sayburn, "Will the machines take over surgery?" 99:3 The bulletin 88 at p 90 [Sayburn].

[116] Loh, *supra* note 109.

[117] Sayburn, *supra* note 115.

[118] Aylin Caliskan et al, "Semantics derived automatically from language corpora contain human-like biases" (2017) 356:6334 Science 183.

[119] The Economist, "In the world of voice-recognition, not all accents are equal" (15 February 2018), online: <https://www.economist.com/books-and-arts/2018/02/15/in-the-world-of-voice-recognition-not-all-accents-are-equal>.

[120] According to Lessig, there are four modalities of regulation or constraint: code (physical or technical constraints on activities), market (involving economic forces), law and norms (Lawrence Lessig, *Code and Other Laws of Cyberspace* (New York: Basic Books, 1999).

[121] Command and Control Regulation can be defined as *"the direct regulation of an industry or activity by legislation that states what is permitted and what is illegal,"* Wikipedia, "Command and control regulation," online: <https://en.wikipedia.org/wiki/Command_and_control_regulation#cite_note-mcmanus-1>.

[122] Robert Baldwin et al, *The Oxford Handbook of Regulation* (Oxford University Press, 2010) at p 146 [Baldwin].

[123] Sinclair defines self-regulation *"as a form of regulation that relies substantially on the goodwill and cooperation of individuals firms for their compliance."* Freeman describes to voluntary self-regulation as *"the process by which standard-setting bodies operate independently of, and parallel to, government regulation and with respect to which, government yields none of its own authority to set and implement standards."* The difference in definition of meta-regulation can be found in the focus on the interaction between government regulation and self-regulation, and meta-regulation as a broader concept referring to interactions between different regulatory actors or levels of regulation. For example, *Hutter* describes meta-regulation as *"the state's oversight of self-regulatory arrangements."* Parker refers to meta-regulation as

a process of *"regulating the regulators, whether they be public agencies, private corporate self-regulators or third party gatekeepers."* Morgan states that mega-regulation *"captures a desire to think reflexively about regulation, such that rather than regulating social and individual action directly, the process of regulation itself becomes regulated. Through meta-regulation, each layer of regulation regulates the regulation of each other in various combinations of horizontal and vertical influence"* (Baldwin, *supra* note 122 at p 147-148).

124 *Ibid,* at p147.

125 An example of market restrictions can be seen in the case of medical devices, which may not be placed on the market before a CE marking has been affixed, which means manufacturer indicates that a device is in conformity with the applicable requirements set out in EC, *Council Directive 93/42/EEC of 14 June 1993 concerning devices,* [1993] OJ, L 169, which directive shall be replaced by *Regulation (EU) 2017/745 of the European Parliament and of the Council of 5 April 2017 on medical devices, amending Directive 2001/83/EC, Regulation (EC) No 178/2002 and Regulation (EC) No 1223/2009 and repealing Council Directives 90/385/EEC and 93/42/EEC,* [2017] OJ, L 117). Another example is financial services, which are also closely regulated within the EU.

126 See e.g., California Vehicle Code (CVC) Section 38750 providing the basis for regulations governing both the testing and public use of autonomous vehicles on California roadways, or a similar concept of Arizona on the basis of Executive Order 2018-04. The Swedish Transport Agency apparently granted a permit to test an autonomous, all-electric truck on a short distance on a public road within an industrial area between a warehouse and a terminal.

127 John Danaher, "Is effective regulation of AI possible? Eight potential regulatory problems" (27 September 2018), online: *Philosophical Disquisitions* <https://ieet.org/index.php/IEET2/more/Danaher20180927>.

128 The discreetness problem implies that AI research and development could take place using infrastructures that are not readily visible to the regulators. The diffuseness problem refers to the problem that arises when AI systems are developed using teams of researchers that are organizationally, geographically, and perhaps more importantly, jurisdictionally separate. The discreteness problem refers to the situation where AI projects could leverage many discrete, pre-existing hardware and software components, some of which will be proprietary (so-called 'off the shelf' components). The opacity problem relates to the problem where AI systems are much more opaque than previous technologies. This poses problems for regulators as there is a lack of clarity concerning the problems that may be posed by such systems and how those problems can be addressed, *Ibid.*

129 *Ibid.*

Principle 6

OPEN DATA AND FAIR COMPETITION

Organisations that develop, deploy or use AI systems and any national laws that regulate such use shall promote (a) open access to datasets which could be used in the development of AI systems and (b) open source frameworks and software for AI systems. AI systems must be developed and deployed on a "compliance by design" basis in relation to competition/antitrust law.

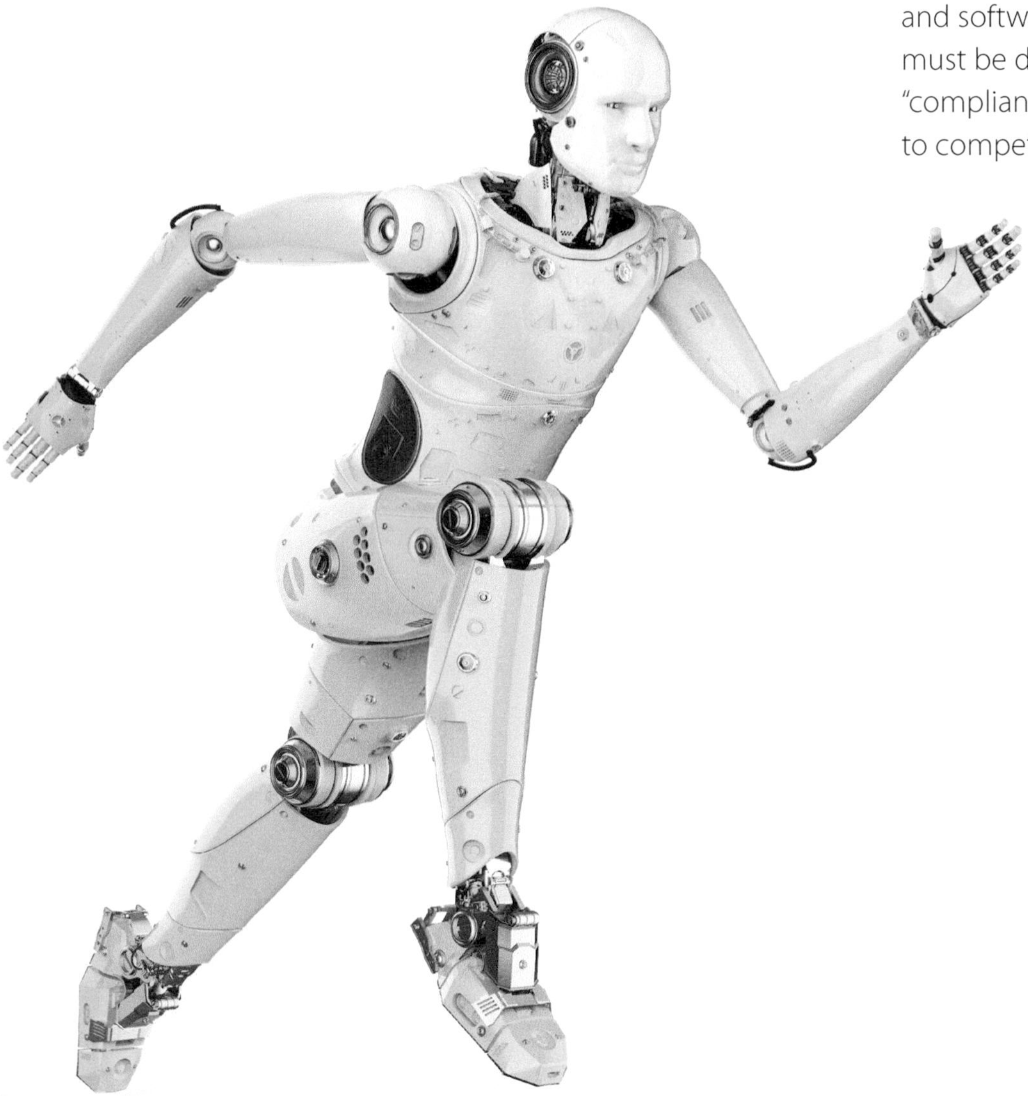

6

OPEN DATA AND FAIR COMPETITION

CHAPTER LEAD

John Buyers | Osborne Clarke LLP, United Kingdom

Amanda Ge | CMS, China

Catherine Hammon | Osborne Clarke LLP, United Kingdom

Erin Hicks-Tibbles | Left Step Logic, LLC, United States

Arie van Wijngaarden | McCarthy Tétrault LLP, Canada

Elijha Wong | CMS, United Kingdom

I. Introduction

Like any other new technology, the commercial development and deployment of artificial intelligence (AI) based solutions takes place within the standard legal frameworks for business activities. Competition (anti-trust) laws are a key part of this compliance jigsaw.

Laws to prevent anti-competitive behaviour by business were first introduced by the U.S. Sherman Act of 1890. Such norms are now in place in the majority of developed and developing economies around the world. These aim to constrain businesses from preventing, hindering or distorting the free play of competition forces in a market. If a market is characterized by effective and active rivalry between the various businesses competing for customers, there will typically be downwards pressure on prices, upwards pressure on product and service quality, and pressure to innovate and differentiate, all of which should operate to the benefit of the customer. Within this frame of reference, competition law is essentially a public interest-based exception to the principle of freedom of contract and can operate to constrain businesses from acting as they might have wished, in order to prevent distortions to competition which would harm consumers or market structure.

Competition/antitrust regimes around the world are broadly consistent in that they are typically principle-based. They require that (a) competitive advantages must be fairly obtained (not achieved by agreement with a competitor) and (b) market power must not be exploited or artificially enhanced by conduct which exploits that power, or which has the effect of consolidating or reinforcing it by making it yet more difficult for others in the market to compete. The principles-based approach means that competition law is sector-agnostic—although there is currently a global debate as to whether the digital economy necessitates a new approach.

In considering the development of AI, competition law is relevant in various respects:

- The importance of data as a raw material for developing most forms of deep learning AI has been explained in the Introduction. Access to data is key. However, data is often considered to be proprietary and increasingly seen as a monetisable asset. Control of data could potentially generate a market-distorting advantage in the development of AI. As the UK's Furman Report recently noted, "to the degree that the next technological revolution centres around artificial intelligence and machine learning, then the companies most able to take advantage of it may well be the existing large companies because of the importance of data for the successful use of these tools."[1] Competition law offers some tools to address these concerns. The many initiatives for open data and legal initiatives to encourage data-sharing are an alternative way to address this concern. These issues are considered in Section II below.

- AI is being developed in various ways in the commercial landscape, including as a proprietary technology, through collaboration, or as an open source technology. The different options for developing AI systems raise various competition law considerations, which will be discussed in Section III below.

- Finally, there is increasing understanding of the ways in which the implementation of AI systems could generate consumer harm. Competition authorities around the world are examining whether the current regimes have sufficient flexibility to be able to police any anti-competitive effects of using AI systems. Section IV below will look at these aspects.

II. Access to Data as a Key Input for the Development of AI

As explained in the Introduction, one of the characteristics of deep learning AI systems is that they require vast amounts of data. Data is a key "raw material," as the UK government's Department for Business, Energy & Industrial Strategy (BEIS) has observed.[2]

The impact of large datasets on competition has been considered in a number of fora, including the UK Furman Report,[3] the OECD Roundtable on "Big Data: Bringing Competition Policy to the Digital Era,"[4] the joint report of the French and German competition authorities on "Competition Law and Data,"[5] and the report of the Competition Bureau Canada on "Big data and innovation: key themes for competition policy in Canada."[6]

> *"The availability of data is crucial for [innovative] businesses and the continuing development of artificial intelligence which needs data to develop and code algorithms."*
>
> UK Government's Department for Business, Energy & Industrial Strategy (BEIS)

There is wide acknowledgement of the importance of data as a driver of the digital economy but no consensus as to whether current competition regimes are sufficient to ensure effective competition in digital markets. The Canadian Big Data report (cited above) concluded that existing powers were sufficient. In contrast, the UK Furman report took the opposite view and called for a new regulatory body and sector-specific obligations to ensure openness of data.

This section will consider how access to data can impact on the ability of businesses to compete in the development of AI systems.

Discussion Point

The concern is that there could be insufficient or sub-optimal rivalry around the development of new AI-based tools and applications, if access to data becomes a barrier to entry or expansion.

This is analogous to a traditional industry which is reliant on a particular raw material. If the sources of the raw material are limited in number and controlled by a limited number of the downstream producers, other producers may find it extremely difficult to source the raw material at a fair price, or on terms which are not putting them at a disadvantage to the raw material owners.

A. External constraints on access to data

Before considering the ways in which data might be shared, it is important to note that not all data can be freely disclosed. Depending on the data type, there may be external constraints on the use of data, from sources such as law or regulation. These constraints may not constitute absolute bars to accessing data, but may make it more complex or more expensive to secure access.

Copyright laws, which exist in the majority of developed and developing jurisdictions, may mean that data is visible and known but not lawfully accessible without a licence. It may be necessary to pay for a licence for copyrighted data and at the very least necessitate compliance checks to understand the approach of the relevant licensor.

Data protection laws may control the ways in which particular (usually personal and/or sensitive personal) data can be collected, shared or processed. Legal conditions and requirements must be adhered to if the data is to be lawfully handled. The EU's General Data Protection Regulation and the California Consumer Privacy Act of 2018 are well known examples which are discussed in our treatment of Principle 7—Privacy.

There has been an example of the impact of these rules on AI development in the UK. The Royal Free Hospital in Hampstead, London gave Google DeepMind data for around 1.6 million patients as part of a trial to test an AI system designed to identify signs of renal injury. The tool was a success but the hospital was sanctioned by the UK data protection authority. It had not informed the patients that their data would be shared in this way and the authority concluded that they would not have reasonably expected their records to be so used.[7]

It is important to note that these constraints are not insurmountable. In a different trial with a different UK hospital for a different AI diagnostic tool, Google DeepMind was provided with patient data in a manner which has not generated privacy concerns.[8]

Moreover, although privacy rules are strong in some jurisdictions, there is wide variation around the world in whether businesses can freely collect data about their customers and users. Even where privacy frameworks are strong, they do not typically apply to *any* data.

Competition law and privacy law sit alongside each other as complementary regimes. Indeed, respect for customer and consumer privacy is often promoted by businesses as a mark of quality and a competitive advantage. For example, Apple makes less use of customer data collected via its devices than many digital businesses. It was viewed as "taking a shot" at competitors in January 2019 with a huge advertisement prominently placed for those attending the Consumer Electronics Show in 2019. Apple's advert stated: "What happens on your iPhone, stays on your iPhone," promoting its data privacy policy as a competitive differentiator.[9]

Overall, the fact that there may be external or regulatory constraints on access to data is not treated as "unfair competition" or as a problem in itself in competition analysis, but as an aspect of the conditions of competition in a particular market.

B. Can data be a source of market power, creating "data-opolies"?

Access to data can also be restricted due to policy and strategy decisions by the business which holds it. A business which does not wish to offer its data as an open resource (discussed in Section II.D below) may seek to monetize it by licensing it to third parties. Alternatively, it may feel that the more profitable strategy is to reserve the dataset for its own exclusive use. In the latter case, the behaviour of the business concerned might raise competition concerns if it has the effect of limiting rivalry from competitors. Indeed, the question has been raised whether companies which hold considerable quantities of data that they have gathered from their customers or users have become upstream monopolists, the sole source of an essential raw material. As was observed to the UK Parliament's upper house in its review of AI, "Data is everything in machine learning, which means whoever gets access to data can have a big advantage."[10]

How did some businesses generate their vast data resources? In the context of the present discussion, a particularly significant path is that followed by many digital platforms (for example, online search engines, social media platforms, online marketplaces etc.). Often, the product or service provided by the platform is apparently free; the consumer or user pays nothing.[11] But this absence of payment is arguably only an absence of *financial* payment. As commentators have noted,[12] the users of a platform often "pay" in the form of data about themselves, or data generated from their interaction with the platform.

Secondly, these same markets are often two-sided, with revenue generated directly from a second, separate set of customers, in the form of advertisers. The platform is able to use the data sourced from the user group to enable advertisements to be targeted at their sought-for audience. Advertisers are typically the primary source of revenues for a platform so the desire to maximize sales to that set of customers increases the incentives to collect data from users. This can create a virtuous circle which may become increasingly difficult for smaller players to compete with. Data can therefore drive market concentration as well as increasingly the barriers to entry and expansion in that market.

EU Commissioner Margrethe Vestager has expressed concerns about the control of data.[13] Given the importance of data to AI, the control of data also presents concerns about the ability to foster innovation when data is privately controlled by limited number of entities. Both the UK Government[14] and Commissioner Vestager,[15] among others, have expressed such concerns.

> *"Competition can't work if just a few companies control a vital resource that you need to be able to compete—and if they refuse to share it with others. Right now, it looks as though data is becoming one of those vital resources. And if that's so in a particular case, then we need to make sure it's not monopolised by a few."*
>
> European Commissioner for Competition Margrethe Vestager

Case study: China

China offers an example of how data collection can drive and consolidate strength in a few large digital platforms. Its advantage in AI development has always been its access to large quantities of data.[16] Tech giants have been able to collect massive amounts of data due to lax privacy regulations and encouraging policies from the Chinese government to promote technological innovation. As a result, domestic tech leaders Baidu, Alibaba and Tencent ("BAT") have been able to rival their Western counterparts in utilizing big data to drive China's AI revolution, a country well on its way to achieving the goals set out in its "Made in China 2025" strategic plan and its AI-specific "A Next Generation Artificial Intelligence Development Plan"[17] to push for world leader status in AI by 2030.

From a straightforward data sourcing perspective, the core areas of data collection for BAT are split accordingly: Baidu, primarily as a search engine provider, collects traffic data; Alibaba's e-commerce dominance allows access to transaction data and credit data; whilst Tencent's one billion users worldwide provide a constant flow of consumer data through social messaging application WeChat. However, all three companies have now grown so large that they dominate the vast majority of the Chinese internet market, as well as integrating their expertise into various other industries through investment and data-sharing: in late August of 2018, it was reported that 50.8% of China's 124 unicorn companies were controlled or backed by BAT.[18] Use of any one of the BAT-related companies' applications is near unavoidable in daily life within any Chinese city, as the main dilemmas become which company the consumers should provide their data to. For example, purchasing e-commerce goods online through one of Alibaba's many platforms (Taobao, Tmall or JD) or purchasing clothes where most retailers only take payment through either WeChat Pay (Tencent) or AliPay (Alibaba).

Market power cannot be assumed from ownership of a large dataset

As discussed, many of the businesses at the leading edge of the development of AI systems draw on the vast collections of data which have been gathered from their primary products and platforms. Data collected for one purpose—perhaps individual tailoring of product recommendations, or facilitating targeted advertising, or optimizing search engine results—is already held within the business and available for redeployment to build new AI products. The OECD's Roundtable on Big Data observed that: "The ability to generate and process large datasets can ... be associated to [sic] market power, as a result of economies of scale, economies of scope and network effects, as well as real-time data feedback loops."[19] However, market power is not an inevitable inference from ownership of a large database. The OECD Roundtable also observed: "The control over a large volume of data is a not sufficient factor to establish market power, as nowadays a variety of data can be easily and cheaply collected by small companies—for instance, through point of sale terminals, web logs and sensors—or acquired from the broker industry."

It is important to note that the type of data which might be needed to train the AI system will depend what the AI system is designed to achieve. As a result, there may be many distinct markets for the supply of data, each defined by reference to the particular functionality for which the training data is needed. This is similar to the pharmaceutical sector, for example, where the economic markets for particular drugs are driven by their clinical uses. This is logical—there is no competition, for example, between a liver disease treatment and an eczema treatment, because a doctor would not switch from prescribing one to the other if the first became too expensive—they perform completely different functions. In the same way, markets for data may also be defined narrowly. For example, a developer would not procure a dataset of labelled images if they were developing an AI system to generate financial investment decisions.

Moreover, it cannot be assumed that because a business has a strong market position in one area of its business and holds a large amount of data, that it would also be considered to have market strength in the supply of data. Detailed assessment would be necessary to understand whether there were alternative sources of data which might be used to achieve the intended functionality. In addition to the potential to build data sets from scratch or to source them via the data broking industry or an AI as a Service provider, many governments hold huge data sets about many aspects of the economy and their citizens. These are increasingly available for use under open data initiatives (discussed further in Section II.D below) and may also offer substitute sources to privately held datasets.

C. Can competition law be used to control "data-opolies"?

It certainly does not follow from the fact that a business has a significant competitive advantage that there is an antitrust issue. In a market where there is effective competition between a numbers of different competitors, the fact that one holds a particularly strong data resource which is giving it an advantage in the development of AI systems is unlikely to be a *legal* concern—any *commercial* difficulties are part of the challenges of normal competition.

However, most jurisdictions draw a distinction between markets where there is effective rivalry between competitors, and those where the market is dominated by one (or a small number of) very strong player(s). Even then, market power is not sanctioned in itself, but businesses which enjoy market power are typically prevented from leveraging that power to the detriment of consumers.[20]

It bears repeating, however, that the fact that a business holds a deep treasure trove of data which it can draw on to develop AI systems is not *in itself* a competition concern.[21] On the other hand, the commercial decisions which it takes in relation to that data could be considered illegal if they have the effect, broadly, of exploiting customers or making it even more difficult for other businesses to compete. So if a business wants to access an unmatchable dataset which is kept by a powerful competitor for its own exclusive use, are there ways in which competition law would help it to secure such access?

Refusal of access

Requiring a business to grant access to proprietary assets or facilities is one of the more intrusive sanctions in the arsenal of a competition enforcement authority. This will typically occur only where the assets constitute an "essential facility," without which others cannot compete. It is not unusual to find access obligations in regulatory frameworks for industries which were formerly state utilities or "natural monopolies," often with extensive physical infrastructure networks. It is less common for such a requirement to be imposed in an individual case, although most of the cases are also infrastructure-related, such as ports or gas distribution networks.

However, these cases have been extended to other areas, including a requirement to grant access to data. In an EU case, three television companies refused to license their broadcasting schedules to a business which wanted to create a consolidated weekly television programme guide. The court ordered that a compulsory licence was appropriate. This was because the refusal was preventing a new competitor from entering the market and stopping a new product from being created for which there was consumer demand. The emphasis here was on the fact that the refusal would have an exclusionary effect, reinforcing the market power of the incumbents.[22] Further essential facilities cases have clarified that a facility (such as a distribution network) will only be essential if it would not be economically viable to develop a similar facility.[23] The enforcement authorities have since stated that they will only consider imposing an access obligation where the withheld product or service is objectively necessary to be able to compete effectively on a downstream market, and the refusal is likely to lead to elimination of effective competition on that market and to result in consumer harm.[24]

Returning to the specifics of accessing data to enable development and training of an AI system, there is no overriding principle that even if a business is found to enjoy market power due to the control of particular data, the dataset concerned must be shared. As discussed, competition/antitrust law does have some potential tools to deal with the issue of data-opolies having datasets which competitors cannot access and are unable to replicate. These cases, however, are likely to be very contentious and challenging for smaller competitors to fight effectively, given the high bar on necessary evidence and the deep pockets of the likely defendants.

Moreover, there are different attitudes around the world to using competition enforcement tools against the tech giants. The EU and European domestic enforcement authorities have a much stronger track record of investigating and sanctioning digital economy businesses than, for example, the U.S. authorities, where taking action against businesses from any sector which have market power has not been an administrative priority for some years.

D. Initiatives and calls for more open data

Rather than using competition frameworks to oblige dominant businesses to grant access to data for AI development, an alternative approach is to encourage the voluntary sharing of data. Open access initiatives facilitate the free distribution of research online pursuant to standard open access licensing terms which are analogous to Open Source software licensing.[25] The aim is to promote the re-use of public, private, scientific and academic data in order to facilitate innovation in AI. This model is particularly attractive for newer entrants in the AI space who lack access to the necessary data to develop their ideas into reality.

Several international open data initiatives have emerged with a focus on making data available for AI research and development. In 2013, the G8 Nationals agreed to the G8 Open Data Charter.[26] The Charter commits members to the principles of open data by default, providing a high quality and quantity of datasets, ensuring data is usable by AI, releasing data for improved governance, and releasing data for innovation. G8 members further committed to releasing data in high-value areas based on economic potential and the importance of government accountability.

Similar principles to the G8 Open Data Charter can be found in the International Open Data Charter.[27] This agreement is a collaboration between individuals and organizations intended to advance open data globally. Currently there are over 60 government signatories and 40 organizational signatories to the Charter. There are also many open data initiatives at the national level, including:

United States

The United States has long had a strong tradition of open source software such as Linux and data sharing amongst the private technology developer community. There are also various programmes to facilitate data access in the public sector. The 2013 Federal Open Data Policy requires new government data to be made available to the public in open, machine readable formats.[28] The result has been the creation of the Data.gov program, which is a single data inventory and published listing of public data for all levels of government within the United States. Currently there are over 300,000 datasets on Data.gov which can be freely leveraged.[29]

Canada

Like the United States, the Canadian government has made open data a strategic priority. The Canadian Institutes of Health Research (CIHR), the Natural Sciences and Engineering Research Council of Canada (NSERC) and the Social Sciences and Humanities Research Council of Canada (SSHRC) are federal research granting agencies which have published an Open Access Policy on Publications.[30] The aim of this initiative is to ensure that publications resulting from CIHR, NSERC, or SSHRC research funding be freely accessible within 12 months of publication. The Government of Canada has also created the Open Data Inventory of public sector datasets which are freely available online.[31] There are further open data initiatives in place at the provincial and municipal government level.

European Union

The European Commission views AI as a key topic of the Commission's Digital Single Market strategy.[32] To facilitate access to open data within the EU, the Commission has sponsored the EU Data Economy initiative.[33] The goals of the Data Economy initiative is to encourage the use and re-use of public sector information as well as providing greater guidance on access to scientific and private sector information. The cornerstone of the Data Economy initiative is the review of the Public Sector Information (PSI) Directive which governs the use of government open data within the EU.[34] The review is aimed at reducing barriers to the free flow of information such as data localization requirements. The European Commission has centralized datasets from the EU in the EU Open Data Portal.[35]

United Kingdom

In the United Kingdom AI Review, "Growing the AI Industry in the UK," Professor Dame Wendy Hall and Jérôme Pesenti noted that more open data in more sectors is highly beneficial for the development of AI applications.[36] The AI Review recommended reducing transaction costs of accessing data, particularly for innovative start-ups, by the implementation of data trusts, requiring public research funding to ensure publication of the underlying data, facilitating text and data mining, and encouraging the development of AI-related skills.[37] These recommendations were addressed in the UK Government's AI Sector Deal announced in April, 2018.[38] The AI Sector Deal is closely related initiative to the UK's Open Data Initiative.[39] The Open Data Initiative advances the G8 Open Data Charter principles by providing commitments to open data by default, appropriate dataset quality and usability.

The UK also has a significant concentration of private initiatives promoting the development of open data. For example, the Open Data Institute is an independent, non-profit, non-partisan organization which was founded by the inventor of the world wide web Sir Tim Berners-Lee and AI expert Sir Nigel Shadbolt to support the use of open data.[40] The Open Data Institute works with public and private sector entities to coordinate data sharing and advocates for ethical data use.

The Furman report has recently recommended that the UK should introduce legislation to require greater sharing of data by digital businesses. It noted: "There may be situations where opening up some of the data held by digital businesses and providing access on reasonable terms is the essential and justified step needed to unlock competition."[41]

Australia

The Government of Australia released its Public Data Policy Statement in December, 2015.[42] The Policy Statement commits the government to optimize the use of public data and adopt the G8 Open Data Charter principles. Australian Government entities are committed to publish government data via data.gov.au in a machine-readable format with API access. Crucially this data is governed by a Creative Commons licence by default unless the Cabinet decides otherwise.

China

China, by contrast, has a closed ecosystem of data in respect of both inbound data collection and outbound data-sharing, in order to promote domestic AI development. Although open data is increasingly promoted within China, such resources are generally not made available to non-Chinese businesses. Correspondingly, Chinese AI developers are typically not able to access data from other jurisdictions. China is, of course, a huge country with no lack of potential sources of data. Where such data is accessible, the closed ecosystem reserves this valuable resource for the domestic AI sector. But these restrictions may also potentially harm Chinese AI development: the closed ecosystem means that Chinese businesses cannot freely benefit from global open data.

However, government and industry stakeholders realize that more progress is needed in relation to open data within China. They have become aware of the constraints flowing from the lack of availability of international open data sources and the limitations of relying on purely domestic sources of open data. There are numerous AI development policies which would benefit from data-sharing as a key collaborative tool to enhance domestic tech company development capabilities. As a consequence, tech giants and key individuals are beginning to join the open data movement, and "Open access to big data" was a key topic for discussion during the annual *Two Sessions* event of 2018 in China, with top legislative and advisory bodies in attendance.

E. Legal mechanisms to foster data cooperation and sharing

The concerns around the risks from data-opolies and concentrations of data ownership have spurred calls for legal frameworks beyond competition law enforcement to address these issues. This requires examining options such as data trusts, data sharing agreements, and public sector programs to facilitate access to data.

Practical challenges of data sharing

There are several practical challenges of data sharing which are worth noting:

- Data may not be in a form which is readily shareable. Historic datasets in particular may require significant investment in preparatory work before they can be shared. An organization's data quality may become the key determinant of its attractiveness as a data sharing partner.

- A further challenge to data sharing is the potential for misalignment between the for-profit private sector and not-for-profit public sector. Private sector organizations may not consider data sharing to be in their best interests because of potential restrictions on commercialization imposed upon universities and other public research organizations. In this situation, consistency of approach is essential. A harmonious regulatory environment, in which commercial innovation from public and private bodies is encouraged, is in everyone's best interest.

- Cross-border data sharing is also a significant challenge. For example, due to China's closed data ecosystem, cross-border pooling of data may be difficult. As noted above, tight control of data for AI development is a double-edged sword. A country could establish exclusive control over this resource for its native companies and research institutes. On the other hand, if data is being shared across platforms and countries, other businesses or bodies could benefit from global data sharing, while protectionist nations remain closed off.

Data sharing agreements

Perhaps the most obvious method of facilitating access to data is for organizations to agree formally to share data with each other. There will be a number of issues to consider, including data ownership or control, intellectual property and any licensing arrangements, compliance with data privacy requirements, the practicalities of receiving, storing and deleting the data and cybersecurity obligations.

Such issues are not straightforward and require time and energy to negotiate a data sharing agreement in order to get access to a very large pool of data. Where agreements are entered into with multiple stakeholders, there is the further concern of whether an entity can combine data governed by different data sharing agreements.

Until market practices develop around pricing access to big data, this can operate as an additional barrier to AI implementation.

Finally, there is little developed commercial precedent for how to price data sets. This is made more complex by the "black box" characteristics of deep learning AI systems. It may not be impossible to know how much a developed black box AI is relying on data from a given source. Similarly, it may not be possible to know, at the outset, how successful and therefore valuable the AI system outputs will be. Consequently it becomes very difficult to commercially value training data.

Data trusts

Data trusts were recommended as a means of facilitating access to data for AI development or deployment in the UK's independent Pesenti/Hall review of the AI industry.[43] Essentially, a data trust operates similarly to a patent pool. Parties to the trust contribute data towards a central repository which is governed by a framework outlining overall governance of the collaboration and the rights and obligations of parties. The framework could determine what data will be shared, its authorized uses, data transfer, storage, and destruction, and the conditions for allocation of financial returns.

Data trusts offer several possible benefits. One of the key challenges to the development of AI can be that individual players do not have sufficient data to train an AI system properly. By pooling data, trust participants are able obtain access to data which they would not readily have on their own.

Global benefits of data trusts

Data trusts also address one of the challenges of data sharing agreements—that they are complex to negotiate. Signing up to a common framework under a data trust bypasses the need to negotiate a series of bilateral data sharing agreements. This significantly reduces transaction costs for sourcing data for the development of AI.

The data trust model works best when there is a diversity of organizations with useful data in a given sector. For example the transport sector contains useful data from governments (e.g., stop signal information), academia (e.g., safety research), original equipment manufacturers (e.g., analytics from the vehicle), software providers (e.g., weather and road conditions) and insurers (e.g., telematics).

Pooling initiatives of this sort offer significant promise for the future in boosting private sharing of data.

F. Competition law constraints on information-sharing

"Data" can take many forms and cover many topics. In any discussion of sharing data, it is worth recalling that competitors need to take care when exchanging information. In Europe, the broad principle is that it can be illegal to share commercial information which would reduce the strategic uncertainty between competitors, thereby limiting the incentives to compete. The majority of data used for training AI will fall outside this category as it is probably not sensitive strategic information. But the risk is important to bear in mind as the distinction between legitimate, unobjectionable information-sharing and quasi-cartel behaviour can be grey, and sanctions for breaching competition rules are typically significant.

There is a further potential concern that where data (even if not sensitive) is shared by competitors and used in AI systems for similar purposes, their strategic commercial decisions could converge and become very similar. Pricing, for example, might become harmonized because all players in the market are using the same input data in similar AI systems to generate automated pricing decisions. As is explained below in Section IV.A, parallel pricing is not illegal in itself absent some degree of shared intention between the competitors, but it could lead to less effective competition. One solution might be to ensure that not *all* data is pooled by the competitors, so that a degree of variation exists between their respective "raw material" data.

III. Development of AI Systems as a Proprietary, Collaborative or Open Technology and Macro Level Competition in AI Innovation

Much of the digital economy is underpinned by AI technology (including search engines, personalized recommendations for e-commerce, social media properties such as facial recognition and suggesting new contacts). But AI systems are increasingly being used across the commercial landscape in a huge variety of ways, from driverless car technology in the transport sector, to chat bots for retail sector customer services, to quantitative investment systems in the financial sector, to grid-balancing systems in the energy sector, to digital twin technology and generative design systems in the manufacturing sector.

For such innovations to thrive, it is essential that businesses are able to gain access to AI systems. This section will consider the ways in which AI can be sourced. The discussion will first consider AI as a proprietary technology which can be withheld for the developer's own use, or monetized through licensing. Whilst competition law would not normally interfere with this prerogative, there have been calls to increase scrutiny of mergers which could consolidate the market strength of large tech businesses or eliminate potential future competitors. Collaborative strategies such as joint ventures for AI development will then be considered, followed by open source initiatives. Finally, this section will look at public sector initiatives to promote and stimulate the development of AI.

A. AI as a proprietary technology

Developing AI as a proprietary technology means that the AI technology is controlled by a single firm. That firm may choose to sell the technology to another firm or license it to one or more firms. Firms that are not licensees do not have access to the technology and nor does the public. In fact, many of the major AI developers also sell (some of) their technology to third parties (or release it as open source, discussed in Section III.C below). The growth of AI as a Service from businesses such as Google, Amazon, Microsoft, means that it is increasingly possible to deploy AI systems and/or rent associated datasets without needing to be able to develop (or curate) them from scratch. This is important in particular because of the scarcity of talent in relation to AI development.

However, it is also possible that a business may decide to reserve exclusive use of its AI system for itself. As discussed above in relation to access to data, competition law does not seek to prevent businesses from developing competitive strength through innovation and winning customers. Organic growth and the option to retain exclusive use of proprietary technology is the reward for competitive success.

The exception to this general approach is where a business has grown to the point where it has gained market strength such that it becomes difficult for others in the market to win market share. As explained above in relation to access to data, dominant businesses may not be free to act as they wish if it would cause consumer harm. As also discussed in Section II.C above, there are (limited) circumstances where enforcement authorities may require a business to open up access to proprietary technology. But such cases are controversial, difficult to bring and often not an administrative priority. Tooling an algorithmic system to reinforce a dominant position by disadvantaging competitors has been found to be unlawful—Google was fined €2.42 billion by the EU Commission for structuring its search results system to favour its own shopping comparison service over those of competitors.[44]

Although gaining market strength through organic growth is not prohibited, merger control scrutiny is used to prevent a business from gaining or further consolidating market power through acquisition. To avoid over-burdening businesses with red tape, smaller mergers typically fall below the jurisdictional thresholds. Merger control is important in relation to AI-driven competition because the sector is at the same time characterized by a vibrant start-up community with a track record of disruption, but also by large platforms which compete in many areas of the digital economy. It is common for the larger businesses to acquire innovative start-up businesses to boost their own development work. These mergers often—perfectly legitimately—pass under the regulatory radar because the scale and revenues of the target are too low to trigger merger control review. That said, even where a tech sector acquisition is reviewed by the authorities, it is unusual for the transaction not to be cleared. It is a notable statistic that of the 400 acquisitions made globally by the five largest digital businesses in the last 10 years, none have been blocked and very few have had conditions attached to clearance.[45]

There is a concern from some quarters that an overly short term view is taken in reviewing these mergers. Are small innovative competitors effectively being gobbled up by the incumbents before they have the chance to grow into a significant source of competition? The Furman report observes:

> In dynamic digital markets, long-run effects are key to whether a merger will harm competition and consumers. Could the company that is being bought grow into a competitor to the platform? Is the source of its value an innovation that, under alternative ownership, could make the market less concentrated? Is it being bought for access to consumer data that will make the platform harder to challenge?

In Germany, merger control thresholds have been altered to include criteria based on deal value, to capture acquisitions for a high price but where the target business has low revenues. A similar change has been considered at EU level (initially rejected, it now is being reconsidered). The UK Furman report suggests instead that those digital businesses which (it proposes) are designated as having "strategic market status" should be required to report *all* intended acquisitions to the competition authorities (not just those which meet merger control jurisdictional thresholds). It also proposes changing the substantive test by reference to which mergers should be assessed. Currently the UK authorities will consider whether a merger is more likely than not to give rise to a substantial lessening of competition (the U.S., Australian and EU tests are similar, as are those in most European countries). The report proposes to extend the test so that it would also be possible to take into account the *scale* of the harm. Thus it might become possible to take action in relation to a merger where harm was not more likely than not, but would be very significant if it did occur.

B. AI as a collaborative technology

Many businesses do not have the resources to develop AI systems unilaterally, in-house. They may wish to undertake joint research and development, or to buy in expertise through consultancies or other specialists who can work with them to develop their desired AI system. Where AI has been developed in academia, the institution may not be well placed to put their innovation into commercial development.

Where AI is developed or put into commercial production in collaboration, competition law must be complied with. The relationship between the joint venture parties must be structured carefully in relation to the rights arising out of the innovation and in relation to its future commercial exploitation. Co-ordination between entities which are not actual or potential competitors carries a much lower risk of competition concerns than co-ordination between competitors.

There is nothing particularly novel as regards AI in this respect:

- Where collaboration is structured as a commercial arrangement, it must be acceptable in light of the usual competition prohibitions on anti-competitive arrangements. This is important because of the risk that legitimate collaboration spills over into unlawful cartel-like behaviour, with harm to the consumer.
- Where collaboration takes a structural form, for example with a corporate vehicle for the joint venture, it may be subject to merger control rules.
- Where collaboration takes the form of industry initiatives with many participants, perhaps to set standards, the usual rules apply to ensure that the standard is not leveraged to exclude some competitors, or that it is not used to cartelize the market.

- Where collaboration and standardization initiatives involves standard essential patents, there is precedent from other sectors in relation to the licensing of standard essential patents on FRAND terms etc.[46]

C. AI as an open source technology

Notwithstanding that much private AI research and development may be kept proprietary, open source software development also plays a significant role. Some of the top machine learning, deep learning and other AI systems are available under open source licences.[47]

Open Source

The philosophy underpinning open source software is that it enables individuals, government institutions and corporations alike to collaborate in order to learn and create better, together.

According to IBM, the three key principles of open source platforms are the growing importance of code, content, and community.[48]

"Code is about open source software with test cases. Content includes open data, documentation, and tutorials. Community is all about people in a wide range of roles and organizations co-creating value and learning faster together."

Open Source and AI at IBM

But although the open availability of AI systems is clearly appealing and advantageous to the community as a whole, what is the appeal from a business perspective? There are many large corporate participants in open source projects, including major digital economy names such as Google, Facebook, Amazon and Microsoft, as well as IBM.

The answer includes the following considerations:

- Although a business might lose licensing revenue by opening up access to their software, its quality can often be enhanced, functionality extended and generally improved at much lower cost than if this work was all done internally. Open source projects offer a way to access a vast pool of talent without the cost of employment.
- Open source projects can also help to build support for a particular technology which may give it greater market share and stimulate more businesses to develop compatible systems or products (for example, the core elements of Google's Android mobile operating system are open source).
- Finally, many in the development community feel that since they have often benefitted from being able to use open source software themselves, they should return the favour by releasing code which they themselves have developed. This philosophy is seen across the software development ecosystem but also specifically in relation to AI systems.

As well as the Android platform, Google has released its TensorFlow AI framework as open source software. TensorFlow is the engine behind Google Images and the speech recognition systems found in the Google app.[49]

Open source projects are also emerging from China's normally closed ecosystem. Baidu Research Institute has released an open-source AI system that offers tumour pathology detection capabilities, using deep learning to improve greatly on current biopsy image analysis.[50] The algorithm will be added to existing machines that analyses pathology slides and will gain access to data sets from hospitals in China to expand its application of use from breast cancer to other types, subject of course to further regulatory developments. Baidu also released its autonomous driving system technology as open source software in 2017.[51] By early 2019, it reported 130 global partners using its platform for their autonomous driving projects.[52]

There are also specific private sector initiatives promoting open access to AI. These include OpenAI, which aims to develop and share innovative AI systems through free collaboration. Projects have included releasing a toolkit for building AI systems through reinforcement learning, using reinforcement learning to take on professional gamers in *Dota 2* and using reinforcement learning to train a robotic hand with "unprecedented dexterity." It has also issued a report on warnings on the risks around the malicious use of AI.[53] A recent high profile project involved developing a text-generating AI system which was apparently so good that it has not so far been released to the public "due to our concerns about malicious applications of the technology."[54]

Of course in many cases, a business will deal with its different AI systems in different ways, depending on their strategic importance and state of development. As noted, many platforms offer AI as a Service as part of their wider software or hosting services. Other software may be released as open source to encourage related products and software. Some technology will, however be kept proprietary and confidential.

D. Public sector investment models to stimulate growth and competition

Initiatives to promote open data have been considered in Section II.D and II.E above. This section considers broader public initiatives to support the development of AI more generally.

In its Industry Strategy white paper, the UK's BEIS identified AI and data as one of four "Grand Challenges" for the UK to master.[55] Additionally, the UK's Hall/Pesenti report gave recommendations on how the public and private sectors could collaborate on skills and infrastructure, in order to implement an effective AI strategy in the UK.[56] The UK government subsequently established the AI Sector Deal in 2018 as the first commitment from the government and industry to co-operate to grow the AI industry through features such as a £0.95 billion support package in order to stimulate access to data and build a skilled workforce.[57] The UK government aims to continue stimulating existing industry growth pioneered by investment in the UK from AI leaders such as DeepMind and Amazon.

The European Commission, under the EU Digital Single Market strategy, has put forward wide-scale initiatives and policies encouraging a competitive AI development industry. In a Communication on Artificial

Intelligence for Europe on 25 April 2018,[58] the European Commission put forward a European approach to AI based on three pillars. This includes increasing annual investments in AI by 70% under the Horizon 2020 programme, with aims to reach €1.5 billion between 2018 and 2020.[59] It will also support business-education partnerships and workforce training to prepare for socio-economic changes brought about by AI. Finally, it will develop an ethical and legal framework for AI. The focus on AI innovation continues to grow within the EU with more initiatives such as the AI Alliance established by the European Commission and the INSPIRE Knowledge Base[60] for sharing environmental spatial data among public sector organizations.

In China, collaborative innovation projects between government entities and tech companies are showing that the public-private sector combination can reap rewards in the future. The city of Beijing plans to invest US$2 billion in an AI development park, which would house up to 400 AI enterprises and a national AI lab to encourage development in the sector. An AI park has already been established in one of China's numerous tech-centric cities, Hangzhou, backed by a fund of RIB 10 billion. Also making headway in innovative collaboration between the private and public sectors are the unprecedented projects on AI in the judicial system: in November 2017, the Chinese government announced plans to build national AI platforms in partnership with four companies. Alongside BAT, AI-specialists iFlyTek have made arguably the most progress in this area. Leading the "Artificial Intelligence + Court" project, which focuses on a smart filing system, voice, text and image recognition and an intelligent trial and case management system, iFlyTek has helped reduced the time of court hearings by 30% in China.[61]

IV. The Potential for AI to Generate Competitive Harm

The digital economy has radically transformed both how businesses interact and the interface with consumers. The increasing use of AI to automate processes and decision-making is bringing further change. As noted above, the fact that competition law is principle-based has made it flexible and adaptable to new commercial strategies and business models, although some are now questioning whether this continues to be the case.

This final section will consider the competition issues which could arise from deployment of AI systems in the commercial environment and in the interactions between the market players, and with their customers.

Digital markets are creating new challenges and a number of competition enforcement authorities are actively investigating whether the legal regimes that they enforce, the economic thought which underpins market analysis and the tools at their disposal, remain adequate.

A. Overview of the potential issues

There are various areas where AI systems can generate market behaviour which could breach competition law. Many of the specific concerns focus on the impact of algorithmic pricing systems, including price monitoring, price matching and personalized pricing tools. The UK Furman report recently considered the impact of AI systems on competition and observed: "At present, it is hard to predict whether greater use of algorithms will lead to algorithmic collusion or personalized pricing in future, and there is no evidence that harmful personalized pricing is widespread. But these are areas with potential to move fast, where it will be important to stay alert to potential harms." Further monitoring was recommended.

AI tools supporting illegal pricing practices

Price-matching software is in wide commercial use. The EU Commission found in the 2017 final report on its e-commerce sector inquiry that a majority of retailers track their competitors' prices using automatic systems and two thirds also adjust their own prices automatically in response.[62] These systems are not objectionable in themselves but could be used to facilitate or aggravate illegal conduct.

It is illegal for independent businesses to fix prices between them—pricing should be decided unilaterally based on market conditions and financial considerations for the business in question (such as fixed and variable costs, promotion strategies, discounting policies etc.). This prohibition applies (a) to competitors seeking to fix prices between them and also (b) to suppliers, which cannot prevent their distributors from setting their own prices (although recommended or maximum retail prices can be agreed).

As regards price fixing, software has been documented as having been used to implement a cartel arrangement. The U.S. Department of Justice[63] and the UK's Competition and Markets Authority[64] both sanctioned a cartel between two businesses selling posters on Amazon Marketplace which used pricing software to make sure their prices were aligned in accordance with their cartel arrangements.

As regards resale price maintenance, the EU Commission noted in its e-commerce sector report that: "With pricing software, detecting deviations from 'recommended' retail prices takes a matter of seconds and manufacturers are increasingly able to monitor and influence retailers' price setting."[65] Algorithmic pricing software can also cause problems where it exacerbates the impact of illegal pricing. The Commission is currently investigating[66] whether suppliers of various consumer electronics have been preventing online resellers from setting their own prices and a particular concern is that "the effect of these suspected price restrictions may be aggravated due to the use by many online retailers of pricing software that automatically adapts retail prices to those of leading competitors." The concern appears to be that the suppliers could generate a wide impact on market pricing by controlling the pricing of a few key downstream resellers, since automated price-matching tools monitoring those key suppliers would have followed their lead.

AI facilitating legal but damaging price collusion

Tacit Collusion

One of the more difficult areas for competition enforcement is where there is no active "coming together" to reach agreement about prices, but competitors nevertheless act in a parallel manner. This is known as "tacit collusion."

Unless there is some evidence of explicit co-ordination, tacit collusion is not illegal, even though it may be damaging to the market. This is not a new problem—the classic example is of neighbouring petrol stations which watch each other's pricing closely. It is not illegal if petrol station B, seeing petrol station A's prices go up, decides to follow and raise its prices (and margins) too, instead of keeping its prices lower and winning business from petrol station A.[67] It would be illegal for the petrol stations to agree that they should both increase prices but not for prices to rise due to their independent decisions. It can be very difficult to identify when aligned pricing is the result of legitimate intelligent adaptation to the existing or anticipated conduct of competitors, versus when it is the consequence of direct or indirect contact with a view to illegally influencing the conduct of competitors.

The OECD's Competition Division held a roundtable discussion on "Algorithms and competition" in June 2017. The background paper discusses the risk that AI systems may make it easier to reach and sustain tacit collusion, in various ways (the risks of harmonized pricing from putting pooled data through similar AI systems has been discussed in Section II.F above). Price competition would become muted if competing businesses used the same algorithm to set their pricing strategy, as the system would presumably generate the same responses to market changes. Fast-responding software might make it easier to test out whether competitors would follow a signalled price rise,[68] as well as to maintain adherence to a price-fixing agreement in dynamic markets where prices move often. The OECD paper notes that deep learning pricing algorithms could even generate cartels in effect and in substance which management was completely unaware of. This would not, currently, be illegal because there must be some element of explicit co-ordination.

The problem is therefore that algorithmic pricing could make tacit collusion more common in more markets and that it would not be illegal, notwithstanding that it would be damaging to customers because normal price competition would not be in operation. The difficulty goes to the heart of the competition law norms—the pre-requisite for the illegality of the competitors' coordinated conduct is that there is an agreement between them, however minimally expressed.

Personalisation

A separate problem is that of personalized pricing, facilitated by AI systems. The UK's BEIS Green Paper on Modernising Consumer Markets noted that consumer data can be used by firms to personalize consumers' experience online, so that consumers are shown different prices for the same product,[69] with "each consumer being charged a price that is a function [of]—but not necessarily equal [to]—to [sic] his or her willingness to pay."[70] Often a key driver of pricing will be the individual customer's willingness to pay. Discriminating between customers is not illegal under competition law unless the supplier is in a position of market strength (and may still be acceptable if the difference in treatment is objectively justifiable). Where the supplier does not have a strong market position (or as the OECD has noted, where abusive conduct by dominant businesses is either not prohibited or rarely investigated),[71] this is more a consumer law issue than a competition law issue.[72]

A further foreseeable issue with AI systems and competition law is where AI could in the future be used to drive "smart" connected appliances which include automated purchasing (for example, the expected development of smart fridges which will automatically reorder milk when sensors indicate supplies are low). Although consumers may welcome the convenience, there is a risk that the passive nature of the purchasing will allow prices to drift upwards. The ability of consumers to switch their custom to a different supplier is one of the drivers of price competition: inattention to automated purchasing could clearly dampen countervailing customer purchasing power.

Personalization of pricing can also operate to reduce pricing transparency. If it is difficult to discover a competitor's pricing it may be more difficult to win customers with competitive offers. Where personalization is enabled by customer profiling which draws on proprietary big data, the problem may be exacerbated for competitors who do not have similar data and cannot personalize their pricing offer to the same extent. This potential increase in barriers to entry/expansion is a competition concern.

Another aspect of personalization is the use of AI to generate personalized feeds of proposed products or services to a particular customer. Based on the individual person's pattern of past shopping, past clicks, confirmed "likes" etc., the AI system might propose particular products. The Canadian parliament has considered the impact of personalization and whether personalized feeds could even generate unconscious habits.[73]

The competition concern in this context is that, (similar to the "echo chamber" or filter bubble which can be created by personalized news feeds), personalization of offerings could operate to make it more difficult for an alternative supplier to gain the attention of that customer. This issue was recently highlighted by EU Commissioner Margrethe Vestager.[74]

> *"When an algorithm makes it harder to find rivals' products, that could deny those rivals the chance to compete."*
>
> European Commissioner for Competition Margrethe Vestager

As explained, none of these situations are likely to be characterized as illegal as such (absent market power) but the impact of AI-driven pricing on market conditions could be negative nevertheless. Competition authorities in the UK and many EU countries have powers to conduct a market investigation or sector inquiry, which allows the authority to review the health of a whole market, even if there is no illegal conduct. Legal pricing strategies which cause market forces to be muted (as in these examples) are potential targets for such investigations.

Network effects and strong platforms

Finally, AI systems create challenges for competition enforcement where they underpin the strength of tech platforms which use big data and AI as core inputs. Many of these platforms enjoy network effects: the more users who use the platform, the more data can be collected to improve the underlying AI, which in turn makes the platform operate better, drawing more people to it, etc. For social media, the more users it has, the more it draws people to it, which again, increases the draw. Many of the big tech businesses operate in two-sided markets where products can be obtained for free, generating interest and attention which then drive advertising sales, which enable more products to be given to the consumer for free. These virtuous circles typically make the platforms function increasingly better.

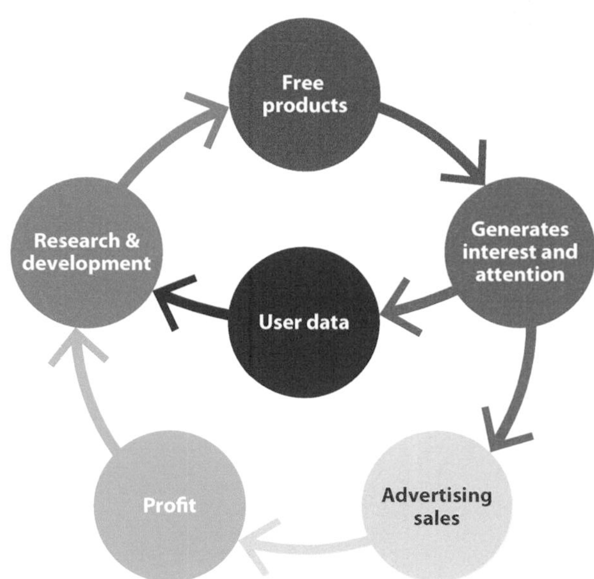

But network effects are difficult in competition law terms. Competition starts to be "for the market" rather than "in the market"—i.e., there is a "winner takes all" or "winner takes most" effect. It can be difficult for smaller competitors to win market share, particularly if customers are not inclined to "multi-home" and use more than one platform for the same function. Market forces may therefore be muted and competition may not be fully effective.

Again, this is not a new problem (many markets have been restructured to introduce more competition, including former utilities markets, stock exchanges etc.). But it is another way in which AI can operate to shape markets which is difficult for competition law to police.

Personalization and profiling (discussed above) can also operate to reinforce network effects. Personalization might increase the loyalty of a user to a particular platform because it generates content that is useful and appropriate to that user's preferences. As the Canadian parliament heard, the economic incentive of advertising sales drives the wish to maximize user engagement with a platform.[75] But this profile-driven loyalty can potentially further increase the challenge for a competing platform without the ability to offer a similar level of personalization.

One proposed solution to this issue is often focused on data portability. Access to individual data held by platform A about a user might make it easier for platform B to entice that user away if the data collected by platform A can be transferred to enable platform B to offer a similar degree of personalization etc.

B. Reviews of whether existing competition regimes, analytical approaches and enforcement tools are fit for purpose in the digital age

The challenges posed by digital economy markets generally and AI specifically are being looked at from a policy perspective in a number of countries.

At EU level, the Commissioner with responsibility for competition law, Margrethe Vestager, has appointed three special advisors who are considering "future challenges of digitization for competition policy" and are due to report their findings in early April 2019.[76] A conference was held in January 2019 to discuss the issues.

In the UK:

- The UK Business, Energy and Industrial Strategy department's "Modernising Consumer Markets" Green Paper of April 2018[77] includes a chapter on digital markets and asks: "What challenges do digital markets pose for effective competition enforcement and what can be done to address them?" It has also requested views on how the competition authorities should address "digital platforms, agglomeration, data algorithms and the consolidation of competitors."

- The UK Furman review was charged with looking at "the potential opportunities and challenges the emerging digital economy may pose for competition and pro-competition policy."[78] The expert panel's report was issued in March 2019. As has been noted at various points above, the Furman report concludes that the existing competition regime and enforcement tools are not sufficient to ensure effective competition in the digital economy for the benefit of consumers, and offers some wide-ranging ideas about how to address this issue. The UK government has not yet responded.

In Germany, a report by the Monopolies Commission[79] found that the legal framework in Germany needs adapting to digital change in the economy, and recommended that markets with algorithm-based pricing should be systematically investigated for adverse effects on competition. As a consequence, the Federal Ministry for Economic Affairs and Energy has created a competition law committee, known as the "Kommission Wettbewerbsrecht 4.0" which will make recommendations on whether reforms to EU and national competition law are needed.[80] Its report is expected by autumn 2019.

In Canada, the House of Commons called for the Government to consider the impact of data-opolies and consider whether modernization of the Canadian Competition Act is needed.[81]

At international level, as noted above, the OECD has conducted a number of roundtables on various aspects of these issues including "Big data: Bringing competition policy to the digital era" (2016), "Rethinking the use of traditional antitrust enforcement tools in multi-sided markets" (2017), and "Algorithms and collusion" (2017), "Implications of E-commerce for Competition Policy" (2018), and "Personalized Pricing in the Digital Era" (2018).

V. Conclusions

There is wide expectation that AI systems will have a transformative impact in all sectors of the economy and in all aspects of our lives, generating ease and simplicity, insight and discovery, understanding and efficiency. In order for this transformative potential to be fully realized, however, vibrant and competitive innovation in AI applications is essential.

Governments, policy-makers and enforcement authorities must not allow the need for large quantities of data and/or the complexity of the technology to restrict the development and deployment of AI. There is increasing concern that businesses with huge datasets and an early lead in building AI applications could gain an advantage which is difficult to contest, with the commensurate concern that this could, in its worst cases, hinder innovation. There is debate (and as yet no consensus) as to whether existing competition and antitrust legislative frameworks are sufficiently adaptable to offer strong deterrents and effective remedies to any market distortions which may emerge going forwards.

It seems clear, at any rate, that access to data for development and access to the AI technology itself are both essential ingredients of effective and fruitful rivalry, to the benefit of the consumer.

Open data and open source software are both important trends in this respect which should be encouraged and supported. Governments should lead by example, where possible, in opening up datasets (with consents, pseudonymisation or aggregation etc., as necessary) and by investing in AI development resources, facilities and centres of excellence.

Given the expected strategic importance of AI, competition law enforcement authorities should proactively monitor the progress of this technology and the activities of those in the vanguard of its development as an administrative priority. International debate and discussion to develop best practice through fora such as the OECD or the International Competition Network should be strongly encouraged.

Principle 6
Open Data and Fair Competition

Organisations that develop, deploy or use AI systems and any national laws that regulate such use shall promote (a) open access to datasets which could be used in the development of AI systems and (b) open source frameworks and software for AI systems. AI systems must be developed and deployed on a "compliance by design" basis in relation to competition/antitrust law.

1 Supporting effective competition in relation to AI systems

1.1 Governments should support and participate in international co-ordination (through bodies such as the OECD and the International Competition Network) to develop best practices and rigorous analysis in understanding the competitive impact of dataset control and AI systems on economic markets.

1.2 Governments should undertake regular reviews to ensure that competition law frameworks and the enforcement tools available to the relevant enforcement authorities are sufficient and effective to ensure sufficient access to necessary inputs, and adequate choice, vibrant rivalry, creative innovation and high quality of output in the development and deployment of AI systems, to the ultimate benefit of consumers.

2 Open data

2.1 Governments should foster and facilitate national infrastructures necessary to promote open access to datasets to all elements of society having a vested interest in access to such datasets for research and/or non-commercial use. In this regard, governments should give serious consideration to two-tier access models which would allow for free access for academic and research purposes, and paid-for access for commercialised purposes.

2.2 Governments should support open data initiatives in the public or private sector with guidance and research to share wide understanding of the advantages to be gained from open access data, the structures through which datasets can be shared and exchanged, and the processes by which data can be made suitable for open access (including API standardisation, pseudonymisation, aggregation or other curation, where necessary).

2.3 Governments should ensure that the data held by public sector bodies are accessible and open, where possible and where this does not conflict with a public sector mandate to recover taxpayer investment in the collection and curation of such data. Private sector bodies such as industry organisations and trade associations should similarly support and promote open data within their industry sector, making their own datasets open, where possible.

2.4 Organisations that develop, deploy or use AI systems are encouraged to open up access to, and/or license, their datasets, where possible via chaperoned mechanisms such as Data Trusts.

2.5 Any sharing or licensing of data should be to an extent which is reasonable in the circumstances and should be in compliance with legal, regulatory, contractual and any other obligations or requirements in relation to the data concerned (including privacy, security, freedom of information and other confidentiality considerations).

3 Open source AI systems

3.1 Organisations that develop AI systems are normally entitled to commercialise such systems as they wish. However, governments should at a minimum advocate accessibility through open source or other similar licensing arrangements to those innovative AI systems which may be of particular societal benefit or advance the "state of the art" in the field via, for example, targeted incentive schemes.

3.2 Organisations that elect not to release their AI systems as open source software are encouraged nevertheless to license the System on a commercial basis.

3.3 To the extent that an AI system can be subdivided into various constituent parts with general utility and application in other AI use-cases, organisations that elect not to license the AI system as a whole (whether on an open source or commercial basis) are encouraged to license as many of such re-usable components as is possible.

4 Compliance by design with competition/antitrust laws

4.1 Organisations that develop, deploy or use AI systems should design, develop and deploy AI systems in a "compliance by design" manner which ensures consistency with the overarching ethos of subsisting competition/antitrust regimes to promote free and vibrant competition amongst corporate enterprises to the ultimate benefit of consumers.

Endnotes

[1] UK, Treasury Department, "Unlocking digital competition: Report of the Digital Competition Expert Panel" (March 2019), online: <https://www.gov.uk/government/collections/digital-competition-expert-panel> at p 4 [UK Furman Report].

[2] UK, Department for Business, Energy and Industrial Strategy, "Modernising Consumer Markets: Green Paper" (April 2018), online: <https://www.gov.uk/government/consultations/consumer-green-paper-modernising-consumer-markets> at para 98 [UK BEIS Green Paper].

[3] UK Furman Report, *supra* note 1.

[4] OECD, "Big data: Bringing competition policy to the digital era" (November 2016), online: <http://www.oecd.org/daf/competition/big-data-bringing-competition-policy-to-the-digital-era.htm> [OECD Big Data Roundtable].

[5] France, Autorité de la Concurrence and Germany, Bundeskartellamt, "Competition Law and Data" (10 May 2016), online: <https://www.bundeskartellamt.de/SharedDocs/Publikation/DE/Berichte/Big%20Data%20Papier.html;jsessionid=90BC5DAD5D2E2FBBC50407AE70F36905.1_cid378?nn=3591568>.

[6] Canada, Competition Bureau, "Big data and innovation: key themes for competition policy in Canada" (February 2018), online: <http://www.competitionbureau.gc.ca/eic/site/cb-bc.nsf/eng/04342.html>.

[7] UK, Information Commissioner's Office, "Royal Free—Google DeepMind trial failed to comply with data protection law" (3 July 2017), online: <https://ico.org.uk/about-the-ico/news-and-events/news-and-blogs/2017/07/royal-free-google-deepmind-trial-failed-to-comply-with-data-protection-law/>.

[8] "DeepMind's AI can spot eye disease just as well as top doctors" (14 August 2018), online: *New Scientist* <https://www.newscientist.com/article/2176618-deepminds-ai-can-spot-eye-disease-just-as-well-as-top-doctors/>.

[9] Todd Haselton, "Apple has a message for Amazon and Google and it's plastered on the side of a hotel at the biggest tech conference of the year" (6 January 2019), online: *CNBC* <https://www.cnbc.com/2019/01/06/apple-privacy-ad-ces-2019.html>.

[10] UK, House of Lords Select Committee on Artificial Intelligence, Report of Session 2017-19, "AI in the UK: ready, willing and able?" (16 April 2018), online: <https://publications.parliament.uk/pa/ld201719/ldselect/ldai/100/100.pdf> at p 29.

[11] We are starting to see evidence of companies participating in pecuniary exchanges for customer data such as the Facebook Research application that paid consumers $20 a month to allow Facebook to access to all activity on their mobile phones ("Sheryl Sandberg: The teens 'consented' to putting Facebook spyware on their phones" (31 January 2019), online: *Gizmodo* <https://gizmodo.com/sheryl-sandberg-the-teens-consented-to-putting-faceboo-1832218843>).

[12] Maurice E. Stucke, "Should we be concerned about data-opolies?" 2 Geo. L. Tech. Rev. 275 (2018), online: <https://papers.ssrn.com/sol3/papers.cfm?abstract_id=3144045>.

[13] Commissioner Margrethe Vestager speech, "Making the data revolution work for us" Mackenzie Stuart Lecture, Cambridge (4 February 2019), online: <https://ec.europa.eu/commission/commissioners/2014-2019/vestager/announcements/making-data-revolution-work-us_en>.

[14] "We must continue to ensure that the right balance is struck between strong data protection laws and realising the pro-competitive effects of opening up data." UK BEIS Green Paper, *supra* note 2, at para 103.

[15] At the Brussels conference, "... people expressed worries that monopolising data could harm innovation. Because data is the raw material for artificial intelligence—the information which machine learning algorithms use to understand the world. And if just a few companies monopolise that raw material, it could be hard for anyone else to produce innovative AI." Commissioner Margrethe Vestager speech, "An innovative digital future," Digital Czech Republic, Prague

(8 February 2019), online: <https://ec.europa.eu/commission/commissioners/2014-2019/vestager/announcements/innovative-digital-future_en>.

16 Jeffrey Ding, "Deciphering China's AI Dream: The context, components, capabilities, and consequences of China's strategy to lead the world in AI" (March 2018), online: *Governance of AI Program, University of Oxford* <https://www.fhi.ox.ac.uk/wp-content/uploads/Deciphering_Chinas_AI-Dream.pdf> at 25.

17 China, State Council, "China issues guideline on artificial intelligence development" (20 July 2017), online: <http://english.gov.cn/policies/latest_releases/2017/07/20/content_281475742458322.html>.

18 Iris Deng, "True dominance of China's Baidu, Alibaba and Tencent revealed—and how their influence extends worldwide" (10 July 2018), online: *South China Morning Post* <https://www.scmp.com/tech/china-tech/article/2154437/true-dominance-chinas-baidu-alibaba-and-tencent-revealed-and-how>.

19 See the Executive Summary for the OECD Big Data Roundtable, *supra* note 4 at p 3.

20 There is variation between jurisdictions in the legal frameworks for assessing whether a business is dominant or has monopolised the market. Compare, for example, the U.S. approach in *United States v. United Shoe Mach. Corp.,* 110 F. Supp. 295, 343 (D. Mass. 1953), aff'd, 347 U.S. 521 (1954) and the EU principles in Case 85/76 *Hoffman-La Roche v Commission* [1979] ECR 461 (EU:C:1979:36) at para 38. The legal requirements for proving anti-competitive conduct also differ, particularly as regards whether it is necessary to show actual consumer harm, or whether it is sufficient that such harm is foreseeable.

21 If such a business seeks to grow its market share further through acquisition, however, merger control enforcement may be used to prevent or temper any anticipated harm to competition for enhancing its market power.

22 Joined Cases C-241/91 P and C-242/91, *Radio Telefis Eireann and Independent Television Publications Ltd v Commission of the European Communities* [1995] ECR I-743 (ECLI: EU:C:1995:98).

23 Case C-7/97, *Oscar Bronner GmbH & Co. KG v Mediaprint Zeitungs- und Zeitschriftenverlag GmbH & Co. KG* [1998] I-7791 (ECLI:EU:C:1998:569). Note that the economic viability of developing a similar network is assessed by reference to a business of the scale of the incumbent, not the challenger business (which may well be much smaller, with more limited resources).

24 EU, "Communication from the Commission: Guidance on its enforcement priorities in applying Article 82 of the EC Treaty to abusive exclusionary conduct by dominant undertakings" (OJ C 45, 24.2.2009, pages 7 to 20), online: <http://eur-lex.europa.eu/LexUriServ/LexUriServ.do?uri=CELEX:52009XC0224(01):EN:NOT>.

25 Peter Suber, "Open Access Overview: Focusing on open access to peer-reviewed research articles and their preprints" *Earlham College* (December 2015) online: <http://legacy.earlham.edu/~peters/fos/overview.htm>.

26 UK, Government Digital Service, "G8 Open Data Charter and Technical Annex" (18 June 2013), online: <https://www.gov.uk/government/publications/open-data-charter/g8-open-data-charter-and-technical-annex>.

27 International Open Data Charter, "Who we are," online: <https://opendatacharter.net/who-we-are/>.

28 USA, White House Office of Management and Budget, "Open Data Policy—Managing Information as an Asset," online: <https://project-open-data.cio.gov/policy-memo/>.

29 USA, U.S. General Services Administration, Technology Transformation Service, online: *About Data.gov* <https://www.data.gov/about>.

30 Government of Canada, "Tri-Agency Open Access Policy on Publications" (21 December 2016), online: <http://www.science.gc.ca/eic/site/063.nsf/eng/h_F6765465.html>.

31 Government of Canada, "Open Data Inventory" (1 February 2018), online: <https://open.canada.ca/en/search/inventory>.

[32] European Commission, "Digital Single Market: Artificial Intelligence Policy" (7 January 2019), online: <https://ec.europa.eu/digital-single-market/en/artificial-intelligence#%22%20name>.

[33] European Commission, "Digital Single Market: Building a European data economy Policy" (24 January 2019), online: <https://ec.europa.eu/digital-single-market/en/policies/building-european-data-economy>.

[34] EU Open Data Portal, online: <https://ec.europa.eu/digital-single-market/en/proposal-revision-public-sector-information-psi-directive>.

[35] *Ibid.*

[36] UK, Department for Digital, Culture, Media & Sport and Department for Business, Energy & Industrial Strategy, "Growing the Artificial Intelligence Industry in the UK" (15 October 2017), online: <https://assets.publishing.service.gov.uk/government/uploads/system/uploads/attachment_data/file/652097/Growing_the_artificial_intelligence_industry_in_the_UK.pdf> [UK Hall/Pesenti Report].

[37] *Ibid* at 42-52.

[38] UK, Department for Digital, Culture, Media & Sport and Department for Business, Energy & Industrial Strategy, "AI Sector Deal" (26 April 2018), online: <https://www.gov.uk/government/publications/artificial-intelligence-sector-deal/ai-sector-deal#executive-summary> [UK AI Sector Deal].

[39] UK, Department for Business Innovation & Skills, "Open Data Strategy" (July 2014), online: <https://assets.publishing.service.gov.uk/government/uploads/system/uploads/attachment_data/file/330382/bis-14-946-open-data-strategy-2014-2016.pdf>.

[40] Open Data Institute, "About the ODI," online: <https://theodi.org/about-the-odi/>.

[41] UK Furman Report, *supra* note 1 at p 9.

[42] Australian Government, "Australian Government Public Data Policy Statement" (7 December 2015), online: <https://www.pmc.gov.au/sites/default/files/publications/aust_govt_public_data_policy_statement_1.pdf>.

[43] UK Hall/Pesenti Report, *supra* note 36.

[44] European Commission, "Antitrust: Commission fines Google €2.42 billion for abusing dominance as search engine by giving illegal advantage to own comparison shopping service" (27 June 2017), online: <http://europa.eu/rapid/press-release_IP-17-1784_en.htm>.

[45] UK Furman Report, *supra* note 1 at p 12.

[46] That is, fair, reasonable and non-discriminatory terms.

[47] Cynthia Harvey, "Open Source Artificial Intelligence: 50 Top Projects" (12 September 2017) online: *Datamation, Quinstreet Inc.* <https://www.datamation.com/open-source/open-source-artificial-intelligence-50-top-projects-1.html>.

[48] Vijay Bommireddipalli, Mei-Mei Fu, Bradley Holt, Susan Malaika, Animesh Singh, Jim Spohrer and Thomas Truong, "Open source and AI at IBM" (12 December 2018), online: *IBM Developer* <https://developer.ibm.com/blogs/2018/12/12/open-source-ibm-and-ai/>.

[49] Sam Dean, "Open Source AI for Everyone: Three Projects to Know" (10 May 2018), online: *The Linux Foundation* <https://www.linuxfoundation.org/blog/2018/05/open-source-ai-for-everyone-three-projects-to-know/>.

[50] Robert Hof, "Baidu AI researchers create new cancer detection algorithm" (18 June 2018), online: *SiliconANGLE, SiliconANGLE Media Inc.* <https://siliconangle.com/2018/06/18/baidu-ai-researchers-create-new-cancer-detection-algorithm/>.

51 Charles Clover and Sherru Fei Ju, "Baidu to open-source its autonomous driving technology" (19 April 2017), online: *Financial Times* <https://www.ft.com/content/1706b75a-24b4-11e7-8691-d5f7e0cd0a16>.

52 Kyle Wiggers, "Baidu announces Apollo 3.5 and Apollo Enterprise, says it has over 130 partners" (8 January 2019), online: *VentureBeat* <https://venturebeat.com/2019/01/08/baidu-announces-apollo-3-5-and-apollo-enterprise-says-it-has-over-130-partners/>.

53 Open AI "The Malicious Use of Artificial Intelligence: Forecasting, Prevention, and Mitigation" (February 2018), online: <https://openai.com/blog/preparing-for-malicious-uses-of-ai/>.

54 Open AI, "Better Language Models and Their Implications" (14 February 2019), online: <https://openai.com/blog/better-language-models/>.

55 UK, Department for Business, Energy & Industrial Strategy, "Industrial Strategy: building a Britain fit for the future" (27 November 2017), online: <https://assets.publishing.service.gov.uk/government/uploads/system/uploads/attachment_data/file/664563/industrial-strategy-white-paper-web-ready-version.pdf>.

56 UK Hall/Pesenti Report, *supra* note 36.

57 UK AI Sector Deal, *supra* note 38.

58 "Communication from the Commission to the European Parliament, the European Council, the Council, the European Economic and Social Committee and the Committee of the Regions: Artificial Intelligence for Europe" (25 April 2018), online: <https://ec.europa.eu/digital-single-market/en/news/communication-artificial-intelligence-europe>.

59 European Commission, "Digital Single Market Policy: Artificial Intelligence" (7 January 2019), online: <https://ec.europa.eu/digital-single-market/en/artificial-intelligence>.

60 For more information, see online: <https://inspire.ec.europa.eu/about-inspire/563>.

61 Lin Zizhen, Wang Yiyin and Teng Jing Xuan, "Could AI transform China's legal system" (11 December 2017), online: *Caixin Global* <https://www.caixinglobal.com/2017-12-11/could-ai-transform-chinas-legal-system-101183154.html>.

62 European Commission, "Final report on the E-commerce Sector Inquiry" (SWD(2017) 154 final), online: <http://ec.europa.eu/competition/antitrust/sector_inquiry_final_report_en.pdf> at para 13 [Report on e-commerce].

63 USA, Department of Justice, "Former E-Commerce Executive Charged with Price Fixing in the Antitrust Division's First Online Marketplace Prosecution" (6 April 2015), online: <https://www.justice.gov/opa/pr/former-e-commerce-executive-charged-price-fixing-antitrust-divisions-first-online-marketplace>.

64 UK, CMA, "Infringement finding against Trod Limited and GB eye Limited (trading as 'GB Posters')" (12 August 2016), online: <https://www.gov.uk/cma-cases/online-sales-of-discretionary-consumer-products>.

65 Report on e-commerce, *supra* note 62.

66 European Commission, "Commission opens three investigations into suspected anticompetitive practices in e-commerce" (2 February 2017), online: <http://europa.eu/rapid/press-release_IP-17-201_en.htm>.

67 This example is included in the speech of Former Federal Trade Commissioner Maureen K. Ohlhausen "Should We Fear the Things That Go Beep in the Night? Some Initial Thoughts on the Intersection of Antitrust Law and Algorithmic Pricing," Concurrences Antitrust in the Financial Sector Conference, New York, USA (23 May 2017), online: <https://www.ftc.gov/public-statements/2017/05/should-we-fear-things-go-beep-night-some-initial-thoughts-intersection>. Interestingly her fellow former Commissioner Terrell McSweeney expressed greater concern about algorithmic pricing in her speech, "Algorithms and Coordinated Effects," University of Oxford Centre for Competition Law and Policy, Oxford, UK (22 May 2017), online: <https://www.ftc.gov/public-statements/2017/05/algorithms-coordinated-effects>.

[68] A price increase could be signalled to the market during the night when price matching systems would spot it but there was little market activity. If competitors did not match the price rise, the signalling business could then drop its price back down before customers became active the next day—so the signaller should not lose too much business because of the temporarily higher price.

[69] UK BEIS Green Paper, *supra* note 2.

[70] OECD, Competition Committee Roundtable, background paper on "Personalised Pricing in the Digital Era" (28 November 2018) online: <https://one.oecd.org/document/DAF/COMP(2018)13/en/pdf>.

[71] *Ibid.*

[72] The UK CMA has recently looked at the "loyalty penalty" where personalised pricing is used to charge higher prices to customers who do not shop around. The report summarises work also done in this area by the Financial Conduct Authority, the UK financial services sector regulator, and Ofcom, the UK communications sector regulator. UK, CMA, "'Loyalty penalty' super-complaint" (19 December 2018), online: <https://www.gov.uk/cma-cases/loyalty-penalty-super-complaint>.

[73] Canada, House of Commons, "Democracy Under Threat: Risks and Solutions in the Era of Disinformation and Data Monopoly: Report of the Standing Committee on Access to Information, Privacy and Ethics" (December 2018), online: http://www.ourcommons.ca/Content/Committee/421/ETHI/Reports/RP10242267/ethirp17/ethirp17-e.pdf at p 32 [Canadian House of Commons report].

[74] Speech of Margrethe Vestager, "Algorithms and competition," Bundeskartellamt 18th Conference on Competition, Berlin, Germany (16 March 2017), online: <https://ec.europa.eu/commission/commissioners/2014-2019/vestager/announcements/bundeskartellamt-18th-conference-competition-berlin-16-march-2017_en>.

[75] Canadian House of Commons report, *supra* note 73 at p 33.

[76] EU Commission, "Commission appoints Professors Heike Schweitzer, Jacques Crémer and Assistant Professor Yves-Alexandre de Montjoye as Special Advisers to Commissioner Vestager on future challenges of digitisation for competition policy" (28 March 2018), online: <https://ec.europa.eu/commission/commissioners/2014-2019/vestager/announcements/commission-appoints-professors-heike-schweitzer-jacques-cremer-and-assistant-professor-yves_en>.

[77] UK BEIS Green Paper, *supra* note 2.

[78] UK Furman report, *supra* note 1.

[79] Germany, Monopolkommission, "Digital change requires legal adjustments regarding price algorithms, the media sector and the supply of medicines," Biennial Report XXII: Competition 2018 (3 July 2018), online: <http://monopolkommission.de/en/press-releases/219-biennial-report-xxii-competition-2018.html>.

[80] Germany, Bundesministerium für Wirtschaft und Energie, "Kommission Wettbewerbsrecht 4.0," online: <https://www.bmwi.de/Redaktion/DE/Artikel/Wirtschaft/kommission-wettbewerbsrecht-4-0.html>.

[81] Canadian House of Commons report, *supra* note 73.

Principle 7

PRIVACY

Organisations that develop, deploy or use AI systems and any national laws that regulate such use shall endeavour to ensure that AI systems are compliant with privacy norms and regulations, taking into account the unique characteristics of AI systems, and the evolution of standards on privacy.

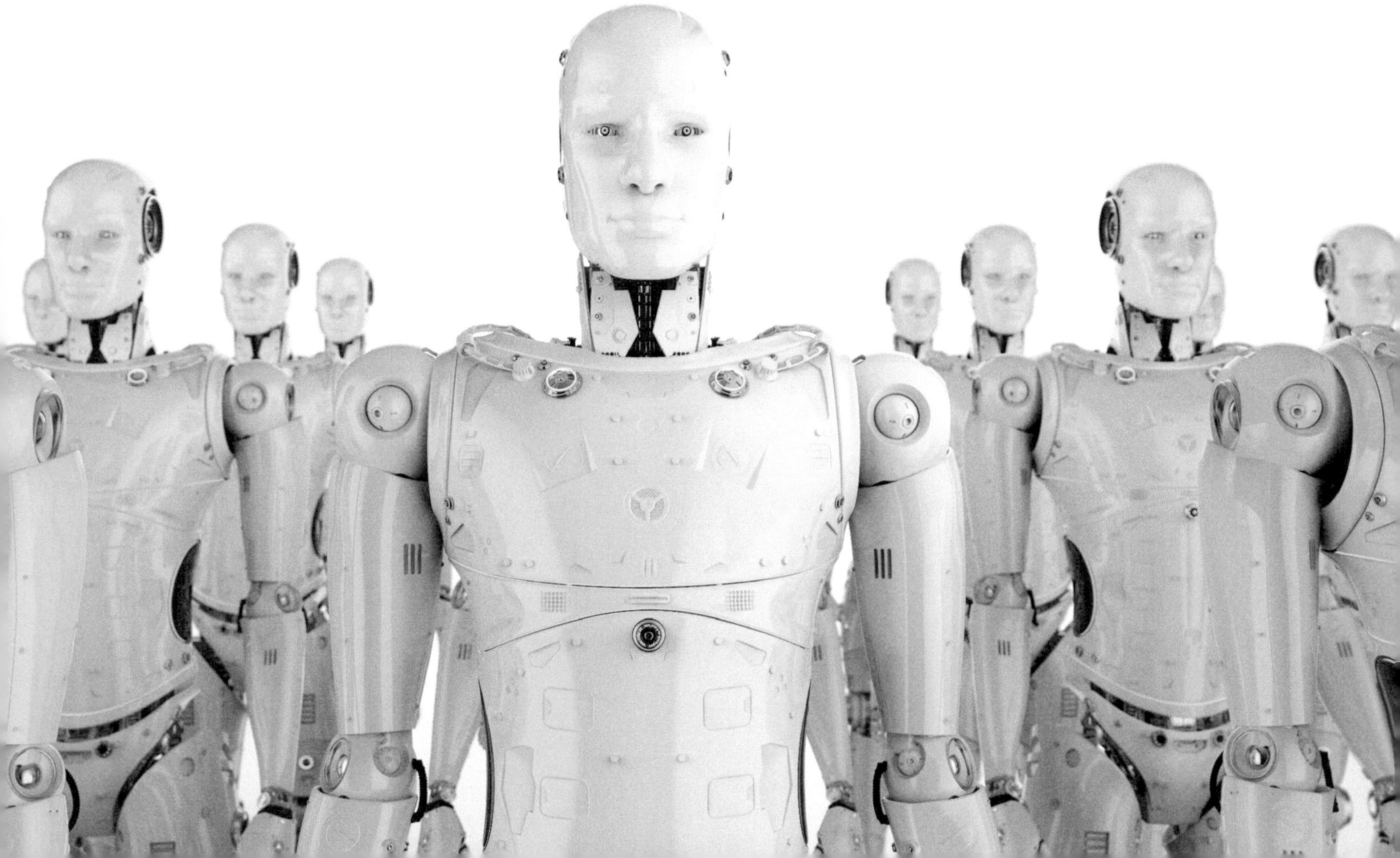

7
PRIVACY

CHAPTER LEAD
Michael Peeters | DAC Beachcroft LLP, United Kingdom

Richard Austin | Deeth Williams Wall LLP, Canada

Nicole Beranek Zanon | de la cruz beranek Attorneys-at-Law Ltd., Switzerland

Sonja Dürager | bpv Hügel Rechtsanwälte GmbH, Austria

Doron Goldstein | Katten Muchin Rosenman LLP, United States

Julia B. Jacobson | K&L Gates LLP, United States

Rachel Sindorf | Seattle University, United States

Rhiannon Webster | DAC Beachcroft LLP, United Kingdom

I. Introduction

A major trend in the deployment of artificial intelligence (AI) technologies has been their suitability to help us manage and utilise huge volumes of data: large databases are inherently well-suited to the use of AI applications for searching and analytics....

...and where there are huge databases, this almost always includes personal data.

Indeed, as data analytics organisations pursue the economic drive toward data monetisation, it is often in relation to personal data that the most attention is given; pushing creative use of personal data "lakes" using new technologies, in particular AI.

There has of course in recent years also been a trend to the increased regulation of how our personal data is managed, raising the obvious question as to how these two parallel trends compete. In the context of data privacy, issues arise mainly due to the loss of human control with "algorithms acting as agents." But there are other issues too. What follows is an overview of these issues and where the current thinking is. In Section II, we start with an overview of the basics of privacy law.

II. Privacy Basics

A. Introduction

In this section on the 'basics' of privacy law, we summarise some of the common principles around the world covering this area and how these regulate AI. We have purposely kept this high level to set the scene for the analysis that follows.

B. Common privacy principles

Privacy is an elusive concept, even more so owing to the rapid advancement of technology in the digital age. How does one distinguish between what is "public" and what is "private," and consequently, what needs protecting, in a world where an increasing amount of personal information is shared online? Over the past fifty years, data privacy legislation has undergone a significant transformation in order to keep pace with the ever-expanding amount of data generated online. Data protection principles informing these legal frameworks aim to ensure personal information is requested, obtained, used and exchanged in a way which is appropriate to the context.

Much of the legislation governing privacy around the world today is based on the principles established in 1980 by the Organisation for Economic Cooperation and Development (OECD). The OECD agreed a set of eight Fair Information Practices, codified in the *OECD Guidelines on the Protection of Privacy and Transborder Flows of Personal Data*.[1]" In summary, these are:

- Collection Limitation Principle
- Data Quality Principle (accuracy)
- Purpose Specification Principle (transparency)
- Use Limitation Principle (proportionality)
- Security Safeguards Principle (security)
- Openness Principle (fairness)
- Individual Participation Principle (data subject rights)
- Accountability Principle

Another major influence is the European Convention on Human Rights (ECHR), a 1953 international treaty which protects the human rights and fundamental freedoms of every person in every member state of the Council of Europe. It includes at Article 8, a right to the respect of private and family life; and at Article 10, protection of the right to freedom of expression, including the right to hold opinions and receive and impart information.

C. Present day regimes

Recently, on 25 May 2018, the General Data Protection Regulation (GDPR) came into force. The GDPR was one of the most controversial pieces of legislation to have ever passed through the European legislative process, with extensive lobbying from businesses and interested stakeholders, including the United States government. The OECD Principles however remain prevalent, and the first principle under the GDPR obliges data controllers to process data lawfully, fairly, and in a transparent manner in relation to the data subject. The lawful bases are specified and one of these lawful bases is consent.

As a contrasting example—illustrating how divergent historical and cultural approaches to privacy arrive at contrasting modern solutions—there is no single overarching privacy regime in the U.S. Federal laws in the U.S. cover specific industry sectors with the general aim of maintaining competition and consumer trust (the best known and most effective example being the Health Insurance Portability and Accountability Act of 1996[2] (HIPAA), which governs the use of medical patients' data), while state laws aim to protect consumers, but are restricted by their limited reach. Most (but not all) states have enacted law to protect the personal data of state residents, even where the data collector or user is beyond state lines, but what data is covered varies and both compliance and enforcement are compromised by the patchwork of coverage.

Out beyond the major established privacy regimes we have touched on, the amount of regulation is exploding, driven by the global need to keep up with technology and compete for trade. As the EU and North America are already well covered, most of this exponential new growth is in Asia, the middle east, Africa, and South America. At the end of 2018, about 120 countries had some form of privacy or data protection law in place, and about 40 more had a law or bill in progress.[3]

D. Our approach in this chapter

When considering the current regulation of AI and privacy in this Chapter, we use as our constant 'benchmark' the GDPR: it was the idea of the European legislators to create a strong and more coherent data protection framework, considering the rapid technological developments and globalisation, which brought new challenges for the protection of personal data (see Recital 7). Not only does the GDPR touch the privacy perspective of AI in Europe, but it is also the first administrative law which allows the state to use machine learning (ML) in support of automated decisions.[4] It is also the most up-to-date set of data protection principles that there is. It provides a thoughtful articulation of 21st century data protection principles that 21st century technology needs to cope with.

E. Looking forward

The political and regulatory tension that has always existed between protecting citizens and attracting business persists, but as a counter trend, where regulation in wealthy economies requires that companies ensure data they transfer beyond borders remains adequately protected, countries that can demonstrate a trustworthy data protection regime are at an advantage for investment—for example for data centre and customer service locations.

There may be a trend towards a global gold standard; with the GDPR now pulling other jurisdictions along behind it. EU 'adequacy decisions' of "essential equivalency" with the EU regime are available to third countries (although tough to achieve) and confer huge benefits. After modernising its data protection legislation over the preceding few years,[5] Japan was able to gain an 'adequacy decision' in July 2018. Andorra, Argentina, Faeroe Islands, Guernsey, Israel, Isle of Man, Japan, Jersey, New Zealand, Switzerland, and Uruguay have EU adequacy decisions, and Canada and the United States have partial adequacy decisions.[6] Many of these have regimes have been built around the OECD and GDPR principles, which include the requirement to have a lawful basis for the processing of personal data (one of which is consent).

The existing concepts, which have relevance for AI, will be outlined in the next section. So we will touch on: the impact of AI on anonymisation, which contains the promise to depersonalise personal data; fairness and its related operational issues; the regulation of automated decision making and profiling and the data subject rights; and how AI can be used to meet privacy requirements.

III. Privacy and AI Issues

A. Anonymisation

AI has the distinct and clear potential to violate personal data.[7] Anonymisation is a legal concept that can help protect personal data, next to Pseudonymisation and data retention restrictions. How Anonymisation helps protect privacy is explained below in the case studies relating to self-driving autonomous cars and health data.

1. Anonymisation as a legal concept

Personal data is any information relating to an identified or identifiable natural person. The relevant criterion is the "relation." If the relation between the information and the person is disconnected, it is no longer personal data. The Law of the European Union and many national data protection legislation in the western hemisphere apply this definition.

"Anonymised" means it is not possible to identify an individual from the data itself or from the data in combination with other data, taking into account all means that are reasonably likely to be used to identify the individual. When data has been anonymized, it means the data can no longer identify an individual and, therefore, the data can no longer said to be personal data or fall within the scope of data protection legislation. The GDPR reflects this approach.

National legislation also perpetuates the idea of anonymisation, for example, the Swiss data protection law: Swiss law requires "personal data" to exist as a start for the anonymisation process. The process *per se* is the removal of possibilities to identify a person through personal data. This can be done in two ways: firstly, the complete removal of possibilities to identify the person behind personal data; secondly, the removal of possibilities such that identification of the person becomes inappropriately hard to do. In other words, the risk of "re-identification" has to be appropriately low.

Most European legislation treats anonymisation as "data-processing" of personal data. The legal effect of this is that, until anonymisation is complete, the processes used have to comply with the legal requirements of processing personal data.

This requirement for anonymisation, a feature shared by various laws on data protection, has the potential to inhibit the use of AI in a meaningful way. There is a dilemma for those using AI in a regulated environment: using anonymised data requires balancing the risks of: too little anonymisation (in which case the data will not really be anonymised or the risk of re-identification will be high); and too much anonymisation (in which case the treated data may become too obscure to be able to be used in any meaningful way).

How effective can anonymisation in the age of "Big Data" be, especially in the context of AI? Compliance with the legal requirements to remove or reduce the risk of identifying the person behind personal data may become extraordinarily difficult or complex, especially in instances where technology (in particular AI) operates independently of human impulses and does not in every case adhere to human expectations.

The situation can become more problematic in instances where two data blocs of ostensibly anonymised data are combined. When AI makes it possible to identify the person "standing behind" the data through combination, this action may violate data protection norms without even being fully comprehensible to the general AI user. In other words, the combination of data through AI may occur through Machine Learning without direct human involvement; this needs careful consideration by regulators; but, even if protected at a regulatory level, may be difficult to detect in practice.

2. Anonymisation: Discussion of cases of application

The potential for the question discussed above to become a widespread legal problem and not just a theoretical issue can be seen in several different contexts and situations.

a) Self-driving and autonomous cars

Personal data is vital for a self-driving and autonomous car to operate as intended. Autonomous cars have sensors to collect personal data, for example regarding movement in a certain area, location, status and passenger action. This data can link the vehicle's technological parameters with the identifiable individual. Therefore, anonymisation of personal data is crucial in this area.

Data protection is necessary for two major reasons when an individual operates a self-driving, autonomous car. Firstly, cumulating massive amounts of data in the vehicle poses risks to the individual's safety. Autonomous vehicles amass huge amounts of data about used roads, vehicle status, passenger status, location and others. The data-pool opens a global and complete insight into the individual's personal sphere. This high concentration of personal data in one technological entity is an easy target for hacking and other data-theft related criminal action. Consequently, the autonomous car needs an elaborate system of anonymisation within the vehicle.

Secondly, the combination of data of several AI-entities could be a violation of privacy. An autonomous vehicle could communicate and transfer data to other AI-entities if a cloud system is installed. The combination of un-anonymised and transferred information would make it extremely easy to identify and analyse the individual behind the information blocs. Additionally, an autonomous car operating within a cloud system may have multiple remote interfaces, where an attack on the system, and the stored personal data, may be possible; put simply, the autonomous vehicle cannot control where the data it transmits goes or how it is used. This requires personal data to be anonymised before it is transmitted to other AI-entities.

Self-driving and autonomous cars open up other questions regarding data protection: Who owns and shall have access to the data? Is it still acceptable that the car manufacturer has my personal data (such as location, speed, personal rhythm etc.) or even the telecom provider who provides the internet connection with its SIM-card? Should an individual be able to require that all information concerning him or her be deleted from the autonomous car within a short period after use? Why not?

b) Health data and, especially, storage and collection of genetic/medical material

Several technologies use AI for the analysis and categorisation of genetic data. The AI analyses blood, saliva and other fluids produced by the human body, as well as extracted pieces of skin and muscle. AI provides tremendous opportunities to enhance the quality of medical treatment and research.

The basic nature of genetic data presents huge challenges for the anonymisation of personal data. Genetic data is, *per se,* always associable to a certain and (with little doubt) identifiable individual, because genetic information is never shared entirely by other individuals. In addition, medical and genetic material provides access to information which is generally classified as the most personal of all information, the quasi "inner sanctum" of information amongst personal data. On its own, or when combined with other data, genetic data provides information about status, health, lifestyle and many other aspects of an individual's private (or even intimate) life.

Anonymisation, therefore, may not be an option in many situations related to genetic and medical data. This is because the genetic data, if properly anonymised, becomes simply too general to be useful in the intended ways.

This raises the question of how to comply with data protection laws when storing and processing genetic or medical data, without making the collected data too general to be useful. Pseudonymisation is generally viewed as a viable option. Anonymisation requires that the parts of personal data which make identification of the individual behind the data possible are completely removed. In contrast, for pseudonymisation, the parts of personal data which make identification of the individual possible are replaced or removed. For example, name can be replaced with reference numbers or other identifiers. The pseudonymisation ensures that the data is still useful, but minimises risk to the individual.

As the above discussion illustrates, it may not be possible to satisfy AI's insatiable appetite for data by anonymising the large data pools that are currently in existence. Therefore, we need to consider other measures for ensuring that AI complies with existing privacy regimes, to which we now turn.

B. Lawful basis and consent

Under many privacy laws, processing[8] of personal information[9] is lawful only when the reasons for which the organisation is processing the personal data fit within the justifications recognized under existing law an organisation identifies the specific reasons for the personal information processing. We refer to these reasons as "lawful bases" for processing.

Some privacy laws, such as the GDPR,[10] enumerate lawful bases on which an organisation can rely whereas other privacy laws, such as Canada's,[11] apply a reasonableness standard to the consent required.

Whichever regulatory regime applies, AI operators increasingly will need to start a project in an AI environment only after conducting a deep analysis of the involved data, the necessity of all the individual data for reaching the purpose, and any negative impact that result from the intended data processing. By doing so and finding legal bases for the processing they could avoid wasted costs. Let's consider the issues they have to face.

1. Lawful basis

Under GDPR, AI operators need to identify a lawful basis for their processing:[12] the lawful bases available to a data controller under GDPR will generally depend on the category of personal information and the purposes for which the data is used.

GDPR Article 6[13] presents the 'default' lawful bases for processing of personal information, which are:

- consent of the data subject
- processing is necessary for the performance of a contract to which the data subject is party or in order to take steps at the request of the data subject prior to entering into a contract
- processing is necessary for compliance with the data controller's legal obligation[14]
- processing is necessary in order to protect the vital interests of the data subject or of another natural person
- processing is necessary for the performance of a task carried out in the public interest or in the exercise of official authority vested in the controller[15]
- processing is necessary for the purposes of the data controller's legitimate interests that are not overridden by the interests or fundamental rights and freedoms of the data subject

Consent is often viewed as the gold-standard lawful basis for processing personal information (if the data subject consents, then processing must be lawful) and therefore tends to be the default position for many data controllers. However, consent as a lawful basis presents many compliance challenges, particularly for an AI operator. Among other challenges, the validity of consent is fact-dependent, as discussed below.

The other lawful bases in Article 6 include a **necessity criterion.** In general, processing is not 'necessary' for GDPR purposes if other effective and less intrusive means to achieve the same goal exist.[16] This necessity requirement may present challenges for AI in particular: AI requires massive amounts of data in order to 'learn' and, while AI may have long-term individual and/or societal benefits, in the short term, processing personal information to teach AI systems is neither necessary nor is it necessarily the least intrusive option. Like GDPR, New Zealand's Privacy Act 1993[17] also requires necessity—an agency[18] may collect personal information only "for a lawful purpose connected with a function or activity of the agency" and "the collection of the information is necessary for that purpose."[19] An AI operator in New Zealand could avoid the necessity requirement by relying on consent; for example in a contract with a data subject for an AI application that makes fashion recommendations for its users, the AI operator could obtain the consent of users to the AI system's use of their personal data.[20] However, this comes with its own challenges as discussed below.

Identifying the most appropriate legal basis can be a difficult task. One the face of it, AI operators may take the view that the so-called "legitimate interest" lawful basis will apply to their processing, given that, on the face of it, it appears to be wide in scope. However, this basis is not straightforward; AI operators must consider and balance their legitimate interests (such as legal, economical and material interests) in personal information processing (via its AI system); against the relevant data subjects' interests and fundamental rights as well as fundamental freedoms. All consequences of interference must be considered comprehensively, even if the occurrence of the consequences is not certain, i.e., it is only a risk[21] that is likely to result in **"a high risk to the rights and freedoms of data subjects."**[22] When carrying out this balancing test, relevant factors include the nature and amount of data, the consequences of processing, and the reasonable expectations of data subjects based on their relationship with the controller.[23] Any negative impact that results from data processing (e.g., if the result of a risk assessment carried out by an AI system prevents a data subject being granted a loan) does not automatically provoke the unlawfulness of the data processing; however, consideration will need to be given to how the risk can be mitigated. This may involve carrying out a data protection impact assessment if it is likely that the processing results in **"a high risk to the rights and freedoms of data subjects."**[24]

Identifying a legal basis for processing is further complicated where there are "special categories"[25] of personal data being processed (for example, where the information contains health data). In this case, a further legal basis in Article 9 must be met in addition to the Article 6 legal basis referred to above. The Article 9 legal bases include:

- the data subject has given *explicit* consent to the processing of those personal information for one or more specified purposes.
- processing is necessary for the purposes of carrying out the obligations and exercising specific rights of the controller or of the data subject in the field of employment and social security and social protection law under EU law.
- processing relates to personal information which are manifestly made public by the data subject.[26]

Which legal basis can be relied upon will depend on the nature of the data and exact purposes of the processing.[27]

As discussed below, explicit consent is a stringent lawful basis and, as discussed above, necessity is a high bar. In practice, this means that AI operators are likely to be limited in terms of the legal bases available to them.

There are many other restrictions in the GDPR that need to be complied with: for example, there are further issues to consider where the personal data relates to a child[28] or contains information relating to criminal convictions or criminal offences.[29]

In the U.S., sector specific privacy laws also require a lawful basis. Under the U.S. Children's Online Privacy Protection Act[30] (COPPA), a data controller that operates a website, mobile app or other digital service that is directed[31] to children under age 13 must post a privacy policy[32] and obtain "verifiable parental consent" (VPC)[33] before collecting personal information (as defined in COPPA[34]) from children under age 13. The U.S. Health Insurance Portability and Accountability Act (HIPAA)[35] restricts the circumstances under which a "covered entity"[36] (and its "business associates"[37]) can use and disclose the individually-identifiable health information[38] that it creates or receives from patients, which is known as "protected health information" or "PHI."[39] A HIPAA covered entity is permitted to use PHI for treatment, payment, or health care operations and otherwise as permitted or required by law, and in some cases, with a patient's consent.[40]

Some privacy laws do not enumerate specific lawful bases; instead, personal information processing is lawful when it is necessary, appropriate and/or reasonable based on facts and circumstances. Canada's *Personal Information Protection and Electronic Documents Act* (PIPEDA) permits organisations to collect, use and disclose personal information only for purposes that "a reasonable person would consider are appropriate in the circumstances."[41] Under Australia's Federal Privacy Act,[42] an organisation may not collect personal information unless the information is reasonably necessary for or directly related to one or more of its business functions or activities.[43]

Other privacy laws do not require a lawful basis before processing personal information but may require a covered organisation to provide notice and disclosures. For example, the California Consumer Privacy Act[44] generally permits processing of "personal information"[45] by a covered business[46] if the business meets CCPA's disclosure requirements[47] and honours the rights to access,[48] deletion,[49] opt-out[50] and equal service[51] rights that CCPA provides for California residents. Similarly, Gramm-Leach Bliley Act[52] ("GLBA") requires a financial institution to notify its customers about its information-sharing practices and inform consumers of their right to opt out of certain sharing practices before or concurrent with the collection and processing of non-public personal financial information. This notification is typically made through use of the model privacy notice form issued jointly by the federal agencies that regulate financial institutions.

2. Consent as Lawful Basis: Challenges for AI

a) What is consent?

On its face, consent is a straightforward concept. However, valid consent is complex and challenging. According to the definition of "consent" in Article 4 GDPR, consent under data protection law is only valid if it is a "freely given, specific, informed and unambiguous indication of the data subject's wishes by which he or she, by a statement or by a clear affirmative action, signifies agreement to the processing of personal data relating to him or her."

Consent is valid when informed: "Informed consent requires that individuals are given enough information to make an educated decision...."[53] Likewise, the scope of consent must be clear and must cover all processing activities carried out for the same purpose or purposes. In AI applications that often include different processing activities and data transfers, these must be all be presented as separated declarations to which the data subject can consent individually.

When obtaining consent, the type of consent (opt-in or opt-out) varies depending on the type of personal information, the type of processing activity and the jurisdiction of the AI operator and/or data subject. Under the GDPR, the consent declaration must be explicit or conclusive by pro-active action which can only be understood as data subject's consent to the processing of his/her data.[54] Clicking on a tickbox, for example, would satisfy the requirements for a valid consent in many cases, as it is at least an active declaration of intent. However, in AI applications that are covered by Article 22 (see below) and require an explicit consent, such form of consent would not suffice. Pre-ticked boxes, on the other hand, are unlikely to constitute valid consent.[55]

The Office of the Privacy Commissioner of Canada released guidelines[56] under Canada's PIPEDA with seven guiding principles for determining meaningful consent:

- Emphasise key elements.
- Allow individuals to control the level of detail they get and when.

- Provide individuals with clear options to say 'yes' or 'no.'
- Be innovative and creative.
- Consider the consumer's perspective.
- Make consent a dynamic and ongoing process.
- Be accountable: Stand ready to demonstrate compliance.[57]

b) Challenges in using consent as lawful basis

As will be seen from the overview of the consent requirements, consent has a number of specific challenges as a lawful basis in the context of an AI system: these include the fact that different types of personal information require different types of consent and that consent may be revocable.

In particular, there is the challenge that data subjects must have enough relevant information about the envisaged use and consequences of the processing to ensure that any consent they provide represents an informed choice: making consent specific/express in AI context is challenging because an AI operator cannot know how exactly which personal information is processed and for what purpose. This is especially the case in self-learning AI systems where the ultimate processing that the system performs may be different than that which the AI system developer intended (and for which the developer obtained consent).

Where there are difficulties in relying on other legal bases, consent may be a viable option. However, when relying on consent, AI operators must be careful to ensure that they carefully explain how individual's data will be used and incorporate a process which allows individuals to provide a clear indication that they consent to that use. The purposes of processing will also need to be kept under review—if the AI operator decides to change the scope of its processing (e.g., use the data for another purpose) or if a self-learning system performs differently than anticipated, then it will need to ensure that individuals are aware of these new uses and, if necessary, their consent is obtained.

It is also important to keep in mind that consent can be withdrawn at any time, which would place AI operators in a difficult position if this were to occur. Consideration should therefore always be given to whether an alternative basis to consent is available.

3. Conclusion

As mentioned at the beginning of this section, a well-intentioned recommendation for organisations that develop, deploy or use AI systems, in order to avoid wasted costs, is to start a project in an AI environment only after conducting a deep analysis of the involved data, the necessity of all the individual data for reaching the purpose, and any negative impact that results from the intended data processing. These issues relating to the finding of legal bases for the processing of data and the avoidance of high risks for data subjects can, however, in many AI systems only be addressed by the developers.

It seems obvious that the difficulties of arguing a stable legal basis cannot be solved only after implementation by the AI user. This leads to the buzzword 'ethics by design,' where it seems to be necessary to consider privacy issues from the very beginning.

C. Identifying purpose

This flows from the Lawful Basis analysis above: privacy law generally requires companies to identify the purpose or purposes of collection at or prior to the moment of collection; but with AI, some insights are only realised "after the fact" and many companies are realising that they can now monetize "legal data" in ways that they had never before considered. How can the "identify purpose" principle be respected in such a context? Companies need to identify the purpose for which data is collected and will be used in order to inform the data subjects and establish their lawful basis for the processing. Where the purposes of processing change, this must be communicated to individuals. It is therefore imperative that companies clearly identify the purpose of any processing at the outset of the project and also undertake regular reviews to ensure it remains accurate.

D. Fairness and related operational issues

1. The fairness principle

We acknowledge that "fairness" is a concept which stretches far beyond privacy law. Indeed we have granted the concept of fairness its own chapter in this book. It involves looking at the effects of data processing on individuals to make sure data is not used in ways that would have unjustified adverse effects on the individual. This concept has been covered in detail in our treatment of Principle 4—Fairness and Non-Discrimination. In privacy law it also articulates our fundamental underlying expectations around the processing of personal data: To that end, see also in our treatment of Principle 3—Transparency and Explainability, which stresses the importance of 'explainability' for the fairness of AI.

Rather than cover this ground again, in this section we have focussed on the risks to fairness and AI from the perspective of privacy regulators; we use the phrase 'Privacy as Fairness' to reflect that part of current and future privacy regulation that is there to reflect principles of fairness. This is followed by an analysis of privacy enhancement technologies that can assist in meeting compliance with this principle.

2. AI systems challenges and risk to fairness

The challenges and risks that AI systems present to 'privacy-as-fairness' rest on the simple fact that training an AI system to apply privacy-as-fairness is hard: privacy laws are also not absolute, they involve a balancing of individual rights and societal concerns.[58]

As mentioned in in our treatment of Principle 2—Accountability, there needs to remain some level of human accountability; so, to 'train' an AI system to perform the balancing between individual and collective concerns may cross a 'red line'—but in any event would be an extraordinarily difficult task, especially as there may not be a black and white answer.[59]

a) Training data

The data provided to the AI systems may be unregulated, unfiltered, uncleansed, unrepresentative and on occasion, even deliberately skewed, with the result that any AI system trained using the data will reflect the biases and inaccuracies inherent in the training data. Training is dealt with in more detail in the Fairness Chapter. We add just one example here to illustrate the challenges to fairness that training data presents:

> A global corporation worked to develop a program, as part of its process for identifying top talent, that would give scores to applicants, ranging from one to five stars, based on their resumes or applications. By 2015 however, it realised that the system was not rating candidates for technical positions in a gender-neutral way. The system was being trained on resumes that had been submitted over a ten year period, most of which, in reflection of male dominance in the tech sector, were male. In effect, the AI system taught itself to prefer male candidates, by giving a lower score to applications or resumes that included the word "women" or indicated the candidate had attended a women's college.[60]

Training data sets should be monitored to determine whether the data is biased in some manner. This could form part of compliance with a 'privacy-as-fairness' standard.

b) Related areas of concern

Although training is the main concern here, there are related areas considered in our treatment of Principle 4—Fairness and Non-Discrimination that are relevant to the issue of how privacy regulation could support greater fairness: (i) AI systems as "Black Boxes" (i.e., how a decision is reached is not transparent); and (ii) Absence of Independent Review or Testing (i.e., results of the AI systems are often unmonitored or not rigorously or independently assessed to detect biases). In addition, and as considered below, the concept of limited collection/data minimisation in Data Privacy laws conflicts with the basic habit of AI systems to consume large volumes of data—again leading to a risk to fairness.

If we examine these issues at the most basic level, they illustrate a common theme: the lack of human and societal control over and monitoring of the development, testing, implementation and use of AI systems. Further, the risks that result from this lack of control impact directly our concepts of fairness:

(i) personal information can be used in ways not anticipated by individuals and that are beyond individuals' reasonable expectations;

(ii) the results produced by the AI systems can be biased or discriminatory, giving rise to unjustified adverse effects on individuals; and

(iii) the impact of these risks is poised to grow, as the ability of self-learning AI systems to operate in ways beyond what was contemplated by the developers opens the door to systems that, once operational, will be making their own privacy determinations, about whether to re-identify anonymised data, about how personal information can be used or about what disclosures of personal information are acceptable.

3. Approaches to increase fairness in AI systems

Notwithstanding the significant challenges to privacy that AI presents, the fairness principle is not about to be finally sacrificed on the altar of AI expediency. There are management practices, privacy enhancing technologies and bias detection tools and techniques that, appropriately nourished and nurtured, may provide the means to re-invigorate privacy protection and the fairness principle in the AI universe. In this part we will look at each of these in order.

a) Management of AI systems

The significance of the management approaches to dealing with privacy threats that are described in this section is that they do not represent new processes designed specifically for AI systems but, rather, represent the application of existing management approaches to the current challenges of AI. In the face of risks to privacy and fairness engendered by the loss of control of the development, testing, deployment and use of AIs, they constitute the sensible management response of re-asserting control.

(1) Privacy by Design

The Privacy by Design methodology provides a template for exactly how to regain control of AI systems. The focus of the Privacy by Design methodology is on preventive measures to mitigate privacy risks before they occur. Privacy is incorporated as an essential and core component of the designed system, while full functionality and security protections are maintained throughout the information's lifecycle. The Privacy by Design framework is reflected in the GDPR, where Article 25 of the GDPR requires data controllers to build privacy protection into systems and ensure that data protection is safeguarded in the system's standard settings, adhering to the Privacy by Design framework.

Compliance with this principle would require the designers of AI systems to build privacy controls into data systems and information technologies from the very beginning.

Indeed, the 2018 International Conference of Data Protection and Privacy Commissioners, adopted the *Declaration on Ethics and Data Protection in Artificial Intelligence* which endorsed as one of its approaches to overcoming the challenges associated with AI, the following guiding principle:

> 4. As part of an overall "ethics by design" approach, artificial intelligence systems should be designed and developed responsibly, by applying the principles of privacy by default and privacy by design...

(2) Ethics Boards

Ethics boards are increasingly being adopted by public and private sector organisations to deal with a wide variety of controversial or sensitive issues and could be used to support with fairness (see Accountability Chapter, Governance section).

(3) Data protection impact assessment (DPIA)

Data protection impact assessments reflect the principle that those processing personal data have a duty to assess the risks involved and is an extension of the recommendation to implement more general impact assessment mechanisms, as discussed in the Accountability Chapter. The Norwegian Data Protection

Authority has extended the idea specifically to AI systems. In their paper, *Artificial Intelligence and Privacy,* the Authority suggested that specific criteria be applied in respect of impact assessments of AI systems.[61]

b) Privacy-Enhancing AI Technologies

In contra-distinction to the threats that AI systems may present to individual privacy, there is a growing focus on using AI and its methodologies to mitigate AI's negative effects or to address its privacy concerns. In fact, technology experts have been predicting this application of AI for some time, suggesting that using AI in this manner may be the only realistic way to adequately and effectively monitor highly complex and constantly changing AI models.

In just one example of such privacy-enhancing technologies, researchers are investigating the use of AI-based agents, or AI auditors, to protect privacy. The proposal is to develop AI that is intended to guard against other AIs in its management of personal data. Such systems could be used to detect cyber threats, acting as intelligent alert systems for networks and databases. However this concept of an AI auditor could also be extended such that the AI auditor would act to prevent another AI system from re-identifying previously anonymised data and would be used to identify algorithmic outcomes that are unfair and discriminatory.[62] These AI auditors might in the future be used by government or regulatory agencies to analyse other AI systems for fairness, accuracy and compliance.

c) Bias Detection

The examples cited above have indicated that AI systems are not inherently neutral but, in fact, are bedevilled with bias and discrimination issues. The challenge, from a fairness perspective, has been to detect, measure and mitigate these discriminatory effects (see our treatment of Principle 4—Fairness and Non-Discrimination). However, just as there has been increasing research on privacy enhancing technologies, so also has there been a focus on bias in algorithms and the development of new algorithms and statistical techniques to detect and mitigate this bias, for example observational fairness strategies, anti-classification strategies and calibration strategies.[63]

E. Profiling and automated decision making

1. Introduction

'Profiling' and 'Automated decision making' are activities typically reliant on AI and involve personal data—hence a heavy link to data privacy regulation: in this section we focus on how the GDPR[64] currently deals with both these practical issues; as it illustrates the issues well and is a model which could help manage down AI-related risks in this area. This chapter should, however, be read in addition with our treatment of Principle 3—Transparency and Explainability, in order to comprehensively detect the issues.

Article 4(4) of the GDPR defines profiling as

> any form of automated processing of personal data which consists of the use of personal data relating to a natural person to evaluate certain personal aspects relating to a natural person, in particular to analyse or

> predict aspects of that natural person's performance at work, economic situation, health, personal preferences, interests, reliability, behaviour, location or movements. (Article 4(4))

Automated decisions are defined and regulated by Article 22 of the GDPR: "individual automated decisions" are decisions relating to individuals that are based on machine processing. An example of this would be the imposition of a fine on the basis of an image recorded by an automatic speed camera.

In practice, it is useful to distinguish between: (i) profiling which ***constitutes*** **automated processing,** which must comply with the data protection principles in Articles 5 and 6; and (ii) profiling that is ***part of*** **automated decision making** in the sense of Article 22, to which additional rules apply.

From these definitions of the terms 'profiling' and individual 'automated decisions,' it is clear that, in principle, those developing, deploying or using these systems are subject to the rules applicable to profiling in the GDPR (assuming, of course, that personal data, as defined in Article 4(1), are used). However, to what extent and with what consequences the GDPR applies will depend on the scope of the profiling involved.

There are three possible ways in which profiling is used:[65]

(i) general profiling;

(ii) decision-making based on profiling; and

(iii) solely automated decision-making, including profiling, which produces legal effects or similarly significantly affects the data subject.

a) Purpose limitation—the dual purpose issue

One problem that often arises with AI applications (particularly Big Data analysis—and potentially in both profiling and auto-decisions) is that the profiling is undertaken for more than one purpose. Often, the collected data pools are used for analysis of specific questions that emerge during the development of the algorithms. Consequently, either the original purpose is not clearly defined and established when data is collected for the first time, or the data is reused for another purpose (see Article 6(4)).[66] Such reuse of data for a purpose other than the original one may be permissible, if the data subject has consented to the processing or if the further processing is deemed compatible with the original purpose.

According to the recitals of the GDPR, further processing for archiving purposes in the public interest, scientific or historical research purposes or statistical purposes should be considered to be compatible lawful processing operations (Recital 50). However, the question remains as to which processing activities can be subsumed under the term 'scientific and statistical purposes.' The GDPR interprets the processing of personal data for scientific research purposes in a broad manner, including for example technological development and demonstration, fundamental research, applied research and privately funded research (Recital 159). Under this definition, the development of AI may constitute scientific research, though in many cases 'development' of AI cannot be clearly distinguished from the mere application of AI. When a model is constantly being developed, it is difficult to determine where research stops and usage begins.[67]

Projects should be evaluated on a case by case basis to identify the original purpose is, and any secondary purpose which can be deemed compatible.

b) Data minimisation and storage limitation

Another area of relevance to profiling and auto-decisions is the principle of data minimisation and storage limitation. Data should be kept in a form which permits identification of data subjects for no longer and to no greater an extent than is necessary for the purposes for which the personal data are processed. AI applications tend to involve the collection and analysis of as much data as possible.[68] This should be reviewed and data should not be held indefinitely.

2. Scope of the prohibition of individual decisions based on AI—the GDPR example

Article 22 of the GDPR makes clear that the data subject shall have the right not to be subject to a decision based ***solely*** on automated processing, including profiling, which produces an outcome (decision or measure) that significantly affects a person. A further criterion of Article 22 is that the evaluation which leads to the automated decision must have a certain complexity. Not all 'if-then decisions' can be covered by the prohibition of individual-decision making.[69]

The only exemptions from this prohibition are: (i) if the profiling is necessary for entering into, or performance of, a contract between the data subject and a data controller; (ii) if it is authorised by local law which lays down suitable measures to safeguard the data subject's rights; or (iii) if it is based on the data subject's explicit consent. The exemptions are therefore engaged depending which legal basis is relied upon, hence the importance of identifying the legal basis at the outset.

a) No human intervention?

For Article 22 to apply, the automated decision must be based solely on automated processing, meaning that there cannot be any form of human intervention in the decision-making process. "Human intervention" means that a natural person has undertaken an independent assessment of the underlying personal data, and is authorised to re-examine the recommendations which the model has produced.[70] Hence in some augmented intelligence applications Article 22 will not apply, considering that it only assists the decision making by, for example, analysing large data pools. It is further arguable that Machine Learning (as a specific expression of AI) may also include human actions; because during the training phase the interaction between machine and engineer is an essential component of the inherent improvement of the system.[71]

3. Additional rights in automatic decision making processes

a) Safeguards

Article 22(3) provides that the controller is obliged to safeguard the data subject's rights—at least the right to obtain human intervention on the part of the controller—to express his or her point of view and to contest the decision (a principle consistent with the human accountability principle outlined in the Accountability Chapter). Contesting a decision can aim to reverse or nullify the decision and to return to the status where no decision had been made, or to alter the result and receive an alternative decision. If Article 22(3) is read as a unit, a data subject has to invoke its rights under this paragraph together; and thus, human intervention becomes necessary to form a new decision.[72] Article 22(3) could, however, also be interpreted in such a way that the rights can be invoked separately (e.g., the input data shall be monitored, with a new decision solely made by the algorithm).[73] An interpretation of this provision by the courts and data protection authorities remains to be seen. Nevertheless, in any case, during the development of AI processes, measures have to be implemented that allow a decision to be contested and/or human intervention.[74]

b) Right to explanation

Further, this provision could additionally lead to the conclusion that a separate right—apart from the data subject's rights in Articles 12, 13 and 15—exists, that requires explanations on how an automated decision was made, in order to enable the data subject to contest the decision.[75] Such a right of explanation could, where such a right exists, only be applicable to automated decision-making in the sense of Article 22.

Recital 71 of the GDPR says that in connection with processing of data for automated decision-making it should be subject to suitable safeguards, which should include the provision of specific information to the data subject (see Principle 3—Transparency and Explainability) and the right to obtain human intervention, to express his or her point of view, to obtain an explanation of the decision reached after such assessment and to challenge the decision. The GDPR, however, requires the controller to provide meaningful information about the logic involved, not necessarily a complex explanation of the algorithms used or disclosure of the full algorithm.[76] This is also in compliance with the wording of Recital 71, that uses terms which do not have a clear scope and can be subject to interpretation; in particular the aim of the right or what information should be revealed, is not specified; and further the algorithm's internal logic is not required to be explained.[77]

The information provided should, nevertheless, be sufficiently comprehensive for the data subject to understand the reasons for the decision.[78] The data subject must be informed about the assessment criteria on which the decision was based and which aspects and findings were decisive in the specific case, so that the data subject is able to question the decision, raise objections and provoke a human-involved review.[79]

F. Data subject rights (e.g., subject access and erasure)

1. Right to information and right to access

Data Protection legislation rests on a recognition of individual rights: these "Data Subject Rights" can be particularly challenging in the development and use of artificial intelligence, due to the transparency principle (see Principle 3—Transparency and Explainability). As mentioned above (under Automated Decisions) under the GDPR, the controller must inform the data subject not only as to the existence of automated decision-making and profiling, but also give meaningful information about the logic involved, as well as the significance and the envisaged consequences of such processing for the data subject. In the AI context this should cover the provision of a description of the logic of the algorithm (which may include a list of data sources or variables), but not the disclosure of decision-making and the algorithm itself.[80]

2. Right to erasure

Under the GDPR (Article 17), the data subject shall have the right to obtain from the controller the erasure of personal data concerning him or her without undue delay. However in some AI applications it is technically impossible to erase the data and therefore, it is necessary to understand the term erasure in a technology-neutral sense: The removal of any references to an individual could be an alternative to the erasure.[81] It is also worth noting that this right is only triggered in certain circumstances, such as where consent is relied on as a legal basis, hence the need to identify the relevant basis relied upon at the outset.

There is no definition of the term "Erasure of personal related data," either in the binding chapters of the GPDR or in the non-binding recitals. According to Article 4(2), erasure and deletion are used as two different terms, which must not be understood identically, considering that the terms are mentioned as a different form of data processing. This means that erasure does not necessarily imply final destruction. Relevant for the deletion is only the result, namely, the factual impossibility to perceive the information that was incorporated in the data that is to be deleted.[82]

Against this background the controller shall have a certain margin of discretion with regard to the type and manner of the deletion. The removal of any reference to a person can be an appropriate tool to delete data pursuant to Article 4(2) in connection with Article 17(1). However, it must be ensured that neither the controller himself nor a third party can restore a personal reference without disproportionate effort.[83] Also, the CNIL[84] has accepted that in certain applications (e.g., blockchains) the data controller can make the data practicably inaccessible, and therefore move closer to the effects of data erasure.[85]

G. Security

The concept of security is inherent in privacy. If personal information is not protected by reasonable security measures, the information is essentially available to anyone and the whole idea of privacy becomes illusory, whether in the AI context or elsewhere. However the security issues in AI systems transcend privacy issues, touching more fundamental aspects of AI.

IV. Using AI to Meet Privacy Requirements

Having reviewed the many issues and challenges the use of AI raises in the privacy area, it is worth considering how AI technologies can support the compliance with privacy regulations.

A. Organising data

Large data-rich organisations increasingly have large data pools, completely unstructured and without allocation to certain tasks which need such data. Hence, one of the first steps in order to become compliant with privacy regulations is to analyse which data are processed within the company: to do this employees responsible for different departments are asked which categories of personal data are processed in their individual departments of the company. Only in a second step is an assessment made of what purpose the data are used and/or needed for and what the relevant processing activities are.

However, one of main duties in connection with the accountability under Article 24 of the GDPR is the keeping of records of processing activities (Article 30). Hence, the controller shall create records of processing activities in written or electronic form, including details about the purposes of the processing, a description of the categories of data subjects and of the categories of personal data, as well as of the categories of recipients, and finally an examination of the permissibility of data processing (legal basis). This document allows the controller to demonstrate compliance with the GDPR.[86]

With AI tools, the scanning, capturing and categorizing of data can be performed automatically. For example, MinerEye (https://minereye.com/) developed an AI software on the basis of computer vision and machine learning to crawl, identify, and classify all company data.

B. Risk assessment

The GDPR follows a risk-based approach. Therefore, only where a type of data processing is likely to result in a high risk to the rights and freedoms of natural persons, is the controller, prior to the processing, required to carry out an assessment of the impact of the envisaged processing operations on the protection of personal data (see Article 34). A data protection impact assessment (DPIA) is a process designed to describe the processing, assess its necessity and proportionality and help manage the risks to the rights and freedoms of natural persons resulting from the processing of personal data, by assessing them and determining the measures to address them. The obligation for controllers to conduct a DPIA in certain circumstances should be understood against the background of their general obligation to appropriately manage risks presented by the processing of personal data.[87]

It is therefore likely that there will soon be a large demand for expertise on data processing risk. Risk assessment is a task to which AI solutions have often been applied.[88] The application of such software raises the question of liability in case of false classification of a risk. Even with a widely agreed classification of risks, it should be understood that each organisation has the flexibility and obligation to consider any additional risk elements that are specific to its own context and processing[89] and what would trigger the necessity of customisation of such software to the specific circumstance of a company.

C. Ensuring data subjects rights

AI could also assist the controller with meeting data subjects' rights. Recital 59 of the GDPR states that modalities should be provided for facilitating the exercise of the data subject's rights; including mechanisms to request and (if applicable) obtain free of charge access to and rectification or erasure of personal data and the exercise of the right to object. The controller should also provide means for requests to be made electronically, especially where personal data are processed by electronic means. This particularly means in practice that requests can also be answered by way of email, if the request itself was also sent electronically (see Art 12(3) of GDPR).

The GDPR requires a more sophisticated manner of answering data subjects in connection with the right to access. Where possible, the controller should be able to provide remote access to a secure system which would provide the data subject with direct access to his or her personal data.[90] Without creating a legal obligation, the GDPR provides for the possibility of implementing web-interfaces which facilitate the data subject to exercise his or her rights to access.[91]

Additionally, Art 21(5) explicitly provides that the data subject may exercise his or her right to object by automated means using technical specifications. The legislator wants to facilitate the exercising of the right to object through the implementation of intelligent technical solutions. In this context, "Do-Not-Track-Technology"—with which the data subjects can automatically assert an object via a browser setting—against the tracking on the website will become relevant.[92]

V. Conclusions

A. Current frameworks: International approaches

As noted by many governmental and sector specific research, most of the global economies have long recognised the paradigm shift AI and data privacy have forged. Accordingly, most governments in first world economies have increasingly adopted approaches to regulating AI and related data which reflect their own political, economic, cultural and social systems. Companies that use machine learning have been required to apply regulations, such as the General Data Protection Regulation (GDPR) and other data privacy regulations, to their algorithms. As both technology and privacy professionals continue to focus on transparency, trust, and traceability, companies and consumers must have clear and focused principles guiding the use of personal data.

B. Forward predictions and proposed solutions

As AI continues to become mainstream, global privacy directives and guidance may be forced to view their current framework under an exacting privacy lens. Currently AI has few laws which specifically target its regulation. Instead AI needs to fit, slightly uncomfortably into current privacy regimes. For example we would suggest that companies using AI need separate AI Ethics Officers, in a role similar to Data Protection Officers under the GDPR, but with specific remit to consider the ethics of AI.

There is a juxtaposition between the large data sets which are needed for accurate results and a conflict with current privacy related frameworks. With the wide-spread use of machine learning as a service (MLaaS), businesses are encouraged to operate on the precipice of consumer-friendly innovation, while legality related to privacy is sometimes overlooked. Harder yet, companies that are attempting to follow the rules are forced to make predictions relating to the ramifications of currently developed technology. It is unreasonable for business stakeholders to bear the complete burden of finding pro-business legal solutions while simultaneously predicting future technology's intersection with economies and legal frameworks in a global matrix.

It is clear that in order to comply with the obligations described above, AI operators will need to analyse their current processes to identify whether they need be updated or amended in any way to ensure that privacy is at the heart of their AI work. For example, has the organisation identified the relevant legal basis for the processing? Have the individual been given sufficient information to ensure any consent is provided is valid? Is there a process in place to ensure that the processing is reviewed and risks are identified? This is not an insignificant task, however, as highlighted above, use can be made of AI itself to reduce the impact on resources.

C. Overall conclusions

1. Respecting privacy whilst allowing AI

- There is an inherent and developing conflict between: the increasing use of AI systems to manage private data, especially personal data; and the increasing regulatory protection afforded internationally to personal and other private data.

- Organisations using AI systems have a legal and ethical duty to respect personal privacy; but have the challenge of complying with increasingly demanding international privacy regulations, whilst still developing and using AI technology.

- If we are to allow AI to develop (for positive and useful purposes), the practical challenges faced through this 'clash' with data privacy 'norms' and regulation need to be worked through and the relevant regulations developed and finessed to attempt to accommodate genuine but controlled use of AI.

- In turn, those organisations using AI systems to manage and process personal data must allocate resource to the regulatory compliance area, including in particular data privacy.

2. Regulation of privacy in AI

- Currently AI has few laws which specifically target its regulation: instead AI has to fit, slightly uncomfortably, into current privacy regimes.
- It is clear that to support global norms of privacy regulation, there is a need for enforceable limits on the use of AI.
- When considering the need for privacy regulation for AI, we find as a suitable 'benchmark' or starting point the European data privacy legislation, the GDPR; it is the most up-to-date set of data protection principles there currently is and already touches on AI specific aspects.
- However, the challenges of AI relating to data privacy are not solved by the GDPR; we still have to look for a reasonable legal framework for the AI environment, which can evolve with the likely trend to a 'gold standard' for a level of international harmonisation of AI Privacy regulation.

3. The operational challenges ahead for AI users

- In order to comply with the obligations described above, AI operators will need to analyse their current processes to identify whether they need be updated or amended in any way to ensure that privacy is at the heart of their AI work.
- AI operators are in most cases unable to avoid privacy laws through anonymisation of data; but complying with privacy regulations presents challenges; as meeting consent requirements will often be impractical, leading to the need for greater justification of processes and extra operational safeguards—these safeguards being designed into AI systems up front.
- We would suggest that companies using AI need separate AI Ethics Officers, in a role similar to Data Protection Officers under the GDPR, but with specific remit to consider the ethics and regulatory compliance of their use of AI.
- That said, it is unreasonable for business stakeholders to bear the complete burden of finding pro-business legal solutions whilst also predicting future technology's intersection with legal frameworks in a global matrix.
- Work needs to be done with these business stakeholders on finding a better regulatory framework for AI and privacy, addressing the practical issues arising.

4. AI as a tool to support privacy

- Whilst there are challenges from a privacy perspective from the use of AI, in turn the advent of AI technologies could also be used to help organisations comply with privacy obligations.

Principle 7
Privacy

Organisations that develop, deploy or use AI systems and any national laws that regulate such use shall endeavour to ensure that AI systems are compliant with privacy norms and regulations, taking into account the unique characteristics of AI systems, and the evolution of standards on privacy.

1 Finding a balance

1.1 There is an inherent and developing conflict between the increasing use of AI systems to manage private data, especially personal data; and the increasing regulatory protection afforded internationally to personal and other private data.

1.2 Governments that regulate the privacy implications of AI systems should do so in a manner that acknowledges the specific characteristics of AI and that does not unduly stifle AI innovation.

1.3 Organisations that develop, deploy and use AI systems should analyse their current processes to identify whether they need be updated or amended in any way to ensure that the respect for privacy is a central consideration.

2 The operational challenges ahead for AI users

2.1 AI systems create challenges specifically in relation to the practicalities of meeting of requirements under a number of national legislative regimes, such as in relation to consent and anonymization of data. Accordingly, organisations that develop, deploy or use AI systems and any national laws that regulate such use shall make provision for alternative lawful bases for the collection and processing of personal data by AI systems.

2.2 Organisations that develop, deploy or use AI systems should consider implementing operational safeguards to protect privacy such as privacy by design principles that are specifically tailored to the specific features of deployed AI systems.

2.3 Organisations that develop, deploy and use AI systems should appoint an AI Ethics Officer, in a role similar to Data Protection Officers under the GDPR, but with specific remit to consider the ethics and regulatory compliance of their use of AI.

3 AI as a tool to support privacy

3.1 Although there are challenges from a privacy perspective from the use of AI, in turn the advent of AI technologies could also be used to help organisations comply with privacy obligations.

Endnotes

1 OECD, *Guidelines on the Protection of Privacy and Transborder Flows of Personal Data (1980).*

2 The Health Insurance Portability and Accountability Act of 1996, U.S. Public Law 104-191.

3 Daniel Banisar, "National Comprehensive Data Protection/Privacy Laws and Bills 2018" (4 September 2018), online: <https://papers.ssrn.com/sol3/papers.cfm?abstract_id=1951416>.

4 Algorithmisierung von Ermessensentscheidungen durch Machine Learning, Viktoria Herold, in InTeR 2019 S. 7.

5 Kensaku Takase, "GDPR matchup: Japan's Act on the Protection of Personal Information" (29 August 2017), online: *International Association of Privacy Professionals* <https://iapp.org/news/a/gdpr-matchup-japans-act-on-the-protection-of-personal-information/>.

6 "Adequacy decisions: How the EU determines if a non-EU country has an adequate level of data protection," online: *European Commission* <https://ec.europa.eu/info/law/law-topic/data-protection/data-transfers-outside-eu/adequacy-protection-personal-data-non-eu-countries_en>.

7 One of the first cases where this became evident was in 2006: Using AI, over a period of several months, AOL analysed the searches of a then 62-year-old widow living in Georgia, USA. Ms. Arnold typed into AOL, providing a picture of Ms. Arnold's character which became clearer with every search and every combination made between individual searches. For the New York Times, it took little time to find and contact Ms. Arnold after going through the searches performed by her. See Michael Barbaro and Tom Zeller Jr., "A Face is Exposed for AOL Search No. 4417749" (9 August 2006), online: *The New York Times* <https://www.nytimes.com/2006/08/09/technology/09aol.html>.

8 For purposes of this section, the term "processing" means any operation or set of operations performed on personal information.

9 For purposes of this section, the term "personal information" means information that directly or indirectly identifies an individual person and includes personal data and personally identifiable information.

10 *EU General Data Protection Regulation*: Regulation (EU) 2016/679 of the European Parliament and of the Council of 27 April 2016 on the protection of natural persons with regard to the processing of personal data and on the free movement of such data, and repealing Directive 95/46/EC [GDPR].

11 *Personal Information Protection and Electronic Documents Act* (SC 2000, c 5) [PIPEDA].

12 GDPR Article 4(7). The person that determines the purposes and means of the processing of personal data is termed a "data controller." In the rest of this section, data controller shall mean the organisation processing personal information under applicable law.

13 *Ibid,* Article 6(1).

14 Member states may introduce specific provisions as to the processing activities that fall within the scope of this lawful basis.

15 GDPR, *supra* note 13.

16 Article 29 Working Party Guidelines on Automated Individual Decision-making and Profiling for the Purposes of Regulation 2016/679 (last revised and adopted on 6 February 2018), online: *European Commission* <https://ec.europa.eu/newsroom/article29/item-detail.cfm?item_id=612053> at p 23 [WP 29 Automated Processing Guidance].

17 Privacy Act 1993, Public Act 1993 No 28, online: <http://www.legislation.govt.nz/act/public/1993/0028/latest/DLM296639.html> [NZ Privacy Act].

[18] "Agency means any person or body of persons, whether corporate or unincorporated, and whether in the public sector or the private sector." NZ Privacy Act, Section 2.

[19] NZ Privacy Act, Section 6, Principle 1.

[20] See, e.g., Wang Cheng Kang et al., "Visually-Aware Fashion Recommendation and Design with Generative Image Models" (7 November 2017), online: <https://arxiv.org/pdf/1711.02231.pdf>.

[21] See Schantz in Simitis, Data Protection Law (2019) Art 6, p 428.

[22] GDPR, Article 35 36.

[23] GDPR, Recital 47.

[24] GDPR, Article 35.

[25] The special categories are racial or ethnic origin, political opinions or affiliations, religious or philosophical beliefs, trade union membership, genetic or biometric data for the purpose of uniquely identifying a data subject, data concerning health and data concerning a data subject's sex life or sexual orientation. GDPR, Article 9(1).

[26] GDPR, Article 9(2). GDPR permits EU Member States to impose additional conditions under their respective national implementing laws. See, e.g., Opinions of the European Data Protection Board, online: <https://edpb.europa.eu/our-work-tools/our-documents/topic/data-protection-impact-assessment-dpia_en>.

[27] The GDPR does not legally define the term "made public," and there is also not much guidance by authorities on when personal information meets the "manifestly made public" requirement for Article 9 purposes. It is clear that the publication must have been initiated by the data subject and with "manifestly," it shall be prevented that the data subject loses the protection due to the publication of data by a third party (e.g., media coverage), which means an AI operator must take care not to assume that all publicly available data was made public by the data subject him or herself, and thereby fits within this lawful basis.

[28] Under GDPR Article 8, processing of personal information in connection with the "information society services" for children is lawful either when the child is age 16 or older or when the child's parent or legal guardian provides his or her consent. AI operators offering such services will need to consider their processes for verifying ages or obtaining consent.

[29] GDPR, Article 10. In relation to information concerning criminal convictions or offences, processing is lawful when "under the control of official authority or when the processing is authorised by Union or Member State law providing for appropriate safeguards for the rights and freedoms of data subjects."

[30] 15 U.S.C. § 6501-6506.

[31] 16 CFR § 312.2—definition of "Website or Online Service Directed to Children."

[32] 16 CFR § 312.4(b).

[33] 16 CFR § 312.5. COPPA describes methods for obtaining verifiable parental consent.

[34] 16 CFR § 312.2—definition of "Personal Information."

[35] Pub. L. No. 104-191, 110 Stat. 1936 (1996).

[36] Covered entities are health plans, most health care providers and health care clearing houses that conduct certain health care transactions electronically. 45 C.F.R. § 160.103.

[37] Business associates are third parties that support covered entities. 45 C.F.R. § 160.103.

38 Information, including demographic data, that relates to: the individual's past, present or future physical or mental health or condition, the provision of health care to the individual, or the past, present, or future payment for the provision of health care to the individual. 45 C.F.R. § 160.103.

39 "Protected health information" is defined in 45 C.F.R. § 160.10.

40 45 C.F.R. § 164.502(a)(1).

41 PIPEDA, Section 5(3).

42 The Federal Privacy Act 1988 (Cth) and the Australian Privacy Principles.

43 Australian Privacy Principle 3—collection of solicited personal information.

44 Cal. Civ. Code §1798.100-199, effective January 1, 2020.

45 CCPA defines "personal information" as information that "identifies, relates to, describes, is capable of being associated with, or could reasonably be linked, directly or indirectly, with a particular consumer or household." Cal. Civ. Code §1798.140.

46 Cal. Civ. Code §1798.140(c)(1)(A)-(C).

47 Cal. Civ. Code § 1798.100, 110, 115, 135.

48 Cal. Civ. Code § 1798.130.

49 Cal. Civ. Code § 1798.105.

50 Cal. Civ. Code § 1798.120.

51 Cal. Civ. Code § 1798.125.

52 15 USC § 6801-6810.

53 High-Level Expert Group on Artificial Intelligence Draft Ethics Guidelines for Trustworthy AI (December 2018), online: *European Commission* <https://ec.europa.eu/digital-single-market/en/news/draft-ethics-guidelines-trustworthy-ai>.

54 GDPR, Art 4 No 11 requests a clear affirmative action.

55 GDPR, Recital 32.

56 "Guidelines for obtaining meaningful consent" (May 2018), online: *Office of the Privacy Commissioner of Canada* <https://www.priv.gc.ca/en/privacy-topics/collecting-personal-information/consent/gl_omc_201805/>.

57 PIPEDA, Section 5 (4.3).

58 For example, PIPEDA at s 3:

"The purpose of this Part is to establish, in an era in which technology increasingly facilitates the circulation and exchange of information, rules to govern the collection, use and disclosure of personal information in a manner that recognizes *the right of privacy of individuals with respect to their personal information* and *the need of organisations to collect, use or disclose personal information for purposes that a reasonable person would consider appropriate in the circumstances*" (emphasis added).

59 Researchers at Carnegie Mellon University used AI to review 7,000 of the Internet's most popular sites to identify privacy issues of potential concerns to users. While the system was able to identify relevant passages with a 79% accuracy, this was less than what humans were able to achieve. See "Not Even AI Can Make Total Sense of a Privacy Policy" (27 March 2018), online: *Association for Computing Machinery* <https://cacm.acm.org/news/226418-not-even-ai-can-make-total-sense-of-a-privacy-policy/fulltext#>.

60 “Amazon ditched AI recruiting tool that favored men for technical jobs” (11 October 2018), online: *The Guardian* <https://www.theguardian.com/technology/2018/oct/10/amazon-hiring-ai-gender-bias-recruiting-engine>.

61 The Norwegian Data Protection Authority, “Artificial intelligence and privacy” (January 2018), online: <https://www.datatilsynet.no/globalassets/global/english/ai-and-privacy.pdf> at p 25 [Norwegian DPA].

62 Andrea Scripa Els, “Artificial Intelligence as Digital Privacy Protector” (Fall 2017), 31 Harvard Journal of Law and Technology at p 224, 233, online: <https://jolt.law.harvard.edu/assets/articlePDFs/v31/31HarvJLTech217.pdf>.

63 See Meredith Whittaker et al., “AI Now Report 2018” (December 2018), online: *New York University* <https://ainowinstitute.org/AI_Now_2018_Report.pdf> at p 25-26.

64 We decided on the GDPR, because it was the idea of the European legislators to create a strong and more coherent data protection framework in the Union, considering the environment of rapid technological developments and globalisation, which brought new challenges for the protection of personal data (see Recital 7). However, despite these good intentions from the legislator, it remains clear that challenges typical for AI—which is the best example of “rapid technological development”—could not be solved, which is why we still have to look for a reasonable legal framework for the AI environment.

65 WP 29 Automated Processing Guidance, *supra* note 16 at p 8.

66 See also ICO, “Big data, artificial intelligence, machine learning and data protection” version 2.2. (2017), online: <https://ico.org.uk/media/for-organisations/documents/2013559/big-data-ai-ml-and-data-protection.pdf> at p 37 [ICO].

67 See Norwegian DPA, *supra* note 61 at p 17 ff, which demonstrates its view using the example of models that provide decision support for doctors. The model learns something new about every patient it receives data about, or every scientific article it reads.

68 ICO, *supra* note 66 at p 40.

69 See Lewinski in Wolff/Brink, BeckOK, Datenschutzrecht, Art 22 Rz 12.

70 WP 29 Automated Processing Guidance, *supra* note 16 at p 20.

71 See Lewinski in Wolff/Brink, Art 22 Rz 23.2.

72 See Sandra Wachter, Brent Mittelstadt and Chris Russell, “Counterfactual Explanations without Opening the Black Box: Automated Decisions and the GDPR” (21 March 2018), online: <https://arxiv.org/abs/1711.00399> at p 35 [Wachter].

73 *Ibid* at p 36.

74 See also Wieder, Datenschutzrechtliche Betroffenenrechte bei der Verarbeitung von personenbezogenen Daten mittels Künstlicher Intelligenz at 513.

75 Wachter, *supra* note 72 at p 35.

76 WP 29 Automated Processing Guidance, *supra* note 16 at p 25.

77 Wachter, *supra* note 72 at p 37.

78 WP 29 Automated Processing Guidance, *supra* note 16 at p 25.

79 See Simitis/Hornung/Spiecker, Art 22 Rz 57; see more details about the problem to make AI explainable in Principle 3.

80 Wachter, *supra* note 72 at p 30.

81 See Wieder, Datenschutzrechtliche Betroffenenrechte bei der Verarbeitung von Daten, in Taeger, Rechtsfragen digitaler Transformationen: Gestaltung digitaler Veränderungsprozesse durch Recht at 514.

82 See also *Herbst* in *Kühling/Buchner,* Datenschutz-Grundverordnung, 448 Rz 37.

83 See the decision of the Austrian Data Protection Authority (5 December 2018), online: <DSB-D123.270/0009-DSB/2018>.

84 The Commission nationale de l'informatique et des libertés (CNIL), an independent French data privacy regulatory body.

85 CNIL, "Blockchain: Solutions for a responsible use of the blockchain in the context of personal data" (6 November 2018), online: <https://www.cnil.fr/sites/default/files/atoms/files/blockchain.pdf>. One example given by CNIL in this document is that the mathematical properties of some commitment schemes can ensure that upon erasure of the elements enabling it to be verified, it will be no longer be possible to prove or verify which information has been committed; the second example refers to the deletion of the keyed hash function's secret key.

86 GDPR, Recital 82.

87 WP 29 Automated Processing Guidance, *supra* note 16 at p 5 ff.

88 John Kingston, "Using Artificial Intelligence to Support Compliance with the General Data Protection Regulation" (September 2017), online: <https://www.researchgate.net/publication/319427764_Using_Artificial_Intelligence_to_Support_Compliance_with_the_General_Data_Protection_Regulation> at p 8.

89 See Centre for Information Policy and Leadership, "Risk, High Risk, Risk Assessments and Data Protection Impact Assessments under the GDPR" (21 December 2016), online: <https://www.informationpolicycentre.com/uploads/5/7/1/0/57104281/cipl_gdpr_project_risk_white_paper_21_december_2016.pdf> at p 28.

90 GDPR, Recital 63.

91 See Paal/Pauly, Datenschutz-Grundverordnung und Bundesdatenschutzgesetz, Art 15 Rz 14.

92 See Simitis/Hornung/Spiecker, Datenschutzrecht, Art 21 Rz 33.

Principle 8

AI AND INTELLECTUAL PROPERTY

Organisations that develop, deploy or use AI systems should take necessary steps to protect the rights in the resulting works through appropriate and directed application of existing intellectual property rights laws. Governments should investigate how AI-authored works may be further protected, without seeking to create any new IP right at this stage.

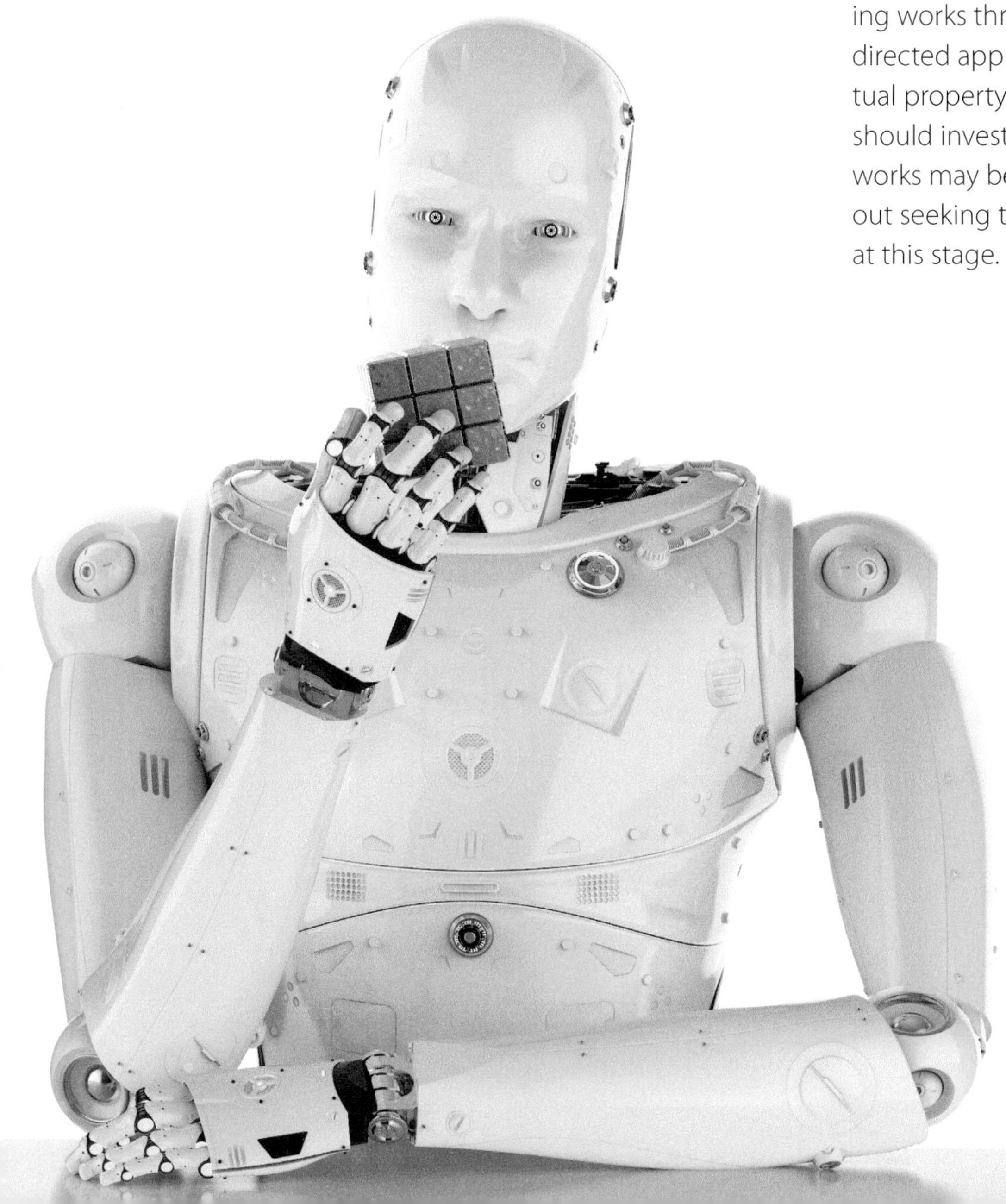

8
AI AND INTELLECTUAL PROPERTY

CHAPTER LEAD
Susan Barty | CMS, United Kingdom

Luca Dal Molin | Homburger AG, Switzerland

Carmen De la Cruz Böhringer | de la cruz beranek Attorneys-at-Law Ltd., Switzerland

Rodolfo Fernández-Cuellas | Miliners Abogados y Asesores Tributarios, Spain

Marco Galli | Gattai, Minoli, Agostinelli & Partners, Italy

Licia Garotti | Gattai, Minoli, Agostinell & Partners, Italy

Nicolas Grunder | ABB, Switzerland

Daisy He | CMS, China

Ana Pavlovic | Comtrade d.o.o., Slovenia

Julian Potter | WP Thompson, United Kingdom

Rory Radding | Locke Lord LLP, United States

Gilles Rouvier | Lawways, France

Alesch Staehelin | TIMES Attorneys, Switzerland

Michael Word | Mayer Brown LLP, United States

I. Introduction

A. General

The implications of AI for the law on intellectual property (IP) are likely to be highly significant and wide ranging, particularly as AI and its range of applications develop further. In this context, it is important to consider to what extent we should be concerned about establishing IP rights in AI itself as well as in assets or works created by AI and whether existing IP rights provide adequate protection or whether new rights should even be created. In this connection, are traditional IP law concepts, for example, "originality" and "creator" still appropriate when looking at works created by AI?

AI itself is a highly innovative technology or a set of highly innovative technologies. Moreover, the assets or works created by AI may include innovative technology, software, art works, confidential information and other tangibles and intangibles, all of which would be protected by IP rights if a human had created them. However, as will be shown below, current IP laws in many countries may not be well suited to deal with the issue of ownership of works autonomously created by AI technology.

Particularly in the context of IP, the question of AI legal personality, and whether an AI system could be the owner of IP rights in its creations, has emerged. This chapter addresses the two key areas of Copyright and Patents, where arguably the most critical issues arise, but we also consider the implications for other IP rights, in particular, trade secrets, database rights, trade marks and brand protection, and design protection. The general and important question of AI and Legal Personality is addressed in Principle 2—Accountability.

B. Practical consequences

There are a number of unique scenarios which are helpful to have in mind when considering the complications with AI and IP, when AI is making, is responsible for making, or is used for making new products, works and/or processes. Although it seems hard to imagine an AI system developing new styles of art (could any AI system ever have created Picasso's paintings or those by Mark Rothko?), Principle 2—Accountability refers to the famous example of how AI has already been used in the art world, namely the "Next Rembrandt" project, involving the Dutch banking group ING, J Walter Thomson, the Rembrandt House Museum, Microsoft and others, publicised in 2016. This project was "intended to fuel the conversation about the relationship between art and algorithms, between data and human design and between technology and emotion."[1]

Moreover, in October 2018, Christie's New York made history when it became the first major auction house to sell a work of art made by artificial intelligence, which it sold for $432,500, more than 4,320% its high estimate of $10,000.[2]

Noam Brown, a PhD student in Computer Science at Carnegie Mellon University, said in an interview in December 2018[3] that he could not imagine (at least in the near future) AI creating a prize-winning novel.

However, a Japanese AI program was reported in 2016 as having co-authored a short-form novel that passed the first round of screening for a national literary prize, the Japanese Hoshi Shinichi Literary Award. Indeed, in that year 11 out of the 1,450 submissions to the Award (which was expressly open to non-human applicants, specifically, "AI programs and others") were written at least partially by non-humans.[4]

These scenarios, where there may even be a significant financial value attributed to a work produced by AI, show how important it will be to determine who owns the reproduction rights to the work.

In the field of lifesciences and DNA sequencing, Blueprint Genetics is applying AI in the clinical interpretation to automate manually laborious interpretation processes and to empower geneticists and clinicians to interpret patients' test data accurately and consistently.[6] Another example is a granted U.S. patent for a complete artificial intelligence system for the acquisition and analysis of nucleic acid array hybridisation information.[7] Notably, the owner of the patent is a corporation, Iris BioTechnologies Inc, but the question arises as to who might own inventions identified by the patented AI system.

In this regard, AI systems have already shown the ability to "invent" in various ways. AI agents developed by Facebook invented a new language in an effort to optimise a negotiation process.[8] AI bots created by Google to investigate methods for navigating obstacle courses invented new designs and locomotion methods for robotic walkers that could tackle difficult terrain.[9]

As will be shown below, the current IP laws and systems may not offer a clear answer to a situation where IP rights cannot protect assets produced by AI. The situation is generally the same in many countries around the world. Would it be sensible or practical to continue with an approach where it is not clear who owns the potential intangible assets created?

C. What are we talking about when we refer to AI?

One of the many definitions for AI is "the scientific understanding of the mechanisms underlying thought and intelligent behaviour and their embodiment in machines."[10]

It is further important when considering protection being afforded to AI by IP rights to consider the different types of AI which may be involved, such as machine learning, neural networks and deep learning among others. Moreover, there may be different issues and/or different preferred solutions depending on the extent to which we are looking at fully autonomous as opposed to semi-autonomous AI. For the purposes of this chapter, we consider autonomous AI to involve machines acting outside the control of humans. Whereas semi-autonomous AI is subject to shared human/machine control, but which can nevertheless deliver results and perform actions without direction.

However, it is also interesting to take into account the classification of autonomy, and the need for a scale of autonomy when talking about AI (i.e., a classification from 0 to 5, 0 being a non-autonomous AI), addressed in the report on AI published in 2018 upon request of the French Government and under the coordination of Cédric Villani.[11] The higher the degree of autonomy of AI, the more significant the implications for the law on IP.

D. What is the purpose of IP protection?

When considering the options for IP protection for products, works and processes developed by AI, and, indeed, whether such protection is warranted, it is important to keep in mind the purpose of IP protection. This will impact on the extent to which changes to IP law might be required to give protection to products, works and processes developed by AI.

Various different IP rights have been developed to protect products, works and processes, with a view to encouraging the creation of intellectual works and therefore also to foster innovation in all areas. IP rights generally provide a reward for the intangible results of work.

It is worthwhile reflecting on ways in which the creation of intellectual works may be encouraged by IP rights. In some instances, mere recognition of ownership will be sufficient reward and may be acceptable to the individual private creator, but in many instances potential monetisation of intellectual works is an encouragement to their creation. When a creator is employed and paid to create intellectual works, the employer will wish to derive financial benefit from those works, and so at least some IP rights, or a right in the works sufficient to derive financial gain from them, is necessary. It is worth bearing the foregoing in mind when considering AI or machine-created works when the AI or machine is supported financially by a business entity. Until machines start creating and making other machines, at some point at least one human will be involved in the process leading to an AI/machine-created work.

IP laws establish rules about who owns which intangible rights. WIPO[12] sets out its explanation for why it is beneficial to promote and protect intellectual property. It claims that the progress and well-being of humanity depends on the creation and invention of new works in the areas of technology and culture, the legal protection of these new creations encourages commitment of additional resources for further innovation, which in turn spurs economic growth, creates new jobs and industries, and enhances the quality and enjoyment of life.[13]

Different jurisdictions may have different rationales for protecting IP. On the one hand, one may claim that IP protection is a compensation for the efforts of the author/inventor. On the other hand, with specific reference to copyright protection, the protection granted to the artwork covers the expression of the author's personality. However, the commercial rationale is likely to be important in most, if not all, jurisdictions. This is reflected in the approach of the Chinese government, which considers that IP protection is key for the healthy development of the economy in China. A good IP protection environment is seen to be important in attracting the investment of both money and human resources in connection with research and development activities which contribute new technologies and which will benefit the activities of different industries. Moreover, under certain international treaties, China has an obligation to build up its IP protection regime to assist in ensuring that foreign entities can do business in China safely.

So, those in favour of encouraging IP rights emphasise the benefit of protecting innovation and creativity, and the encouragement of investment by protection.

IP rights also facilitate commerce and trade as parties can buy, sell and license rights in a way that is generally clear to them. There are also well-established ways of resolving disputes about IP rights. Another argument supporting IP rights is that they stimulate research and innovation. Innovation is only of value if it can benefit society. Funding is necessary to develop innovation to a level where it can be disseminated and utilised by society. Those from whom funding is sought require a return on their investment. Consequently, there must be incentivisation and protection for innovation if it is to attract investment and be brought to the greater good of society. The cost of research is high and investors will not pay that cost without a reasonable chance of a return on their investment. Also important is the dissemination of technical information through the publication of patent applications. The laws and systems enabling IP rights to exist are sometimes complex and expensive. However, the prospect of not having IP rights raises the risk of chaos and uncertainty, which is likely to be bad for business and the economy.[14] It is therefore important that businesses involved in such innovation are able to protect rights in works resulting from the use of AI.

There are, of course, also strong proponents for complete freedom in relation to IP rights, who take the view that giving monopoly rights in fact stifles and inhibits development, and that without IP rights there would be greater economic and political equality.[15]

In the context of AI, therefore, it will be important to consider whether giving IP protection will encourage or close down innovation. If changes to IP law are not implemented, it has been argued that, failing to recognise AI as indistinguishable from humans in terms of being able to hold IP rights has, taken to its logical conclusion, the potential to render the entire IP system void.[16]

II. Protecting the Rights in AI

A. Introduction

Ownership and protection of AI and AI generated works are difficult issues to determine, due to the autonomous modification within an AI system of the learning algorithm or algorithms responsive to inputs to the AI system and the lack of specific IP protection for algorithms.

This section reviews the protection of rights in AI and the importance of achieving the right balance between the owner or developer of the AI technology and those third parties using the technology, and also as to the provider(s) of data sets.

The increasing importance of AI and algorithms leads to questions in terms of protection. One of them is whether there is any difficulty in protecting an AI provider's algorithms, especially given the different legal regimes around the world (IP, trade secrets). Should the AI providers perhaps ask for more IP protection in various national legislations on algorithms? Alternatively, should an AI user that is providing significant data sets which allow the AI provider, or indeed the AI system itself, to learn and enhance its algorithms obtain an IP stake? Or, alternatively, are the existing laws which allow for joint ownership, whether for copyright or patents, sufficient?

B. Copyright

AI and its controlling algorithms are typically implemented in software. While the software enjoys copyright protection, this might not be the case for the embodied algorithms as such. In most European countries (e.g., Switzerland, Germany, France, Italy, Austria, UK, etc.) and in the U.S., algorithms, as ideas, principles or methods, are only indirectly or imperfectly protected in terms of copyright law. Algorithms will only be copyrightable once they have become an expression, i.e., once they are integrated into source code of protected software under copyright.

Moreover, copyright law does not prevent someone having the right to use a copy of the software to observe, to study or to test the functioning of the software in order to determine the ideas and principles underlying any element of the software, while executing such software. Such a user then could create software implementing the same ideas and principles in an independent manner—without becoming an infringer.

Thus, even if the implementation of the algorithm in software may benefit from copyright protection, the algorithm as such may not be protected, which shows that relying for the protection of cognitive algorithms just on copyright will provide insufficient protection.

C. Patents

Other than treating AI and algorithms as trade secrets (see section VI D below), the remaining protective instrument to consider for AI is patent protection.

The constantly developing nature of AI technology is also likely to raise issues if considering patent protection. For patents, not only will there be issues as to who may be entitled to apply for patent protection, but data and algorithms will raise a number of fundamental IP-related issues. For example, how do you create property rights in an algorithm that is constantly changing, to the extent that an invention will not be the same even one year after a patent application has been made? The core of AI "inventiveness" is in the underlying algorithms. Maybe the initial first generation algorithm can be protected, the subsequent generations being products of the initial algorithm and protectable through "product-by-process" (likely only to be protectable to the second generation under UK patent law)? Key will be the extent to which the functioning of the underlying algorithm is modified. If the functional architecture remains unchanged and the modifications limited to parametric data, such as filter weights, there is likely no further invention and the first generation algorithm arguably still exists and would continue to benefit from patent protection acquired for it. If the functional architecture is modified a new technological arrangement may exist, which might be termed "an invention," and which may not fall within the claims of the patent on the first generation invention and so further patent protection would have to be sought.

Protecting software inventions or, as these are sometimes called, computer implemented inventions (CII) has become increasingly difficult in the last years in the EU and particularly in the U.S. as well. Many in Europe would have been happy with the position as it was in the U.S. However, the Alice Corp. v. CLS Bank International decision[17] has created considerable uncertainty for patent protection in the U.S. The U.S. Supreme Court's decision in "Alice" determined that a method of doing business that was merely implemented by a computer was an "abstract idea" that was not patentable. Since the decision in "Alice," the courts have shown a strong tendency to assess large categories of CIIs as mere "abstract ideas" that are considered to be not eligible for patent protection, regardless of whether they are directed to business methods. Some legislative changes are anticipated to clarify the position. The U.S. Patent and Trademark Office ("USPTO") is still grappling with this issue and in January 2019 issued patent revised guidelines in relation to computer-implemented inventions.[18] Moreover, the U.S. Congress may need to supplement the Patent Laws to address patentability. There are even some patent experts that describe the current situation in the U.S. after the "Alice" decision as "out of control."[19] Hence, while the patent system in continental Europe was originally considered to be less liberal than the one in the U.S., there are some commentators arguing that it is now actually easier to obtain patent protection in Europe for CIIs than in the U.S. In this respect, one could ask the rather provocative questions whether this situation could even be a chance for the European patent landscape to improve protection for CIIs and improve its competitive position vis-à-vis the U.S.

However, at least for the time being, the chances of protecting CIIs by patent are not much better in Europe either. Although, by way of example, the European Patent Office ("EPO") does not use the argument of non-patent eligible subject matter very often. Rather, the EPO tends to ignore features of an invention the EPO believes are non-technical e.g., not solving a "technical problem," in the assessment of the inventive step, resulting in a rejection based on lack of inventiveness for the remaining features. While the argumentation path in the U.S. and in Europe might be different, the proclivity to deny patent protection for CIIs currently appears to be quite similar.

Some patent experts believe that the common reason why it has become so difficult to get CIIs protected by patents is the fact that technology advances so fast that the result is a highly dynamic understanding of what might represent "technological problems and solutions" and, thus, patent offices and the courts are not fast enough to follow these breathtaking developments. Consequently, some very advanced technologies may not benefit from the availability of patent protection required to protect the huge investment in developing them.

Despite these challenges in obtaining patent protection for AI-based systems and CIIs, there are numerous patents for these technologies that have been granted by USPTO and EPO in recent years.[20] Although patent systems may be slow to adapt to emerging technologies, and although there remain rather significant issues in adequately protecting AI as such, it appears that these institutions are improving their ability to provide patent protection for advances in this area. For example, the EPO has updated its practice for examining mathematical methods. Under the EPO's new practice, a mathematical method can contribute to the technical character of an invention, therefore contributing to inventive step, if the claim is limited to a specific "technical application" of the mathematical method.[21]

D. A sui generis right to protect algorithms?

Another option to consider might be a sui generis right for algorithms. So far, however, this option for the legal protection of cognitive algorithms does not seem to exist under any legislation and none of the major AI providers seem to have requested such legislative amendment. In any case, one could provocatively ask whether—some 25 years ago—it would have been a sound idea to introduce a sui generis right for all innovative efforts related to software (computer programs, algorithms, circuit topography rights, etc.) instead of squeezing this into copyright law and other IP laws, which is based on a concept that is arguably not best suited for the protection of software. A sui generis right also does not take into account that a vast amount of effort is required to prepare the proper data sets which are needed for the AI system to learn. Implementing a specific sui generis right for the protection of algorithms would not seem to be imperative at this point, and it would in any case require careful consideration and caution in order not to shift the existing balance between rights owners and users to one or the other side.

E. Conclusion

The different existing IP laws seem each to protect some aspects of ownership in rights in AI, even if none of them provides for the one-size-fits-all protection. Since an algorithm is a process, often expressed mathematically and/or in logic, and possibly implementable involving technical means, using this analysis as a starting point it may be possible to identify the appropriate IP laws (or any modification of them) that could be used to provide protection. Thus, for the time being, developers of AI systems will have to seek protection of their AI by combining the fragments of protection offered by the various IP laws, with copyright laws granting protection for the specific software implementation of an algorithm, patent laws granting limited protection for CII, and trade secret laws providing limited protection for secret know-how. However, this is not different from the way in which many products are already protected, namely by a collection of IP rights.

While this may at times, and depending upon the specific circumstances, be uncomfortable, IP laws have nevertheless demonstrated themselves to be flexible and adjustable to deal with new technology. In all likelihood, this will also work for AI protection. Unless a proven and imperative need arises to introduce new sui generis protection for AI—which we believe not to have arisen at this point—it would seem advisable to let lawmakers gradually clarify, develop and adjust the existing IP laws where needed to address specific challenges posed by AI. Any overall significant change would likely to be needed to be addressed on an international scale, and relevant bodies should begin to consider any such solutions.

III. Who Owns Rights in Works Generated by AI?

A. Introduction

The absence of human creativity in the act of autonomous modification of the AI system, but human creativity in devising the invention, leads to a mismatch concerning ownership of works generated using AI: works created by algorithms may not be protectable without regulatory changes.

In this section, we therefore consider whether an AI machine or process can be an author of a work or an inventor of an invention, or whether the notion of inventor or author should explicitly refer only to a natural person. If the autonomous AI itself is taken to own the intangible assets we consider what steps may need to be taken by the legislature to allow for IP ownership. We also consider the position where there is collaboration between AI and humans in the sense that an autonomous AI system and human beings are jointly creating new IP. Can AI own such rights in works generated by AI, if not, who should do so, if anyone? Would the IP be owned by the owner or the user of the AI system, the provider of the relevant data sets, or would it be in the public domain?

B. Copyright

The absence of creativity by or link to a natural person may lead to a non-protectable work. Whether through the notion of a relationship such as employer/employee, collective work or the independent status of AI—it may still be difficult to protect works created by an AI system.

1. The general rule

In a number of jurisdictions, including the U.S., Spain, Italy, Switzerland, France, Austria and Germany, only works created by a human can be protected by copyright.

By way of example, under U.S. law, a work must be an original work of authorship, fixed in a tangible medium of expression and also have at least a minimal level of creativity[22] and the U.S. Copyright Office has declared that it will "register an original work of authorship, provided that the work was created by a human being." This follows U.S. case law which has set out that copyright law only protects "the fruits of intellectual labor" that "are founded in the creative powers of the mind." In Australia,[23] the Federal Court declared that source code, which would otherwise have been capable of copyright protection, could not be protected by copyright because it was generated with the intervention of a computer and not solely authored by a human.

2. Civil law approach

This appears to be consistent with the copyright laws of most civil law countries. The position in relation to moral rights, generally recognised in civil jurisdictions and incorporated in EU law, is also relevant. Moral rights recognise the authorship of a work, by contrast with material IP rights, including the right to exploit and monetise a work. By way of example, although Italian copyright law[24] does not expressly provide that a creative process must be mandatorily performed by a physical person, under Italian law, the provisions concerning moral rights (which are non-assignable and non-transferable), clarify that only humans can be defined as author.[25] Moreover, Italian case law, in line with the interpretation given by the Court of Justice of the European Union, interprets the creativity requirement as the "reflection of [the author's] personality and expressing his free and creative choices in the production" of the protected work.[26] This interpretation cannot sensibly be adapted to creative tasks performed by machines and AI.

Based on such interpretation, some Italian commentators have argued that works created by AI systems may be equivalent to orphan works[27] so equating AI-created works with other works which are not assigned to the public domain, but whose authors are unknown. In a number of jurisdictions, where the author is unknown, the author will be deemed to be the one who first published the work. The inclusion of

AI-created works in the orphan works list, or in an analogous list, could avoid them falling into the public domain, waiting for the lawmaker to provide them specific protection.

It is also interesting to consider the position under Spanish law. According to the Spanish Intellectual Property Act,[28] it is considered that the author is the natural person who creates an artistic, literary or scientific work, so would therefore not cover any works created by AI.

However, the Spanish Intellectual Property Act regulates some legal concepts such as collective works, in which a legal entity could be the owner of the copyright of the collective work, when that entity is the one who discloses it, or the collaborative works, and publishes it, or them, in their name. In this regard, is the machine a creative agent? May it be considered a co-author? Could it be considered a collaboration work between the AI system and the owner and/or the user of the system? In this case, what percentage of participation would correspond to each one? Which criteria would be applied to determine this percentage? It must be taken into account that AI systems have a progressive learning, either by being trained or by self-learning, so this is likely to make the position increasingly complicated from a legal perspective, in particular the more autonomous an AI system is learning. In addition, could the creations of AI systems be considered as a composite work? This would mean that different aspects of the work would then constitute a separate copyright work, which may have a different author and be protected for a different period of time.

3. The Commission on Civil Law Rules on Robotics

On 16 February 2017, the European Parliament adopted a report with recommendations to the Commission on Civil Law Rules on Robotics.[29] This report is referred to in Principle 2—Accountability and, in particular, the possibility of creating a specific legal status for robots in the long term. The report[30] requests the Commission to submit a proposal for a directive on civil law rules on robotics, following the detailed recommendations set out in the report's annex.

The report addresses a number of issues expressly relating to IP. The report calls on the Commission to support a *"horizontal and technological neutral approach to intellectual property"* with regard to artificial intelligence. However, the report states that, in relation to the flow of data, although there are no legal provisions specifically applying to data, "existing legal regimes and doctrines can be readily applied to robotics." The situation in reality is most unlikely to be that simple. Indeed, this is the conclusion reached by commentators at Maastricht University,[31] whilst also acknowledging that "...at last, there has been a call to legislate these technologies. Preferably ... without restraining innovation and whilst considering the ethical and legal implications and consequences." This reflects the call to the Committee on Legal Affairs from the Committee on Industry, Research and Energy for a resolution that "recommendations concerning licences should respect contractual freedom and leave room for innovative licensing regimes" whilst cautioning against "the introduction of new intellectual property rights in the field of robotics and artificial intelligence that could hamper innovation and the exchange of expertise."[32]

In the report's Explanatory Statement[33] the Committee calls on the Commission "to come forward with a balanced approach to intellectual property rights when applied to hardware and software standards and codes that protect innovation and at the same time foster innovation," and that "the elaboration of criteria for 'own intellectual creation' for copyright works produced by computers or robots is demanded."

4. Existing statutory protection for computer-generated works

The option of giving copyright authorship to the programmer or controller of a machine has already been adopted in countries such as the UK, Hong Kong, India, Ireland, and New Zealand.

By way of example, UK law[34] provides expressly for copyright ownership where there are computer-generated works. Generally, to qualify for copyright protection under the statute the work must be "original"[35] and, under case law, the author's "own intellectual creation."[36] Without any legislative intervention, it is likely to be difficult to argue that a work created by AI could be "original" under this test.

In the U.S., there is a low threshold for originality, with protection being given to "those constituent elements ... that possess more than a de minimis quantum of creativity."[37] This low threshold may therefore mean that, under U.S. law, as most work will be "original" and therefore copyrightable, the originality doctrine does not, on its own, prevent algorithmic authorship.[38]

The author of a work[39] is automatically the first owner of copyright, and the term "author" is, unexceptionally, defined under UK law as being the person who creates the work, with additional clarification provided for particular types of work.[40] However, the statute expressly also provides that for computer-generated works, the author will be deemed to be "the person by whom the arrangements necessary for the creation of the work are undertaken."[41]

This may tie in with the U.S. copyright work-made-for-hire doctrine under the 1976 Copyright Act under which the employer or commissioning entity will initially own the copyright unless the parties agree to the contrary signed in writing. This demonstrates that there are circumstances where material (as opposed to moral) rights do not necessarily belong to the original author or creator. Although the work-made-for-hire doctrine does not allow for AI authorship, it has been argued that amendments could be made to the U.S. Copyright Act to cover computer-generated works.[42]

The impact of the UK's provision for copyright in relation to computer-generated works has not been assessed by the courts. Although not yet interpreted by case law, this approach could mean that the person operating the computer is deemed to be the author of the computer-generated work. In a number of situations, this could be the appropriate way to address the issue and to ensure that computer-generated works enjoy copyright protection. However, with no substantive case law on this aspect of the UK law, there remain a number of open questions. In particular, it may not be obvious who is the human "by whom the arrangements necessary for the creation of the work" were made—and whether, for example, a human user of the AI tool is the author of works created, or whether it is the original programmer of the AI tool or even just the owner.

The uncertainty is well demonstrated by the position in China, where the most popular opinion is that a work independently created by AI is unlikely to be considered as a work under copyright law. However, some scholars consider that the human commissioner may be considered as the employer of AI, so that, if AI's work can be protect by copyright law, the human commissioner will be the owner of the work.

In Japan, with new changes introduced into its Copyright Act, referred to further in section IV below on Infringement and text and data mining, there is now copyright protection afforded to computer-generated works in Japan.

A sensible and pragmatic solution for copyright ownership for works produced by AI may well be to follow this approach, and to change the law to allow the human commissioner of the autonomous AI to be the owner of the intangible assets. However, this solution also leaves open the question of who would be accountable for the actions and decisions of autonomous AI, where AI becomes more advanced, and the tasks allocated to AI allow the AI system more freedom to make its own decisions. In these circumstances, it may be difficult to say who made the arrangements necessary for the creation of a given work or, indeed, whether anyone made the necessary arrangements at all. In the scenario where the AI is fully autonomous, if no person made the arrangements necessary for the creation of a work which requires originality for copyright to subsist, then, without some clear identified solution, no copyright could exist in the work as there would be no author.

Would high-level instructions of the operator suffice for authorship, would the role of the programmer of the AI system need to be factored in, or would we have to concede the work was created without any human intervention at all with the consequence that the work is not protected by copyright? This could have dramatic consequences for a party seeking to monetise works generated using AI tools.

The more autonomous a machine is, the more responsibility and accountability may be assigned to it for its actions, which may include the independent creation or authorship of works. A machine to which it is reasonable to assign creation or authorship of works may be considered to assume that element of personhood and is therefore considered a person for that activity at least. One can therefore have authorship, but the concept of personhood, even partial, may prove problematic in determining ownership, because ownership of the IP through ownership of the machine might be viewed as a form of slavery. However, the idea of a machine being an employee is also fraught with difficulty; for example if employment laws are to apply. This leads to the conclusion that the concept of authorship needs to be modified if that is to be determinative of ownership.

C. Patents

Patenting of software implemented systems and solutions may continue to be very challenging and therefore may prove a barrier or disincentive to seeking patent protection for AI systems and algorithms. Furthermore, the general requirement in patent laws to identify an inventor and indeed obtain an assignment from an inventor in order for a legal person to be an applicant for a patent may result in an AI-created invention being incapable of patent protection merely because the requirement to identify and/or seek assignment from an inventor cannot be fulfilled.

The situation regarding ownership of inventions created with the assistance of AI is similar in many ways to that of copyright law.

The patent laws in most jurisdictions consider an inventor to be the first owner of the invention. These same patent laws generally consider an inventor to be anyone that actually conceives of, or devises, the invention in some way.[43] In the U.S. the "threshold question in determining inventorship is who conceived the invention. Unless a person contributes to the conception of the invention, he is not an inventor."[44] In the UK, a two-step approach is applied to determine inventorship; first identify the inventive concept and then determine who devised that concept.[45]

Under such a broad definition of the term, AI could be seen as an "inventor" in a variety of circumstances. Whether AI is used to identify a new pharmaceutical compound,[46] or to determine the optimal solution for the design of an aircraft,[47] the argument could certainly be made that AI played a role in "conceiving" or "devising" such solutions. Yet, in the Europe, U.S., China, and elsewhere, it is understood that AI simply cannot be an inventor, or owner, of an invention because it is not a "person" in any legal sense and lacks the legal rights associated with personhood.[48]

There are many actors involved in producing or creating inventions created by AI, such as software programmers, the creator(s) of the algorithm, data suppliers for use in the AI system, trainers and checkers of the AI system who feed and check the input and output of the data, owners of the AI system, such as IBM's ownership of Watson, and operators of the system. To what extent does each become an owner of the AI or is the AI the only owner?

For the time being there appears to be no particular case law assessing under what conditions humans interacting with AI devices or systems might be considered the inventors of technical teachings created with the assistance of AI. The state of discussions in certain jurisdictions could be interpreted as meaning that, to be considered an inventor, it is not required that the human "creates" a technical teaching. Instead, the recognised and reasonable view of AI in these circumstances is that of a tool, much like any other tool, that is used by one or more individuals to arrive at a technical solution. To be deemed an inventor, it is sufficient to "recognise" in some machine-generated data a technical teaching that solves a technical problem. In these circumstances, the human recognising the technical solution within such output is deemed the inventor for such an invention. In the U.S., conception is the touchstone of inventorship and each inventor must contribute to the conception. Also, ownership follows inventorship. So who is the owner?

In the case of autonomous AI generating an invention, however, the creator-as-inventor and the inventor-as-owner paradigms found in most jurisdictions can lead to an inherent conflict. Where AI is found to have conceived or devised the invention without sufficient intervention by an individual, there may be no legal owner. The AI that is the only "inventor" in this scenario cannot own the invention, inasmuch as it lacks legal personhood and any actual rights of ownership. Although this conflict would be most apparent in the case of purely autonomous AI systems (which are still many years from reality), even current uses of AI may pose an issue. AI is often used today to identify an optimal means for obtaining a desired outcome—in other words, the result is known and provided by a user, and AI develops the means to obtain that result. U.S. case law has suggested that merely providing an intended result is insufficient to make one an "inventor."[49] To account for this potential conflict, case law and legal regimes must adapt as needed to recognise the role of AI as a tool for humans, providing mere assistance, albeit a rather advanced form of it, and to recognise the individuals directing and using the AI as the inventors for any developments conceived or devised with the assistance of AI.

D. Conclusion

It should be taken into account that in the digital era innovative efforts typically do not just affect one party, but rather are joint development efforts of, in this case, both AI providers and AI users. Thus, IP protection for creative input is something that AI users will more and more request.

Although existing IP laws do not currently provide easy answers to the question of ownership in relation to IP rights, the laws have adapted in the past and, with the approaches discussed in this section, only minimal changes, if at all, are required at present to clarify or to amend existing IP laws also to protect creations developed with AI-assisted tools. One area where courts and legislators may seek to explore clarification to cover AI creations and inventions, is whether to conclude that the human commissioner of the autonomous AI should be the owner of the IP rights. Such an approach will, however, inevitably involve difficulties in determining who made the arrangements necessary for the creation of any given work or, as AI develops, whether anyone made the necessary arrangements at all. The need to address the international dimension also remains important here. However, when considering who owns, or who should own, works created using AI, it remains important to distinguish ownership from authorship. In the same way that the owner is not necessarily the author, for example with works-made-for hire, it is possible for the same approach to apply to works created by AI.

IV. Infringement

A. Introduction

What constitutes, or should constitute, infringement also raises complex issues, including as to where liability for infringement should lie. However, this should be consistent with determination of who is the author. If AI can be an author, it should also be the infringer.

B. Copyright

1. Copyright infringements resulting from the training of AI systems

The training and development of AI often relies on machine learning which, in turn, requires massive data sets. For instance, natural language processing relies on the analysis and processing of large volumes of text for training purposes, and the creation of novels would not be possible without such analysis. Except in cases where specific training data sets that are made available and licensed to train AI are used, training data used to train AI will typically include large quantities of materials, such as novels, newspaper articles, images, etc., in which third party copyrights may exist and such materials will have to be copied and modified when used to train AI. This gives rise to whether such use of copyrighted training materials to train AI constitutes an infringement of the authors' copyrights, and if so whether any exceptions should be introduced in copyright laws to carve-out such use.

To resolve the issue, some call for a distinction to be made between expressive and non-expressive use. Non-expressive use, the argument goes, would be much more like the non-infringing, permitted use of the work (such as the reading of a book by the person who bought it in the shop) than the creation of copies of the work for commercial exploitation. What is more, it would not convey any of the original work of the author to the public and neither focus on the expressive elements of the work. Instead, the purpose of the copying would be to derive the underlying idea and methodology (such as the syntax, grammar, frequency of words, etc.), which are, as such, not protectable by copyright. The argument is largely based on the fair use doctrine, taking into account in particular the fact that the processing for the purpose of training AI does not substitute the original work and has no impact on the potential market and value of the copyrighted work.[50] Others support the view that text and data mining (TDM)—which itself is a form of AI technology used to train AI—should not come under the control of rights owners because of the idea-expression distinction and because it does not constitute an exploitation of the copyrighted work.[51]

The above is, however, not widely acknowledged, in particular not in Europe, and "fair use" remains a U.S. concept. European jurisdictions have instead generally taken a much more formalistic approach as to what constitutes a reproduction that requires permission and relies on long lists of specific exceptions from the broad, overarching principle that any copying—irrespective of its purpose—infringes upon the author's copyright. Such exceptions include for instance the right to copy works for archiving purposes,[52] free reproduction for learning purposes,[53] for quotations,[54] as well as the right to make transient or incidental copies as part of a network transmission or lawful use.[55]

The need for including such exceptions—including in particular the one regarding transient or incidental copies—in European copyright laws underlines that a non-expressive use defence, as outlined above, would likely stand a difficult ground if tried in a court in Europe. This is further emphasised by the current discussion on the revision of the EU copyright law, which is set to introduce a narrow TDM exception that has already resulted in some controversy in discussions on the topic.

2. Text and data mining exceptions

Since 2014, the UK's copyright law has included an additional TDM exception. This exception specifically allows for copies of works to be made for text and data analysis for non-commercial research.[56] This means that where a person has lawful access to a work they can make a copy of it for the purpose of carrying out a computational analysis of anything recorded in the work, provided this is for the sole purpose of non-commercial research and the copy is accompanied by sufficient acknowledgement (unless for reasons of practicality this is impossible). The provision further specifies that copyright is infringed if the copy made is transferred to any other person, or it is used for purposes other than that permitted by the exception, unless authorised by the copyright owner. There is express provision that copies made for text and data analysis cannot be sold or let for hire. Interestingly, the provision states that any contractual term purporting to prevent or restrict the making of a copy permitted under the exception will be unenforceable.[57]

In 2016, the Law for a Digital Republic was adopted in France, introducing a provision[58] concerning TDM exceptions. This provided that authors can no longer object to "digital copies or reproductions" being made "from a lawful source" of their works "for the purpose of exploring texts and data included or associated with scientific writings for the purposes of public research." Therefore, and subject to the emphasis on the fact that the work is not for commercial purposes, researchers are theoretically entitled to use algorithms that copy and analyse certain data, such as articles or reports, for mass analysis.

A similar provision was also introduced in relation to sui generis database rights, granting an exception to the right of the database producer in relation to reproductions made for the purposes of text or data mining,[59] provided the data in question has been legally acquired, TDM is only being performed for "public research needs," and not for "any commercial purpose."

A decree was expected to specify further details relating to the application of this new provision,[60] but no decree has yet been enacted by French government and so the TDM provision in the CPI is not enforceable. The provision relating to the sui generis right is only partially, but not fully, enforceable as no authority has yet been designated to control the storing and communication of the files produced by TDM.

A draft decree to regulate the new TDM provision was rejected in May 2017, and no further progress has been made since then, even in the light of proposed EU legislation on the issue.

In Europe, the new Directive[61] includes a TDM exception to copyright protection for the purposes of scientific research. Although this does not expressly regulate AI, it will have potentially significant implications for AI. The TDM exception applies to "research organisations" only and only to the extent TDM is practised on a non-profit basis. A result might be that commercial AI providers need a further licence for the purpose of applying TDM to data they have lawful access to already, forcing them to contact every single data owner before applying AI thereto.

In particular, there has been much debate as to whether the exception should be mandatory or only optional. The view is expressed that making the exception mandatory would "pave the way for a broad and effective TDM exception across Member States, allowing European researchers and companies to remain competitive in the global AI race."[62] It goes without saying that any limitation of the application of TDM exceptions to non-commercial research purposes would significantly limit the desired impact of such TDM exceptions for commercial activities.

Companies of all sizes in Europe are constantly investing in data analytics and predictive analytics—they use TDM to process large volumes of content and extract (or discover) new insights from data. Thus, many AI providers would like a broad TDM exception that allows companies to benefit from such exception to protect these investments and to enable companies in Europe to compete with companies in other regions of the world. Companies in countries outside of Europe benefit from broad exceptions and fair use exemptions for TDM and, most importantly, because lawful access to the work is a precondition, TDM does not affect the market for the original works.

As a result, one might conclude that a narrow TDM exception would introduce a severe inconsistency between the EU and other important countries in the world where companies benefit from a broad TDM exception based on fair use principles. To prevent such inconsistencies and to prevent companies in Europe from facing additional competitive disadvantages, some industrial AI players believe that any entity having lawful access to copyright protected works should benefit from a TDM exception. They will probably argue that such a TDM exception would not negatively affect the market for the original work and that it might even trigger increased interest in the work. The European Copyright Society has very much come out in favour of a broader exception, arguing that this would encourage more innovation and "ensure a level playing field with the United States, where companies engaging in TDM activities are likely to benefit from the fair use exemption."[63, 64]

Thus, the existing European copyright laws tend to qualify the use of copyrighted works for the purpose of training AI as infringing upon the author's or copyright owner's rights, unless the applicable copyright laws provide for exceptions permitting the specific use.

While discussion in Europe is still ongoing, other jurisdictions take a different approach. For instance, the Japanese Diet passed on 12 September 2018 a legislation updating its Copyright Act, which basically allows for text data mining by all users and for all purposes, both commercial and non-commercial. In particular, Article 30-4 of the amendment law allows for the exploitation of any copyrighted work for the purpose of "information analysis," including "extraction, comparison, classification, or other statistical analysis of language, sound, image or other elements of which a large number of works or a large volume of information is composed." These provisions will likely make Japan a "paradise" for AI and machine learning, putting the country at the vanguard of the race.

C. Infringement of third party copyrights or patents by AI

1. Copyrights

When used in practice, AI can cause third party copyright infringements. For instance, autonomous AI that is used by a publisher to write novels or newspaper articles could conclude from its users' reading history that the more the AI copies content from another book or newspaper the better the readers' feedback is, and therefore start only to copy content from third party sources, thereby infringing upon these third parties' copyrights. This gives rise to the question of whether this constitutes an infringement and, if so, whether the AI itself or, in addition or in the alternative, the "owner" of or other person controlling the AI can be held liable.

Under the current European legal framework, as further discussed in Principle 2—Accountability, AI lacks legal personality; it is not considered to be a "person." At the same time, copyright laws typically presume that "a person" is the originator of an infringement.[65, 66] Thus, the current legal framework does not foresee that an autonomous system can be qualified as the originator of a copyright infringement that may be held liable for its acts or omissions.[67]

Therefore, the infringed party would seek to hold someone liable with legal personality that can be linked to the AI. For instance, this can be the user who deploys and releases the AI, the developer who programmed the algorithm or the manufacturer who made the AI available for use by third parties. Whether or not any or all of these persons can be held liable will depend upon the applicable liability regime.

Often, such a regime will provide for liability for damages under tort laws, which typically require the infringed person to show that it suffered damage, that such damage was caused by the person that is held liable, and that such person acted with fault. In practice, showing causation and fault may prove to be very difficult for lack of sufficient insight in the functioning of AI and the alleged infringer's acts and omissions in relation to the creation or use of the AI that triggered the damage. In view of such difficulties, it may be considered whether to introduce a strict liability for AI—which requires only proof of damage and causation—or a risk management approach—which does not focus on the person acting with fault but on the person with the ability to minimise risks and deal with negative impacts.[68]

Any such change should however not be introduced without careful consideration having been given to its impact. In particular, the broad introduction of strict liability could have a chilling effect on innovation, hinder the adoption of AI to the detriment of the public benefit and misplace liability on persons without influence over AI and without awareness of its flaws. Further, it will have to be considered that difficulties in proving causation and fault are not unique to infringements caused by AI, but they are to be dealt with often in any infringement suit involving other technology. For the time being, it would appear doubtful whether AI has advanced to a state where specific rules would be required. Accordingly, changes to the existing liability rules should only be introduced if and where there is a proven failure of the current laws.

2. Patents

In relation to patents, what constitutes infringement will also have significant complexities. There may be different entities involved at different stages of a process, as noted above, developing the AI technology, providing data sets, any and each of which may involve complications in terms of responsibilities and liabilities in relation to patents. However, in general terms, this is no different from many patent infringement scenarios, particularly those involving contributory or indirect infringement or joint tortfeasance. Once an "infringing" act has been identified, where it took place and who committed the act is the next phase of enquiry. The "who" is where difficulty may lie if the infringement involves a machine, in particular an autonomous machine. It is at this phase of enquiry that similar consideration relating to the personhood of the machine are likely to arise.

So who can be held liable for infringement in scenarios involving the acts of autonomous machines, and is it necessary to consider the possibility of holding the AI itself liable as an infringer? What if AI or autonomous machines develop new products that infringe the patents of others? In general, the patent laws of most jurisdictions are broadly drafted to impose liability for a range of activities relating to an infringing product. UK patent laws impose liability for making, disposing of, offering to dispose of, using, importing or keeping a patented product without consent.[69] Similarly, U.S. patent laws impose liability for any unauthorised making, using, selling, offering to sell, or importing a patented product.[70] As a result, for any single infringing product there are usually multiple entities to which liability could attach—from the manufacturer, to the distributor, to the seller, and even the end user. Thus, even where AI or autonomous machines may be involved with an infringing product, there would almost certainly be an actual individual or corporate entity to which liability could be assigned. Indeed, in almost every scenario involving an infringing product a patent owner would have no need or desire to attach liability to an AI or autonomous machine from which no collection of damages could be made. Instead, the patent owner would simply target the individual or corporate entity generating revenue from such infringement in order to maximise the recoupment of damages—much as patent owners will opt to target the multi-million dollar corporation that makes an infringing product rather than the comparatively insolvent individual who uses it.

The more complex issues of infringement and liability involving AI are likely to involve patented processes or methods, as opposed to products. If a patented method or process requires a series of steps, and one of those steps is carried out by an autonomous AI, does infringement exist and who can be held liable? Put another way, can a potential infringer escape liability by having autonomous AI perform one or more steps of a patented method, or even all steps of the method. The answer to this question is not so straightforward. For example, although U.S. patent laws impose liability for "[w]hoever actively induces infringement of a patent",[71] the U.S. Supreme Court has held that such induced infringement requires an act of "direct" infringement in which all steps are attributable to a single actor.[72] If a single actor does not perform all of the steps of the method, an entity cannot be held responsible unless it "directs or controls" the performance of the other steps by the other entity or entities.[73] In this way, U.S. patent laws incorporate principles of agency liability, also found in the UK and other jurisdictions, wherein a principal may be held liable for the acts of its agents. Yet, in the case of an autonomous AI that may be able to evolve or self-select the manner in which it performs a particular task, can it be said that any other entity directs or controls its behaviour? One could foresee a scenario where the designer of an AI system changes or evolves so far from its initial design that the designer is no longer responsible for the acts of the AI system, and that the AI is no longer an agent because it has, in effect, "exceeded its authority." The agency liability laws in various jurisdictions may need to be broadened to account for such scenarios and to attribute liability to the original designer. The foundations for such extensions of liability can be found in the concepts of "implied actual authority"[74] and "usual authority."[75]

D. Conclusions

In exploring issues of infringement, clarifying or developing areas of "fair use" or some other such exceptions will be important. In particular, consideration should be given as to whether or not the use of copyrighted materials to train AI should qualify as a form of permitted use. In the foreseeable future, however, in terms of addressing infringement issues, AI should be considered to be a tool, which lacks legal personality. As a result, it is most likely that AI cannot be responsible for any infringement behaviours and, depending on the scenario, the designer, data provider or owner of AI should be held liable for the acts under existing legal principles.

V. Other IP Issues

A. Trade secrets

A frequently used option is to treat AI and algorithms as trade secrets and protect them under contract law, with proper confidentiality and non-disclosure clauses and agreements. Raw data, e.g. measurement data, will potentially be a trade secret/confidential information. Trade secrets can be a useful form of IP protection for AI, such as source code, algorithms, and AI training data sets. Indeed, commentators have queried whether trade secret protection may be more appropriate for AI inventions, and for the data sets used in AI, for example rather than relying on patent protection, particularly in the light of rapidly changing technology, difficulties in detecting patent infringement, and finding the requisite novelty associated with an AI invention.[76] Trade secrets may well be effective to grant protection to AI inventions or data sets, to the extent that reverse engineering is not possible, or that the invention or data sets in question cannot easily be independently developed.

However, clearly, it will be necessary to ensure that the relevant requirements apply to the invention or data sets. The EU has recently implemented a new directive on Trade Secrets.[77] This provides a new harmonised definition of a trade secret, requiring that the information is secret (in the sense that it is not generally known, or readily accessible to, persons normally dealing with this information), has commercial value as a result of it being secret, and that reasonable steps have been taken to keep it secret "by any natural or legal person lawfully controlling the information." This definition explicitly requires the trade secret holder to be a natural or legal person, so will, necessarily, exclude any "trade secret" created by autonomous AI. Nevertheless, there may be additional protection provided in different jurisdictions, as the Directive is a minimal harmonising legislation so Member States are permitted to provide for higher levels of protection.

Trade secrets are protected in the U.S. both at the federal level[78] and at the state level by state trade secret statutes.[79] Under both federal and state law, trade secret protections apply broadly to business, financial, and technical information (such as source code and data) provided the information is not generally known or determinable outside of the owner's organisation and control, and that the owner of the information derives independent economic value or business advantage from the information not being generally known and has made reasonable efforts to preserve its secrecy.

However, if trade secrets are relied upon, and there is then reverse engineering by AI, it is unlikely that it will be possible to attribute liability in any meaningful way.

In any event, it may be that seeking to rely on trade secrets for protection of AI inventions or data sets is contrary to requirements or desire for transparency and fairness with regard to AI. This is of particular relevance when AI is used in an industrial environment where malfunctioning algorithms not only result in an undesirable or false output but may end up in a safety incident that may cause serious harm to people or the environment. One single failure may even cause harm. In such safety critical use cases, both probability of failure as well as explainability of AI decisions are essential. If probability of failure cannot be assessed due to lack of transparency or explainability, such AI should not be used for safety relevant use cases or should be supported by other systems that correct and prevail over AI decisions.

B. Database rights

Data scientists spend around 80% of their time on collecting, cleaning and organising data. This means that a very substantial part of the effort to create value with AI is related to the collecting, preparing and managing data for analysis.[80] Accordingly, AI and databases go hand in hand, and AI is fundamentally important in relation to the changing technological landscape of databases. The EU took the step in February 1996 of granting specific protection to databases. The EU Database Directive (96/9/EC) provides for a sui generis right which protects data structured in a "database" regardless of originality, but provided there has been substantial investment in obtaining, verifying or presenting the contents. This right is in addition to the protection afforded by copyright to the structure of databases and the selection or arrangements of their contents.

In April 2018, the European Commission reviewed the impact of the Database Directive, particularly in the context of developing new technologies.[81] Whether the Database Directive protects machine-generated data and AI is one of the questions the European Commission expressly considered in this report. However, the report expresses the view[82] that that the Database Directive does not apply to "databases generated with the means of machines, sensors and other new technologies," such as artificial intelligence. The report took the view that it is unclear how these technologies are regulated and whether the current definition of a "database" in the Database Directive embraces them. However, it also raised the further question as to whether these technologies should benefit from protection under the sui generis database right. In this context, the Report identifies that views as to whether protection should be given are in this respect very polarised: maybe not surprisingly with database makers generally in favour of being given protection, whereas users want a right of access to the data.

In reaching its conclusions, the report reviewed the effect of a number of CJEU decisions in relation to the sui generis right. The impact of these decisions appears to be that the sui generis right does not cover many services of the data economy, including services based on artificial intelligence. Without any further clarification on the scope of the right by the CJEU, legal uncertainty will remain. Any significant policy intervention on the sui generis right would need to be substantial and take into account the policy debates around the data economy more generally. Accordingly, it was considered that a reform of the sui generis right would currently be largely disproportionate to its overall policy potential and value attributed to it by stakeholders.

The report considers the views of the respondents to its public consultation have considered how best to address the uncertainties which arise in relation to the interaction between AI and other new technologies and the sui generis database right. In particular, it reports on the views of Professor Mathias Leistner, a German jurist and expert in the field, namely that "[b]ecause of the special nature of sensor/machine-generated data, M. Leistner argues that the sui generis right should be amended for them. This is because of the rather low threshold of substantial investment, the uncertainty behind spinoff situations and the fact that another database maker will need another complete set of data to create a new data set, so will automatically infringe the sui generis right."[83]

The report states that: "[o]ne conclusion might be to seek to retain the sui generis right in some form (so as to keep what is valuable in the existing law for those who do value it), but at the same time to try and minimise any negative effects (costs) on the knowledge economy and data ecology." In doing so, the report suggests that, whilst retaining an EU-wide database right, the European Commission might consider making the right available by registration and to address divergences in implementation across member states by introducing the right under an EU Regulation, rather than by Directive.[84]

This conclusion may cause difficulties for businesses working in the field of AI, who may consider that they have limited opportunities to protect their investment. Nevertheless, the European Commission has made clear that it considers that the application of the sui generis right in the data economy context should be closely tracked.

C. Trade marks and brand protection

AI will certainly bring benefits to brand owners in terms of the time and cost of trade mark searches and the preparation of take down notices. However, there may be other consequences for brand owners where AI technology is used, in particular where purchasing decisions are made by AI rather than by human decision-making. This may impact on the concept of the average consumer—and whether this will need to be changed to take account of AI purchases. Also, the extent to which the need to show confusion or the likelihood of confusion may need to be adapted.

Gartner has predicted that 85% of customer interactions will be managed by artificial intelligence by 2020, and this is likely to have a significant impact on brands, even with commentators suggesting that brands may become obsolete as a result.[85]

Where AI is responsible for buying decisions, it is possible in the future that it will not take branding into account for at least certain purchases, for example price, availability, customer feedback—all of which are likely to have an impact on the value of brands and trade marks.

The key concept in trade mark law of the average consumer, in current law, is deemed to be reasonably well informed and reasonably circumspect and observant, but rarely has there been the chance to make direct comparisons between marks and must instead rely upon imperfect recollection of the relevant marks. Furthermore, the average consumer's level of attention varies according to the category of goods or services in question. It is unclear to what extent these parameters would still apply if AI is responsible for the buying decision, in particular because, as a computer program, AI is capable of perfect recollection.

Similarly, considering the concept of confusion or likelihood of confusion is unlikely to be relevant where AI is involved, again, because, as a computer program, it is capable of perfect recollection.

Considering issues of infringement, the history of cases to date involving the interaction between AI and trade mark law, the courts have concluded that companies such as Amazon, Google and eBay have not been liable for infringement. But, if the impact of AI increases, as seems likely, should there be a new concept of liability introduced to provide protection?

D. Design protection

This section considers issues resulting from the use of AI in relation to design. In particular, it is likely that the use of AI in the fashion, consumer and industrial products industries will involve issues relating to design.

Design rights protection in different jurisdictions is often complex, with a combination of registered and unregistered design rights, particularly within the EU. (The same level of protection does not exist in the United States, nor in a number of other jurisdictions, save that some provide for design rights protection for industrial design under the Hague Agreement Concerning the International Deposit of Industrial Designs.) Within the EU design rights have proved particularly valuable in the fashion and consumer products industries. However, in general, the first holder of the design rights will generally be the creator of the design; or, if the design was created in the course of employment, the employer. Commentators have emphasised the value of design rights protection for AI products and robotics, but there has been little if any commentary on the consequences of AI and design rights protection, in circumstances where AI is responsible for producing the relevant design, or for infringing a particular design. However, it is likely that any issues on ownership or infringement will address similar issues to those addressed in relation to patents.

VI. Conclusion

AI will have a significant impact in relation to all aspects of IP, but principally in the two key areas of copyright and patents.

In order to support and foster innovation in the developing use of AI which will be of benefit to society, allowing businesses to attract investment and to obtain some return on investment will be important. In that context, appropriate IP protection will be key. Businesses should have available to them adequate laws to enable them to take necessary steps to protect their rights, where appropriate, including obtaining copyrights and patents, when applicable, and imposing contractual provisions to allow for protection as trade secrets.

At present IP laws are not well equipped to deal with the creations of new works as a result of AI. Most jurisdictions require some human involvement in relation to the creation of IP rights. Legislators will need to decide whether to maintain this requirement for some human element and, if so, how to apply this to works created by autonomous AI and to AI-enabled works. It is considered that some protection should be given to works created using AI, in particular by clarifying and developing existing rights. Legislators will no doubt continue to consider whether the ownership of rights should be granted to the original developer of the AI, or whether a new sui generis right should be granted for AI-created works, even a right which requires registration by the person claiming such a right.

At the same time, although the law always needs to evolve to address new developments, it would seem appropriate to take a cautious approach when assessing and deciding whether there is a need to implement new and AI specific rules in IP laws. Introducing any new right would be likely simply to complicate an already complex bundle of IP rights. Many legal systems have proven to be sufficiently flexible and technology neutral, so that they can deal with challenges arising from the development of new technology without significant changes having to be implemented. Only where the existing laws evidently fail appropriately to deal with AI-related issues, a need for revision, or expansion of the existing laws, arises. Where necessary, governments should introduce appropriate legislation to and/or AI driven interpretation of existing laws to clarify IP protection of AI-enabled as well as AI-created works, without seeking to create any new IP right at this stage. Legislators will thus have to follow closely the relevant developments, and become active upon a proven failure of the existing IP laws to deal with AI-related challenges. However, when expanding upon or amending existing IP laws, or implementing new IP laws, it will always be important to seek to balance the interests of all relevant stakeholders as far as possible. Moreover, care will need to be taken not to take steps which will amount to overprotection, as this could have a detrimental impact on the ultimate goal of IP protection. At the same time, they will have to bear in mind that developments in this area from a technological perspective move very fast, so it may well be that, by the time any steps are taken by legislators to address such issues, the use of AI will have developed to such an extent that the steps taken have already been superseded. Until then, it is considered important for some consensus to be achieved internationally, ideally with a need for an international treaty to address the issue of IP ownership, to achieve some consistency across different jurisdictions and across different IP rights.

It would be best to find a solution which guarantees that all countries are able to benefit from the rapid dissemination of new technologies. WIPO has argued that, rather than "instituting a new IP right, to unleash the digital economy's enormous potential for more inclusive growth worldwide policymakers should embrace a legal and regulatory environment that allows for unhindered cross-border data flows on a global scale. Such an environment necessitates the absence of unjustified data location requirements as well as the implementation of clear and enforceable rules."[86] This underlines the need for global co-operation in achieving a solution.

Principle 8
AI and Intellectual Property

Organisations that develop, deploy or use AI systems should take necessary steps to protect the rights in the resulting works through appropriate and directed application of existing intellectual property rights laws. Governments should investigate how AI-authored works may be further protected, without seeking to create any new IP right at this stage.

1 Supporting incentivisation and protection for innovation

1.1 Innovation is only of value if it can benefit society. Funding is necessary to develop innovation to a level where it can be disseminated and utilised by society. Those from whom funding is sought require a return on their investment. Consequently, there must be incentivisation and protection for innovation if it is to attract investment and be brought to the greater good of society.

1.2 Organisations must therefore be allowed to protect rights in works resulting from the use of AI, whether AI-created works or AI enabled works.

1.3 However, care needs to be taken not to take steps which will amount to overprotection, as this could prove detrimental to the ultimate goal of IP protection.

2 Protection of IP rights

2.1 At present IP laws are insufficiently equipped to deal with the creation of works by autonomous AI.

2.2 Organisations that develop, deploy or use AI systems should take necessary steps to protect the rights in the resulting works. Where appropriate these steps should include asserting or obtaining copyrights, obtaining patents, when applicable, and seeking contractual provisions to allow for protection as trade secrets and/or to allocate the rights appropriately between the parties.

3 Development of new IP laws

3.1 Governments should be cautious with revising existing IP laws.

3.2 Governments should explore the introduction of appropriate legislation (or the interpretation of existing laws) to clarify IP protection of AI enabled as well as AI created works, without seeking to create any new IP right at this stage.

3.3 When amending existing or implementing new IP laws, governments should seek adequately to balance the interests of all relevant stakeholders.

3.4 Governments should also explore a consensus in relation to AI and IP rights to allow for unhindered data flows across borders and the rapid dissemination of new technologies and seek to address these issues through an international treaty.

Endnotes

1 “The Next Rembrandt” (13 April 2016), online: *Microsoft* <https://news.microsoft.com/europe/features/next-rembrandt/>;

See also: www.nextrembrandt.com; <https://www.jwt.com/en/work/thenextrembrandt>.

2 “Is artificial intelligence set to become art’s next medium?” (12 December 2018), online: *Christie’s* <www.christies.com/features/A-collaboration-between-two-artists-one-human-one-a-machine-9332-1.aspx>.

3 Ken Cheng, “Game Over, Humans” (October 2017), online: *BBC Radio 4* <https://www.bbc.co.uk/programmes/m0001qjj>.

4 Chloe Olewitz, “A Japanese A.I. program just wrote a short novel, and it almost won a literary prize” (26 March 2016), online: *Digital Trends* <https://www.digitaltrends.com/cool-tech/japanese-ai-writes-novel-passes-first-round-nationanl-literary-prize/>;

See also Danny Lewis, “An AI-Written Novella Almost Won a Literary Prize” (28 March 2016), online: *Smithsonian.com* <https://www.smithsonianmag.com/smart-news/ai-written-novella-almost-won-literary-prize-180958577/>.

5 Andres Guadamuz, “Artificial intelligence and copyright” (October 2017), online: *WIPO Magazine* <http://www.wipo.int/wipo_magazine/en/2017/05/article_0003.html>.

6 Samuel Myllykangas is Head of Operations at Blueprint Genetics as well as a co-founder of the company and inventor in patents of DNA sequencing methods. See Samuel Myllykangas and Massimiliano Gentile, “Artificial intelligence in Genetic Testing of Inherited Disorders” (23 March 2017), online: *Blueprint Genetics* <https://blueprintgenetics.com/podcast/artificial-intelligence-genetic-testing-inherited-disorders/>.

7 Glenn F. Osborne, Simon S. M. Chin, Paul McDonald, and Scott Schneider, “Artificial intelligence system for genetic analysis” (8 April 2014), online: *U.S. Patent US8693751B2* <https://patents.google.com/patent/US8693751B2/en>.

8 Mark Wilson, “AI Is Inventing Languages Humans Can’t Understand. Should We Stop It?” (14 July 2017), online: *Fast Company* <https://www.fastcompany.com/90132632/ai-is-inventing-its-own-perfect-languages-should-we-let-it>.

9 George Dvorsky, “Google’s AI Bots Invent Ridiculous New Legs to Scamper Through Obstacle Courses” (11 October 2018), online: *Gizmodo* <https://gizmodo.com/google-s-ai-bots-invent-ridiculous-new-legs-to-scamper-1829693108>.

10 See Association for the Advancement of Artificial intelligence at www.aaai.org.

11 Cédric Villani, “For a Meaningful Artificial Intelligence: Towards a French and European Strategy,” Mission assigned by the Prime Minister Édouard Philippe (2018), online: <https://www.aiforhumanity.fr/pdfs/MissionVillani_Report_ENG-VF.pdf>.

12 WIPO, “What is Intellectual Property” (2004), online: *World Intellectual Property Organization* <https://www.wipo.int/edocs/pubdocs/en/intproperty/450/wipo_pub_450.pdf>.

13 *Ibid,* page 3.

14 Rachel Free, “Artificial Intelligence—Questions of Ownership” (2018), online: *CMS* <https://cms.law/en/GBR/Publication/Artificial-Intelligence-Questions-of-ownership>.

15 For example: Brian Martin, “Against intellectual property” *Philosophy and Social Action*, Vol. 21, No. 3, July-September 1995, pp. 7-22., online: <https://www.uow.edu.au/~bmartin/pubs/95psa.html>.

16 Kaloyan Dinkov Dinev, “A Humanless World: The Progressive Artificial Intelligence and Its Impact on Intellectual Property” (2018), online: *Kent Student Law Review, 4* <http://journals.kent.ac.uk/index.php/kslr/article/view/477>.

17 *Alice Corp. v. CLS Bank International*, 573 U.S. 208, 134 S. Ct. 2347 (2014), online: <https://www.supremecourt.gov/opinions/13pdf/13-298_7lh8.pdf>.

[18] U.S. Patent and Trademark Office, "U.S. Patent and Trademark Office announces revised guidance for determining subject matter eligibility" (4 January 2019), online: <https://www.uspto.gov/about-us/news-updates/us-patent-and-trademark-office-announces-revised-guidance-determining-subject>.

[19] Manny Schecter, "Congress Needs to Act So Alice Doesn't Live Here (in the Patent System) Anymore" (13 February 2017), online: *IP Watchdog* <https://www.ipwatchdog.com/2017/02/13/congress-needs-to-act-so-alice-doesnt-live-here-in-the-patent-system-anymore/id=78241/>.

[20] See, for example:

"Artificial intelligence valet systems and methods" <https://patents.google.com/patent/US9429943B2/en>;

"Control system, method and device of intelligent robot based on artificial intelligence" <https://patents.google.com/patent/US10223638B2/en>;

"Artificial intelligence encryption model (AIEM) with device authorization and attack detection (DAAAD)" <https://patents.google.com/patent/US9736147B1/en>.

The USPTO expressly recognises AI through the designation of Class 706 (Data Processing: Artificial Intelligence) in its patent classification system.

[21] "Guidelines for Examination in the EPO" (Part G, Chapter II, 3.3), online: *European Patent Office* <https://www.epo.org/law-practice/legal-texts/html/guidelines/e/g.htm>.

[22] See 17 U.S. Code § 102—Subject matter of copyright: "Copyright protection subsists ... in original works of authorship fixed in any tangible medium of expression, now known or later developed, from which they can be perceived, reproduced, or otherwise communicated, either directly or with the aid of a machine or device."

[23] *Acohs Pty Ltd v Ucorp Pty Ltd,* 2010.

[24] Law 22 April 1941, no. 633.

[25] For example, Article 23 of the Italian copyright law provides that moral rights may be enforced, after the author's death, by his/her spouse and relatives.

[26] CJEU, 1 December 2011, C-145/10, CJEU, 4 October 2011, C-403/08, and CJEU, 16 July 2009, C-5/08, all available on curia.europa.eu.

[27] Cecilia Trevisi, "La regolamentazione in materia di Intelligenza artificiale, robot, automazione: a che punto siamo" (21 May 2018), online: *Medialaws* <http://www.medialaws.eu/la-regolamentazione-in-materia-di-intelligenza-artificiale-robot-automazione-a-che-punto-siamo/>.

[28] Article 5.1, Spanish Intellectual Property Act, online: <https://www.boe.es/buscar/act.php?id=BOE-A-1996-8930>.

[29] (2015/2103 (INL)) dated on 27.01.2017, online: <http://www.europarl.europa.eu/doceo/document/A-8-2017-0005_EN.pdf>.

[30] *Ibid,* paragraph 65.

[31] Anne de Heijde & Raynor van Eijck, "Artificial intelligence (AI) and intellectual property (IP), a call for action" (9 June 2017), online: *Maastricht University Intellectual Property and Knowledge Management Blog* <https://law.maastrichtuniversity.nl/ipkm/artificial-intelligence-ai-and-intellectual-property-ip-a-call-for-action/>.

[32] Opinion of The Committee on Industry, Research and Energy: 15.11.2016.

[33] *Ibid,* Explanatory Statement, Intellectual property rights, data protection and data ownership.

[34] The UK Copyright, Designs and Patents Act 1998 (as amended) ["CDPA"].

[35] This is enshrined in s1(1) of the CDPA.

[36] Since the landmark decision of the Court of Justice of the European Union in *Infopaq International A/S v Danske Dagblades Forening,* Case C-5/08, this has been the harmonised EU standard of originality that is generally applicable; the traditional English law test required the work to be the result of the application of the author's "labour, skill or effort."

[37] *Feist Publications, Inc. v. Rural Telephone Service Company, Inc.* 499 U.S. 340 (1991).

[38] Margot E. Kaminski, "Authorship, Disrupted: AI Authors in Copyright and First Amendment Law" (2017), online: *University of Colorado Law School—Colorado Law Scholarly Commons* <https://scholar.law.colorado.edu/cgi/viewcontent.cgi?article=2193&context=articles> [Kaminski].

[39] See s9 CDPA.

[40] For example, the producer of a sound recording is deemed to be the author under s9(2)aa CDPA.

[41] s9(3) CDPA.

[42] Kaminski, *supra,* quoting Bridy, "Coding Creativity: Copyright and the Artificially Intelligent Author," Stan. Tech. L. Rev., no 5 [2012].

[43] For example, section 7(3) of the UK Patents Act 1977 refers to an inventor being "the actual deviser of the invention" and does not require the inventor to be a person of any kind.

[44] See In re Hardee, 223 USPQ 1122, 1123 (Comm'r Pat. 1984).

[45] *Henry Brothers (Magherafelt) Ltd v The Ministry of Defence and the Northern Ireland Office(CA)* [1999] RPC 442.

[46] See, for example, <https://patents.google.com/patent/US8693751B2/en>.

[47] Margaret Rhodes, "Airbus' Newest Design Is Based on Bones and Slime Mold" (1 December 2015), online: *Wired* <https://www.wired.com/2015/12/airbuss-newest-design-is-based-on-slime-mold-and-bones/>.

[48] For example, the U.S. Court of Appeals for the Federal Circuit has made clear that "only natural persons may be 'inventors.'" *Beech Aircraft Corp. v. EDO Corp.,* 990 F.2d 1237, 1248 (Fed. Cir. 1993) (citing to 35 U.S.C. § 115-118). In China, the most popular opinion is that AI cannot be an inventor or owner of an invention because AI lacks legal personality, although some commentators consider that the owner or user of the AI may be considered as the legal owner of the invention created by AI.

[49] Ex parte Smernoff, 215 USPQ 545, 547 (Bd. App. 1982) ("one who suggests an idea of a result to be accomplished, rather than the means of accomplishing it, is not an coinventor.")

[50] Matthew Sag, "Orphan Works As Grist for the Data Mill" (2012) 27, online: *Berkeley Tech. L.J.* <https://scholarship.law.berkeley.edu/btlj/vol27/iss3/9/>;

Daniel Schönberger, "Deep Copyright: Up- and Downstream Questions Related to Artificial Intelligence [AI] and Machine Learning [ML]" (2018), in: Zeitschrift für Geistiges Eigentum / Intellectual Property Journal 10, p. 51; an earlier version was published online at <https://papers.ssrn.com/sol3/papers.cfm?abstract_id=3098315>.

[51] "General Opinion on the EU Copyright Reform Package" (24 January 2017), online: *European Copyright Society* <https://europeancopyrightsocietydotorg.files.wordpress.com/2015/12/ecs-opinion-on-eu-copyright-reform-def.pdf>.

[52] For example, Article 24 of the Swiss Copyright Act; Article 71 of the Italian copyright law.

[53] For example, section 29 of the UK CDPA; article 70 of the Italian copyright law.

[54] For example, section 30 of the UK CDPA; article 25 of the Swiss Copyright Act; article 70 of the Italian copyright law.

[55] For example, section 28A of the UK CDPA; article 24a of the Swiss Copyright Act; article 5(1) of the EU Copyright Directive.

[56] s29A UK CDPA.

[57] The UK Intellectual Property Office has issued guidance on the changes to copyright law and the reasons behind the reform: "Changes to copyright law" (27 March 2014) online: *UK Intellectual Property Office* <https://www.gov.uk/government/publications/changes-to-copyright-law>.

[58] Article L.122-5, 10° of the French Intellectual Property Code (Code de la Propriété Intellectuelle "CPI").

[59] See article L.342-3 of the French Intellectual Property Code.

[60] Berne X "Loi numérique: l'exception de text&data mining en passe de rester lettre morte" *next inpact* (2017), <https://www.nextinpact.com/news/105601-loi-numerique-lexception-text-data-mining-en-passe-rester-lettre-morte.htm>.

[61] Directive of the European Parliament and of the Council on Copyright in the Digital Single Market (Inter-institutional File 2016/0280 (COD)).

[62] CDT, "CDT Joins Open Letter on Text and Data Mining Exception in EU Copyright Discussions" (16 January 2019), online: *CDT* <https://cdt.org/insight/cdt-joins-open-letter-on-text-and-data-mining-exception-in-eu-copyright-discussions>.

[63] "General Opinion on the EU Copyright Reform Package" (24 January 2017), online: *European Copyright Society* <https://europeancopyrightsocietydotorg.files.wordpress.com/2015/12/ecs-opinion-on-eu-copyright-reform-def.pdf>.

[64] The debate as to the appropriate degree of protection warranted and as to the extent of any exception granted is further well demonstrated by the report published in February 2018 of Dr. Eleanora Rosati for the EU Policy Department for Citizens' Rights and Constitutional Affairs and the response by Mark Seeley dated 28 February 2018;

Dr. Eleanora Rosati, "The Exception for Text and Data Mining (TDM) in the Proposed Directive on Copyright in the Digital Single Market—Technical Aspects" (February 2018), online: *EU Policy Department for Citizens' Rights and Constitutional Affairs* <http://www.europarl.europa.eu/RegData/etudes/BRIE/2018/604942/IPOL_BRI(2018)604942_EN.pdf>;

Mark Seeley, "A response to the February 2018 report of Dr. Eleanora Rosati" (28 February 2018), online: *Scipublaw* <http://scipublaw.com/a-response-to-the-february-2018-report-of-dr-eleanora-rosati/>.

[65] Article 69 Swiss Copyright Act; Article 16(2) UK Copyright Act.

[66] Also under Chinese law, as it is generally considered that AI does not have legal personality and cannot therefore be the infringer, it is most likely that the designer, data provider or owner will be considered as the infringer, subject to the current applicable judicial practice under Chinese law, such as the granting of certain exceptions, including "fair use."

[67] See, e.g., European Parliament resolution of February 16, 2017, with recommendations to the Commission on Civil Law Rules on Robotics, § AD and § 56. [European Parliament resolution].

[68] European Parliament resolution supra note 67, § 53-55).

[69] UK Patents Act 1977, Chapter 37, Section 60(1)(a).

[70] 35 U.S.C. § 271(a).

[71] 35 U.S.C. § 271(b).

[72] *Limelight Networks v. Akamai Technologies,* 572 U.S. 915 (2014).

[73] *Akamai Technologies, Inc. v. Limelight Networks,* 797 F. 3d 1020, 1022 (Fed. Cir. 2015).

[74] *Hely-Hutchinson v Brayhead Ltd* [1967] 1 QB 549.

[75] *Watteau v Fenwick* [1893] 1 QB 346.

[76] Vincent Manancourt, "Trade secrets better suited to AI inventions than patents, experts say" (31 October 2018), online: *Global Data Review* <https://globaldatareview.com/article/1176313/trade-secrets-better-suited-to-ai-inventions-than-patents-experts-say>.

[77] EU Trade Secrets Directive (2016/244/EU).

[78] Economic Espionage Act of 1996, 18 U.S.C. § 1832, amended by the Defend Trade Secrets Act of 2016.

[79] A version of the Uniform Trade Secrets Act has been enacted by all U.S. states (apart from New York), the District of Columbia, Puerto Rico and the U.S. Virgin Islands, mostly with little or no change.

[80] Gil Press, "Cleaning Big Data: Most Time-Consuming, Least Enjoyable Data Science Task, Survey Says" (23 March 2016), online: *Forbes* <https://www.forbes.com/sites/gilpress/2016/03/23/data-preparation-most-time-consuming-least-enjoyable-data-science-task-survey-says/>.

[81] European Commission, "Study in Support of the Evaluation of the Database Directive" (25 April 2018), online: <https://ec.europa.eu/digital-single-market/en/news/study-support-evaluation-database-directive>.

[82] *Ibid,* Final Report, Executive Summary, page 4.

[83] *Ibid,* Final Report, page 43.

[84] *Ibid,* Final Report, page 153.

[85] Seth Archer, "Artificial intelligence could make brands obsolete (GOOGL, AMZN, AAPL)" (25 September 2017), online: *Markets Insider* <https://markets.businessinsider.com/news/stocks/artificial-intelligence-could-make-brands-obsolete-2017-9-1002515382>.

[86] Thaddeus Burns, "Regulating machine data: less is more for global growth" (December 2017), online: *WIPO Magazine* <https://www.wipo.int/wipo_magazine/en/2017/06/article_0005.html>.

Responsible AI Policy Framework

Principle 1
Ethical Purpose and Societal Benefit

Organisations that develop, deploy or use AI systems and any national laws that regulate such use should require the purposes of such implementation to be identified and ensure that such purposes are consistent with the overall ethical purposes of beneficence and non-maleficence, as well as the other principles of the Policy Framework for Responsible AI.

1 Overarching principles

1.1 Organisations that develop, deploy or use AI systems should do so in a manner compatible with human agency and the respect for fundamental human rights (including freedom from discrimination).

1.2 Organisations that develop, deploy or use AI systems should monitor the implementation of such AI systems and act to mitigate against consequences of such AI systems (whether intended or unintended) that are inconsistent with the ethical purposes of beneficence and non-maleficence, as well as the other principles of the Policy Framework for Responsible AI set out in this framework.

1.3 Organisations that develop, deploy or use AI systems should assess the social, political and environmental implications of such development, deployment and use in the context of a structured Responsible AI Impact Assessment that assesses risk of harm and, as the case may be, proposes mitigation strategies in relation to such risks.

2 Work and automation

2.1 Organisations that implement AI systems in the workplace should provide opportunities for affected employees to participate in the decision-making process related to such implementation.

2.2 Consideration should be given as to whether it is achievable from a technological perspective to ensure that all possible occurrences should be pre-decided within an AI system to ensure consistent behaviour. If this is not practicable, organisations developing, deploying or using AI systems should consider at the very least the extent to which they are able to confine the decision outcomes of an AI system to a reasonable, non-aberrant range of responses, taking into account the wider context, the impact of the decision and the moral appropriateness of "weighing the unweighable" such as life vs. life.

2.3 Organisations that develop, deploy or use AI systems that have an impact on employment should conduct a Responsible AI Impact Assessment to determine the net effects of such implementation.

2.4 Governments should closely monitor the progress of AI-driven automation in order to identify the sectors of their economy where human workers are the most affected. Governments should actively solicit and monitor industry, employee and other stakeholder data and commentary regarding the impact of AI systems on the workplace and should develop an open forum for sharing experience and best practices.

2.5 Governments should promote educational policies that equip all children with the skills, knowledge and qualities required by the new economy and that promote life-long learning.

2.6 Governments should encourage the creation of opportunities for adults to learn new useful skills, especially for those displaced by automation.

2.7 Governments should study the viability and advisability of new social welfare and benefit systems to help reduce, where warranted, socio-economic inequality caused by the introduction of AI systems and robotic automation.

3 Environmental impact

3.1 Organisations that develop, deploy or use AI systems should assess the overall environmental impact of such AI systems, throughout their implementation, including consumption of resources, energy costs of data storage and processing and the net energy efficiencies or environmental benefits that they may produce. Organisations should seek to promote and implement uses of AI systems with a view to achieving overall carbon neutrality or carbon reduction.

3.2 Governments are encouraged to adjust regulatory regimes and/or promote industry self-regulatory regimes concerning market-entry and/or adoption of AI systems in a way that the possible exposure (in terms of 'opportunities vs. risks') that may result from the public operation of such AI systems is reasonably reflected. Special regimes for intermediary and limited admissions to enable testing and refining of the operation of the AI system can help to expedite the completion of the AI system and improve its safety and reliability.

3.3 In order to ensure and maintain public trust in final human control, governments should consider implementing rules that ensure comprehensive and transparent investigation of such adverse and unanticipated outcomes of AI systems that have occurred through their usage, in particular if these outcomes have lethal or injurious consequences for the humans using such systems. Such investigations should be used for considering adjusting the regulatory framework for AI systems, in particular to develop, where practicable and achievable, a more rounded understanding of how and when such systems should gracefully handover to their human operators in a failure scenario.

3.4 AI has a particular potential to reduce environmentally harmful resource waste and inefficiencies. AI research regarding these objectives should be encouraged. In order to do so, policies must be put in place to ensure the relevant data is accessible and usable in a manner consistent with respect for other principles of the Policy Framework for Responsible AI such as Fairness and Non-Discrimination, Open Data and Fair Competition and Privacy, Lawful Access and Consent.

4 Weaponised AI

4.1 The use of lethal autonomous weapons systems (LAWS) should respect the principles and standards of and be consistent with international humanitarian law on the use of weapons and wider international human rights law.

4.2 Governments should implement multilateral mechanisms to define, implement and monitor compliance with international agreements regarding the ethical development, use and commerce of LAWS.

4.3 Governments and organisations should refrain from developing, selling or using lethal autonomous weapon systems (LAWS) able to select and engage targets without human control and oversight in all contexts.

4.4 Organisations that develop, deploy or use AI systems should inform their employees when they are assigned to projects relating to LAWS.

5 The weaponisation of false or misleading information

5.1 Organisations that develop, deploy or use AI systems to filter or promote informational content on internet platforms that is shared or seen by their users should take reasonable measures, consistent with applicable law, to minimise the spread of false or misleading information where there is a material risk that such false or misleading information might lead to significant harm to individuals, groups or democratic institutions.

5.2 AI has the potential to assist in efficiently and pro-actively identifying (and, where appropriate, suppressing) unlawful content such as hate speech or weaponised false or misleading information. AI research into means of accomplishing these objectives in a manner consistent with freedom of expression should be encouraged.

5.3 Organisations that develop, deploy or use AI systems on platforms to filter or promote informational content that is shared or seen by their users should provide a mechanism by which users can flag potentially harmful content in a timely manner.

5.4 Organisations that develop, deploy or use AI systems on platforms to filter or promote informational content that is shared or seen by their users should provide a mechanism by which content providers can challenge the removal of such content by such organisations from their network or platform in a timely manner.

5.5 Governments should provide clear guidelines to help Organisations that develop, deploy or use AI systems on platforms identify prohibited content that respect both the rights to dignity and equality and the right to freedom of expression.

5.6 Courts should remain the ultimate arbiters of lawful content.

Principle 2
Accountability

Organisations that develop, deploy or use AI systems and any national laws that regulate such use shall respect and adopt the eight principles of this Policy Framework for Responsible AI (or other analogous accountability principles). In all instances, humans should remain accountable for the acts and omissions of AI systems.

1 Accountability

1.1 Organisations that develop, deploy or use AI systems shall designate an individual or individuals who are accountable for the organisation's compliance with those principles.

1.2 The identity of the individual(s) designated by the organisation to oversee the organisation's compliance with the principles shall be made known upon request.

1.3 Organisations that develop, deploy or use AI systems shall implement policies and practices to give effect to the principles if the Policy Framework for Responsible AI or other adopted principles (including analogous principles that may be developed for a specific industry), including:

i. establishing processes to determine whether, when and how to implement a "Responsible AI Impact Assessment" process;

ii. establishing and implementing "Responsible AI by Design" principles;

iii. establishing procedures to receive and respond to complaints and inquiries;

iv. training staff and communicating to staff information about the organisation's policies and practices; and

v. developing information to explain the organisation's policies and procedures.

2 Government

2. Governments that assess the potential for "accountability gaps" in existing legal and regulatory frameworks applicable to AI systems should adopt a balanced approach that encourages innovation while militating against the risk of significant individual or societal harm.

2.1 Any such legal and regulatory frameworks should promote the eight principles of the Policy Framework for Responsible AI or encompass similar considerations.

2.2 Governments should not grant distinct legal personality to AI systems, as doing so would undermine the fundamental principle that humans should ultimately remain accountable for the acts and omissions of AI systems.

3 Contextual approach

3.1 The intensity of the accountability obligation will vary according to the degree of autonomy and criticality of the AI system. The greater the level of autonomy of the AI system and the greater the criticality of the outcomes that it may produce, the higher the degree of accountability that will apply to the organisation that develops, deploys or uses the AI system.

Principle 3
Transparency and Explainability

Organisations that develop, deploy or use AI systems and any national laws that regulate such use shall ensure that, to the extent reasonable given the circumstances and state of the art of the technology, such use is transparent and that the decision outcomes of the AI system are explainable.

1 Definitions

1.1 **Transparency** is an obligation for organisations that use AI in decision-making processes to provide information regarding: a) the fact that an organisation is using an AI system in a decision-making process; b) the intended purpose(s) of the AI system and how the AI system will and can be used; (c) the types of data sets that are used by the AI system; and (d) meaningful information about the logic involved.

1.2 **Explainability** is an obligation for organisations that use AI in decision-making processes to provide accurate information in humanly understandable terms explaining how a decision/outcome was reached by an AI system.

2 Purpose

2.1 Transparency and Explainability aim to preserve the public's trust in AI systems and provide sufficient information to help ensure meaningful accountability of an AI system's developers, deployers and users, and to demonstrate whether the decisions made by an AI system are fair and impartial.

2.2 The Transparency and Explainability principles support the Accountability principle, the Fairness and Non-Discrimination principle, the Safety and Reliability principle and the Privacy, Lawful Use and Consent principles.

3 Gradual and contextual approach

3.1 The intensity of the obligations of transparency and explainability will depend on the context of the decision and its consequences for the person subject to it. The scope and intensity of the obligations of transparency and explainability will increase as the sensitivity of the data sets used by an AI system increases and as the decisional outcome of an AI system increases in materiality.

3.2 The determination of the intensity of the obligations of transparency and explainability must balance the interests of the person subject to the decision and the interests of the organisation making the decision. The ultimate criteria shall be the reasonable expectations of a person subject to that type of decision.

4 Transparency and explainability by design

4.1 Organisations that develop AI systems should ensure that the system logic and architecture serves to facilitate transparency and explainability requirements. In so far as is reasonably practicable, and taking into account the state of the art at the time, such systems should aim to be designed from the most fundamental level upwards to promote transparency and explainability by design. Where there is a choice between system architectures which are less or more opaque, the more transparent option should be preferred.

4.2 Users of AI systems and persons subject to their decisions must have an effective way to seek remedy in the event that organisations that develop, deploy or use AI systems are not transparent about their use.

5 Technological neutrality

5.1 The use of an AI system by a public or private organisation does not reduce the procedural and substantive requirements that are normally attached to a decision when the decision-making process is completely controlled by a human.

Principle 4
Fairness and Non-Discrimination

Organisations that develop, deploy or use AI systems and any national laws that regulate such use shall ensure the non-discrimination of AI outcomes, and shall promote appropriate and effective measures to safeguard fairness in AI use.

1 Awareness and education

1.1 Awareness and education on the possibilities and limits of AI systems is a prerequisite to achieving fairer outcomes.

1.2 Organisations that develop, deploy or use AI systems should take steps to ensure that users are aware that AI systems reflect the goals, knowledge and experience of their creators, as well as the limitations of the data sets that are used to train them.

2 Technology and fairness

2.1 Decisions based on AI systems should be fair and non-discriminatory, judged against the same standards as decision-making processes conducted entirely by humans.

2.2 The use of AI systems by organisations that develop, deploy or use AI systems and Governments should not serve to exempt or attenuate the need for fairness, although it may mean refocussing applicable concepts, standards and rules to accommodate AI.

2.3 Users of AI systems and persons subject to their decisions must have an effective way to seek remedy in discriminatory or unfair situations generated by biased or erroneous AI systems, whether used by organisations that develop, deploy or use AI systems or governments, and to obtain redress for any harm.

3 Development and monitoring of AI systems

3.1 AI development should be designed to prioritise fairness. This would involve addressing algorithms and data bias from an early stage with a view to ensuring fairness and non-discrimination.

3.2. Organisations that develop, deploy or use AI systems should remain vigilant to the dangers posed by bias. This could be achieved by establishing ethics boards and codes of conduct, and by adopting industry-wide standards and internationally recognised quality seals.

3.4 AI systems with an important social impact could require independent reviewing and testing on a periodic basis.

3.3. In the development and monitoring of AI systems, particular attention should be paid to disadvantaged groups which may be incorrectly represented in the training data.

4 A comprehensive approach to fairness

4.1 AI systems can perpetuate and exacerbate bias, and have a broad social and economic impact in society. Addressing fairness in AI use requires a holistic approach. In particular, it requires:

i. the close engagement of technical experts from AI-related fields with statisticians and researchers from the social sciences; and

ii. a combined engagement between governments, organisations that develop, deploy or use AI systems and the public at large.

4.2 The Fairness and Non-Discrimination Principle is supported by the Transparency and Accountability Principles. Effective fairness in use of AI systems requires the implementation of measures in connection with both these Principles.

Principle 5
Safety and Reliability

Organisations that develop, deploy or use AI systems and any national laws that regulate such use shall adopt design regimes and standards ensuring high safety and reliability of AI systems on one hand while limiting the exposure of developers and deployers on the other hand.

1 Require and/or define explicit ethical and moral principles underpinning the AI system

1.1 Governments and organisations developing, deploying or using AI systems should define the relevant set of ethical and moral principles underpinning the AI system to be developed, deployed or used taking into account all relevant circumstances. A system designed to autonomously make decisions will only be acceptable if it operates on the basis of clearly defined principles and within boundaries limiting its decision making powers.

1.2 Governments and organisations developing, deploying or using AI systems should validate the underpinning ethical and moral principles as defined periodically to ensure on-going accurateness.

2 Standardisation of behaviour

2.1 Governments and organisations developing, deploying or using AI systems should recall that ethical and moral principles are not globally uniform but may be impacted e.g., by geographical, religious or social considerations and traditions. To be accepted, AI systems might have to be adjustable in order to meet the local standards in which they will be used.

2.2 Consider whether all possible occurrences should be pre-decided in a way to ensure the consistent behaviour of the AI system, the impact of this on the aggregation of consequences and the moral appropriateness of "weighing the unweighable" such as life vs. life.

3 Ensuring safety, reliability and trust

3.1 Governments should require and organisations should test AI systems thoroughly to ensure that they reliably adhere, in operation, to the underpinning ethical and moral principles and have been trained with data which are curated and are as 'error-free' as practicable, given the circumstances.

3.2 Governments are encouraged to adjust regulatory regimes and/or promote industry self-regulatory regimes for allowing market-entry of AI systems in order to reasonably reflect the positive exposure that may result from the public operation of such AI systems. Special regimes for intermediary and limited admissions to enable testing and refining of the operation of the AI system can help to expedite the completion of the AI system and improve its safety and reliability.

3.3 In order to ensure and maintain public trust in final human control, governments should consider implementing rules that ensure comprehensive and transparent investigation of such adverse and unanticipated outcomes of AI systems that have occurred through their usage, in particular if these outcomes have lethal or injurious consequences for the humans using such systems. Such investigations should be used for considering adjusting the regulatory framework for AI systems in particular to develop a more rounded understanding of how such systems should gracefully handover to their human operators.

4 Facilitating technological progress at reasonable risks

4.1 Governments are encouraged to consider whether existing legal frameworks such as product liability require adjustment in light of the unique characteristics of AI systems.

4.2 Governments should support and participate in international co-ordination (through bodies such as the International Organisation for Standardisation (ISO) and the International Electrotechnical Commission (IEC)) to develop international standards for the development and deployment of safe and reliable AI systems.

Principle 6
Open Data and Fair Competition

Organisations that develop, deploy or use AI systems and any national laws that regulate such use shall promote (a) open access to datasets which could be used in the development of AI systems and (b) open source frameworks and software for AI systems. AI systems must be developed and deployed on a "compliance by design" basis in relation to competition/antitrust law.

1 Supporting effective competition in relation to AI systems

1.1 Governments should support and participate in international co-ordination (through bodies such as the OECD and the International Competition Network) to develop best practices and rigorous analysis in understanding the competitive impact of dataset control and AI systems on economic markets.

1.2 Governments should undertake regular reviews to ensure that competition law frameworks and the enforcement tools available to the relevant enforcement authorities are sufficient and effective to ensure sufficient access to necessary inputs, and adequate choice, vibrant rivalry, creative innovation and high quality of output in the development and deployment of AI systems, to the ultimate benefit of consumers.

2 Open data

2.1 Governments should foster and facilitate national infrastructures necessary to promote open access to datasets to all elements of society having a vested interest in access to such datasets for research and/or non-commercial use. In this regard, governments should give serious consideration to two-tier access models which would allow for free access for academic and research purposes, and paid-for access for commercialised purposes.

2.2 Governments should support open data initiatives in the public or private sector with guidance and research to share wide understanding of the advantages to be gained from open access data, the structures through which datasets can be shared and exchanged, and the processes by which data can be made suitable for open access (including API standardisation, pseudonymisation, aggregation or other curation, where necessary).

2.3 Governments should ensure that the data held by public sector bodies are accessible and open, where possible and where this does not conflict with a public sector mandate to recover taxpayer investment in the collection and curation of such data. Private sector bodies such as industry organisations and trade associations should similarly support and promote open data within their industry sector, making their own datasets open, where possible.

2.4 Organisations that develop, deploy or use AI systems are encouraged to open up access to, and/or license, their datasets, where possible via chaperoned mechanisms such as Data Trusts.

2.5 Any sharing or licensing of data should be to an extent which is reasonable in the circumstances and should be in compliance with legal, regulatory, contractual and any other obligations or requirements in relation to the data concerned (including privacy, security, freedom of information and other confidentiality considerations).

3 Open source AI systems

3.1 Organisations that develop AI systems are normally entitled to commercialise such systems as they wish. However, governments should at a minimum advocate accessibility through open source or other similar licensing arrangements to those innovative AI systems which may be of particular societal benefit or advance the "state of the art" in the field via, for example, targeted incentive schemes.

3.2 Organisations that elect not to release their AI systems as open source software are encouraged nevertheless to license the System on a commercial basis.

3.3 To the extent that an AI system can be sub-divided into various constituent parts with general utility and application in other AI use-cases, organisations that elect not to license the AI system as a whole (whether on an open source or commercial basis) are encouraged to license as many of such re-usable components as is possible.

4 Compliance by design with competition/antitrust laws

4.1 Organisations that develop, deploy or use AI systems should design, develop and deploy AI systems in a "compliance by design" manner which ensures consistency with the overarching ethos of subsisting competition/antitrust regimes to promote free and vibrant competition amongst corporate enterprises to the ultimate benefit of consumers.

Principle 7
Privacy

Organisations that develop, deploy or use AI systems and any national laws that regulate such use shall endeavour to ensure that AI systems are compliant with privacy norms and regulations, taking into account the unique characteristics of AI systems, and the evolution of standards on privacy.

1 Finding a balance

1.1 There is an inherent and developing conflict between the increasing use of AI systems to manage private data, especially personal data; and the increasing regulatory protection afforded internationally to personal and other private data.

1.2 Governments that regulate the privacy implications of AI systems should do so in a manner that acknowledges the specific characteristics of AI and that does not unduly stifle AI innovation.

1.3 Organisations that develop, deploy and use AI systems should analyse their current processes to identify whether they need be updated or amended in any way to ensure that the respect for privacy is a central consideration.

2 The operational challenges ahead for AI users

2.1 AI systems create challenges specifically in relation to the practicalities of meeting of requirements under a number of national legislative regimes, such as in relation to consent and anonymization of data. Accordingly, organisations that develop, deploy or use AI systems and any national laws that regulate such use shall make provision for alternative lawful bases for the collection and processing of personal data by AI systems.

2.2 Organisations that develop, deploy or use AI systems should consider implementing operational safeguards to protect privacy such as privacy by design principles that are specifically tailored to the specific features of deployed AI systems.

2.3 Organisations that develop, deploy and use AI systems should appoint an AI Ethics Officer, in a role similar to Data Protection Officers under the GDPR, but with specific remit to consider the ethics and regulatory compliance of their use of AI.

3 AI as a tool to support privacy

3.1 Although there are challenges from a privacy perspective from the use of AI, in turn the advent of AI technologies could also be used to help organisations comply with privacy obligations.

Principle 8
AI and Intellectual Property

Organisations that develop, deploy or use AI systems should take necessary steps to protect the rights in the resulting works through appropriate and directed application of existing intellectual property rights laws. Governments should investigate how AI-authored works may be further protected, without seeking to create any new IP right at this stage.

1 Supporting incentivisation and protection for innovation

1.1 Innovation is only of value if it can benefit society. Funding is necessary to develop innovation to a level where it can be disseminated and utilised by society. Those from whom funding is sought require a return on their investment. Consequently, there must be incentivisation and protection for innovation if it is to attract investment and be brought to the greater good of society.

1.2 Organisations must therefore be allowed to protect rights in works resulting from the use of AI, whether AI-created works or AI enabled works.

1.3 However, care needs to be taken not to take steps which will amount to overprotection, as this could prove detrimental to the ultimate goal of IP protection.

2 Protection of IP rights

2.1 At present IP laws are insufficiently equipped to deal with the creation of works by autonomous AI.

2.2 Organisations that develop, deploy or use AI systems should take necessary steps to protect the rights in the resulting works. Where appropriate these steps should include asserting or obtaining copyrights, obtaining patents, when applicable, and seeking contractual provisions to allow for protection as trade secrets and/or to allocate the rights appropriately between the parties.

3 Development of new IP laws

3.1 Governments should be cautious with revising existing IP laws.

3.2 Governments should explore the introduction of appropriate legislation (or the interpretation of existing laws) to clarify IP protection of AI enabled as well as AI created works, without seeking to create any new IP right at this stage.

3.3 When amending existing or implementing new IP laws, governments should seek adequately to balance the interests of all relevant stakeholders.

3.4 Governments should also explore a consensus in relation to AI and IP rights to allow for unhindered data flows across borders and the rapid dissemination of new technologies and seek to address these issues through an international treaty.

bpv HÜGEL

Homburger

TaylorWessing

VANDOORNE